SAM ADAMS

Painted by Johnston   Aet. 72.   Engᵈ by H.B.Hall.

Samᵈ Adams

SAM ADAMS

Pioneer in Propaganda

JOHN C. MILLER

STANFORD UNIVERSITY PRESS
STANFORD, CALIFORNIA

Stanford University Press
Stanford, California
Copyright 1936 by John C. Miller; copyright
renewed 1964 by John C. Miller
Printed in the United States of America

First published in 1936 by Little, Brown,
and Company. Reissued in 1960 by Stanford
University Press. Reprinted 1966.

To my Mother and Father

In the course of my research I have been accorded many kindnesses by the librarians of the Massachusetts Historical Society; the Massachusetts Archives; the Harvard College Library; the New York Public Library; the New York Historical Society; and the Congressional Library in Washington, D. C. I am deeply indebted to Professor Samuel Eliot Morison of Harvard University, and to Professors Lawrence J. Henderson and Charles Pelham Curtis, Jr., of the Society of Fellows of Harvard University, for their stimulating criticism of my work.

The substance of this book was delivered in lectures at the Lowell Institute during October 1935.

JOHN C. MILLER

The preparation of this study, in which it has been reported that numerous ... has been attended upon ... unnumbered ... Michael Scott, the Massachusetts Center for ... studied, ... Michael the ... New York, The ... Oxford ... New York, H. Douglas Greene, and the Department of ... for ... H. Watkins, ... E. H. ... Carl, Herman ... Oh ... James Russell Starr, Mr. R. S. ... and ... University, and the ... Sciences ... Lawrence S. ... ... and ... S. Cox ... and ... for ... by ... S. ... Oh ... the ... the ... publishers ... and my wife, ... that for their assistance in ... Taiwan, ... as ... to ... for the ... through ... 1958.

John E. Elliot

CONTENTS

ILLUSTRATIONS

SAM ADAMS

I

A BOSTON ADAMS

THE character of Sam Adams is so unlike that of other members of the Adams Family that it is difficult to find him a place within the family circle. In that distinguished gathering there seems no room for a propagandist, democrat, and backstairs politician. Still, Sam was an Adams, although not, it is true, of the Quincy breed. During the eighteenth century, there were two distinct branches of the Adams Family in New England — the town and the country Adamses; and there were striking differences in talent and temperament between the townsmen and their country cousins. Most of the descendants of Henry Adams, the founder of the Adams Family in New England, remained obscure yeomen almost a half century after the Boston Adamses had become prominent merchants and politicians. While the Quincy clan were still not far removed from the dirt-farmer stage, the Bostonians gave promise of becoming one of the most influential families in Massachusetts Bay. Although the country Adamses outstripped the Boston branch before the century was out, it is significant that when rank in Harvard College was determined by social position, Sam Adams, a Bostonian, was placed fifth in his class, while his country cousin, John Adams, the first important Adams to come out of Quincy, ranked sixteenth on his graduation a few years later — and such prominence as he enjoyed was owing to the fact that his mother was a Boylston.[1]

Sam Adams, the greatest of the Boston Adamses, was born on the "sixteenth day of Septbr at twelve of the Clock at noon, being Sabbath day, 1722." His father, Samuel Adams, Senior, was a prosperous brewer and merchant, whose trim house,

[1] John T. Morse, Jr., *John Adams* (1885), 3.

brewery, and wharf on Purchase Street marked him as one
of the substantial citizens of Boston's South End. Beside
manufacturing beer, the elder Adams was a pillar of the Congregational Church. By the time of Sam's birth, "Deacon"
Adams, as he came to be known, had acquired a comfortable
estate and made a reputation as a "godly man." [2]

Little is known of Sam Adams until he reached middle age.
Even the Tories who went over his career with a fine-tooth
comb, determined to show he was a scoundrel, were unable to
prove that he had spent an abnormal childhood. For eight
years he attended the Boston Latin School, where little more
than Latin and Greek was drilled into the students. Whatever
its shortcomings, this instruction admirably fitted them for
Harvard College. When the Reverend Mr. Thacher delivered Sam Adams's funeral sermon many years later he said
that Sam had distinguished himself in his youth as one of the
best scholars of his day. Although it is doubtful if he really
shone so brilliantly in the classroom, he did well enough to
give his parents high hopes for him in the ministry. Admitted
to the class of 1740, Sam was packed off to Harvard College
at the age of fourteen, where it was expected he would prepare
himself for the Church. But here Deacon and Mrs. Adams suffered the first of many disappointments in their son. Sam's
morals were good and he was seldom missing from the family
pew on Lord's Days, yet he showed little interest in theology or
metaphysics. He had not been long at Harvard College before
it was clear that Deacon Adams would never have the gratifica-
tion of seeing his son in a pulpit.

Such rebellion did not spare young Sam the torments of
metaphysics, which was crammed into students at Harvard
during the eighteenth century regardless of their choice of
profession. But Adams put to good purpose in Cambridge all
the Latin and Greek he had learned at the Boston Latin School.
Freshmen studied Cicero, Virgil, the Greek Testament, and
Hebrew. Although the curriculum was heavily weighted with

[2] William V. Wells, *The Life and Public Services of Samuel Adams* (1865),
III, 427–428 (Appendix).

Greek and Latin, the college fulfilled in a great measure its purpose of instructing in "ye Learned Languages, ye Liberal Arts & Sciences"; and Adams became well grounded during his seven years at Cambridge in geography, arithmetic, geometry, astronomy, physics, logic, rhetoric, and natural philosophy. Only in English literature was he conspicuously ignorant — a fault common to most educated New Englanders of his generation.[3]

After his junior year at Harvard College, Adams was permitted to live "wholly out of Commons," which allowed him to board at a private home in Cambridge — a privilege accorded to delicate students who required different fare from that served in the Commons or to "swells" who turned up their noses at college food. Then Deacon Adams lost his money in the Land Bank crash and young Sam was forced to come down in life and serve as one of the waiters for the lower table in the college dining hall, where his duties consisted in being ready "when the Bell tolls at meal time to receive the Plates and Victuals at the Kitchen Hatch & carry the same to the severall tables." Although Adams seems to have taken no part in the "shamefull & scandalous Routs and Noises" in the college yard, — such as whittling lead from the roofs of the college buildings, tearing up the yard fences for bonfire fuel, and setting off "Squibs or Crackers" at midnight, — he was hardly a classroom saint.[4] Harvard College demanded that its scholars lead "sober, righteous & godly Lives," and the drinking of brandy, rum, or other distilled liquors in college rooms was strictly prohibited. Those detected in such revels were fined, degraded in class, or rusticated. During his senior year, Sam Adams was caught drinking rum; and, while he escaped with a five-shilling fine, several of his less fortunate companions were both rusticated and degraded.[5]

[3] *Records of the College Faculty*, I, 178, MS. Harvard College Library. *Harvard College Records, Publications of the Colonial Society of Massachusetts*, II, 557.

[4] *Records of the College Faculty*, I, 116, 132, 162. *Publications Col. Soc. of Mass.*, II, 543, 544, 568, 598.

[5] *Records of the College Faculty*, I, 123, 124.

Life in New England was certainly not humdrum during
Sam Adams's youth. While he was at Harvard College, the
Great Awakening swept over the country and Harvard became
"a new Creature" filled with devout young men who had experienced the "New Birth."   George Whitefield was welcomed
in New England as "an Angel of God and Messenger of Jesus
Christ," and there were few students at Cambridge able to
resist his hot gospeling. Harvard again became a citadel of
righteousness and the clergy exulted over "the sweet Work
going on at Cambridge." When Whitefield first visited the
college he was dismayed by the laxity he found: tutors did
not pray with their pupils and their favorite theologian was
Tillotson, whom Whitefield declared "knew less of Christianity
than Mahomet." [6] But after the religious awakening of 1740,
it was said that only "Voices of Prayer and Praise" were to be
heard in students' rooms and Tillotson and Clark were cast
aside for Flavel and the Mathers. Indeed, the piety of the
college became so formidable that even "divers gentlemen's
Sons" who came to Harvard prepared to spend four years
in sloth and pleasure were suddenly seized with remorse and
became so "zealous for Christ's Cause as to devote themselves
entirely to Studies of Divinity." [7]   In Boston, where the Congregational clergy had for many years past seen the Devil
making long strides, the Great Awakening brought about a
"Week of Sabbaths": taverns, dancing schools, and assemblies
"which have always proved unfriendly to serious Godliness"
were deserted for prayer meetings and sermons, and religious
conversation became "almost fashionable." At every opportunity, Whitefield put "a Damp upon Polite Diversions" and
beseeched his hearers to shun the snares Satan had laid for them
in fashionable dress. His exhortations produced startling
changes in Boston. Young men and women cast off their
finery and walked along the fashionable Boston Mall, built in

---

[6] *Christian History* (1740), II, 282. *Massachusetts Historical Society
Proceedings*, LIII, 214. Benjamin Colman to Dr. Benjamin Colman to Dr.
Watts, *Ibid.*, LIII, 196. *Christian History*, II, 282. *New England Weekly
Journal*, May 20, 1740.

[7] Benjamin Colman to George Whitefield, July, 1741, *Mass. Hist. Soc.
Proceedings*, LIII, 196.

imitation of St. James's Park in London, wearing the sombre dress seen in the heyday of Puritanism.[8]

But this revival of Puritanism proved exceedingly short-lived. George Whitefield was followed in New England by a host of lesser "New Lights," such as Gilbert Tennent of New Jersey, who edified his audience by "roaring out and bellowing *Hell* and *Damnation*" at the top of his lungs, and by James Davenport of Long Island, who shrieked hell-fire on the Boston Common until his followers were tumbling and howling "more like a Company of Bacchanalians after a mad Frolick, than sober Christians." [9] The Congregational clergy soon found that instead of bringing back the days of Cotton and Winthrop, the Great Awakening had ushered in a wild, disorderly religious frenzy which split the Congregational Church into bitterly hostile factions — the "Old Lights" and the "New Lights." Far from harking back to Puritanism, the Great Awakening was the first of the backwoods revivals that were to sweep America during the eighteenth and nineteenth centuries.[10] But, as will be seen, this "Puritanism" of the early period of the Great Awakening left a profound impression upon Sam Adams.

Despite his repute as a merchant and staunch Congregationalist, Deacon Adams's liveliest interest was in neither rum nor religion, but in Boston politics. After accumulating a moderate fortune in business, the elder Adams turned his attention almost wholly to politics and became one of the most prominent public men in Massachusetts Bay — "a true New England Man; an honest Patriot." Beginning at the bottom of the political ladder, he ascended the stages of tithingman,

[8] Benjamin Colman to Dr. Watts, 1740, MS. Mass. Hist. Soc. *Christian History*, II, 282. *Diary of Paul Dudley, New England Historical and Genealogical Register* (1881), 29. Jonathan Belcher to Richard Waldon, Oct. 27, 1740, Belcher MSS., Mass. Hist. Soc.

[9] George Whitefield, *Vindication and Confirmation of the Remarkable Work of God in New England* (1741), 8. *Boston Evening Post*, Aug. 2, 1742.

[10] John C. Miller, "Religion, Finance and Democracy," *New England Quarterly*, March 1933, 29–58. Charles Chauncy, *Seasonable Thoughts on the State of Religion in New England* (Boston, 1743), 184. Chauncy, *Religious Commotions in New England* (Preface), 18.

constable, assessor, and selectman, to become at last one of the
Boston representatives in the General Court.   Only the veto
of a royal governor prevented him from reaching the Massachusetts Council, which was regarded as the particular preserve
of the first families of the province.[11]   Whenever a vigorous
statement of colonial rights was required, Deacon Adams's pen
was pressed into service.   In 1731, for example, he urged the
Boston representatives to use their "utmost Endeavor that the
Great Priviledges we Enjoy by the English Constitution & the
Royal Charter may be preserved from all Enchroachments"
— words which his son was to reëcho in his revolutionary
manifestoes.   Deacon Adams drew up Boston's declarations of
grievances against the British government and the royal governor; wrote the town's instructions to its representatives; and
denounced British impressments of New England seamen as
"breaches of Magna Charta, the Charter of this Province, and
an Act of Parliament." [12]

Deacon Adams's political success was owing to his influence
in the Boston Caucus, of which he probably was a charter member.   This club of small shopkeepers, mechanics, and North
End shipyard workers (it is possible that "caucus" is a corruption of "caulker") held a tight grip on town offices and filled
with its nominees all the snug berths, from hogreeve to selectman and representative.   Bostonians nominally decided their
concerns in the town meeting, but under Deacon Adams, and
still more under his son and successor in the leadership of the
Caucus Club, the political bosses laid their plans and thoroughly
cut and dried all the town's important business long before the
citizens met in the town meeting — there usually to do as the
Caucus Club bid.   During the eighteenth century, the Caucus
became so powerful that Sam Adams turned it into a revolutionary machine and with its aid made himself "Dictator" of
Boston.

Sam Adams grew up in an atmosphere heavily charged with

[11] *Boston Records*, 8th Report of the Record Commissioners of the City of
Boston (1879), 70, 77, 170. William Bennett, *History of New England*,
Sparks MSS., Harvard College Library, 145.

[12] *Boston Records*, 12th Report of the Record Commissioners (1885), 23–
24; 14th Report, 84–85.

politics and, from his earliest years, the dangers that threatened New England's liberties were deeply impressed upon his mind. Deacon Adams made his house a gathering place for Boston politicians, from petty "bosses" to such leaders as Elisha Cooke, "the greate Darling of his Country" and standard bearer of the Massachusetts Country Party. When the Crown demanded a fixed salary from the Massachusetts General Court for the royal governors, Elisha Cooke and Deacon Adams led the colony's resistance, with the result that the King and the governor were worsted in the struggle. Sam's biographers have supposed that he was allowed to sit at Elisha Cooke's feet; if so, no rebel could have had better schooling. Governor Jonathan Belcher, who certainly had no reason to love Cooke, said he had "a fixt enmity to all kingly government" and "endeavoured, to poyson the Minds of His Countreymen, with his republican notions, in order to assert the Independency of New England" — the accusation later brought against Sam Adams by the royal governors of Massachusetts.[13] There is little doubt that had Cooke lived two generations later, he would have been a leader in the struggle for American independence. His attitude toward the mother country reveals strikingly on what uncertain tenure Great Britain held the allegiance of the chiefs of the popular party in New England. Elisha Cooke expressed the traditional spirit of Massachusetts that had taken root when the colony was virtually an independent state recognizing only a shadowy sovereignty in the mother country. This heritage of the seventeenth century was handed down from one generation to another, and it was chiefly through Elisha Cooke that Sam Adams became imbued with the spirit that was to make him a revolutionary leader.

During the struggle between aristocrats and common people to establish a Land Bank in Massachusetts, Sam Adams was brought into direct contact with political radicalism. In 1740, shortly after he had graduated from Harvard, the colony reached the crisis of an economic depression. Throughout the greater part of the century, the lack of a stable currency embittered Massachusetts politics and divided parties on class

[13] C. K. Shipton, *Sibley's Harvard Graduates*, IV, 352, 353, 354.

lines: debtors against creditors, and inflationists against the
"sound money" mercantile aristocracy.   As commerce began
to decline and farmers and town artisans found themselves in
a "pretty Pickle" because of the currency shortage, hostility
mounted everywhere in the colony against the wealthy Boston
merchants who, by paying their debts in England with colonial
silver, made the scarcity more acute at home.   The common
people denounced them as "griping and merciless usurers" who
"heaped up vast Estates" and made themselves "Lords of
Mannors" by profiteering at the small farmers' expense.
Another excellent reason for hating the Boston aristocracy was
that they were creditors in the colony to the tune of "Hundreds
of Thousands" and were not inclined to ease their debtors'
burden by accepting payment in depreciated paper money.[14]
Under these circumstances, the merchants became almost as
unpopular in Massachusetts as did the Tories in the next generation.   It was widely believed that they would "swallow up
thousands of Families" and strip half the farmers in the province
of their property; if they continued to dominate Massachusetts,
it was said that yeomen would be forced into the degradation
of "Husbandmen, Laborers and Tenants."   Even a French
invasion and the rule of "Papists" were pictured as preferable
to remaining as the "Slaves and Vassals" of these mercantile
overlords.[15]

In 1740, it was clear that a popular upheaval was imminent
in the colony.   The crisis led to the resurrection of an old
scheme known as the "Land Bank" which promised hard-
pressed farmers and town mechanics a Utopia of paper money
backed by real estate.   The promoters of the Land Bank were
frankly inflationists who proposed to bring back prosperity by
flooding the country with paper bills and, at the same time, to
"humble the Merchants" by taking the control of currency
out of their hands.   With these rosy promises attracting thousands of distressed yeomen and mechanics, the Land Bank

[14] *Boston Gazette*, Jan. 28, 1740. *Colonial Currency Reprints*, edited by
Andrew McFarland Davis, *Publications Prince Society*, IV, 223. *New England Weekly Journal*, Sept. 23, 1740; Aug. 19, 1740. *Boston Evening Post*,
Sept. 22, 1740.
[15] *Colonial Currency Reprints*, IV, 42, 78, 79.

reached portentous dimensions. It quickly became the rallying point of a political party whose objective was to bring the government within the grasp of the common people. The "numerous swarm of the village" everywhere menaced the power of the aristocracy; and the metropolis fell under the sway of the "Boston Chaps who rule the roast." In the House of Representatives, the Land Bankers piled up a large majority and threatened to take possession of the Council, leaving only the royal governor as a brake upon the people's fury against the merchants. To the dismayed gentlemen of Boston it was clear that the question which lay at the root of the struggle was whether the common people or wealthy gentry were henceforth to control the political life of the colony; in their eyes, the balance trembled between the "Idle and Extravagant who want to borrow money at any bad Lay" and "our considerable Foreign traders and rich Men." [16]

One of the most important of those "Boston chaps" who held the metropolis for the Land Bank was Deacon Adams. As a director of the bank, Adams sunk most of his fortune in the scheme and was among the first "martyrs" to be deprived of office by the royal governor for activities in the Land Bank. Immediately after Governor Belcher's proclamation threatening all officeholders under the governor's commission with removal if they passed Land Bank money, Adams resigned as justice of the peace and sent a scorching letter to Belcher, in which he declared that upon the Land Bank "the Interests of our Native Country so much depends as to Require the Utmost of our Endeavours" to promote it. For this defiance, Adams was promptly dismissed from office, along with a large number of militia officers and justices of the peace who did business with the prohibited bills. Adams continued to accept Land Bank money at his shop, although it was rumored that he was wary of overloading himself with large sums. When stories began to circulate that Adams was refusing to take Land Bank bills,

---

[16] Thomas Hutchinson, *History of the Province of Massachusetts Bay* (1767), II, 394. *Colonial Currency Reprints*, II, 46; IV, 257, 258, 305. *Belcher Papers*, *Mass. Hist. Soc. Collections*, Sixth Series (1894), II, 222. Massachusetts Archives, 102, *Pecuniary Papers*, 29, 90.

a disastrous panic was threatened because if the most prominent
director of the scheme and deepest plunger had lost confidence,
it behooved the rank and file to make sure they did not scorch
their fingers with worthless currency.   Adams immediately advertised in the newspapers that he would give five pounds to
the person who pointed out the author of this slander.   To
Adams's consternation, his offer was accepted; one Benjamin
Pollard declared he had spread the story and volunteered to
produce his proof.   To crown the Deacon's embarrassment,
Pollard claimed the five pounds reward.[17]

The mercantile aristocracy regarded the Land Bank as
nothing more than a scheme of "desperate and fraudulent"
debtors to cheat their creditors after they had firmly seated
themselves in the political saddle.   Governor Belcher in particular "exerted himself to blast this fraudulent undertaking" by
means of royal authority.   In spite of his labor, the Land
Bankers continued to gather up the threads of power so rapidly
in Massachusetts that Belcher and the Boston merchants became
convinced that nothing less than Parliamentary intervention
could prevent the "ruin of government and people" at the
hands of Deacon Adams and his followers.   In Boston, the
"quarrelsome, mobbish Spirit and Impatience under Government that has so long been growing" gave rise to fears of outright insurrection.   The House of Representatives, which now
swarmed with Land Bankers, treated the Crown with "all
possible rudeness and ill-Manners" by flatly ignoring royal
instructions regarding paper money.   Indeed, the popular
party in the colony seemed inclined to pull the royal beard so
lustily that Belcher doubted whether it would leave "Jupiter
a hair upon his face, but will bid defyance to his imperial resentment."   Outside the General Court, yokels and town laborers
screwed up the politicians' courage by declaring that free-born
New Englanders could do as they pleased since they were
"pretty much out of the reach of the government at home."
Few Crown officers doubted that unless Parliament came to
the rescue, royal authority would crumble and the colony would

[17] *Boston Evening Post*, Feb. 16, 1741.   Mass. Archives, 102, *Pecuniary
Papers*, 29, 90.

soon be "ripe for a smarter sort of government" in which republicans such as Deacon Adams would hold the reins.[18]

Unquestionably, two distinct social classes were arrayed against each other by the inflationist sentiment that had swept over the colony. The bulk of the Land Bank Party was composed of that class which Boston gentlemen called "the Mobility," "the Idle and Extravagant," "the needy part of the Province," or "the Rabble." The Land Bank's rolls show that wharfingers, shipwrights, bricklayers, weavers, tanners, and yeomen predominated, with a thin sprinkling of "Gentlemen" and physicians.[19] It was from these materials that Sam Adams later built the revolutionary Whig Party in Massachusetts; and the social cleavage in 1740 was very similar to that of 1775. In both, a small aristocracy stood at bay against a large majority of the common people; and in both, the aristocracy appealed to the King and Parliament for protection against colonial radicalism. In leading the Land Bank Party, Deacon Adams foreshadowed his son's later career, and even the quarrel with Parliament was not lacking to complete the resemblance.

In May 1741, the Land Bank Party reached the "height of its Malignity." The clergy were still dreaming of the new Puritan Age that was to emerge from the Great Awakening, but there was little in the temper of the people to remind one of the days of Cotton and Winthrop. "They are grown so brassy and hardy," wrote Governor Belcher, "as to be now combining in a body to raise a rebellion." It was said that thousands of farmers would march to Boston on election day to join forces with the town Land Bankers. The embattled farmers, assisted by their urban allies, would then "force the currency of the Land Bank Bills" and demand grain from the merchants; "if corn was there and the merchants would not let them have it they would throw them into the dock." [20]

---

[18] *Belcher Papers*, II, 349, 364, 386, 387, 388; Rev. William Williams to Benjamin Colman, July 1, 1740, MS. Mass. Hist. Soc.

[19] Hutchinson, II, 394. *Colonial Currency Reprints*, II, 46; IV, 305. Mass. Archives, 102, *Pecuniary Papers*, 103; a list of all such Persons as have mortgaged any part of their Estates in the County of Suffolk to the Directors of the Manufactory Company, Dec. 19, 1740.

[20] *Belcher Papers*, II, 388. *Publications Col. Soc. of Mass.* (1910), IV, 20.

What might have gone down in history as the Great Massachusetts Rebellion was nipped in the bud. Governor Belcher, who had been busily ferreting out radicals, learned that certain extremists were planning a desperate attempt to beat down opposition to the Land Bank. He struck quickly and hard. The leading conspirators were rounded up and jailed. Election day passed without a sign of the threatened uprising. But though the people did not openly revolt, they gave the Land Bankers such an overwhelming victory at the polls that when the new House of Representatives met, Deacon Adams and other prominent members of the popular party were elected to the Council and were prevented from entering that aristocratic stronghold only by the governor's veto. There was no question that the Land Bank had the support of the vast majority of Massachusetts voters and that the leadership of the Boston aristocracy had been completely repudiated. Yet just as the Land Bank Party was taking the reins of government in Massachusetts, it was learned that Parliament had responded to the pleas of Belcher and the merchants and had outlawed the Land Bank by extending the Bubble Act to the colonies.

The first impulse of the Land Bankers upon learning that the House of Commons had signed the death warrant of their bank was to defy Parliament. The people were "ripe for tumult and disorder" and confident that Parliament could not execute the act in the face of determined opposition. The severity of the Bubble Act was a strong argument for resistance. Parliament struck down the popular party in Massachusetts with so little regard to justice that for a generation the memory rankled in the colony, and particularly in the Adams household. The Bubble Act of 1720 had never applied to the colonies and certainly had nothing to do with the Massachusetts Land Bank, which was not a joint stock company. Yet Parliament declared in 1741 that the Bubble Act had been in force in the colonies from the beginning, thus making the Land Bank illegal *ab initio*. When Deacon Adams and his fellow directors established the bank they had no reason to suppose they were acting unlawfully, for as late as 1734 a New Hampshire Land Bank had been approved by the Board of Trade.[21] Nevertheless, Parliament now declared them criminals and liable to the punishments of the Statute of Provisions and Praemunire. All the directors were made personally responsible for the face value of all the Land Bank money that had been issued, on pain of forfeiture of estate or imprisonment. By this means, Deacon Adams and other directors were put at the mercy of any enemy who could gather up bills, demand payment, or insist they be punished according to the letter of the law. It was no wonder, then, that the Land Bank was dissolved with great difficulty and that many directors "appeared very stout" for disobeying Parliament. The Land Bank was brought to an end by the vote of a bare majority of moderates; but it was not until Governor Belcher, who had been chiefly responsible for Parliament's intervention, was removed and William Shirley put in his place that a serious clash between Massachusetts and the mother country was averted.[22]

Had the Bubble Act been carried out in its full severity in Massachusetts Bay, Deacon Adams would have been utterly ruined. The greater part of his fortune was in the Land Bank, and he had many enemies, particularly among the mercantile aristocracy, who would have been overjoyed to assist the royal authorities in clapping him in irons and confiscating his estate. Fortunately, the Massachusetts General Court eased the penalties prescribed by Parliament for the Land Bank directors. But even with this mitigation, the Adamses, father and son, were forced to withstand for twenty years the efforts of the Land Bank Commissioners to seize the remainder of Deacon Adams's estate to pay his obligations as director.

Sam Adams remained at Harvard College during the months when the Land Bank and Great Awakening were threatening the social and religious foundations of New England. After his graduation in 1740 he continued at Cambridge until 1743, when he received his degree of Master of Arts. Already his preoccupation with politics and government had begun to

[21] A. McF. Davis, *Publications Col. Soc. of Mass.*, III, Transactions 1895–97, 29, 31, 32, 41. Mass. Archives, 26, *Hutchinson Corr.*, II, 370.
[22] Mass. Archives, 26, *Hutchinson Correspondence*, II, 370.

crowd all other interests from his mind. Adams read deeply in Locke, Harrington, and Pufendorf; and in his choice of subject for his Master's degree he revealed strikingly in what channel his mind was running. He undertook to debate the affirmative of the question "whether it be lawful to resist the Supreme Magistrate, if the Commonwealth cannot be otherwise preserved." It is probable that Adams's choice of subject was inspired by the resistance to Great Britain contemplated shortly before by the Land Bankers, whose plans he had no doubt heard discussed in his own household. It has been supposed that Adams showed remarkable courage in defending a point so unpalatable to the Crown officers and blue-blooded conservatives who attended Harvard commencements. These gentry are pictured as thunderstruck by the young orator's "bold denial of British power." [23] But such subjects were not uncommon at Harvard College commencements; in 1738, for instance, a candidate had argued a question even more explosive than Sam Adams's: "Are we bound to observe the mandates of kings, unless they themselves keep their agreements with their subjects?" [24] Conservatives frequently found their toes trod upon by Harvard commencement speakers; and Sam Adams's political radicalism was in the best Harvard manner. Unfortunately, no copy of his thesis has been found: evidently it was not remarkable enough to be preserved in hearers' notes or in the newspapers. But if this early work was like his later political tracts, Adams probably began with the Greeks and Romans and ran the whole course of political theory down to John Locke. Although his address may not have struck his audience as "incipient 'treason,' " doubtless it showed that in Deacon Adams's son the Massachusetts patriot party possessed a promising recruit. Had his audience been composed of Land Bankers instead of Boston bigwigs, no doubt those disgruntled financiers and politicians would have cheered to the echo young Adams's premise that the supreme magistrate could be resisted.

Having fired this parting shot at political conservatism, it

[23] Wells, I, 10, 11.
[24] Edward J. Young, *Mass. Hist. Soc. Proceedings* (1881), XVIII, 125. Subjects for Master's Degree at Harvard College, 1655–1791.

JOHN ADAMS AS A YOUNG MAN

THOMAS HUTCHINSON

PAINTED BY EDWARD TRUMAN, IN THE POSSESSION OF THE
MASSACHUSETTS HISTORICAL SOCIETY, BOSTON

became necessary for young Sam to find a profession. His mother's opposition prevented serious study of law; but the Whig Party in the colonies was so well provided with lawyers during the American Revolution that Adams's lack of legal training was not missed: he was, indeed, far more valuable to the Whigs as a popularizer of political ideas and as a man who possessed deep "understanding of liberty and her resources in the temper and character of the people." [25] Adams's first venture was as a businessman, and here he had the blessing of both parents. He was sent to Thomas Cushing's counting-house with high hopes of becoming a prosperous merchant. But Sam was not happy in trade and he soon showed that although he had inherited his father's passion for politics, he was woefully lacking in business ability. He lasted only a few months in Cushing's offices before his employer broke the news to the Deacon that his son would never make a merchant. Mr. Cushing remarked somewhat starchily that he was training young men for business, not for politics — which gives an inkling where Adams's wits had been woolgathering while he was expected to be conning figures and accounts. Decidedly, Sam was becoming a problem to his parents, and no doubt there were numerous worthies who solemnly shook their heads and prophesied a bad end to a young man who did not like business. When his father loaned him a thousand pounds with which to go into business for himself, Sam Adams prodigally loaned most of his money to a friend, who, in turn, promptly lost it. Sam never attempted to get his money back; and Deacon Adams provided in his will that his son should not be compelled to repay the loan. This unlucky incident ended Sam Adams's career as a financier: his father took him into the malt business and, under Deacon Adams's watchful eye, Sam settled down to the life of a merchant and brewer.

But his heart was not in beer, rum, and molasses. He had drunk in so much political talk at home and among friends that he was bursting with ambition to follow Elisha Cooke's footsteps and lead the Massachusetts Country Party in its struggle against the royal governors. In 1748 Sam made his

[25] *The Works of John Adams* (1850), II, 163.

first appearance as a political writer. He and a few close
friends of similar political views swore themselves to secrecy,
organized a club, founded a newspaper called the *Independent
Advertiser*, and began to pepper the royal governor, William
Shirley—a popular English-born politician whose chief
anxiety was to keep the colony quiet and establish an "era of
good feelings" while he made his reputation fighting French
and Indians on the frontier. During King George's War
(1741–1748) a truce had been patched up between the governor
and the popularly elected legislature in order to meet the
menace of an attack from Canada. In 1748, when the war
came to a close, Sam Adams believed the time was ripe to renew
the quarrel between royal and popular authority in the colony.
Although he failed in his first attempt to kindle a flame in
Massachusetts Bay, his work in 1748–1749 sheds significant
light upon his later career as a revolutionist.

Throughout his life, Sam Adams was strongly disposed to
"view with alarm," and his friends of the *Independent Advertiser* club shared his apprehensions to a man. They feared
that the growing wealth and luxury in Massachusetts Bay were
snuffing out the "good old *New England* Spirit" of the early
settlers.[26] By 1748, all signs of the Puritanism of the Great
Awakening had been swept away by a wave of materialism
that reached its peak in Boston and other large seaports. Sam
Adams and his friends were in revolt against the commer-
cialism and money-making spirit that followed the religious
excitement of the early 1740's, not only because it led to a
sharp deviation from puritan morality, but because they believed it sapped the love of liberty that had enabled the early
settlers to defend their liberties against the assaults of the
British government. They did not doubt that, when Puritanism declined, "our Morals, our Constitution, and our Liberties
must needs degenerate," and that New England would fall an
easy prey to its enemies. The first of Sam Adams's many efforts to revive Puritanism was made in the *Independent Advertiser* when he was a young man of twenty-four years.

At Harvard College, Sam had read deeply in Roman history

[26] *Independent Advertiser*, Dec. 5, 1748; March 20, 1749.

and literature: and it was later said of him that he began "by the Greeks and Romans, to get at the Whigs and tories." [27] He was thoroughly familiar with Plutarch, Cicero, and the Roman historians. Because of this saturation in the learning and history of antiquity, even his political writings, designed to rouse the common people of New England against British oppression, are heavy with classical allusions that no present-day revolutionist would inflict upon his followers. But Sam Adams was appealing to an audience which, like himself, had been educated in the shadow of the Latin world and which knew the literature of Rome far better than it did that of England. In the *Independent Advertiser*, he repeatedly revealed the influence of his classical education. Characteristically, he used the decline of Rome as a "dreadful example" of what New Englanders might expect if they lost the puritan virtues, and he drew a close comparison between the best days of the Roman Republic and the early period of New England settlement. In Adams's mind, a Roman Senator would have quickly made himself at home in seventeenth-century Puritan New England because Rome and New England were spiritually built upon common ground. Adams became known as the "Cato" of the American Revolution because from youth to old age he preached the necessity of returning to an earlier and simpler way of life: his first revolt was against materialism and his first hatreds were against those whom he believed hostile to the rebirth of the Puritan or "Old Roman" spirit in New England.

For New England's moral decay, Sam and the *Independent Advertiser* club held Governor Shirley responsible. Instead of combating the evils they protested against, Shirley allied himself with the mercantile aristocracy and encouraged the growth of the colony's commercial prosperity at the expense of its religious well-being. Moreover, the governor entrenched himself in power by means of a political machine which effectively kept the Country Party, or popular party, out of office. Because the legislative body in Massachusetts was popularly elected, the royal governor was compelled to fight the leaders of the Country Party with their own weapons

[27] Marquis de Chastellux, *Travels in North America* (1787), I, 275.

and to create by means of patronage a political following of
his own in the General Court. Adams and his friends exclaimed that Governor Shirley had used his powers of granting commissions in the militia, and nominating judges, justices,
and sheriffs, to the injury of the people; and they urged that
the governor's influence be curbed to make way for a more
democratic form of government.

It was in the pages of the *Independent Advertiser* that Sam
Adams fired his first shots at the "prerogative party" of town
gentlemen and country squires who had "an Itch for riding the
Beasts of the People." [28] He was to have the satisfaction, many
years later, of driving these gentry from the province, but in
1748 he was unable to raise a storm against them.   He had no
potent economic grievances from which to manufacture political capital such as his father had had during the Land Bank.
Indeed, the attack upon Shirley gave Adams no more than some
valuable practice in shooting at royal governors; he gained no
reputation as a political writer from it because the meetings of
the *Independent Advertiser* club were kept secret: members
boasted that their identity was "utterly unknown" to the public
and even to their best friends.   And, in spite of young Sam's
gloomy forebodings of the decline and fall of New England,
popular liberty did not appear to be threatened.   There were
few indeed who became enthusiastic over his plan of turning
back to Puritanism and adopting the frugality of the founding fathers.

The *Independent Advertiser*, although it closed shop a little
more than a year after beginning publication, did keep alive
the principles of the Massachusetts Country Party at a time
when the power of the aristocracy and royal governor seemed
to have reached a new high-water mark.   Tories feared Sam
Adams because he never permitted the people to lose sight of
the struggle for liberty; and his work in the *Independent Advertiser* was similar to his efforts during the darkest days of
the revolutionary period.   Moreover, Adams's newspaper did
good service in popularizing John Locke's political thought in
New England by giving its readers extensive quotations from

[28] *Independent Advertiser*, May 8, 1749.

his works. A large part of Sam Adams's contributions is based
directly upon Locke. Even more significant was Adams's
interpretation of the Massachusetts Charter of 1691 as a "Sacred
Ark" against all encroachments by the British government.
Sam and his friends were wholehearted New England patriots,
and it is clear that as early as 1749 they believed the Massachusetts General Court possessed authority in the colony similar to
that exercised in England by the British Parliament. Because
the Massachusetts Charter gave the royal governor the power
of negativing elections of members of the Council, or upper
house of the legislature, the *Independent Advertiser* demanded
that the governor be stripped of this right, since "the KING AT
HOME cannot *negative* or *suspend* any Member of the upper
House called the House of Lords." [29] Sam Adams and his followers already regarded the Massachusetts General Court as a
local parliament, and they insisted it be given equal dignity with
the British Parliament. They justified their demand that the
royal governor's power be curtailed in Massachusetts on the
ground that the King did not have as extensive authority when
dealing with the British Parliament. But most Englishmen
put the Massachusetts General Court on no higher plane than
a local corporation, and few of them suspected that Bostonians
were nourishing the idea in the public press that it was a parliament. Thus, in England and Massachusetts, two irreconcilable
theories of imperial government were slowly taking form. The
Independent Advertiser contains the germ of the ideas for which
Adams was to fight for the greater part of his life, ideas which
were later to form the political testament of the Whig Party
in the American Revolution.

[29] *Independent Advertiser*, Jan. 23, 1749.

II

SAM ADAMS AND THE MASSACHUSETTS COUNTRY PARTY

WHILE Sam Adams was familiarizing New Englanders with colonial rights and John Locke's political theory by means of his newspaper, he was also playing an active part in politics, although until the outbreak of the revolutionary movement in Massachusetts his progress was painfully slow. It is true his father's influence in the Caucus Club opened for him that select circle of bosses and wire pullers, but, like the Deacon, Sam was forced to content himself with humble offices for many years. He won his first political office in 1746 when, at the age of twenty-four, he was elected one of the clerks of the Boston market, where he served with two other future members of the Massachusetts House of Representatives. After the death of Deacon Adams in 1748, however, Sam fell upon lean years, and he held no office in Boston until 1753, when he was elected a town scavenger — hardly one of those political plums on which he had his eye. Finally, in 1756, he was elected collector of taxes for the town of Boston, which led to one of the worst scandals attaching to the name of a signer of the Declaration of Independence.[1]

For nearly a decade after his election as tax collector, Adams seemed destined to remain an obscure Boston politician to the end of his days. He failed to rise higher in politics at this time, not because his ability was inferior, but because the period was one of almost continuous war. While French and Indians were burning up the New England frontier, ambitious politicians like Sam Adams, whose success depended upon picking quarrels with

[1] *Boston Town Records*, 14th Report of the Records Commissioners (1886), 110, 287.

Parliament and the royal governor, found themselves in bad odor. With the province straining every nerve to muster enough men and money to drive the French out of Canada, it became a patriotic duty to bury the hatchet with which Elisha Cooke had harassed the King's government and scarred more than one royal governor. Moreover, when French and Indians menaced the colonies, Americans always displayed a sudden burst of loyalty to the mother country. During the Seven Years' War in particular, British protection was highly prized in New England because a flood of money and supplies was poured into the Northern colonies by the home government. As a result, scarcely a ripple disturbed Massachusetts politics, and Sam Adams was forced to bide his time until peace should resurrect the Country Party and permit him to face the royal governor upon the ancient battleground of colonial rights.

Sam Adams was nevertheless fully occupied during this period in defending his estate against seizure by the Land Bank Commissioners. In 1758, a decade after Deacon Adams's death, these officials put the estate up at auction for the fourth time.[2] Owing to Sam's mismanagement and indifference to business, precious little remained of it besides the house and brewery on Purchase Street, now sadly weather-worn and in disrepair. His only defense against the Commissioners was his pen, which, as most of his enemies were to find, was an uncommonly sharp weapon. Thomas Hutchinson, who felt its sting more than any other man, declared that Adams was at first "but an indifferent" writer who learned the art by dint of hard work and native skill in "artfully and fallaciously insinuating into the minds of his readers a prejudice against the characters of all whom he attacked."[3] His first move was always to win the support of public opinion; and the Land Bank affair gave excellent training to a man who was to spend the greater part of his life working with the popular mind. He employed the

[2] "To be sold at public Auction at the Exchange Tavern in Boston. To-morrow at noon. The Dwelling House, Malt-House, and other buildings, with the Garden and lands adjoining, and the Wharf, Dock and Flats before the same, being part of the estate of the late *Samuel Adams*, Esq., deceased. . . ." (Wells, I, 26.)

[3] Hutchinson, III, 295.

same methods against the Land Bank Commissioners that he later used against royal governors: "Put your adversary in the wrong," he said, "and keep him there." He swore that the Commissioners had admitted privately that the money which they now demanded from him was an unjust debt and that he was not "truly indebted" to the Land Bank. They not only were hounding him for debt, he protested, but were bleeding the public for large salaries and wasting time in order to prolong their work. Indeed, this propaganda was so forceful that the Commissioners lost their jobs as a consequence.

Adams's shrewdest defense against this confiscation of his estate was to demonstrate to those who had no interest in the Land Bank controversy that one of the most vital principles of the British Constitution was at stake. If his property was forfeit, Adams said, a dangerous blow would be struck at the "Security of English Property." He attempted to show that the Land Bank Commissioners' action was an invasion of property rights in which every property holder had vital interest. Adams knew that his misfortunes would not catch the public eye unless they appeared as wrongs done to a principle, not to an individual: hence his portrayal of himself to the public as a "good and loyal" subject of King George II, who was threatened with the loss of his rights and estate "contrary to all Reason, and the Spirit of common Law, by which British Subjects are secured in the *quiet* Possession of their own Property." [4] Perhaps even more timely was his warning to prospective buyers of the Adams estate of his intention to prosecute the sheriff and all purchasers who attended the sale. He reminded Bostonians that although his property had been advertised for sale four times, no one had been so ill-advised as to attempt to buy it. As a result, the sale fell through and Adams was allowed to enjoy what remained of his brewery.

Although Adams was thus subjected by the British House of Commons to ten years of persecution for a debt he had not personally incurred, this harsh treatment is not a touchstone by which to explain his later career. He became a revolutionary leader in 1765 because he was a New England patriot who,

[4] *Boston Gazette*, Aug. 14, 1758; Aug. 21, 1768. Hutchinson, III, 294.

having received the torch from Elisha Cooke, carried on New England's traditional attitude toward imperial authority. To understand his rebellion against the mother country it is necessary to take into account the history of New England from its settlement, and the rapid growth in the colonies, after the fall of Canada, of an assertive, independent spirit toward Great Britain — a spirit to which Adams himself gave full expression.

Another cause of Adams's inability to make headway in politics until the beginning of the revolutionary movement in 1765 was the domination of Massachusetts by the "Shirlean Faction" — a "motley mixture of high Church men, and dissenters" who monopolized public office at the expense of the Country Party.[5] Governor Shirley had made his position in the colony almost invulnerable by entrenching himself behind the "Court Party," composed largely of wealthy merchants, country squires, and political appointees. The steady growth of Shirley's influence in Massachusetts Bay aroused Sam Adams's fears that the governor was plotting to destroy the colony's charter rights. Although Boston — always the hotbed of opposition to royal governors — quarreled with Shirley, Adams and his friends were unable to pry him from office and put a more easily managed governor in his place. Shirley remained in power in Massachusetts for sixteen years; and during this period the New England patriots, Sam Adams among them, cooled their heels outside political office.

Thomas Hutchinson, the "Prime Minister" of the Shirlean faction and leader of the party that later fought desperately against Sam Adams and American independence, was one of the finest examples of the pre-revolutionary aristocracy of Massachusetts. A scholar whose *History of the Province of Massachusetts Bay* marks the beginning of modern historical writing in New England and whose private collection of manuscript was one of the largest in the colonies, he was no recluse, but an active politician, merchant, and judge. In person he was "a tall, slender, fair-complexioned, fair-spoken, 'very good Gentleman,' " whose good looks, his enemies lamented, had "captivated

[5] Jasper Mauduit, *Letter Book, Mass. Hist. Soc. Collections,* LXXIV (1918), James Otis to Jasper Mauduit, Oct. 28, 1762, 76–77.

half the pretty Ladies in the colony" and whose polished manners had won him "more than half the pretty Gentlemen." [6] Beside cutting the finest figure in Boston and setting "female" hearts fluttering, Hutchinson was an aristocrat and the most resolute of Massachusetts conservatives in keeping his class in power. The greater part of his life was spent in holding the lid tightly on colonial radicalism. By means of appeals to Parliament, he and his father had crushed Deacon Adams and the Land Bank in 1741; and in 1750 Hutchinson gave the Massachusetts inflationist party its death blow by outlawing paper money through Parliamentary legislation. In later years, Hutchinson had reason to take pride in calling himself the father of the Massachusetts currency system, but the immediate effect of the suppression of paper money was to bring upon him the rage of colonial radicals. A "great part of the people was in a fury" and he was forced to barricade his house against the Boston mob; when his house caught fire, the citizens stood by cursing him and crying, "Let it burn!" [7] In the House of Representatives he joined the Court Party and opposed his colleagues, who, like Deacon Adams, took the popular side; and after his conservatism had cost him his popularity in Boston and his seat in the House of Representatives, he moved to the Council, where he became a pillar of strength to the royal government in the colony. Thomas Hutchinson made it abundantly clear that he stood for everything that Sam Adams opposed: the rule of a few, well-born gentlemen over the lower classes; the suppression of colonial radicalism; the placing of loyalty to Crown and Empire above local patriotism; and the existence of a privileged aristocracy barred tightly against Sam Adams and his kind.

By 1760, Thomas Hutchinson's office grabbing had aroused Sam Adams's fears that Massachusetts was to be ruled by a narrow oligarchy. Hutchinson was president of the Massachusetts Council, lieutenant governor of the province, captain

---

[6] *Boston Gazette,* Jan. 31, 1763.

[7] *Publications Col. Soc. of Mass.,* III, Transactions 1895–97, 16. *The Diary and Letters of Thomas Hutchinson,* edited by Peter Orlando Hutchinson (1883), I, 53, 54. *Mass. Hist. Soc. Proceedings* (1899), XII, Second Series, 449. Mass. Archives, 26, *Hutchinson Corr.,* II, 87.

of Castle William, and judge of probate of Suffolk County. Moreover, he had used his influence to load the Supreme Court, the inferior courts, and most of the choice political jobs in the colony with his friends, relations, and political followers, until the Hutchinsons and Olivers had become the ruling families of the province. Hutchinson sincerely believed that the people were never happier than when they were ruled by gentlemen of birth and ability. But his power rankled Sam Adams and James Otis, who found themselves excluded from all share in the government. For twenty years, Otis exclaimed, the province had "groaned under his Tyranny" as he made "enormous strides in power." This "amazing ascendency of one family" violated the principle, highly prized by the Massachusetts patriots, that legislative, judiciary, and executive powers should not be placed in the same hands. James Otis believed that when the same person held judicial and executive powers, as did Thomas Hutchinson, the government was "hastening fast to its ruin, and the mischiefs and miseries that must happen before that fatal period, will be as bad as those felt in the most absolute monarchy." Sam Adams had no doubt that Hutchinson planned to destroy "the Democratical part" of the Massachusetts government; and he feared Hutchinson the more because he used "soft words, a smiling countenance, fair promises, and other tickling blandishments" to gain his purposes. Whatever differences existed between leaders of the popular party in Massachusetts, they stood upon common ground in their conviction that Thomas Hutchinson and his fellow "oligarchs" must be overthrown.[8]

If Sam Adams could not be a political leader of Massachusetts Bay, he set his countrymen an example of an "Old Roman" who lived austerely, despised money, and neglected his own business for the public's. He had run his father's brewery to the ground and had allowed the remainder of his small estate to slip through his fingers, until by 1760 he was as

<hr>

[8] Mauduit, James Otis to Jasper Mauduit, Oct. 28, 1762, 76, 77. *The Works of John Adams*, II, 150, 151.   Thomas Cushing to Dennys de Berdt, Dec. 6, 1766, MS. Mass. Hist. Soc. *Boston Gazette*, Jan. 11, 1762; Feb. 28, 1768; May 4, 1772. *The Writings of Samuel Adams*, II, 165.

bereft of worldly goods as any of the "Old Romans" he venerated.   The Tories later ridiculed his incapacity for business and
nicknamed him "Sam the Maltster," but it would have been far
better for them had Sam Adams become a contented brewer instead of a frustrated, restless politician.   With the death of his
wife in 1757, Adams was left with two small children and a
meagre income eked out by his salary as tax collector, which,
at best, was hardly equal to that of a country clergyman.   Unlike Elisha Cooke, who had piled up a sizable fortune outside
of politics, Sam Adams remained a poor man, dependent upon
his political job for a living.   But Adams was incorrigibly indifferent to money-making and, instead of tending his brewery,
he was constantly running off to the Caucus Club or electioneer-
ing in the town meeting.

In 1757, the Shirlean Faction's long domination of Massachusetts came to an end.   Shirley was removed as governor and
Thomas Pownall was sent out by Pitt to put vigor into the
lagging French War.   This young Whig politician, who later
became a stout defender of the colonies in Parliament, determined to win the support of the popular party in Massachusetts
.in order to fight the war more effectively.   Much to the patriots' surprise, they found themselves courted by a royal
governor and invited to honeymoon with the Crown while important business was being settled with the French and Indians
on the frontier.   It was a rare royal governor who left Massachusetts without feeling the sting of Sam Adams's slings and
arrows, yet Pownall's conciliatory methods made him the most
popular governor since the granting of the charter.   Even
Adams left off attacking the governor and joined the rest of the
patriots in basking in the unaccustomed warmth of court favor.
Bostonians praised Pownall's "tender regard" for Massachusetts' civil and religious liberties, and James Otis spoke of
him as "that truly good and worthy gentleman, almost the only
governor whose fate I ever knew much lamented in the colonies." [9]   Pownall's fate that so deeply grieved Otis was his removal in 1760 as governor of Massachusetts to make way for
Francis Bernard, a gentleman with very different opinions of
how royal colonies should be governed.   Years later, when

[9] *Boston Gazette*, April 4, 1763; Aug. 12, 1765.

Massachusetts was caught in the full tide of the revolution, many colonists looked back to Pownall's administration as the happiest period of their lives and declared that if the British government would restore the liberties they had enjoyed under Pownall and give them another such governor, they would be the most peaceable of His Majesty's subjects. Indeed, this desire to return to Pownall's day became so strong in 1770 that Sam Adams, who then believed the colonies had gone too far to turn back to the old imperial system, and who considered Pownall at best a lukewarm supporter of colonial rights, felt compelled to destroy his old friend's reputation as a friend to Massachusetts Bay.

When Francis Bernard became governor of Massachusetts in 1760, the colony seemed to be one of the most loyal of His Majesty's American provinces. In contrast to the indifferent support given by many other colonies during the Seven Years' War, Massachusetts maintained a large army and made immense expenditures to crush the French.[10] Massachusetts might well have been chosen by a royal governor, who, like Bernard, being none too well grounded in the colony's history, wished to enjoy his salary and be "easy and quiet." Indeed, for a time, Bernard believed he had at last found a haven: "This people," he wrote shortly after his arrival in the colony, "are better disposed to observe their compact with the Crown, than any other on the Continent that I know." The Country Party was in such complete abeyance that the governor need have no fears of encountering serious opposition. Boston was noted for its observance of the laws of trade; it was, wrote Bernard to William Pitt, "the most commendable in that respect of any in N America." The people were satisfied with their charter and the Massachusetts House of Representatives "kept more within the Bounds of Moderation & Decency than most other Assemblies on the Continent." [11] Yet, in fact, Massachusetts was one of the unlikeliest spots in which a royal governor would

[10] *The Necessity of Repealing the American Stamp Act Demonstrated* (London, 1766), 11.
[11] Mass. Archives, 26, *Hutchinson Corr.*, II, 30. Hutchinson, III, 199, 254. *Bernard Papers*, II, Sparks MSS., Harvard College Library, Francis Bernard to the Lords Commissioners for Trade, Aug. 18, 1760; Bernard to William Pitt, Oct. 3, 1761; IV, Bernard to John Pownall, July 20, 1765.

find rest and quiet. In 1721, the Lords Commissioners for Trade and Plantations had complained to the Crown that the House of Representatives had such vast power that the province was "and is always likely to continue in great disorder."[12] Massachusetts seldom let slip an opportunity to make her Crown officers as uncomfortable as possible, and the people were so jealous of their charter liberties that the governor and House of Representatives were almost constantly at odds. Sam Adams boasted that in Massachusetts "a governor's station is very slippery"; and none were as adept as Sam at greasing the ways on which royal governors were skidded out of the province.[13]

But what chiefly damped Bernard's hopes of a peaceful administration was the close of the Seven Years' War and the removal of the menace of French and Indian attacks from Canada. As long as French "papists" forced the colonists to look to England for military protection, provincial ambitions were effectively swaddled; but when Canada became British, one of the strongest bonds that held the colonies to the mother country was snapped. After 1760, the colonists began to entertain high notions of their own importance: a great territory to the North and West now lay open to their expansion; population was increasing so rapidly that the colonies seemed destined soon to outstrip the mother country; and wealth was increasing among all classes. These changes produced in America a "higher sense of the grandeur and importance of the colonies."[14] The Seven Years' War enriched Americans because the British government was forced to pour thousands of pounds into the colonies to fight the French — thus creating some of the large colonial fortunes, such as John Hancock's, that were used by the colonists to fight the British themselves during the Revolution. "You cannot well imagine," wrote a visitor to Boston in 1760, "what a Land of health, plenty and contentment this is among all ranks, vastly improved within these ten years. The war on

[12] British Museum, King's MSS. 205, Library of Congress Transcript, *Report of the State of American Colonies* (1721).
[13] *Independent Advertiser*, Jan. 23, 1749.
[14] Hutchinson, III, 85.

this Continent has been equally a blessing to the English Subjects and a Calamity to the French." [15]   It was not surprising therefore that New Englanders began to demand that they be made "co-equal in dignity and freedom with Britons." [16] Even if the British government had not attempted to centralize the administration of the Empire and tax the colonies, it would have encountered great difficulties in ruling British America after 1760.   But, to aggravate the dangers that threatened the Empire, British statesmen chose this critical period in colonial development to unleash that "terrible menacing monster the writs of assistance" upon Massachusetts Bay. [17]

During the Seven Years' War, American merchants found it highly profitable to supply the Spanish and French West Indian islands with necessities which enabled them to resist British sea power.   This practice of putting profit above patriotism outraged Englishmen and led to stricter enforcement of the laws of trade and navigation.   It was clear that if American supplies could be cut off, the foreign West Indies would be quickly starved into submission; and, since Massachusetts was one of the offenders, customhouse officers were ordered to use writs of assistance in stopping the prohibited trade.   These writs enabled the customhouse officers to enter warehouses and private dwellings in search of contraband.   Because Massachusetts was singled out by the British government in its effort to crush illegal trade, while Rhode Island and the neighboring colonies were allowed to smuggle almost at will, a movement was soon on foot — particularly in Boston, where mercantile interests were strongest — to nullify the writs of assistance.   "We want nothing," declared the Boston merchants, "but to be as free as others are, or that others should be restrained as well as we."   Massachusetts would have no complaints, it was said, if smuggling were suppressed generally: "It is because *we only* are severely dealt with, that we complain of unreasonable treatment." [18]

[15] *The Letters of James Murray, Loyalist* (1901), III.
[16] *The Writings of Samuel Adams*, I, 288.
[17] *The Works of John Adams*, X, 247.
[18] *Boston Gazette*, Dec. 7, 1761; Jan. 4, 1762. *Bernard Papers*, II, Bernard to the Lords Commissioners for Trade, Aug. 6, 1761.

It was not Sam Adams but James Otis, Junior, who, as the
Tories said, "first broke down the Barriers of Government to let
in the Hydra of Rebellion" by attacking the writs of assistance.
The Otises of Barnstable were one of the oldest and most conservative families in the province. Colonel James Otis, the
father of the revolutionary patriot, was such a staunch supporter
of the royal governors in the House of Representatives that he
was singled out by the *Independent Advertiser* as one of the
leading reactionaries in Massachusetts Bay. Nevertheless, this
family was to begin the struggle against the British government and the Massachusetts aristocracy that Sam Adams finished
by exiling the aristocrats and separating the colonies from the
mother country.

The Otises took their first step toward radicalism in 1760
when Colonel James Otis saw the political plum on which he
had set his heart — an appointment to the Supreme Judicial
Court — snatched from his hands by Thomas Hutchinson.
Otis had been promised the office by Governor Shirley as a
reward for his political services, and when it became vacant in
1760 he assumed his appointment would follow at once. Otis
had high qualifications for the Supreme Court; he was leader
of the bar in the three southern counties of Massachusetts and
speaker of the House of Representatives. Hutchinson's legal
knowledge, on the other hand, was scarcely greater than that
of many lawyers' clerks. He had been trained as a merchant,
not as a lawyer, and his only legal experience had been gained
as Judge of Probate for Suffolk County. But Hutchinson never
permitted his shortcomings to stand in the way of his ambition.
Before Colonel Otis knew fairly what his rival was about,
Hutchinson secured his own appointment as Chief Justice of
the province.

The Otises were enraged to be done out of office by what they
firmly believed to be Hutchinson's double-dealing. Colonel
Otis quit the governor's party in high dudgeon, and his son,
James Otis, set himself up in Boston as a politician, swearing,
it is said, among other things, to "set the province in a flame"
to be revenged upon Hutchinson. It was indeed galling to
Massachusetts patriots and lawyers that the Chief Justice of

the province was still studying elementary law while many able lawyers found their talents unrewarded. By taking an office for which he seemed utterly unfitted, Hutchinson convinced his enemies that he was determined to make himself the "Cæsar" of New England. "It has been his principle from a boy," exclaimed Sam Adams, "that mankind are to be governed by the discerning few, and it has been ever since his ambition to be the hero of the few."

James Otis stepped forth as a champion of colonial liberty when Massachusetts patriots celebrated the fall of Canada and the end of the French and Indian War by launching a vigorous attack upon the writs of assistance in 1760. Rather than assist the Crown officers in rounding up smugglers with writs of assistance, Otis resigned his lucrative office as King's advocate general of the vice-admiralty court at Boston, and appeared as attorney for the merchants who had united to resist the writs. Otis was "chief Director, Chamber Council, Councellor at the Bar, popular Haranguer, & Assembly Orator" of the popular or smugglers' party in the colony.[19] In his great speech before the Supreme Judicial Court in the Council chamber in Boston he denied the right of the British government to employ writs of assistance in Massachusetts Bay, basing his argument upon natural law. Although Otis spoke with "such a profusion of learning, such convincing argument, and such a torrent of sublime and pathetic eloquence, that a great crowd of spectators and auditors went away absolutely electrified," he could not prevent the use of writs in the colony.[20] Here again Thomas Hutchinson proved he was the Massachusetts patriots' worst enemy, for it was owing to Hutchinson's efforts alone that the writs were pronounced legal in Massachusetts Bay. Most of the judges of the Supreme Judicial Court before whom Otis spoke were inclined to believe he had the best of the argument and were ready to refuse to grant writs in the colony. But Hutchinson exerted his influence as Chief Justice to persuade them to continue the case until the next term in order that he might write to England to secure a copy of the writ and evidence

[19] *Bernard Papers*, IV, Bernard to Lord Shelburne, Dec. 22, 1766.
[20] *The Works of John Adams*, X, 183.

of the Exchequer's procedure in the mother country. This
delay allowed the friends of the British Ministry to rally, and
writs of assistance were issued in the province the following
year. Thus Hutchinson added another black mark to his record
on which Otis and Adams had already noted the Land Bank,
the Currency Act of 1751, the theft of the Chief Justiceship, and
the domination of the province by a few oligarchic families.

Because Otis launched his attack upon the writs of assistance
shortly after Hutchinson made away with the Chief Justiceship under Colonel Otis's nose, his enemies declared he had
become a patriot solely out of spite. This Otis stoutly denied,
and during the next decade he showed that he was actuated by
higher motives than a grudge against Thomas Hutchinson for
stealing a political job, although it is true that he began his
political career by making such a violent attack upon Hutchinson
and the royal government "that he satisfied the People in
Boston he was a proper person to represent them in the General
Court." [21] It was no wonder that conservative gentlemen swore,
when they learned that Otis had been sent to the House of
Representatives, that "out of this election will arise a d——d
faction, which will shake this province to its foundation." [22]
Otis's election meant the revival of the Country Party after
decades of inactivity. Massachusetts was running true to form:
as soon as the war on her frontiers ceased, the scene of battle
was transferred to the State House in Boston, where long-
suppressed political hostilities began to explode with more
violence than at any time since the Land Bank controversy.

When James Otis became the leader of the Massachusetts
Country Party he stepped into the rôle Sam Adams longed to
play. But a decade of failure had tempered Adams's ambition,
and by 1761 he was prepared to serve in the ranks. His ability,
however, soon made him Otis's right-hand man, chief newspaper
agitator and ablest abettor in keeping the flame lighted by the

[21] "Because a Son felt the ungrateful treatment of a Father, real or imaginary," asked Otis, "ought it to be presumed that every Part of his Conduct flows
from the foul Sources of Envy and disappointed Ambition?" (*Boston Gazette*,
April 4, 1763.) Mauduit, Edmund Trowbridge to William Bollan, July 15,
1762, p. 66.
[22] *The Works of John Adams*, X, 248.

writs of assistance burning briskly in the colony.   Between Otis
and Adams, Boston was filled with such "mad rant, and
porterly reviling" against Hutchinson and his party that the
lieutenant governor exclaimed it would put "even a Billingsgate matron to the blush."   Pious countrymen who came down
to Boston were horrified to find that "downright scurrility and
gross impudence, was really the most exalted Patriotism, the
most perfectly refined, disinterested Amor Patriæ."   For its
part, the Shirlean Faction attempted to convince the people that
Otis was "a Rakoon" and "a filthy skunk."   His patriotism, it
was said, sprang solely from "ungoverned passion, disappointed
ambition, and implacable envy of superior merit." [23]

At the beginning of his administration, Governor Bernard
resolved to steer clear of all alignments with factions in the
colony.   The governor was given no opportunity to carry out
his plan.   He was immediately informed by Adams and Otis
that he must join forces with them or be driven from the colony.
They attempted to convince him that they could easily ruin a
royal governor; no Crown officer, they declared, could stand his
ground after they had "opened the trenches against him."
They reminded him of the long list of governors they had sent
packing out of the colony and boasted they had removed three
of the last four governors entirely by their own efforts.   It
was made perfectly clear to Bernard that unless he favored the
Country Party in Massachusetts Bay he would find arrayed
against him some of the best politicians in the colony, particularly
that formidable Boston politician and newspaper writer, Sam
Adams. [24]   But Bernard had not yet felt Adams's sting sufficiently to rate him at his true worth, and he attached little
weight to the patriots' threats.   Hutchinson appeared to be the
most powerful man in the province and Bernard preferred to
cast his lot with him rather than with Otis and Adams.   The
governor therefore went over to Hutchinson so wholeheartedly
that Otis gave up hope of ever weaning him from the lieutenant

[23] *Boston Evening Post*, Feb. 14, 1763; March 28, 1763.
[24] *Bernard Papers*, XII, Bernard to Pownall, Aug. 28, 1773.   Peter Oliver,
Origin and Progress of the American Rebellion (1781), Egerton MSS., Gay
Transcripts, Mass. Hist. Soc., 68.

governor; and, indeed, Bernard seemed to have placed himself at the head of the old Shirlean Faction. With his aid, Hutchinson's influence soared, a strong party of "Governor's friends" was built up by means of patronage, and the "oligarchy" in Massachusetts Bay began to fasten itself deeper upon the province. Otis and Adams needed no more evidence to convince them that all the real power in the colony was in Hutchinson's hands and that every royal governor "must submit to him or live in perpetual broils." [25]

In many respects the revived Country Party, headed by James Otis, was heir to the Land Bank Party which in the previous decade had given Massachusetts conservatives the worst fright they received from the days of Anne Hutchinson to those of Sam Adams. Otis appealed to the old guard of colonial inflationists by calling Hutchinson's destruction of paper money "that fatal shock." Like the Land Bankers, Otis denounced the wealthy mercantile aristocracy "who grind the faces of the poor without remorse, eat the bread of oppression without fear, and wax fat upon the spoils of the people." He declared that his only purpose in opposing Hutchinson was to awaken in his fellow citizens "the true Spirit of Patriotism, and to stir up a manly Opposition against the Attempt of any Governor or Lieutenant Governor whatever, to infringe the Rights of the People." He regarded himself as a defender of the common people against those merchants and politicians who were piling up large fortunes and power by taking advantage of fluctuations in the price of gold to ship colonial currency to England. These men, Otis said, were "forging chains and shackles for their country"; and Thomas Hutchinson, the most arbitrary of this oligarchical crew, must be shorn of his offices before popular liberty would be secure. [26]

Otis and Adams fanned the flames in Massachusetts Bay so vigorously that the "Rage for Patriotism" spread through New England until it was said there was "scarce a cobler or porter

[25] Mauduit, 39, 78, 97. *Boston Gazette*, April 4, 1763. Mass. Archives, 26, *Hutchinson Corr.*, II, 30. *Bernard Papers*, IV, Bernard to the Earl of Shelburne, Dec. 22, 1766.

[26] *Boston Gazette*, Jan. 11, 1762 (Supplement); April 4, 1763.

but had turn'd mountebank in politicks" and set himself up
as a village Hampden. Through the *Boston Gazette,* which
gained the reputation of being the "most factious paper in
America," the Boston patriots "Spit their Venom" at the governor and Thomas Hutchinson. Governor Bernard soon saw the
true nature of the opposition with which he was faced. He
realized that he was dealing with the "genuine Descendants of
the Faction" which had driven out governors Shute, Burnet,
and Belcher, and which, "like a Body corporate," carried on the
tradition of hostility to royal government. It was clear to
Bernard that he would not find the "ease and quiet" he sought
in Massachusetts while Otis and Adams continued to keep the
colony in ferment.[27]

By arousing Massachusetts patriotism, Otis produced a remarkable burst of activity in the clubs and secret societies which
abounded in Boston. The Merchants Club, which met at the
British Coffee House, gave him valuable aid in opposing the
writs of assistance and the vice-admiralty system. The Boston
Masonic Society peppered Hutchinson and the royal government from its meeting place in "Adjutant Trowel's *long Garret,*" where it was said more sedition, libels, and scurrility were
hatched than in all the garrets in Grubstreet.[28] Otis and his
Masonic brethren became such adept muckrakers that Hutchinson's friends believed they must have "ransak'd Billingsgate and
the Stews" for mud to sling at the Massachusetts aristocracy.
No less active was the Monday Night Club, composed of
radical politicians headed by James Otis and Sam Adams, where
the talk ran to "curious anecdotes about governors, counsellors,
representatives, demagogues, merchants, &c." One of Otis's
first steps had been to make allies of those redoubtable "trumpeters of sedition," the "black regiment" of Congregational ministers; and scarcely a patriot club was without a divine who
lent an odor of sanctity to what conservatives believed would
otherwise have been rank treason. "The Garrets . . . were

---

[27] *Boston Evening Post,* March 7, 1763. *Bernard Papers,* IV, Bernard to
Pownall, July 20, 1765; Bernard to the Earl of Shelburne, Jan. 24, 1767.
[28] *Bernard Papers,* II, Bernard to Pownall, July 6, 1761; Aug. 28, 1761.
Boston News Letter, March 24, 1763. *Boston Evening Post,* March 14, 1763.

crowded with the Rabble in full Divan," wrote one of Otis's enemies, "with a Clergyman to praeside, whose Part was to declaim on Politicks & Sedition." Frequently, this "ghostly father" who "huddled promiscuously" with mechanics, lawyers, and porters in some snug attic in North Boston was the Reverend Dr. Samuel Cooper, pastor of the Brattle Street Church which Sam Adams attended.[29] Hutchinson's friends declared the patriots had fooled no one by hiding behind clergymen's skirts while they concocted sedition in backstairs hideouts. They longed to smoke these politicians and priests out of their garrets, but the patriots stoutly refused to come into the open.

By far the most important of these patriot clubs was the Boston Caucus, which was still, as it had been in Deacon Adams's day, the ladder by which politicians climbed into town offices and the General Court. This "venerable Company," of which Sam Adams was among the most prominent, usually met in the garret of Tom Dawes's house on Purchase Street, where they drank flip, chose town officers, and smoked tobacco "till you cannot see from one end of the garret to the other." [30] Like other "Garretters," many members of the Caucus Club were men whom Thomas Hutchinson considered the "rabble" of Boston, but Sam Adams loved democratic company and felt thoroughly at home among the shipyard workers, masons, and politicians who crowded into Tom Dawes's attic. Aristocratic gentlemen often lamented that Boston was a "complete democracy" in which the people's thinking was done for them by Sam Adams and a few other wily politicians who controlled the town offices. At the Caucus Club, moderators, selectmen, assessors, tax collectors, wardens, firewards, and representatives were picked by Adams and his friends several weeks before the election. The nominees were then sent up to the Merchants' Club for approval. Rarely was this ticket agreed upon by the "Grand Corkass" and Merchants' Club defeated in Boston

[29] *The Works of John Adams*, II, 162. Peter Oliver, 102. *Massachusetts Gazette*, Jan. 11, 1776. Mass. Archives, 27, *Hutchinson Corr.*, III, 122. Richard Frothingham, *The Life and Times of Joseph Warren* (1865), 15.

[30] *The Works of John Adams*, II, 144, 219.

elections. For example, when Sam Adams was chosen moderator of the Boston town meeting in May 1774, apparently by the spontaneous decision of the citizens, it had already been decided in the Caucus that Adams should be moderator.[31] The town meeting was little more than a rubber stamp for the Caucus, but Boston voters could not complain they were not given a good show when they cast their votes in Faneuil Hall. "For form's sake (as on College Commencement days)," Adams staged during the town meetings "a number of warm disputes . . . to entertain the lower sort, who are in an exstacy to find the old Roman Patriots still surviving." The people received oratory and Adams and his friends received the town offices — and both sides were satisfied with the exchange.[32]

In the eighteenth-century Massachusetts, a large tavern acquaintanceship was indispensable to a politician. As John Adams said, it was in taverns that "bastards, and legislators, are frequently begotten." [33] There political bosses bought votes with flip and rum and made themselves intimate with the tavern keeper, who himself was a political power to be reckoned with in every election. Travelers who put up at a Massachusetts tavern usually found it full of people "drinking drams, flip, toddy, carousing, swearing; but especially plotting with the landlord, to get him, at the next town meeting, an election either for selectmen or representative." Sam Adams discovered these taverns with their "tippling, nasty, vicious crew" excellent recruiting grounds for the mobs he later raised against the Tories and Crown officers. Adams himself was a familiar figure in Boston taverns; one of his choice nicknames among the Tories was "Sam the Publican." Indeed, Adams seemed equally at home in meetinghouse or tavern: he was as much at ease with deacons and parishioners as he was with the shipyard workers and artisans. From early life, Adams spent much time among the common people of North Boston and he gradually came to be regarded as their spokesman; but his family's social position and his own piety gave him great in-

---

[31] E. H. Goss, *Life of Paul Revere* (1891), II, 643 (Appendix).
[32] *Boston Evening Post*, March 21, 1763.
[33] *The Works of John Adams*, II, 85, 112, 126.

fluence among the middle-class townspeople. Adams dearly
loved a pot of ale, a good fire, and the company of mechanics
and shipyard workers of radical political opinions. Under Sam
Adams, Boston taverns became nurseries of revolution as well
as "nurseries of our legislators." He made the headquarters
of the Revolution the Green Dragon Tavern in Union Street,
where the Boston Caucus Club held its meetings and where
Sons of Liberty from the near-by shipyards, ropewalks, and
docks met to hear him hold forth against British tyranny and
the Tories. At the Bunch of Grapes in King's Street, Adams
and the Whigs discussed the British Constitution and the Massachusetts Charter, and in the Salutation Tavern in Salutation
Alley they plotted the downfall of the royal government.
Thus, the setting of much of the preliminary work of the
Revolution in Massachusetts Bay is under the roof of a
Boston tavern.

It is surprising to find that Sam Adams, who belonged to almost every liberal political club in Boston and carried the
heaviest schedule of "lodge nights" of any patriot, was not a
Mason. Many of his friends were high-ranking Masons and
the Boston lodge did much to foster the Revolution, but Sam
Adams never joined the Masonic Society. It is true there
is no evidence that he was ever asked to become a Mason, but
Adams was one of the most popular clubmen in Boston and it
is hardly possible that the Boston lodge, which was filled with
fiery Whigs, would have missed an opportunity to bring him
in. But Adams disliked secret societies where ceremonial
ritual was practised, and he always distrusted political organizations which he had not had a hand in creating. He preferred to
revolutionize New England through the Whig Clubs, committees of correspondence, and caucuses, — over all of which
his control was certain, — rather than by means of Masonic
groups where his schemes might be disapproved. Notwith-
standing its services in the Revolution, Adams never showed
that he bore any love towards Masonry.

Despite Otis's early success in reviving the Massachusetts
Country Party, it soon suffered a sharp decline. Without a
supply of fresh grievances, Otis found it impossible to keep the

colony in a flame: writs of assistance lost their novelty, and, after an unpromising beginning, Hutchinson became a popular Chief Justice. Otis lost control of the Massachusetts House of Representatives, where the governor's friends outnumbered his party two to one, although Crown officers complained there were still too many "Inkeepers, Retailers, & yet more inferior Orders of Men" to listen to Otis's "mobbish oratory." [34] Governor Bernard again began to believe that Massachusetts Bay was a haven for a royal governor who sought peace and quiet; the government ran along "with the utmost harmony & good humour"; governor and Assembly never met without exchanging compliments and well-wishes; and Bernard seemed likely to become highly popular. He considered the people in general "extremely well disposed to Government." [35] The colony was still riding the crest of war prosperity; there was yet no evidence of British tyranny; and when Hutchinson declared that Massachusetts possessed "as great civil and religious liberties as any people under heaven," he seemed to have the better of the argument against Otis and Adams, who shrieked tyranny against the royal government. Most New Englanders wished to settle down to enjoy the good fortune brought them by the Seven Years' War rather than help Otis and Adams turn the province topsy-turvy because Hutchinson held too many political offices for the people's good. "When God in his mercy is delivering us from our foreign enemies," asked Thomas Hutchinson, "shall we be so ungrateful as to endeavour to raise animosities and civil wars among ourselves?" And most New Englanders answered with a hearty amen. [36]

Otis's failure was due largely to his inability to win control of the Massachusetts Council. Many years before, in the *Independent Advertiser*, Sam Adams had said that the Council was a great stumblingblock to political liberalism; and Otis's experience from 1763 to 1766 completely confirmed this judg-

[34] Peter Oliver, 36, 37.

[35] *Bernard Papers*, IV, Bernard to the Earl of Shelburne, Dec. 22, 1766. Hutchinson, III, 254.

[36] *Bernard Papers*, III, Bernard to Pownall, May 5, 1765. *Massachusetts Gazette*, April 7, 1763.

ment. The Council was a stronghold of conservatism manned by the governor's supporters, who kept a tight rein upon the unruly Lower House. Although its members were elected by the House of Representatives, the governor's friends were usually present in the Lower House in such force that the Council was filled with those well-born gentry who formed the backbone of the Massachusetts Court Party. During such crises as the Land Bank affair, when the representatives elected Deacon Adams to the Council, the governor kept the Council loyal by negativing the radicals. Almost invulnerable in the Council, the royal governor possessed a strong party in the Lower House which, during periods of political tranquillity, held the balance of power. As James Otis learned, it was no easy matter for the Country Party to wrest control of the House of Representatives from the governor's friends, for successive royal governors had strengthened their political fences by handing out offices in the judiciary and militia to their supporters, thereby creating a machine which served to keep the patriots out of power for many years. Militia regimentals had great attraction for country squires and the governor purchased their loyalty with commissions and special favors. Landowners like John Murray of Rutland, whose estates were the largest in Worcester County, received a colonelcy in the militia besides numerous other bounties from the governor; and Timothy Ruggles of Hardwick, likewise a militia colonel and extensive landowner, was the leader of the governor's party in the House of Representatives. Scarcely a country town in Massachusetts was without the governor's appointees; and, as they were chosen from a highly influential class, western Massachusetts became the most loyal part of the province and repeatedly forestalled the Boston Whigs when they attempted to lead the colony into a quarrel with King and Parliament.[37]

Even when the British government unleashed another "menacing monster" upon New Englanders, — fully as terrifying as the writs of assistance, — Otis was unable to awaken patriotic fervor in the province outside of Boston. In 1764,

[37] Jonathan Smith, Toryism in Worcester County, *Mass. Hist. Soc. Proceedings* (1915), XLVIII, 15, 16, 33.

George Grenville, Chancellor of the British Exchequer, began his fatal quest of a colonial revenue by clapping new duties on Spanish wines imported into the colonies and reducing the duty of Spanish, Dutch, and French West India molasses from six-pence to threepence a gallon.   Considering New Englanders' well-known aversion to taxation, it might be supposed that the Sugar Act, as it was called, was warmly welcomed by the "Saints" because it lowered taxes.   But this piece of legislation produced, Governor Bernard wrote, "a greater alarm in this country than the taking of Fort William Henry did in 1757." [88] Boston merchants exclaimed that it was an "unformed Monster that will Devour all before It" and compel every trader and businessman to "hold the Plough, The Syth and Reaping Hook." [39]   New Englanders had no quarrel with the pro-hibitively high rates on foreign molasses established by the Molasses Act of 1733 because no attempt was made to collect them.   His Majesty's officers of the customs in Boston had notoriously short memories of the laws of trade, and it required only a stiff swig of rum to make them forget the existence of the Molasses Act.   Had the Molasses Act been enforced to the letter, New England's commerce would have been destroyed, because the British West India islands were alone unable to supply the New England distilleries with sufficient molasses. But as long as smuggling from the French and West Indian islands was winked at, New England prospered, although the royal revenue from American commerce dwindled until the ex-pense of maintaining the customs had become greater than the income.   By reducing the duty until its collection was feasible, George Grenville proposed to give American customs officers something to do besides drink rum with smugglers and make pocket money by conniving at violations of the laws of trade. His policy spread greater consternation among New England merchants than had the French and Indians during their bloody frontier forays in 1757, because it was realized that he

[88] *Select Letters on the Trade and Government of America* (London, 1774), 9.   *Bernard Papers*, Bernard to Pownall, Dec. 3, 1765.
[39] *John Powell Letters*, MS. Mass. Hist. Soc.; John Powell to Christopher Champion, April 9, 1764.

planned to tighten imperial bounds and centralize its administration. New England's economic well-being depended upon a continuation of the laxity and free play of the early eighteenth-century Empire; and it was apparent that if George Grenville reorganized the British Empire, New England would be forced to pay a heavy penalty for having permitted its maritime and commercial ambitions to overleap the restraints laid by British mercantile policy upon its colonies.

Sam Adams's preoccupation with politics and mismanagement had long since put his own business beyond the power of injury by the British government, but he could protest as a citizen if not as a brewer and merchant. He found ample cause for alarm in the Sugar Act, which, he pointed out, would bring trade "to the lowest Ebb, if not totally obstruct & ruin it," but his anxiety was chiefly caused by the broad lines of policy Grenville laid down in the preamble to the act. Here Grenville gave strong hints of the reorganization of the Empire contemplated by the British Ministry. The preamble states that "Whereas it is expedient that new provisions and regulations should be established for improving the revenue of this Kingdom . . . and whereas it is just and necessary that a revenue should be raised . . . for defraying the expenses of defending, protecting, and securing the same. . . ." It was a new departure for Parliament to lay duties on commodities for the purpose of raising a revenue; and the implication that the taxes realized from the Sugar Act were to be used to support a colonial military establishment was an abrupt break with the traditional policy of the mother country. Taxes on commodities had hitherto been laid by Parliament only for the regulation of trade, and the mother country had shouldered the expenses of the regular army in the colonies. In the instructions to Boston's representatives in the General Court written by Sam Adams in 1764, he denied Parliament's right to impose such taxes upon the colonies. Almost alone of his contemporaries, Sam Adams protested from the first against the Sugar Act on the ground that Parliament was overstepping its authority. If the House of Commons could compel New England to pay ruinous taxes upon such a staple as molasses, Adams believed that the colonies held their liberty on uncertain tenure indeed. Once the tax on molasses were paid, he warned, the colonists would find themselves saddled with more taxes by Parliament: "If our Trade may be taxed why not our Lands?" he asked. "Why not the Produce of our Lands & every thing we possess or make use of? This we apprehend annihilates our Charter Right to govern & tax ourselves. . . . It strikes at our British Privileges." Thus, as early as 1764, Sam Adams raised the cry of no taxation without representation.[40]

The Sugar Act proved that Bostonians had in Sam Adams one of the best watchdogs of colonial liberty in New England, but this tax alone would not have produced a revolutionary movement in the American colonies. Indeed, there was so little resistance that George Grenville was encouraged to believe Americans would tamely swallow all the pills he had prepared for them. In Boston, it was said that the British government had sold Americans to the West India planters, but Bostonians found New England yeomen slow to rally to their aid. In Massachusetts, as in other provinces, there was latent hostility between town and country which occasionally flared into open hatred. This antagonism greatly embarrassed Boston patriots when they stood in need of country support, for without the aid of farmers and back-country politicians, Boston had little political influence. Of the one hundred and twenty members of the Massachusetts House of Representatives, the metropolis sent only four. This meagre representation made it necessary for Bostonians to look to the country for their principal strength in the legislature. When Sam Adams spoke in 1764 of the danger of taxes on land if the Sugar Act were made a precedent, he was attempting to show landowners in the province their community of interest with Boston in protesting against taxes on commodities for the purpose of raising a revenue. Although the Massachusetts House of Representatives petitioned Parliament to repeal the Sugar Act, the country was far slower than the seaport towns in catching fire against Parliamentary trade duties. Bostonians complained that many of the country towns sent representatives to the General

[40] *The Writings of Samuel Adams*, I, 5.

Court "who are profess'd enemies to trade," and Sam Adams found that many rural voters were "so careless in the Choice of their representatives" as to send to Boston men who became Governor Bernard's tools against the patriots.[41] Country delegates to the General Court, like Artemas Ward of Shrewsbury, who later became one of Adams's staunchest adherents in rural Massachusetts, showed little excitement over the Sugar Act.[42] In attempting to arouse Massachusetts farmers against the British government in 1764, Boston agitators bumped their heads squarely against rural conservatism and the strong inclination of countrymen to regard trade as Boston's own concern. It required the Stamp Act to unite town and country and, by giving every class a grievance against the British government, enable Sam Adams to create a formidable revolutionary party in Massachusetts with Boston at its head.

The ill fortune that had overtaken the Massachusetts Country Party deeply dismayed James Otis. Early in 1765, he attempted to give his earlier radical doctrines such a conservative whitewashing that his friends suspected he had sold out to Hutchinson. Otis had been completely unable to remove Hutchinson and the "oligarchs" from their political offices; and Governor Bernard had entrenched himself, in spite of Otis and Adams, behind a party built up by means of patronage and favoritism. In 1765, on the eve of the Stamp Act, James Otis lamented that he had "contended so much in vain" against Hutchinson and the Governor's party; and Hutchinson's friends, believing themselves well out of danger from Otis, said he had never succeeded in raising a flame in the colony: "With all his puffing and blowing," they rejoiced, "he has been able only to raise a smoke." [43] Throughout New England, farmers swore that Hutchinson had been "most damnably abused, and slandered, and belied"; and few had been shaken in their conviction that he was an honest man, a philosopher, an "eminent saint" of the Congregational Church.[44] To so little purpose had

---

[41] Boston Evening Post, May 12, 1760. The Writings of Samuel Adams, II, 165. Boston Gazette, May 14, 1764. Hutchinson, III, 109, 166.

[42] Charles Martyn, Life of Artemas Ward (1921), 33.

[43] Boston Gazette, May 13, 1765. Boston Evening Post, March 28, 1763.

[44] The Works of John Adams, II, 189, 193.

Adams and Otis labored before the attempts of the British government to tax the colonies by means of the Stamp Act and Townshend duties brought about Hutchinson's downfall and destroyed the conservative party in New England.

III

SAM ADAMS AND THE STAMP ACT

IMPERIAL defense was the rock upon which the old British Empire split. The Seven Years' War demonstrated that the colonies were utterly unable to make concerted military effort even when French and Indians were on the warpath along their frontiers. The requisition system by which the colonies had for generations given aid to the Crown — when they felt so disposed — broke down under the strain of a prolonged war. After peace had been made at Paris in 1763, British statesmen might well feel there was acute need of imperial reorganization. Although Great Britain had carved out a huge empire during the war and defeated the combined forces of France and Spain, Englishmen feared that all that had been gained by seven years of war might be lost in a single campaign if the British American colonies were not given strong military protection.[1] Yet England had emerged from the war with a staggering debt and taxpayers groaned at the thought of supporting large armies in the colonies. Unlike modern taxpayers, eighteenth-century British taxpayers had a decisive voice in government, and they let it be known unequivocally in 1763 that however necessary a colonial military establishment, they would no longer foot the bill.

When the British government learned that Englishmen were unwilling to pay for imperial defense, it began to look for other sources of revenue. It was inevitable that British statesmen should turn to the colonies as a promising reservoir. The American colonies were yet untouched by direct taxation

[1] George Grenville, *The Justice and Necessity of Taxing the American Colonies Demonstrated, together with a Vindication of the Authority of Parliament* (London, 1766), 10, 11.

by the British Parliament; they had become wealthy during the
Seven Years' War; and the money that the British government
was seeking was to be used for the colonists' own defense and
spent in the colonies themselves.   Moreover, it was widely
believed in England that the defense of the American colonies
against a French invasion was the sole cause of the recent war
— in which, it was said, all the profits had gone to Americans
while Englishmen paid the bill.[2]   The shortest way to put hard-
pressed English squires into a good humor was to saddle the
colonists with part of the burden.   Englishmen imagined Americans to be prosperous farmers living on the fat of the land or
rich merchants who made fabulous profits in smuggling; and
few doubted that the colonists could easily afford to support
the garrisons that were to be sent them.   Even after Americans
had pleaded poverty in protest against taxation, Englishmen
were unshaken in their conviction that the colonists were
miserly rascals whose bulging money bags were more than
ample to pay their share of imperial expense.

George Grenville, the Chancellor of the Exchequer, who
had begun his imperial housecleaning with the Sugar Act of
1764, proposed in Parliament in 1764 that taxes in the form
of stamp duties be laid upon the colonies to support their
armed establishments.   In order to sugar-coat the pill, Grenville gave the colonies a year of grace in which to inform their
London agents of a more satisfactory method of raising the
desired revenue.   But the colonies frittered away the year
without suggesting any alternative to the stamp duty, other than
reverting to the old requisition system — with the result that
when Parliament met in 1765, Grenville again brought forward
his scheme for colonial revenue.   He believed a stamp duty
on American newspapers, legal documents, and commercial
papers to be "the easiest, the most equal and the most certain
that can be chosen."   Among its advantages — to which Americans were unfortunately quite blind — was that few collection
officers were required, the burden was spread lightly over the

[2] Thomas Whately, *The Regulations Lately made concerning the Colonies,
and the Taxes imposed upon them, considered* (London, 1765), 3, 102.
Grenville, 12.

whole population, and it fell on the colonies in proportion to
their wealth.   Undoubtedly, Grenville considered he was doing the colonists a good turn by favoring them with such a
faultless tax as the stamp duty.[3]

As a result, Grenville and the British Ministry were taken
completely by surprise at the manner in which Americans received the Stamp Act.   Instead of erecting statues to Grenville and hailing him as their benefactor, they burned him in
effigy and promised to string him on the gallows should he
ever set foot in America.   Even more startling was the growth
of colonial unity as a result of the Stamp Act.   Although the
colonial mind always remained a mystery to George Grenville,
he had reason for bewilderment in seeing Americans uniting
against the mother country in 1765 when a few years before they
had displayed a "peevish reluctance to associate and unite"
while the French and Indians were pounding at their frontier.[4]
The Seven Years' War had led many Englishmen to believe
that the provinces were beyond hope of federation, and the reports of English travelers in the colonies confirmed this conviction: "Fire and water," said Andrew Burnaby shortly before the passage of the Stamp Act, "are not more heterogeneous
than the different colonies in North America." [5]   Colonial union
was almost as unexpected to the colonists themselves as to
British statesmen.   Before 1765, it was said, the provinces
were "ever at a variance, and foolishly jealous of each other,"
and united action was "what the most zealous colonists never
could have expected." [6]   Clear-sighted observers on both sides
of the Atlantic believed colonial unity impossible because of
the great differences between the provinces in manners, religion,
and interest.   Nevertheless, when confronted by the Stamp

[3] Whately, 101.   Joseph Galloway, *Historical and Political Reflections on
the Rise and Progress of the American Rebellion* (London, 1780), 12.
[4] Grenville, *An Application of Political Rules to Great Britain, Ireland,
and America* (London, 1766), 80.
[5] Andrew Burnaby, *Travels through the Middle Settlements in North America* (1798), 121.
[6] James Otis, *A Vindication of the British Colonies against the Aspersions
of the Halifax Gentleman, in his letter to a Rhode Island friend* (Boston,
1765).   Frothingham, 21.

Act, colonial particularism began to crumble and America was "awakened, alarmed, restless, & disaffected." [7] "What a Blessing to us has the Stamp Act eventually . . . prov'd," exclaimed Sam Adams. ". . . When the Colonys saw the Common Danger they at the same time saw their mutual Dependence." [8] From the frontier to the seaboard and from Pensacola to Quebec, there was scarcely a family who had not heard of the Stamp Act and who did not regard it with dread, although, as Thomas Hutchinson said, many had little idea what it actually was. [9]

Within a year of the passage of the Stamp Act by the British House of Commons, the American colonies were covered with Societies whose purpose was to nullify the act. The members of these clubs called themselves "Sons of Liberty" — a name derived from Isaac Barré's speech in Parliament in behalf of the colonies during the Stamp Act debate. By forming military alliances between the colonies, driving out the stamp masters and burning the stamps, the Sons of Liberty prevented the execution of the Stamp Act and usurped much of the real power of government in America. During the course of the Revolution they assumed many different names, but whether they called themselves committees of correspondence, committees of safety, or "true-born Whigs," the Sons of Liberty of 1765 were the radicals who led the colonies into revolution against the mother country.

When news of the Stamp Act reached the colonies, these patriotic societies spread rapidly over America. "The whole continent," George Bancroft said, "rang with the cheering name of the Sons of Liberty." But not all of the clubs that called themselves Sons of Liberty were founded spontaneously to resist the Stamp Act. Many had been in existence for years and had been created with no thought of resisting the "tyranny" of the mother country: their purpose was rather to combat the colonial aristocracy and give the unprivileged class a share of political power. The muster rolls of the "Ancient and Honor-

[7] George Bancroft, *History of the United States*, V, 241.
[8] *The Writings of Samuel Adams*, I, 109.
[9] Mass. Archives, 26, *Hutchinson Corr.*, II, 198.

able Mechanical Company" of Baltimore, which had been formed in 1763 and became the Sons of Liberty in 1765, show that its membership was made up almost entirely of small tradesmen and artisans.[10]   In Charleston, South Carolina, the nucleus of the Sons of Liberty was the long-established Fireman's Association; in Philadelphia, it was the "Heart-and-Hand Fire Company."   And in Boston, where Sam Adams became the leading Son of Liberty, the Sons of Liberty sprang from the Caucus Club, which had been in existence for a half-century. Thus, the political machinery with which American patriots opposed British oppression and seized power from the royal government was firmly established before 1765.

The Boston Sons of Liberty, led by Sam Adams, boasted some of the most fiery, unruly Whigs on the continent.   They were recruited largely from the wharfingers, artisans and shipyard workers of North Boston — the class of men who had warmly supported Deacon Adams and his inflationary Land Bank in 1740 and who were eager in 1765 to punish the Tory upper class.   Although many wealthy merchants were known as Sons of Liberty and made an impressive show with their chariots in parades and celebrations, most of them were patriots out of prudence: when Boston swarmed with patriot mobs, it was well to be known as a Son of Liberty.   The true Sons of Liberty — those who controlled the mobs and Boston elections — were a small group of politicians from the Caucus Club who met in a counting room on the second floor of Chase and Speakman's distillery.   This building stood in Hanover Square near the Tree of Liberty — a huge oak that had been planted, it was significantly pointed out, in 1646, three years before the execution of Charles I.   Tories always believed it important that the Liberty Boys had their meeting place conveniently near a liquor supply such as that afforded by Chase and Speakman's distillery, since it was supposed their courage arose chiefly "from the steams of their poisonous rum." [11]

Those Sons of Liberty who met in Hanover Square were

[10] G. W. McCreary, *The Ancient and Honorable Mechanical Company of Baltimore* (1901), 13–19.
[11] *Pennsylvania Journal*, Nov. 21, 1765.

known as the "Loyall Nine." They were John Avery, a distiller and secretary to the club; John Smith, a brazier; Thomas Crafts, a painter; Benjamin Edes, printer of the *Boston Gazette;* Stephen Cleverly, a brazier; Thomas Chase, a distiller; Joseph Field, a ship captain; George Trott, a jeweler; and Henry Bass, a cousin of Sam Adams. When John Adams visited the "Loyall Nine" in their room above Chase and Speakman's distillery, he was entertained with "punch, wine, pipes, and tobacco, biscuit and cheese, &c"; and Sam Adams sat down with them to a "very Genteel Supper" topped off with patriotic toasts.[12] Although neither of the Adamses was a member of the "Loyall Nine," Sam Adams's connection with them was very close. He spent many convivial evenings and ate Sunday dinners with Henry Bass and other Sons of Liberty; and, since the "Loyall Nine" were for the most part young fire-eating Whigs, they looked to Sam Adams, an older and more experienced plotter against the royal government, for leadership. Adams and the "Loyall Nine" spirited up the mobs which terrorized Boston during the revolutionary period. Whenever a riot or meeting of the citizens at Liberty Tree was planned, it was the "Loyall Nine" who placarded the town with notices during the small hours of the night, urging the townspeople to be on hand for the event. They kept their identity secret and wished it to be believed that the mobs they set in motion were spontaneous outbreaks of violence from the "lower sort." [13] But it will be seen that Boston was controlled by a "trained mob" and that Sam Adams was its keeper.

After the full consequences of the Stamp Act were seen, George Grenville's critics accused him of having destroyed Great Britain's best security for keeping intact her colonial empire: the love of the colonists for the mother country and the differences in sentiments and interest that kept the colonies at variance. The Stamp Act did not work such a miracle in America, but it taught the colonists the value of united action against the mother country and began the revolutionary turmoil

---

[12] *The Works of John Adams,* II, 178, 179.   *Mass. Hist. Soc. Proceedings,* XLIV (1911), 688, 689.
[13] *Mass. Hist. Soc. Proceedings,* XLIV (1911), 688, 689.

that was to disrupt the Empire within a decade.   What manner
of "menacing monster" was this that produced such far-reaching
changes in the colonies, hitherto hopelessly disunited and firmly
bound to the mother country?

Despite Grenville's assertion that the stamp duty was an
equable and easy form of taxation, it is true that Parliament had
never before laid a tax of its kind upon the colonies: the only
precedent for Parliamentary taxation was port duties for the
regulation of trade.   The experience of the British government in attempting to impose new forms of taxation upon English taxpayers should have been a warning of the fate of the
Stamp Act in America.   Wise after the event, Englishmen
saw that the novelty of the Stamp Act alone was sufficient to
have aroused the colonists' opposition.   Like all property
owners, New Englanders dreaded an increase in taxes, and
they were reluctant to give up such an admirable scheme as the
requisition system.   The revenue derived from the Stamp Act
was to be used to support armies in the colonies, but Americans
could see no necessity for maintaining a colonial military establishment: the only enemy visible in 1765, they said, was
"a few ragged Indians" and beaten Frenchmen.   It was remembered that in the seventeenth century when Massachusetts
was surrounded with foes the British government had left the
colony to defend itself alone against "the combined powers of
France, hell, Indian Savages, and the corrupt administration
of those times." [14]   It seemed probable to Americans, therefore, that a large share of the Stamp Act revenue would be
used by the Ministry to buy up the British House of Commons,
make jobs in the colonies for Court favorites, and keep "lazy
fellows in ease, idleness, or luxury, in mother Britain's lap."
If Great Britain had run itself into debt during the Seven
Years' War, the colonists believed themselves no more obliged
to assist her with their pocketbooks than was the "Great
Mogul." [15]

The Stamp Act required that all colonial newspapers, legal
documents, and commercial papers bear a stamp which could

[14] *Boston Gazette,* July 29, 1765; Aug. 12, 1765.
[15] *Ibid.,* Aug. 5 and 12, 1765.

be purchased at prices ranging from a halfpenny to upward of twenty shillings from stamp masters stationed throughout the colonies. Although the price of the stamps was not onerous, Grenville required that they be paid for in specie. Paper money as a political issue was almost dead in Massachusetts, but the necessity of paying for stamps in specie was certain to revive it in an acute form. There was so little hard money in the colonies that Americans denounced the Stamp Act as a "devouring monster" that would "inevitably pump and extort from us all the remaining coin of the continent" and plunge them into monetary chaos. It was believed in America that the supply would not last a year after the Stamp Act went into effect, and this dismal prospect gave Sam Adams a strong talking point in urging resistance.[16]

Grenville's argument for the stamp duty — that it fell equally upon all — was one of the chief reasons it produced an outburst in the colonies. By falling upon all, it gave all a grievance: unlike the Sugar Act of 1764, the Stamp Act brought home British "tyranny" to every class. Because deeds, wills, and legal documents were made subject to stamp duties, the cost of litigation was raised in the colonies. Americans of all classes were notorious in the eighteenth century for the frequency with which they haled one another into court; and since the common people were most often involved in lawsuits, it was argued that the Stamp Act would fall most heavily upon them. It was said that even the "meanest peasant" in America would feel the effect of the Stamp Act: James Otis declared the "middling more necessitous and labouring people" would bear its brunt; and Benjamin Franklin characterized it as a tax upon the poor "and a tax upon them for being poor." [17] Moreover, by increasing the expense of lawsuits, the Stamp Act threatened to destroy the practice of colonial lawyers. Thus, at the outset of its quarrel with the colonies, the British government aroused the enmity of one of the most influential classes of men in America.

[16] *Boston Gazette,* Sept. 16, 1765.
[17] *The Examination of Dr. Franklin Relative to the Repeal of the American Stamp Act* (London, 1767), 30.

Vigorous opposition to the Stamp Act did not spring up instantaneously in the colonies, nor were the provinces equally active in resistance. Although it was evident that New Englanders were alarmed when they first learned of the Stamp Act, there was no reason to suppose they would resort to violence to prevent its execution. Governor Bernard believed Massachusetts would save its dignity with a perfunctory protest against Parliamentary taxation and would then swallow the Stamp Act, albeit with a wry face. Hutchinson thought the people would pay the duties, and several patriots were so certain the act would be obeyed that they tried to have themselves or their friends and relations appointed stamp masters. Nor was the Massachusetts House of Representatives' petition to the House of Commons against the Stamp Act calculated to inspire fears of conflict between mother country and colony. Indeed, this petition was so moderate in tone that Sam Adams considered it a serious blot upon the reputation of the Bay Colony.[18]

The "alarum bell" to the Stamp Act was first sounded not in Massachusetts but in Virginia, where in 1765, at the instigation of Patrick Henry, the House of Burgesses adopted the "Virginia Resolves." In contrast to the mild protest made by Massachusetts, the Virginians made a straightforward denial of the right of the British government to impose internal taxes upon the colonies. Indeed, the House of Burgesses went so far beyond the position taken by New Englanders that James Otis was at first shocked by the radicalism of the Virginia resolves and pronounced them treason. Sam Adams had anticipated in 1764 the Virginia doctrine of no taxation without representation, but most Massachusetts patriots seemed indisposed to burn their fingers with the red-hot sedition now flung at the British government by Patrick Henry. Yet it was not long before Adams was joined by all New England patriots, including Otis himself, in praising the Virginians' stand against British tyranny and in lamenting that Massachusetts' protest had

[18] Hutchinson, III, 114–115. Mauduit, 163. *Bernard Papers*, III, Bernard to Richard Jackson, Nov. 17, 1764.

been written in milk and water.[19]   Oxenbridge Thacher, the
Boston representative in the General Court, whose seat Sam
Adams was soon to occupy, exclaimed of the Virginians: "Oh
yes — they are men! they are noble spirits!   It kills me to
think of the lethargy and stupidity that prevails here."   The
"frozen politicians" of Massachusetts Bay were contrasted with
the fiery Southerners, who "first asserted their Rights with
decent Firmness."   Not to be outdone by Virginians, the
Massachusetts patriots launched a vigorous attack upon the
royal government: "It is inconceivable," said Governor Bernard,
"how they (the Virginia Resolves) have roused up the Boston
Politicians, & have been the Occasion of a fresh inundation of
factious & insolent pieces in the popular Newspapers." [20]   Here
began the race between Virginia and Massachusetts for the leadership of the American colonies against British "tyranny."   As
will be seen, this rivalry did much to precipitate the outbreak
of war between the mother country and colonies.

It was not difficult for Sam Adams to raise a storm in Massachusetts against the Stamp Act, because post-war depression
had begun to grip the colony.   Times were hard in New England in 1765 and the citizens were complaining they were already "miserably burthen'd and oppress'd with taxes." [21]   Governor Bernard admitted that Massachusetts was in no position
to stand any considerable taxation by the British government
because the taxpayers were carrying a heavy load from their
expenditures in the recent war.   In Boston, in particular, a
series of business failures gave the townspeople a bitter taste
of depression.   A banker failed for 170,000 pounds; many merchants were forced to close shop; and a "general Consternation"
spread through the province as substantial Boston mercantile houses began to go into bankruptcy.   Even John Han-

---

[19] Peter Oliver, 70.   Hutchinson, III, 119 (note).   Mass. Archives, 26,
Hutchinson Corr., II, 143.   *Boston Gazette*, March 25, 1765; Aug. 11, 1766
(Supplement).   Harbottle Dorr files, Mass. Hist. Soc.
[20] *The Works of John Adams*, X, 287.   *Boston Gazette*, July 8, 1765;
Aug. 11, 1766 (Supplement).   *Bernard Papers*, IV, Bernard to Pownall,
July 20, 1765.
[21] *Boston Gazette*, Feb. 28, 1763.

cock, the wealthiest merchant in the province, felt "a most prodigious shock" and said it was "like an Earthquake, to the Town." Creditors squeezed their debtors so tightly that the whole colony was brought to the verge of panic. Thus, when New Englanders learned they were to be taxed by the British Parliament, they were already deeply indebted to their own provincial treasury and to each other. On the eve of the Stamp Act, there seemed never to have been "a time of more general distress and calamity since the first beginnings of the country." [22]

Sam Adams rode into power on this wave of political and economic unrest that swept over Massachusetts in 1765. The times were bad, Bostonians reasoned, and there was need of a man like Sam Adams who had long been famous for his "great zeal for Liberty." In 1765 he was appointed by the town meeting to draw up instructions for the guidance of the Boston representatives in the General Court. The death of Oxenbridge Thacher shortly after gave Adams the opportunity he had awaited for twenty years. The Boston town meeting was called to elect Thacher's successor and Sam Adams was among the candidates. On the first ballot, Adams failed to win a majority, but the Caucus Club quickly rallied to his support and on the next trial Adams was triumphantly sent up to the General Court. [23]

Boston was ready in 1765 to take a plunge into radicalism and the citizens could not have found a better man than Sam Adams to lead the way. The fact that a prison term for embezzling public funds was hanging over Adams's head certainly had not strengthened his love for the established order. In 1765, at the time of his election to the Massachusetts House of Representatives, Adams stood a defaulter to the town of Boston and county of Suffolk for over seven thousand pounds because of shortages which appeared in his accounts as tax collector. He had gotten himself into this predicament chiefly through lack

[22] *Bernard Papers*, V, Bernard to Richard Jackson, Oct. 22, 1765. *Letters and Diary of John Rowe*, edited by A. R. Cunningham (1903), 75. A. E. Brown, *John Hancock, His Book* (1898), 61. *Boston Gazette*, Sept. 16, 1765.

[23] *Boston Town Records*, 16th Report of the Records Commissioners (1886), 157–158.

of business sense and his habit of keeping his financial affairs in a baffling state of confusion. When Sam Adams had been named tax collector for the town of Boston in 1756, the citizens should have taken warning from his record when, as a young man, he had been financed by his father, but Boston, the Tories said, was a "perfect Democracy" and a place had to be found on the public payroll for such an influential member of the Caucus Club as Sam Adams. In his own defense, Adams could truthfully boast that he had no extravagances and lived as temperately as an old Puritan, although he did take a flyer in Maine lands, like most Bostonians who could scrape a few pounds together. But Maine lands alone do not explain the appalling arrears that began to appear in Adams's accounts as tax collector. Had he speculated in dozens of wildcat schemes or lived in John Hancock's style, he could hardly have shown a greater shortage than that which appeared in 1764. Tories suspected that Adams was a sanctimonious peculator and wondered how they had ever trusted him with a shilling. Yet it is probable that his defalcations were chiefly caused by the ease with which money always managed to slip through his fingers. Adams had already run through his father's estate, and had he been given time, he probably would have brought Boston itself to similar insolvency.

Sam Adams was everything a good tax collector should not be: a kind-hearted, easy-going man who listened sympathetically to hard-luck stories and never pressed his debtors once convinced it would be a hardship for them to pay. He was an ideal collector from the taxpayers' point of view because he seldom made an outright demand for money and was easily put off for weeks, months, and even years. When money was promised on a certain day, Adams was rarely on hand to collect it. Although such methods made him very popular in Boston, they were sure to bring him trouble. His shortages grew alarmingly, and, to make matters worse, he began to take money for his own use from the funds he had collected for the town of Boston and Suffolk County. It was clear that this could not go on long before Adams would be compelled to account for his arrears, but he successfully postponed the reckoning by mingling his last year's collections with those of the year following, thus keeping an apparent balance. But in 1764 the truth was finally discovered and his total deficit was shown to have reached the staggering total of seven thousand pounds. Bostonians liked him so well as a tax collector, however, that even after his defalcations had been exposed they enthusiastically reëlected him tax collector for another term.[24]

Just when Adams's prospects seemed blackest, news of the Stamp Act reached Boston and public attention was diverted from his financial irregularities. Had not the British government attempted to raise a colonial revenue at this critical juncture of Sam Adams's career, he might have stood trial in Boston for embezzlement. As a young man, he longed to change the social and political order in New England; and no doubt the exposure of his defalcations in 1764 reminded him sharply that he had nothing to lose and much to gain by driving out the "oligarchs" and seizing political power.

In the Massachusetts General Court, Sam Adams soon proved himself a thorn in the side of royal government. When the assembly met in October 1765, Bernard was dismayed to find that the "Faction in perpetual opposition to Government" swept everything before it and "what with inflammatory Speeches within doors, & the parades of the mob without entirely triumphed over the little remains of Government." In full possession of the House of Representatives, James Otis and Sam Adams began "driving on at a furious rate." [25] Under Otis's leadership, the House of Representatives appointed a committee of grievances which Governor Bernard uneasily observed was founded upon the precedent set by the last Parliament of Charles I. Within a fortnight of taking his seat, Sam Adams was elected to all the important committees and recognized as Otis's chief lieutenant. Because of his readiness to agree with others' proposals as long as no vital principle was sacrificed, Adams quickly became one of the most popular committeemen

---

[24] William Gordon, *History of the Rise, Progress, and Establishment of the Independence of the United States of America*, I, 348. *Boston Town Records*, 16th Report of the Records Commissioners (1886), 150.

[25] *Bernard Papers*, IV, Bernard to General Conway, Nov. 25, 1765; V, Bernard to Pownall, Oct. 26, 1765.

in the House; and this "pliableness and complaisance in these smaller matters" enabled him to succeed where a less adaptable man would have failed.[26]   Whenever Adams was appointed to a committee he usually "pulled out a set of resolves, ready cut & dryed" for the edification of his fellow committeemen.[27] During his first term in the General Court, Adams produced so many resolves and wrote so many state papers that Hutchinson rightly blamed him for the House of Representatives' aggressive attacks upon the royal government.   Although a newcomer to the House, Adams was the author of the Massachusetts Resolves of 1765 which were regarded in Boston as "the best digested, and the best of any on the continent" and which omit the acknowledgment of Parliamentary sovereignty usually found in the colonial state papers of this period.[28]

Virginia led the way in constitutional protest against the Stamp Act, but Massachusetts was foremost in riots.   In the summer of 1765, Sam Adams determined to terrorize Andrew Oliver, Thomas Hutchinson's brother-in-law, who had been appointed stamp master of Massachusetts Bay, into resigning office in order that the stamps could not be distributed in the colony.   During the night of August 14, 1765, the "Loyall Nine," probably acting under orders from Sam Adams, hung an effigy of Oliver on Liberty Tree, where it was found the next morning by the astonished citizens.   The Crown officers at first supposed it was merely a boyish prank, but when the sheriff reported he could not take down the effigy without risking his life, they began to suspect that this was not altogether child's play.   When one of the spectators at Liberty Tree asked Sam Adams, who was standing under the tree peering up at the effigy, who it was, Adams answered that "he did not know — he could not tell — he wanted to enquire."[29]   Nevertheless, it soon became clear that Sam Adams and the Sons of Liberty

---

[26] Gordon, I, 206.

[27] *Bernard Papers*, V, Bernard to Pownall, Oct. 26, 1765.

[28] Hutchinson, III, 134.

[29] *The Works of John Adams*, II, 150 (note), 180.   *Mass. Hist. Soc. Proceedings*, XLIV (1911), 688, 689.   *Bernard Papers*, IV, Bernard to the Earl of Halifax, Aug. 15, 1765.   *Letters from the Rev. Samuel Mather to his son*, 1759–1785, MSS. Mass. Hist. Soc., Aug. 17, 1765.

planned an eventful evening for Boston: the crowds that gathered on street corners throughout the afternoon grew by nightfall into a large mob that paraded around the Town House where the governor and Council were sitting, giving "three huzzas by way of Defiance" as it passed.   After destroying a building recently erected near the water front by Oliver, which was believed to be designed as a stamp headquarters, the mob marched to Oliver's house and beheaded his effigy.   After giving the stamp master this significant foretaste of what he might expect at their hands, the rioters built a huge bonfire on Fort Hill.   The demonstration was now thought to be over, and the gentlemen and "persons of character" who had been in the mob to keep order, "disguised with trousers & Jackets," went home for the night, leaving the rest of the rioters around the fire.   But a large number of the mob felt they had spent a very tame evening: therefore, no sooner were the gentlemen rioters out of sight than they rushed down Fort Hill to Oliver's house, led by Andrew Mackintosh, a cobbler and chief of the South End mob.   After shattering Oliver's windowpanes with a hail of brickbats, several ruffians broke into the house and began to search for the stamp master, swearing they would kill him if he fell into their hands.[30]   Governor Bernard could do nothing to restore order: when he called for his drummers to beat the alarm, he was told they were in the mob.   Had not Hutchinson already persuaded Oliver to get out of harm's way, he probably would have been roughly handled indeed during the "furious Onset."   But, although Oliver escaped unhurt, the riot accomplished its chief purpose, for the next day he promised to resign as stamp master.

The fourteenth of August, the day on which this riot took place, was celebrated in New England for many years to commemorate "the happy Day, on which Liberty arose from a long Slumber."   Sam Adams said it "ought to be for ever remembered in America" because "the People shouted; and their shout

---

[30] *Bernard Papers*, IV, Bernard to the Earl of Halifax, Aug. 15, 1765. *Letters from the Rev. Samuel Mather to his son*, 1759–1785, Aug. 17, 1765. *Letters from Andrew Eliot to Thomas Hollis*, *Mass. Hist. Soc. Collections*, IV, Fourth Series, 406, 407.

was heard to the distant end of this Continent." [31]   Tories remarked that it was singular to hold in such esteem a riot that
had done little more than terrify an old man out of his wits,
but the patriots continued to make August 14 a day of proces-
sions, feasts, and patriotic toasts.   There was, indeed, good
reason to set this day apart: it marked the first important outbreak of mob violence in British America against the Stamp
Act; and, as the parent day of all the riots in revolutionary Boston, it possessed strong claims to renown.   Inasmuch as it
encouraged rioting in other colonies and provoked violent resistance to the Stamp Act, Bostonians' boast that "the RESIST-
ANCE *of that Day* roused the Spirit of AMERICA" was justified.[32]

When the Whigs saw what a powerful ally they possessed
against the Tories in the Boston mob they determined to use it
against Thomas Hutchinson.   Sam Adams had no intention
of permitting colonial wrath over the Stamp Act to vent itself
wholly upon the British government: his policy was to force
the Tories and Crown officers to share the guilt of George Grenville and the British House of Commons.   The odium of
"British oppression" was always cast upon Hutchinson and his
party by Sam Adams.   In the House of Representatives, James
Otis declared that he knew the very room in Governor Bernard's
house where the Stamp Act was conceived, the time, and the
company responsible.   It was whispered in Boston by Sam
Adams that Hutchinson was the blackest conspirator of all because he had planned the Stamp Act and sent it to England,
where the British Ministry had eagerly leaped at so plausible
a scheme for raising a colonial revenue.   In backstairs gossip,
Governor Bernard was said to wish to enforce the Stamp Act
with his "dear friend" George Grenville "at the head of a
hundred legions." [33]   Adams and Otis poured their suspicions
into the ears of the "black regiment," whereupon the clergy began to dwell in their sermons upon the iniquity of Thomas

---

[31] *The Writings of Samuel Adams*, II, 201.

[32] *Boston Gazette*, Aug. 11, 1766 (Supplement).   *Bernard Papers*, V,
Bernard to Pownall, Nov. 1, 1765.

[33] *Bernard Papers*, IV, Bernard to Lord Shelburne, Dec. 22, 1766.   Mass.
Archives, 26, *Hutchinson Corr.*, II, 151.   *Boston Gazette*, June 1, 1767.
The Works of John Adams, II, 336.

Hutchinson, Governor Bernard, and other contrivers of the
Stamp Act. Between the politicians and the preachers, the
Boston *canaille* was soon raging against the Tories and itching
for an opportunity to lay hands upon Hutchinson and the governor. No doubt their patriotic fervor was whetted by the
consideration that Hutchinson's cellar was extraordinarily well
stocked.

Adams and Otis had no reason to believe that Hutchinson
was behind the Stamp Act other than their conviction that "some
high or low dirty American" always had a hand in plots against
colonial liberty.[34] They were certain that Hutchinson and
Bernard were secretly undermining the Massachusetts charter
in order to clear the way for raising a revenue by Parliamentary
authority from which they would be enriched. Adams did not
doubt that Hutchinson hoped to destroy "the Democratical
part" of the Massachusetts government and forge "chains and
shackles" upon the colonists.[35] But Sam Adams was in search
of good propaganda rather than historical accuracy and he was
never troubled by the flimsiness of his proof of Hutchinson's
guilt. Could Adams find a scapegoat for the Stamp Act within
the province and turn hostility against Great Britain into a
crusade against the New England "oligarchs," he could hope
to drive Hutchinson and his friends from Massachusetts Bay.
The well-being of the Whig Party demanded that Hutchinson
be implicated in the authorship of the Stamp Act regardless of
whether he actually had had a hand in unleashing that "menacing monster" upon the colonies.

In reality, Hutchinson had had nothing to do with the
Stamp Act until its passage by the House of Commons made it
his duty as a Chief Justice of Massachusetts Bay to enforce it.
When the Stamp Act was first proposed, Hutchinson urged that
it be given up; at no time did he advise that it be put in force;
and he did not hesitate to express his fears of its results.[36] Governor Bernard might be acquitted with equal ease of any com-
plicity in the Stamp Act. It had been conceived in England

---

[34] *Boston Gazette*, Aug. 12, 1765.
[35] *Ibid.*, Feb. 28, 1763. *The Writings of Samuel Adams*, II, 165.
[36] Mass. Archives, 26, *Hutchinson Corr.*, II, 139, 149, 153.

by British imperialists who hankered after a colonial revenue, and the entire blame for its passage can be laid upon the British Ministry and House of Commons.   But Hutchinson and Bernard were unable to convince New Englanders of their innocence after Adams's and Otis's propaganda had done its work; Otis once boasted that nine tenths of the citizens of Massachusetts Bay believed that Hutchinson and Bernard had instigated the Stamp Act in spite of their denials.[37]

After the attack upon Andrew Oliver, Boston continued to simmer and the mob restlessly awaited another opportunity to riot.   The day after Oliver's house was ransacked, Boston gentlemen were forced to protect the stamp master from the lower class.   Oliver's promise not to distribute the stamps and to apply for permission to resign was satisfactory to Sam Adams, but the "lower Part of the Mob" clamored for an immediate resignation and were "unwilling to lose their Frolick."   For a fortnight the tension in Boston continued to increase, until, on the night of August 28, boys and negroes began to build bonfires in King's Street and blow the dreaded whistle and horn that sent the Boston mob swarming out of taverns, houses, and garrets.   A large crowd immediately gathered around the bonfires, bawling for "Liberty and Property," which, said Bernard, "is the usual Notice of their Intention to plunder & pull down an House." [38]   After fortifying themselves with rum, the mob started out on its "frolick" by wrecking several houses belonging to the customhouse officers and Court of Admiralty.   This desultory rioting warmed the mob to its real work, and by the time it reached the home of Lieutenant Governor Hutchinson its appetite had been whetted by large quantities of rum and loot.   "The hellish crew fell upon my house with the rage of devils," Hutchinson wrote, and had he not already left the premises he probably would not have escaped alive.   The mob gutted the house, destroyed his furniture, emptied his cellar, robbed his strongbox, and scattered the manuscript of his *History of the Province of Massachusetts Bay* in the mud outside

---

[37] *Boston Gazette*, Nov. 24, 1766.
[38] *Bernard Papers*, IV, Bernard to the Earl of Halifax, Aug. 31, 1765. Peter Oliver, 125.

his door.[89]   All that night the mob ran amuck.   Not since the impressment riots of 1748, when the mob stoned the General Court and held possession of the town for three days, had Boston seen such a wild evening.

Hutchinson had so many enemies in Boston that he scarcely knew whom to blame for this outrage. But it is certain that even his worst enemies, Otis and Adams, had not intended that the mob should go to such lengths. No doubt the demonstration planned by the patriots against the lieutenant governor got out of their control by reason of the large rations of rum handed out to the mob before it attacked. Otis and Adams had no wish to make Hutchinson a martyr, but the morning after the riot he came to court "clothed in a manner which would have excited compassion from the hardest heart." With tears in his eyes, Hutchinson called upon God as witness to his innocence of any hand in the Stamp Act. He swore he had striven "as much as in me lay, to prevent it," and urged the people to close their ears to evildoers who attempted to inflame them against the men who loved the province best. Many agreed with Hutchinson that it was "the most barbarous outrage which ever was committed in America," and for the moment the lieutenant governor seemed likely to become the most popular man in the colony, particularly in the rural districts where "mobbish Boston" was in low repute. But the Boston patriots deprived Hutchinson of the sweets of martyrdom by circulating a story that letters had been found in his house the night of the riot which proved he was responsible for the Stamp Act. For good reason, Sam Adams never produced these incriminating letters.

Adams was alarmed by the destruction of Hutchinson's house, not because he believed the lieutenant governor had been unduly punished, but because he feared the British government would take steps against Boston for having handled a Crown officer roughly. The morning after the riot Adams attended the Boston town meeting and voted with the citizens to assist the magistrates in keeping order in the metropolis. Because the townspeople publicly expressed their grief for Hutchinson's

[89] *Publications Col. Soc. of Mass.* (1927), XXVI, 33.   Hutchinson, III, 125.   Mass. Archives, 26, *Hutchinson Corr.*, II, 147.

misfortune and showed "universal Consternation" when dis-
cussing the riot, Adams believed Bostonians had completely
cleared themselves of all blame; but Hutchinson said many of
the "villains" who had wrecked his house the night before were
the loudest mourners in the town meeting.[40]   Sam Adams immediately wrote a letter to the Massachusetts agent in London
instructing him to ward off punishment from the mother country by showing the townspeople to be innocent of responsibility
for the outrage done the lieutenant governor.   Had George
III read Sam Adams's letter he would have been overjoyed to
learn that a metropolis of such purity as Boston existed within
his dominions.   Adams declared that the riot was a "high
handed Enormity" perpetrated by "vagabound Strangers" such
as were to be found in even the most peaceable seaports.
Hutchinson's house was attacked, he said, "remote from any
Considerations of the Stamp Act" and "solely with a View to
Plunder." [41]   Nevertheless, it was well known in New England
that Adams and Otis had inflamed the mob against the lieutenant governor by picturing him as the author of the Stamp Act.
Had the rioters been merely the town riffraff Adams described,
he would not have taken precautions to prevent their arrest.
However, when Mackintosh, the leader of the South End mob,
was thrown in jail for taking part in the riot at Hutchinson's
house, Adams and his friends informed the sheriff that unless
he was immediately released, no one would stand guard in Boston the next night.   Rather than see the town given over to
pillage, the sheriff released Mackintosh.   The attorney general
was intimidated for prosecuting the rioters and Mackintosh was
rewarded for his services with a Boston town office and command of the Whig "trained mob" that Sam Adams later turned
against the Tories.[42]
The looting of Hutchinson's house was a sharp reminder to
Sam Adams that the Boston mob must be disciplined and kept
under leash before it could be used as a Whig weapon against

---

[40] Hutchinson, III, 125.   *Mass. Hist. Soc. Proceedings* (1860), IV, 49–
50, Mass. Archives, 26, *Hutchinson Corr.*, II, 148.
[41] Mass. Archives, 56, 465.
[42] Hutchinson, III, 126.   Mass. Archives, 26, *Hutchinson Corr.*, II, 184.

Tories. After the rioters had whetted their appetite at the
lieutenant governor's, it was rumored that they had made a list
of fifteen prominent gentlemen whose houses they proposed to
attack. Since it was plain that the mob now contemplated "a
War of Plunder, of general levelling & taking away the Distinction of rich & poor," many of the gentlemen who had taken
part in the riot of August 14 became fearful of their allies.
Governor Bernard said of these that they had raised the devil
and now they wished to lay him again.[43] Sam Adams could
not afford to let the Whig Party take responsibility for the
violence of water-front toughs: therefore he must either bring
the mob under control or wipe his hands clean of any connection with it. Adams was unwilling to give up such a redoubtable ally, yet it was apparent that the Boston mob was not to
be easily tamed. Had there been a single mob in Boston, his
problem would have been simple, but there were two fiercely
antagonistic mobs in the town that seemed more eager to be at
each other's throats than terrorizing Tories. On every fifth
of November — celebrated as "Pope Day" — gangs from the
North and South End of Boston carried popes and effigies to
King's Street, where they met in a pitched battle, each mob attempting to destroy the other's pope. Everything was fair in
this "dirty Contest" and no blow too low: indeed, these zealous
Protestants sometimes belabored each other so furiously with
staves and cudgels that they were carted dying off the field of
battle.[44] Nothing was to be heard in Boston on these eventful
nights but "a confused medley of the rattlings of Carriages, the
noises of Pope Drums and the infernal yell of those who are
fighting for the possession of the Devill." [45] By 1765, the feud
between North and South Boston had become a tradition carried on by rival gangs of battle-scarred veterans. Thus, before the Whigs could harness the Boston mob they had first to
induce the North and South End mobs to settle their quarrel
and belabor the Tories instead of wasting their talents by cracking each other's pates on Pope Days.

   [43] *Bernard Papers*, IV, Bernard to the Earl of Halifax, Aug. 31, 1768.
   [44] *Massachusetts Gazette*, Nov. 5, 1767.
   [45] *Copley-Pelham Letters, Mass. Hist. Soc. Collections* (1914), LXXI, 201.

Sam Adams painstakingly began to bring these gangs of cudgel-boys together. Of the two factions, the South Enders were the most powerful and were expertly led by Alexander Mackintosh. Adams's large acquaintance among the mob — he was an intimate friend of Swift, the leader of the North End, and well known to the rank and file of both parties — made him an important intermediary in the reconciliation that took place shortly after the attack upon Hutchinson's house. It was probably due to Adams's influence that Mackintosh and Swift, with their respective lieutenants, were brought together, feasted, and entertained until they had been convinced that patriotism required them to forget their quarrels and turn their energies to politics. A huge banquet — called the "Union Feast" — was held to commemorate the burying of the hatchet: the two mobs sat down together with Whig merchants and politicians and joined "with Heart and Hand in flowing Bowls and bumping Glasses" until they had completely drowned all memories of their former differences.[46] On November 5, 1765, instead of the usual riot Bostonians were treated to a parade and military revue. Mackintosh led the procession, resplendent in a gilt uniform of red and blue, a gold-laced hat and cane, and a speaking trumpet to give orders to his "troops," who marched and wheeled with impressive proficiency. Arm in arm with "General" Mackintosh walked Colonel Brattle of the Massachusetts militia, complimenting him upon the order kept by his men and assuring him that "his Post was one of the highest in the Government."[47]

Governor Bernard rightly feared that Sam Adams had united the Boston mobs for other purposes than burning a pope. The demonstration in 1765 of "lovely Unity" between the North and South Ends marks the end of the mob as a free lance in the revolutionary movement. Henceforth Boston was controlled by a "trained mob" under Sam Adams's direction. Although the North and South Ends occasionally took up the cudgels against each other after the "Union Feast," it is remarkable how

[46] *Bernard Papers*, V, Bernard to Pownall, Nov. 6, 1765. *The Works of John Adams*, II, 177. *Massachusetts Gazette*, Nov. 14, 1765.
[47] *Bernard Papers*, IV, Bernard to Pownall, Nov. 6, 1765.

seldom the mob got out of control during the revolutionary period. A hierarchy of mobs was established during Sam Adams's rule of Boston: the lowest classes — servants, negroes, and sailors — were placed under the command of "a superior set consisting of the Master Masons carpenters of the town"; above them were put the merchants' mob and the Sons of Liberty, — known to the Tories as Adams's "Mohawks," — upon whom the more delicate enterprises against Tories and Crown officers devolved; and Mackintosh was given one hundred and fifty men "trained as regular as a military Corps" to act as storm troops.[48]　Englishmen found the Boston mob very different from those in England because the Boston rioters acted "from principle & under Countenance" and openly defied the magistrates who attempted to bring them to trial.　Whereas an English mob good-naturedly spared houses where lights were placed in the windows, the only safety for Tories in Boston was to get out of town before the mob attacked.[49]

Governor Bernard firmly believed that after the Boston mob had finished with Oliver and Hutchinson, his turn would be next.　He had no desire, however, to be the first royal governor in the colonies to suffer martyrdom for King and Parliament.　He prudently slipped out of town and hurried to Castle William, where the stamps had been stored for safekeeping, but even here he did not feel secure.　Therefore, to prevent a surprise attack upon the Castle by the Boston Sons of Liberty, he strengthened its defenses as though he expected a foreign enemy to appear in Boston Harbor, locked himself in with the stamps, and wrote to England that the metropolis was in a state of outright rebellion.　Adams and Otis ridiculed a royal governor who "skulked from one Hole to another" and feared his own shadow, but Bernard had good reason for his furtive behavior: he had no means whatever of defending himself should Adams decide that the King's representative was fair game for a "frolick" with the Liberty Boys.

[48] Mass. Archives, 26, *Hutchinson Corr.*, II, 204, 205. *Bernard Papers,* V, Bernard to Pownall, Nov. 1, 1765; IV, Bernard to Lord Hillsborough, May 19, 1768. *Massachusetts Gazette,* Nov. 7, 1765. Hutchinson, III, 136.

[49] *Letters of a Loyalist Lady* (Anne Hulton), 1927, 11.

The British "tyranny" against which Sam Adams protested in 1765 was not the oppressive rule of a strong government prepared to crush resistance with force.   Because Parliament had not foreseen colonial opposition, it made no preparations to enforce the Stamp Act and was caught completely off guard when the Sons of Liberty began to terrorize the stamp masters and Crown officers.   After it was seen that stamps could be forced upon the colonists only at the bayonet's point, the weakness of the British government naturally made it contemptible in Americans' eyes.   Daniel Leonard, the Massachusetts Tory, rightly complained that "if any thing was in reality amiss in government it was its being too lax": instead of finding themselves opposed by a strong government, Americans were frequently permitted to ride roughshod over British authority. When the Sons of Liberty stormed the fort at Charleston, South Carolina, they found only one private awake and the other eleven members of the garrison sound asleep; at Fort Johnson, North Carolina, a garrison of two British troops were hotly besieged by five hundred heavily armed Sons of Liberty; and in New York, the headquarters of British military authority in the provinces, the troops were unable to keep order in the town.[50]   General Gage informed royal governors who clamored for military aid against the patriots that no military force could be collected within a month, and even then it would be at the expense of strategic posts which would be seriously weakened if their garrisons were removed.[51]   The colonial militia was useless to the Crown officers because its ranks were filled with Sons of Liberty who, if called to arms, would be more likely to attack the royal government than suppress patriot mobs. Governor Bernard considered the militia as "worse than no Soldiers at all," against the "incensed & implacable Mob" commanded by "General" Mackintosh.[52]   The "long arm" of Great Britain was so palsied that until British troops were sent to Boston in 1768, Tories and Crown officers were forced to lie low

[50] John Drayton, *Memoirs of the American Revolution* (1821), I, 45. *Colonial Records of North Carolina* (1890), VIII, 169–171, Governor Tryon to General Conway, Feb. 25, 1766. *Pennsylvania Journal*, Nov. 14, 1765.

[51] *Bernard Papers*, X, General Thomas Gage to Bernard, Sept. 6, 1765.

[52] *Bernard Papers*, IV, Bernard to Richard Jackson, Aug. 24, 1765.

or run the risk of facing the Sons of Liberty alone; in 1766, Bernard said with only slight exaggeration that he was "fighting the King's Battles without protection, support or maintenance." [53] The British government was utterly unable to punish even the fiercest rioters and libelers among the Sons of Liberty: when Alexander MacDougall of New York, "the American John Wilkes," was imprisoned in 1770 he became famed as the first Son of Liberty to be put in jail — at least, for patriotic activities. This helplessness to quell the revolutionary movement in the colonies convinced Sam Adams and his followers that the British government was "so contemptibly weak, and the people so superior to the royal authority that they are not a little elated upon their triumph over the defenceless officers of the crown." [54]

With the royal governor "skulking" behind the ramparts of Castle William in terror of his life and the nearest British troops two hundred miles from Boston, Sam Adams and the Sons of Liberty easily made themselves masters of the metropolis. It was not necessary for them to create new political machinery to rule Boston: the machinery was already in existence under the name of the Caucus Club. The Stamp Act brought about little change in the personnel of the ruling clique in Boston, — the Sons of Liberty were simply the Caucus Club writ large, — but it did vastly increase the power of the political bosses. Never before had they known such prosperity as descended upon them in 1765. Petty politicians who had hitherto wrangled for small offices found themselves famous overnight as daring mob leaders and "true-born" Sons of Liberty. Aristocrats who had sneered at them a few months before as "the scum" and "rabble" were now compelled to bow and scrape before them lest the mob be turned against their fine houses. The sheriff's assistants were Sons of Liberty and would not move against their fellow patriots; justices of the peace were "great favourors of them" and paraded beside them through the

[53] *Barrington Bernard Correspondence*, edited by Ed. Channing and A. C. Coolidge, *Harvard Hist. Studies*, XVII, 115.

[54] Francis Bernard, *Select Letters on the Trade and Government of America, and the Principles of Law and Policy, applied to the American Colonies* (London, 1774), 30–31.

streets; juries were packed with Liberty Boys; and the Boston selectmen stood in such awe of them that they did not dare to attempt repression. Whoever was so foolhardy as to oppose the Sons of Liberty in Boston in 1765 was sure to feel the smart of "the Iron Rod of the popular Despotism." [55]

To show Bernard and Hutchinson that "they were as nothing in the Eyes or the Hands of the People," Sam Adams and the "Loyall Nine" ordered Andrew Oliver, the stamp master, to make another resignation at Liberty Tree on the pretext that his promise to give up his duties, made immediately after the attack of August 14, was not sincere. The memory of the riot was too fresh in Oliver's mind to permit him to disobey this command; and in the presence of a huge crowd at Liberty Tree he took the oath administered by Justice Dana. "And a Glorious sight it was, which I beheld," exclaimed a Son of Liberty who watched Oliver — one of the "oligarchs" of the colony — humble himself in the biting wind and rain before Sam Adams and his Mohawks and swear that "he never would, directly or indirectly, by himself or any under him, make use of his deputation, or take any measures for enforcing the stamp act in America." Only by such abasement, Bernard lamented, could His Majesty's servants in the colonies be sure of a whole skin. [56]

Having forced the stamp master out of office and bottled up the stamps, together with the royal governor, in Castle William, Sam Adams proposed to treat the Stamp Act as a "meer nullity." He therefore demanded that business be carried on in the colony without stamps in open defiance of Parliament. The patriots quoted Coke to prove that an act of Parliament against Magna Charta and the rights of Englishmen was void, but even without recourse to political theory it was clear that the Stamp Act could not be obeyed in Massachusetts because the Sons of Liberty had cleared the country of stamps and stamp masters. Either business was to go on without stamps or totally cease for want of

[55] *Bernard Papers*, IV, Bernard to the Lords Commissioners for Trade, Jan. 10, 1766. *Mass. Hist. Soc. Proceedings* (1923), LX, 282.

[56] *Boston Gazette*, Dec. 23, 1765, Note by Harbottle Dorr, MS. Mass. Hist. Soc. *Bernard Papers*, IV, Bernard to General Conway, Dec. 18, 1765. *The Works of John Adams*, II, 156.

them.   Adams was well aware that if business stopped, Parliament's right to tax the colonies would be implicitly acknowledged.   To prevent this surrender of principle, he determined to open all public offices, courts, and customhouses, regardless of the lack of stamps.   In the House of Representatives, Otis and Adams declared that "the courts of Justice must be open immediately, and the law . . . executed"; and although the Crown officers deeply resented the dictatorial tone assumed by the Whig chiefs in laying down the law to His Majesty's governor and Council, they were unable to keep colonial business at a standstill while Parliament deliberated the fate of the Stamp Act.   The customhouse officers were terrified into opening the port to shipping without stamped clearances; courts of common law and even the Court of Admiralty were compelled to transact business as though the Stamp Act had been repealed; and the whole colony jubilantly read unstamped newspapers, married on unstamped licenses, and sued their neighbors on unstamped legal papers.[57]

Tories believed Sam Adams insisted upon opening the courts without stamps simply "to shew ye Power of our new Gov[erno]rs" and to insult Parliament.[58]   Although most Massachusetts Crown officers were frightened into violating the Stamp Act, Thomas Hutchinson refused to give way to Adams and his mob.   When the House of Representatives sent a resolution to the Council declaring that the closing of the courts for want of stamps would "dissolve all the Bands of civil Society," Hutchinson urged the councilors to prove their loyalty to the Crown by withstanding the seditious demands of the Lower House.   Hutchinson was so bitterly attacked by Adams and Otis in the *Boston Gazette* for his speech in Council that he

[57] *Massachusetts State Papers*, edited by Alden Bradford, Answer of the House of Representatives to the Governor's speech, Jan. 17, 1766. *Boston Gazette*, Jan. 27, 1766.   Mass. Archives, 26, *Hutchinson Corr.*, II, 193. *Bernard Papers*, IV, Bernard to the Lords Commissioners for Trade, Jan. 10, 1766.
[58] Mass. Archives, 25, *Hutchinson Corr.*, I, John Cushing to Thomas Hutchinson, Dec. 29, 1765.   *Bernard Papers*, IV, Bernard to the Lords of Trade, March 10, 1766.   *Israel Williams Papers*, MSS. Mass. Hist. Soc., Thomas Hutchinson to Israel Williams, Feb. 20, 1766.

believed another mob was being raised against him; but he escaped a second attack because there was nothing left in his house to destroy.[59] Nevertheless Adams and Otis soon saw an opportunity to punish Hutchinson for his work in the General Court. For many years, the patriot chiefs had attempted to deprive Hutchinson of his numerous offices, but it was not until the Stamp Act that they achieved their first success. British "oppression" was fashioned by the Whigs into a lever with which to pry the New England "oligarchs" from office. Acting under Sam Adams's direction, the Boston town meeting demanded that Hutchinson, as Judge of Probate for Suffolk County, open his court for business without stamps. Hutchinson's veneration for his oath of office was too deep to admit of such flagrant violation. Knowing that he must either resign or flee the country, he chose to give up his office as Judge of Probate. It was, however, one of the least important of his places and he remained lieutenant governor and Chief Justice of the province despite Adams's success in making him the scapegoat of the Stamp Act.

One of the most striking results of the Stamp Act was the congress of representatives from the various provinces which met in New York in November 1765 to make a united protest to King and Parliament. As early as 1763, the Boston patriots had urged the merchants to choose committees for intercolonial correspondence in order to defeat the Sugar Act, and in 1764 Sam Adams had appealed to the Boston representatives in the General Court to unite the colonies against the new molasses duty. "As His Majestys other Northern American Colonys are embarked with us in this most important Bottom," Adams said in his Boston instructions of 1764, "we . . . desire you to use your Endeavors, that their Weight may be added to that of this Province; that by the united Applications of all who are aggrieved, All may happily obtain Redress." [60] In 1765, after the Stamp Act had given the colonies a common cause of action, James Otis followed Adams's suggestion of the previous year by proposing in the Massachusetts House of Repre-

---

[59] Mass. Archives, 26, *Hutchinson Corr.*, II, 205, 206.
[60] *The Writings of Samuel Adams*, I, 6.

sentatives an intercolonial congress. Otis's motion drew sneers
from the conservatives, but it was adopted by a majority of the
House and sent to all the British colonies on the continent.

Although several colonies were not represented in the Stamp
Act Congress and others sent delegates with inadequate powers, it brought together men from all quarters of the colonies
and laid the foundations for the later Continental Congresses.
Many of the delegates were far more conservative than their
constituents, — even in the Massachusetts delegation it was
said there were three men "fast Friends to Government, & prudent and Discrete," — and their petitions to King and Parliament were far too moderate for Sam Adams's taste. Nevertheless, the shortcomings of the Stamp Act Congress could not
conceal the fact that "the united Colonies have Remonstrated."
"Who," asked the Boston patriots in 1766, "dreamt this time
twelve Months of such a UNION of the Colonies?" [61]

An even more significant manifestation of colonial unity was
the secret military alliances formed among the Sons of Liberty
against the British government. When rumors began to circulate late in 1765 that the Ministry would attempt to enforce
the Stamp Act with redcoats and men of war, the Sons of Liberty
made preparations to give the royal troops a warm reception.
On Christmas Day, 1765, the New York and Connecticut Sons
of Liberty ratified a plan of mutual military aid against the expected attack by a British army. The Connecticut and New
York patriots agreed to march to each other's assistance with
their entire force. They declared they would not be "enslav'd
by any power of earth without opposing force to force," and
promised King George's men a hot battle should they take the
field against American Whigs.[62] Colonel Durkee of the Connecticut militia boasted that he could bring ten thousand well-
armed men against the British; and a "noble possy of Jersey

---

[61] *Boston Gazette*, Jan. 13, 1766, Supplement (1873). Bancroft, V, 200.
Bernard Papers, IV, Bernard to the Lords of Trade, 1765. *Boston Gazette*,
May 5, 1766 (Supplement); May 12, 1765; Jan. 20, 1766.

[62] *Belknap Papers*, MSS. Mass. Hist. Soc., Letter from Boston Sons of Liberty, Feb. 3, 1766. *Lamb Papers*, MSS. New York Hist. Soc., N. Y. Sons
of Liberty to Middletown, N. J., Sons of Liberty, April 10, 1766. *Bernard
Papers*, IV, Bernard to General Conway, Jan. 25, 1766.

Folks" and "Eastern Lads" were prepared to march to New York's relief. These military covenants gave the New York patriots assurance of being supported by a yeoman army if the British military machine were turned against New York; and everywhere the people were told that colonial Whigs were a match for the British army and that, even if the seaports fell into the enemy's hands, the patriots could take refuge in the inland country where the British army could never penetrate.[63]

Englishmen had not anticipated such violent opposition from New York and the Southern colonies, but they were probably less surprised to find the New England Saints — "the spawn of Old Cromwellians" — plotting to massacre British armies.[64] To enlist Boston's aid in the coming struggle against British troops, the New York patriots sent agents to New England to stir up the war spirit and learn how many men could be counted upon to march to their defense. The New Yorkers found the Boston Sons of Liberty laying plans to cut off the British army before it could reach Boston overland. Like the Sons of Liberty in the Southern colonies, the Boston patriots felt "the Patriotic Flame glowing in their Bosoms and would esteem it glorious to die for their Country." A Providence Son of Liberty who came to Boston with credentials from his local chapter was admitted to "the most Honourable Privy Council" of the Sons of Liberty and given a seat "at ye Board," where he learned that the Bostonians had made thorough preparations to handle British invaders. The Whigs boasted that with two hours' notice they could bring three thousand men to Liberty Tree "who would go any where for ye preservation of ye Constitution," and that within a few days forty thousand New Englanders would be on the march to the metropolis.[65]

Despite their enthusiasm for a pitched battle with the King's

<hr/>

[63] *Lamb Papers*, Joseph Allicocke to John Lamb, Nov. 21, 1765. *Bernard Papers*, IV, Bernard to General Conway, Jan. 25, 1766. *The Montresor Journals, Collections of the N. Y. Hist. Soc.* (1882), 350. *Belknap Papers*, Boston Sons of Liberty to the New Hampshire Sons of Liberty, Feb. 13, 1766.

[64] *Considerations on the American Stamp Act* (London, 1766), 33.

[65] *Bernard Papers*, IV, Bernard to General Conway, Jan. 19, 1766; V, Bernard to Pownall, June 29, 1766. *Boston Gazette*, Aug. 19, 1765. *Lamb Papers*, Extract of a Letter from Providence, Feb. 17, 1766.

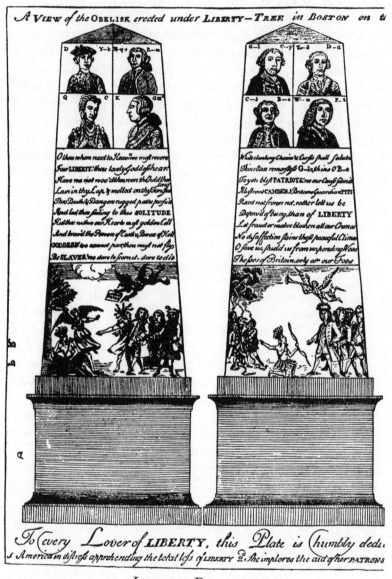

LIBERTY PYRAMID
ERECTED FOR CELEBRATION OF THE REPEAL OF THE STAMP

ACT, MARCH 1776, AND DESTROYED BY FIRE AT THAT TIME

soldiers, Sam Adams and other Sons of Liberty did not regard themselves as disrupters of the British Empire, but as defenders of its constitution. The Sons of Liberty were the "King's Party" in the American colonies. They believed the Stamp Act was an encroachment made by the House of Commons upon George III's "Crown and Dignity," for the King alone was sovereign in the colonies. Royal requisitions and grants, they declared, were the only constitutional forms of colonial taxation: by means of the Stamp Act, Parliament was attempting to strip the colonists of their property and King George of his sovereignty. Thus, to oppose Parliament became the duty of all Americans who truly loved the King and the British Constitution. It is not uncommon to find the Sons of Liberty denying Parliament any power whatever over the colonies, although it required another decade for the mass of Americans to adopt this doctrine.[66]

While the Sons of Liberty were toasting King George in one breath and threatening to massacre royal troops in the next, it was learned in the colonies that the British government had repealed the Stamp Act. For the moment, at least, the crisis that had almost produced bloodshed between opposing armies of British and Americans seemed safely passed. But Englishmen always found it difficult to understand why the colonists should have organized themselves into Sons of Liberty, outraged Crown officers, and prepared to fight the British army. Granting that Parliament had made a serious mistake in imposing a stamp duty upon the colonies, it was not sufficient reason for Americans to make these warlike preparations against the mother country. The colonists seemed to be decidedly hot-tempered gentry, accustomed to reaching for their muskets on the slightest provocation. In reality, however, Americans were not as quick on the trigger as they appeared to Englishmen in 1765. The Stamp Act had almost precipitated an armed revolt in the colonies, not because Americans were particularly

[66] *Lamb Papers,* New York Sons of Liberty to the Middletown, N. J., Sons of Liberty, April 10, 1766; Resolves of the Sons of Liberty at Oyster Bay, N. Y., Feb. 22, 1766. *Belknap Papers,* Boston Sons of Liberty to the Sons of Liberty in New Hampshire, Feb. 13, 1766; Providence Sons of Liberty to the N. H. Sons of Liberty, March 24, 1766.

warlike, but because a century and a half of isolation had so completely estranged them from the mother country that they were prepared to take up arms in defense of their liberties on small aggravation. The Stamp Act had awakened a militant spirit among men who, although in a minority, were the kind of minority that makes revolutions. Particularly in the seaport towns of the North, the Sons of Liberty were recruited from the class that had everything to gain by a social and political upheaval. These men, with Sam Adams at their head, were ready in 1765 to fight Great Britain. And, as Governor Bernard said, it was apparent after the Stamp Act that the "weak patchwork government" in America had no power to prevent colonial independence, "one hour after the people have resolved upon it." [67]

Many years later, George III lamented Parliament's "fatal compliance" in repealing the Stamp Act. It seemed to most Englishmen in 1774 that after Parliament had given way in 1766, the colonists had steadily raised their demands for self-government, made larger claims of exemption from Parliamentary authority, and even attempted to force the King out of his prerogative rights. Looking back from this perspective, it appeared to many British statesmen that England would have done well to have had it out with the colonies in 1766 instead of giving them ten years in which to strengthen themselves for conflict with the mother country. But it is probable that an attempt to enforce the Stamp Act would have proved fatal to the British Empire. Americans were more united in 1766 than in 1776, and England had not yet recovered from the exhaustion of the Seven Years' War. The British government chose to repeal the Stamp Act and blunder into civil war ten years later; but, if military force had been used to cram the stamps down the colonists' throats, it is probable the American Revolution would have begun in 1766.

[67] Bernard, *Select Letters on the Trade and Government of America* (London, 1774), 38, 39.

IV

THE BOSTON WHIGS

The Stamp Act had brought Sam Adams out of obscurity and placed him in the General Court, where he was to remain for the next decade despite the Tories' best efforts to dislodge him. In 1764, Adams seemed destined to remain unknown except, perhaps, for the brief notoriety he had received for embezzling public funds. By 1766, when the Stamp Act was repealed, he had become one of the most important figures in Massachusetts politics, second only to James Otis in popularity. Decidedly, it behooved the Tories to look closely at this man whose rapid rise threatened to destroy their influence in New England.

They saw a middle-aged man, already stricken with palsy, whose clothing was invariably rusty from long use. There was little arresting in his appearance and even to his friends he seemed merely a "plain, simple, decent citizen, of middling stature, dress and manners," who lived frugally and took great pride in his poverty. Tories always professed to see in Adams's face strong traces of the "Malignity" of his heart. An American painter who knew him well is said to have remarked that "if he wished to draw the Picture of the Devil . . . he would get Sam Adams to sit for him." [1] It is singular that this resemblance to Satan which his enemies found so striking does not appear in any of Adams's portraits. It cannot be said that Tory painters did not have opportunity to expose Adams's diabolical qualities, for his best-known portrait is by John Singleton Copley, the greatest of Tory artists, but there is no sign of the cloven hoof in Copley's study of Adams. He has, indeed, long since

[1] *The Works of John Adams*, X, 251, 308; II, 164, 308. *The Writings of Samuel Adams*, IV, 226. Peter Oliver, 54.

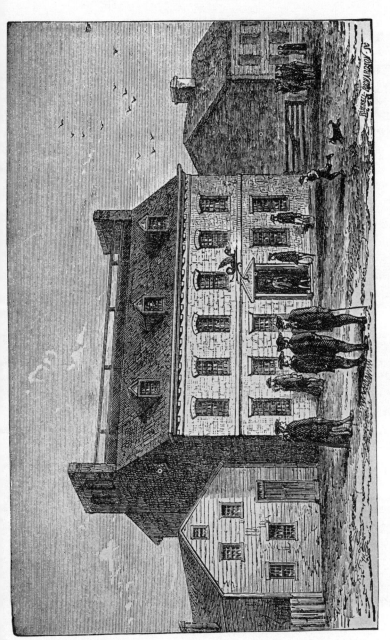

The Green Dragon Tavern

"Headquarters of the Revolution"

MR. AND MRS. JAMES OTIS

PAINTED BY BLACKBURN

ceased to be a terror to conservatives; and those who to-day shriek that Lenin and Stalin are the very devil regard Sam Adams as a holy patriot.

The Adams household consisted in 1764 of Sam's two children by his first wife, a black slave girl, and a Newfoundland dog which, like its master, could not endure the sight of a British uniform. In that year, when his political prospects were darkest and a prison term for embezzlement hung over his head, Adams took as his second wife Elizabeth Welles, who, although she brought her husband no dowry, possessed a loyal spirit and such consummate skill in household management that the Adams family was kept in reasonable comfort even on Sam's meagre income. She was, in fact, said to be the best housekeeper in Boston and made Sam an almost ideal wife: she took upon herself the burdens he shirked, but made no effort to wean him from his first love, Boston politics. Whereas James Otis's wife was a high Tory who gave her husband stinging "curtain lectures" when he came home from the Whig Club, "Betsy" Adams was nearly as stout a Whig as Sam himself. Of Thomas Hutchinson, the leader of the Tory Party, she once wrote: "I believe the most Rancourous Envy and venom Swells the Contaminated veins of the fell tyrant . . . the infamous Hutchinson." [2] Undismayed by her husband's practice of making his home a gathering place for political friends, she made no protest either then or when he kept late hours at the Caucus Club or with the Sons of Liberty. Bravely she bore his long absences at Philadelphia during the Continental Congresses; and while they were separated she kept him closely informed of the latest political developments in Boston. "I am never more happy," she once wrote her husband, "than when I am Reading your Letters or Scribbling to you my Self." During the British occupation of Boston in 1774–1776 she quieted his fears that she would be harmed by telling him she could take care of herself among the redcoats. When Dr. Thomas Young, one of Sam Adams's henchmen, skipped out of Boston somewhat precipi-

[2] *The Works of John Adams*, II, 227. *Samuel Adams Papers*, Bancroft Collection, MSS. New York Public Library, Mrs. Adams to her husband, Sept. 12, 1774.

tately to escape the British dragnet, Mrs. Adams was unable to understand "why he should go just now." [3]

The Adamses were famous even in Boston for their strictness in religious matters. Prayers were said before meals; passages were read from the Bible at bedtime; and the Lord's Day was scrupulously observed in the Puritan manner. By Adams's day, however, the religious fervor that had made Puritanism a way of life had almost completely disappeared in New England; and, although Sam Adams has been called the last of the Puritans, it no doubt would be a shock to seventeenth-century Puritans were they told Sam Adams was one of them. Adams, it is clear, was a good, eighteenth-century Congregationalist who went to church regularly and observed all the formalities of his religion, but he was not a Puritan in the sense in which Winthrop and Cotton understood the name. Nevertheless, in revolutionary Boston, Adams passed as a devout, old-fashioned Puritan, except among the Tories, who believed he had "a religious Mask ready for his Occasions; he could transform his self into an Angel of Light with the weak Religionist, & with the abandoned he would disrobe his self." He was never more angelic than when singing hymns in Dr. Checkley's meetinghouse, where he displayed "an exquisite ear for music, and a charming voice." But Adams found a way of turning even this talent to politics. He organized singing societies among Boston mechanics at which, Tories complained, more revolutionaries were produced than songbirds, because Adams presided over the meetings and "embraced such Opportunities to ye inculcating Sedition, 'till it had ripened into Rebellion." [4] He never overlooked an opportunity to give a religious flavor to his political activities. During crises in the struggle between the House of Representatives and the royal governor, Adams set aside days of fasting and prayer to "seek the Lord"; and by this means he gave the American Revolution the character of a moral and religious crusade. No patriot leader had greater

---

[3] *Samuel Adams Papers*, MSS. Mrs. Adams to her husband, Sept. 12, 1774.
[4] Peter Oliver, 57, 58. *Chalmers Papers*, Sparks MSS., Harvard College Library, III, "A Key to a Certain Publication." *The Works of John Adams*, X, 251.

success than Sam Adams in convincing New Englanders that if they tamely surrendered their liberty to the British government, their religion was certain to be swallowed up by "Popery" or Episcopacy. Thomas Hutchinson said that he made religion a "stalking horse"; and Peter Oliver groaned that Adams had perverted the New England clergy, who, by making their pulpits "Foam with Politicks" and "Unceasingly sounding the Yell of Rebellion in the Ears of an ignorant & deluded People," incited them to revolt.[5]

Sam Adams never forgot those stirring days during the Great Awakening when George Whitefield "thunderd in the Pulpit against Assemblies & Balls" and New Englanders seemed to turn the clock back to the time of Winthrop and Cotton. The glimpse Adams caught of "Puritanism" in 1740 had profound influence upon his later career. It became one of his strongest desires to restore Puritan manners and morals to New England: in his eyes, the chief purpose of the American Revolution was to separate New England from the "decadent" mother country in order that Puritanism might again flourish as it had in the early seventeenth century. Adams hoped to do by means of a political revolution what George Whitefield had done through a religious awakening. Puritanism was his goal: revolution his method of attaining it. But, as Adams was to learn, it was far easier to make New Englanders rebels than "Old Puritans."

One of Sam Adams's most effective ways of arousing patriotic fervor in New England was to appeal to the example of the early Puritans who had lived frugally, loved their liberties, hated the devil, and looked with no friendly eye upon the British government. He always said his purpose was to revive the "ancestorial Spirit of Liberty" in the people rather than to indoctrinate them with newfangled revolutionary principles. Like many other leaders who have precipitated great changes, he regarded himself not as an innovator but as a restorer of the past. When the patriot cause seemed blackest and hardship began to turn the citizens from Whig principles,

---

[5] *New York Gazette and Weekly Mercury*, Oct. 10, 1774. Mass. Archives, 27, *Hutchinson Corr.*, III, 110. *The Writings of Samuel Adams*, II, 336.

Adams rallied his followers by reminding them of the sufferings
their ancestors had undergone to establish liberty in the New
World.   He firmly believed that New Englanders' best security against British tyranny was the Puritan spirit, which, although sadly weakened in the course of a century, might again
be made a bulwark of colonial liberty.   Unwittingly, Thomas
Hutchinson helped Adams turn New Englanders' eyes toward
the past and acquaint them with the heritage they had received
from their Puritan ancestors.   In the winter of 1764, shortly
before the colonies were thrown into turmoil by the Stamp Act,
there appeared the first volume of Hutchinson's *History of
the Province of Massachusetts Bay,* which dealt with the early
period of New England settlement when many of the Puritan
colonists had regarded themselves as bound by only the slenderest ties to Great Britain.   Despite its Tory authorship, Hutchinson's *History* was widely read in New England, and Sam Adams
frequently quoted it to prove his argument that the colonies had
been independent of Parliamentary authority in the seventeenth
century.   The Stamp Act awakened New Englanders' interest
in questions to which they had previously paid little heed; and
Thomas Hutchinson's historical work, in the opinion of Dr.
Ezra Stiles, "contributed more than any Thing else to reviving
the ancestorial Spirit of Liberty in New England on this Occasion." [6]

But few Boston Whigs shared Sam Adams's longing to bring
back Puritanism.   James Otis seems not to have cared a whit
whether New Englanders became "Old Puritans"; and his own
life suggests that he would not have found the Cottons and
Winthrops congenial company.   For Otis was a hearty soul
who rapped out oaths and treated sacred matters so lightly that
his friends complained he "very often bordered upon profaneness." [7]

In this respect, James Otis was a far more typical member
of the Boston Whig Club than was Sam Adams.   The struggle

    [6] *A True copy of the Manuscript Book entitled, the Stamp Act found
among the Literary Remains of Dr. Ezra Stiles,* H. Stevens (1843), 64, MSS.
Library of Congress.
    [7] *The Works of John Adams,* II, 227.

between Whigs and Tories had cast Adams among strange bed-
fellows. He, the "holy man" of Boston, a dour Calvinist who
grumbled that New Englanders had lost their piety and were
"greatly degenerated," worked hand in hand with Dr. Thomas
Young, an avowed freethinker, and with William Molineux,
who went "neither to Mass, Church, nor Meeting." Dr.
Thomas Young had come from Albany to Boston in 1766 with
a reputation as an infidel, unsuccessful land speculator, and
passionate Son of Liberty. He was a close friend of Ethan
Allen and probably collaborated with him in writing *Reason
the only Oracle of Man, or a Compendious System of Natural
Religion.* William Molineux — known among the Sons of
Liberty as "Paoli" Molineux — was a small hardware merchant who became Sam Adams's lieutenant and "first Leader of
Dirty Matters" in Boston.[8] Although a notorious unbeliever,
Molineux was considered by the Tories to have a great deal
in common with Sam Adams inasmuch as both had "*fingered*
the public cash" and persuaded the "unthinking rabble . . .
to vote away the town's money." This singular mixture of
churchmen and infidels in the Boston patriot party was so striking that Hutchinson said it was composed of "mad, abandoned,
atheist fellows" and pious intriguers who, at heart, were no better than their companions. It is significant, however, that Sam
Adams did not permit his religious opinions to stand between
him and his fellow revolutionists. He judged men by their
political rather than by their religious creeds and catechized
his friends upon their Whiggery, not upon their Congregationalism. A man might be "a perfect viper, a fiend, a Jew, a
devil," but if he was orthodox in politics he was admitted into
the party.[9] Although John Wilkes was certainly no "Old Puritan" in private life, Adams reverenced him as a patriot struggling
"in the Cause of public Liberty, and Virtue, through the Rage
of Persecution." As became a follower of John Locke, Adams
believed all religious sects except those which taught doctrines

[8] *Boston Evening Post*, March 23, 1772. *Publications Col. Soc. of Mass.,*
Transactions 1906–07, XI, 17. *The Diary of John Rowe,* 286. *Massachusetts Spy,* Nov. 14, 1771.
[9] Mass. Archives, 26, *Hutchinson Corr.,* II, 514. *The Works of John
Adams,* II, 179; X, 262.

"subversive of society" should be tolerated.   But during the
French Revolution, Tom Paine's irreligion became so brazen
that Adams felt obliged to rebuke his old friend of revolutionary days for contributing to the depravity of the younger generation.[10]

During the early period of revolutionary unrest in Massachusetts, James Otis was a far more important figure than Sam
Adams.   Otis's name was well known in England: one of the
first questions put by the Marquis of Rockingham to travelers
returned from New England was whether James Otis still retained his influence; but Governor Shirley of Massachusetts
was unable to tell "where the Devil this brace of Adamses came
from."   Crown officers dreaded Otis as the "director of all
the Councils of the town of Boston" whose "mobbish eloquence"
and "superior Powers of inflaming and distracting an infatuated
People" made him the most formidable enemy of royal government in America.   When New Englanders toasted American patriots, James Otis's name was usually first on their lips:
throughout the country he was loved as the "American Hampden" by the patriots and feared as "the Great Leviathan" by
the Tories.   Otis's popularity cast Sam Adams in the shade; and
it was not until Otis had been invalided by a crack on the head
in a tavern brawl that Sam Adams emerged as the leader of the
New England patriot party.[11]

Until 1769, Sam Adams acted as Otis's lieutenant and party
"whip" in the House of Representatives, and as proofreader for
Whig newspaper agitators.   Since Otis disliked to revise and
polish his newspaper articles and state papers, he gave them to
Sam Adams, as he said, to "quieu whew" them.   Adams had
a "correct, genteel, and artful pen" and was particularly adept
in polishing the work of others.[12]   Josiah Quincy likewise sent
his manuscripts to the offices of the *Boston Gazette* with instruc-

---

[10] *The Writings of Samuel Adams*, II, 100–101; IV, 412–413.

[11] Mass. Archives, 25, *Hutchinson Corr.*, I, Thomas Hutchinson, Jr., to
Thomas Hutchinson, May 29, 1766.   *The Works of John Adams*, II, 233,
367.   *Bernard Papers*, IV, Bernard to Lord Shelburne, Jan. 24, 1767.   *Massachusetts Gazette*, July 21, 1768.   *Boston Gazette*, Aug. 18, 1766, Harbottle
Dorr Files, Mass. Hist. Soc.

[12] *The Works of John Adams*, II, 163; X, 367.

tions that they be corrected by Sam Adams. As a consequence, many of the newspaper articles in the *Boston Gazette* and the petitions and correspondence of the Massachusetts House of Representatives bear evidence of having been "smoothed with the oily brush of Sam Adams." [13]

Whereas Sam Adams was a popularizer of current political doctrines and a propagandist who was at his best in a rousing piece of sedition, James Otis was an original political thinker. When not lampooning Hutchinson and Bernard in the newspapers, Otis found time to write the *Rights of the British Colonies Asserted*, in which Sam Adams found most of his arguments against the Stamp Act ready-made. Although Otis was a stout imperialist who would have been horrified to learn that he was writing a textbook of rebellion, it was upon natural law, as conceived by Otis, that the American Revolution was ultimately defended.

Unlike modern centralized governments which pay scant respect to the laws of nature, Americans of the revolutionary generation regarded them as decrees of God, scarcely inferior to Biblical revelations. James Otis believed that natural law was superior to all man-made law. If an act of Parliament violated natural law, he said, it was contrary to "eternal truth, equity and justice, and consequently void." In Otis's eyes, the British Constitution was founded upon fundamental principles derived directly from nature; and, since Parliament drew its authority from the constitution, it was likewise bound by natural law. If Parliament attempted to break through the limitations imposed by nature, it overturned the constitution and destroyed its own authority. [14]

Natural law became a dogma among colonial Whigs because it afforded them a defense against British taxation. As James Otis said, the law of nature gave "to all men a natural right to be *free*"; and it was clear that Americans were not free if they were taxed by representatives from Old Sarum and the "cornish barns and ale-houses." Sam Adams proclaimed as one of the

---

[13] Josiah Quincy, *Memoir of Josiah Quincy, Junior* (1875), 21. *The Works of John Adams*, X, 361.

[14] Otis, *The Rights of the British Colonies Asserted and Proved* (1763), 70.

principles "upon which the *British empire is founded*" that no
money could be taken without the subjects' consent.   Since there
could be no rightful taxation without representation, natural
law ordained that the colonists could not be taxed by the British
Parliament in which they were not represented.[15]

Colonial lawyers and patriots never doubted they had been
taken into the confidence of the Almighty and privileged to
read His will in nature.   By their interpretation of these laws,
the colonies won every point in their controversy with the mother
country; indeed, nature seemed to work so exclusively for the
Americans that Englishmen complained that every usurpation
and attack upon government seemed sanctioned by God and
nature.   Americans appealed to the law of nature to prove
their equality to Britons.   Sam Adams believed that God had
decreed that New Englanders were "upon *equal* footing" in
point of liberty and privilege with the inhabitants of Great
Britain.   By thus basing his case upon natural law, Adams
escaped the pitfall which awaited those American patriots who
made colonial charters their chief defense against British oppression.   Without natural law there could have been no political theory common to all the colonies.   The charter-rights
patriots failed utterly to erect an effective barrier to Parliamentary taxation; on the contrary, they succeeded only in imperil-
ing colonial unity.   No common ground could be found in
colonial charters for resisting the mother country: the form of
government established under them differed greatly in the various colonies and some had no charters.   By relying upon natural law, however, Americans could boast that all the charters
in America could be annihilated without injuring their rights
as "men, citizens and British subjects."   For by the law of
nature every British subject was entitled to "all the natural,
essential, inherent and inseparable rights of our fellow subjects
in Great Britain." [16]

James Otis's cure for the ills of the British Empire was to give

[15] Otis, *Considerations on Behalf of the Colonists, Sent to the Publisher by
an unknown Person, from Boston, in New England, by F. A.* (London, 1765),
10.   Otis, *A Vindication of the British Colonies,* etc., 19.   *The Writings of
Samuel Adams,* I, 156, 190, 270, 288, 289.

[16] Otis, *The Rights of the British Colonies, etc.,* 49, 51.

the colonists representation in Parliament.   By this, Otis did not mean that a few "idle scurvey fellows" should be sent over to Westminster to sell themselves to the Ministry, but that there should be created a "thorough beneficial union of these colonies to the realm or mother country, so that all parts of the Empire may be compacted and consolidated, and the constitution flourish with new vigor, and the national strength, power and importance shine with far greater splendor than ever yet hath been seen by the sons of men."   He did not believe that representation would greatly benefit his own generation, but to posterity it would be "an invaluable blessing" inasmuch as it would cause the colonies to "be united, knit, and worked into the very bones and blood of the original system."   When Americans sat at Westminster, Otis said, British ministers would no longer be obliged to get their information of the colonies from "every vagabond stroller, that had run or rid post through America, from his creditors"; and the members of Parliament who knew no more of the affairs of British America than did "savages in California" would be able to hear colonial spokesmen from the floor of the House of Commons.[17]   Yet Otis did not contend that the colonies had any legal right to representation in the British Parliament.   At most, Americans had only reason and equity to support their plea that the House of Commons admit their representatives; and, Otis pointed out, if Parliament "indulged" the colonies by allowing them to return members to Westminster, it would be a favor, not the acknowledgment of a right.   "Upon the reasonableness of an actual American representation," Otis said, "I placed my foot, and built my only hope and desire."

Sam Adams did not share Otis's eagerness for colonial representation in Parliament.   While Otis urged that delegates from the provinces be sent to the House of Commons, Adams declared the scheme was *utterly impracticable* and no better than taxation without representation.   By recognizing the practica-

---

[17] *Boston Gazette*, Aug. 26, 1765.   Otis, *A Vindication of the British Colonies, etc.*, 20.   Otis, *The Rights of the British Colonies, etc.*, 54.   Otis, *Brief Remarks on the Defence of the Halifax Libel, Univ. of Missouri Studies* (1929), II, 174.

bility of such federation, Adams saw that he would throw away one of his strongest arguments for colonial liberty. He based his contention that the King had granted the right of taxation to the colonial assemblies upon the law of nature which made colonial representation in Parliament impossible. When America was separated from Great Britain by three thousand miles of ocean, nature had ordained that the colonies could not be represented in Parliament; and, because there could be no rightful taxation without representation, the British Parliament had no right to tax the colonies. Thus the colonial assemblies were made the sole taxing powers in America. Adams saw also that if American representatives were admitted to Parliament they would be too few in number to carry weight against the "King's Friends"; and, amidst the bribery and corruption of the House of Commons, he believed colonists would be hard put to preserve their virtue. Adams insisted that the only way to preserve the British Empire was to resume the form of government in effect before the passage of the Sugar and Stamp Acts. If the colonial assemblies were recognized as the sole taxing powers in America, Great Britain and the colonies would, he exclaimed, "long flourish in one undivided Empire." [18]

As radicalism gained strength in the colonies, much of Otis's political thought became antiquated and he was compelled to make apologies for his earlier conservatism. When his *Brief Remarks on the Halifax Libel* seemed likely to cost Otis his seat in the House of Representatives, Adams came to his rescue by declaring that there had been "almost a total Change of Opinion with Regard to our Rights" in the six months since Otis had written the *Brief Remarks*. Political theory had leaped forward so rapidly, it was said, that had Otis and other patriots "boldly asserted the truth, they would have been esteemed madmen, and their influence thereby wholly lost." Nevertheless, Otis's backsliding in the *Brief Remarks* could not be wholly explained away by this means. He had *"seemingly* carried the Parliamentary power and authority to the very *apex* of sublimity" and his enemies quoted it to prove that Otis was

[18] *The Writings of Samuel Adams*, I, 39, 40, 161, 171, 174, 175, 218.

really a Tory. Some of Otis's apologists suggested that his essay on the Halifax libel was a *"meer political Humbugg"* printed by the Tories to set honest Whigs by the ears. Otis himself attempted to make amends for having "rant it on the side of prerogative" by attuning his political theory to the radicalism of his followers. In particular, he was compelled to admit in 1765 that American representation in Parliament was doomed because of the colonists' opposition to federation.[19]

Between Sam Adams and James Otis there were differences in character and outlook that were to prove portentous to the peace of the British Empire. Unlike that of Adams, Otis's early background was conservative. Whereas Sam heard in his family circle denunciations of the British Parliament and the Massachusetts "sound money" aristocracy, James Otis was taught to praise the King, Parliament, and royal governors. Moreover, Otis was not born in Boston, the most fertile breeding ground of revolutionaries, but he made up for this shortcoming by attending Harvard College, which was second only to the metropolis in turning out future rebels against George III. Otis, however, never lost his reverence for the mother country. He was as stout a Massachusetts patriot as Sam Adams, but he was a British patriot as well, with a highly developed sense of the grandeur and power of the Empire. "If I have one ambitious wish," he exclaimed, "it is to see Great Britain at the head of the world, and to see my King, under God, the father of mankind." He believed the British Empire to be "founded on the principles of nature, reason and justice, and on the whole best calculated for general happiness of any that has yet risen to view in the world."[20]

James Otis represented an attitude toward the British Empire that was slowly dying in America, while Sam Adams expressed the assertive, independent spirit which, taking its rise from the early period of colonization, gained strength during the eight-

[19] *Boston Gazette*, May 5, 1766; Sept. 2, 1765; Jan. 13, 20, and 27, 1766; Dec. 30, 1765.
[20] James Otis to the Earl of Buchan, July 18, 1768; *Otis Papers*, MS. Mass. Hist. Soc., II.

eenth century and reached its full stature after the French had been driven out of Canada. Sam Adams had little love for the British Empire and, unlike most of his countrymen, he did not regard the mother country as "home." John Adams once said that although he had never been much of a John Bull he had always been very much of a John Yankee. Sam Adams, as well, was a John Yankee whose loyalties and loves were intimately bound up with New England and Boston. Indeed, later in the Revolution, many Americans were to suspect him of being too much of a Bostonian properly to guard the interest of the United States. He was essentially a local patriot whose sympathies had narrow range. Certainly he was not a traveled man: when he set out to attend the first Continental Congress in Philadelphia in 1774 it was the first time he had ventured far beyond Boston Neck.

To express the differences in temperament between Sam Adams and James Otis, John Adams contrasted them with Calvin and Luther, the leaders of the Protestant revolt. Otis, said John Adams, resembled Martin Luther in that he was "rough, hasty, and loved good cheer," while Sam Adams, like Calvin, was "cool, abstemious, polished, and refined, though more inflexible, uniform, and consistent." Tories made less flattering comparisons, although their judgments of Whig leaders are more valuable as picturesque abuse than historical portraits. James Otis, said the Tory propagandist Peter Oliver, was "rash, unguarded, foulmouthed, & openly spiteful," and Sam Adams resembled no one so much as the Devil.[21]

Sam Adams's conduct as clerk of the Massachusetts House of Representatives brought to view striking differences between him and James Otis. The clerk enjoyed the privilege of taking part in the debates and casting his vote with the representatives. It was a post that could be made all-important by a strong man: and none could say that Sam Adams did not take full advantage of his opportunities. During the recesses of the General Court, the London agent of the House of Representatives took orders from Sam Adams, who, as clerk of the House or head of a recess committee, kept the colony's political

<hr>

[21] *The Works of John Adams*, II, 163; X, 190. Peter Oliver, 57, 58.

waters almost as troubled as though the General Court itself were in session. By this means, Massachusetts Crown officers lamented, Sam Adams turned the blaze lighted by James Otis into a "perpetual flame." He had custody of all papers belonging to the House of Representatives and he published them freely in the *Boston Gazette* to keep the people informed of the struggle for freedom waged by their representatives. After Sam Adams had become clerk, Governor Bernard observed that all addresses of the House of Representatives to the royal governor were printed immediately in the newspapers with "the Air of a Manifesto much more than a Message to a Govr." [22] Moreover, it became difficult for the Crown officers to distinguish between Sam Adams's political tracts written for the *Boston Gazette* and the state papers he composed for the House of Representatives. Whether Adams was writing an address to King George or a squib at the Tories, his work seemed "in general designed for the Press & for that Purpose only."

Adams's fondness for publishing the proceedings and state papers of the House of Representatives in the newspapers soon brought him into conflict with James Otis. For many generations, the Massachusetts Assembly had not permitted its addresses to the King or Commons to be printed in the newspapers until they had been received and made public in the mother country. Sam Adams completely upset this traditional procedure. Instead of wasting valuable time waiting for King George and his ministers to ponder the petitions and remonstrances from Massachusetts Bay, Adams rushed them through the press and had them in the *Gazette* before they were stowed aboard ship for England. Such lack of respect for the King and Ministry deeply offended James Otis, who believed it very improper for petitions to be published in the colonial newspapers before they were received in England. When Adams proposed to publish a letter from the House to Lord Hillsborough before that minister had had opportunity to receive it in England, a stormy scene took place in the representatives' chamber between Adams and Otis. An eyewitness reported the dispute to Governor Bernard in the following manner: —

[22] *Bernard Papers*, VI, Bernard to Lord Shelburne, Feb. 7, 1767.

OTIS. "What are you going to do with the Letter to Lord H[ills-borough]?"

ADAMS. "To give it to the printer to publish next Monday."

OTIS. "Do you think it proper to publish it so soon that he may receive a printed Copy before the Original comes to his Hand?"

ADAMS. "What signifies that? you know it was designed for the People and not for the Minister."

OTIS. "You are so fond of your own Draughts that you can't wait for the Publication of them to a proper Time."

ADAMS. "I am Clerk of this House & I will make what use of the Papers which I please." [23]

The letter to Lord Hillsborough appeared in the *Boston Gazette* a few days later.

When James Otis first entered politics in 1760 his enemies had sneered that he was insane and even his friends were soon compelled to admit that his conduct was disconcertingly eccentric. Level-headed John Adams thought Otis "fiery and feverous" and given to unseemly outbursts of passion. He was either very gay or very despondent; when melancholy, he reviled himself for ever having become a Whig; and when in high spirits he was apt to be rash and imprudent. Otis's love for the British Empire was constantly tormenting him with doubts which Sam Adams never experienced. Whenever Otis took a step forward on the slippery path to rebellion he was immediately conscience-stricken. When he returned from the Stamp Act Congress in 1765 he made such a violent speech at the Boston town meeting against Hutchinson that the mob would certainly have swooped down on the lieutenant governor's house again had there been anything left to demolish. Yet, within a few days, Otis outraged the Whigs by declaring that the only way to keep peace in the colony was to take away the Massachusetts Charter, fill the Council with royal appointees, and quarter British troops in Boston. His "mad pranks" at the town meetings began to prove costly to the patriots. At one time he is said to have called the Boston electors "*a pack of d——d stupid fools*" and he began to run off into such "incoherent ravings" that the Tories called him the "mad Dicta-

[23] *Bernard Papers*, IV, Bernard to Lord Hillsborough, July 9, 1768.

tor" of Boston. As moderator of a town meeting, Otis challenged George Grenville to single combat on the floor of the House of Commons to decide whether the colonies were to be free or enslaved by British "tyranny." No doubt the Boston Sons of Liberty would have given heavy odds on the Whig "gladiator," as Otis was called, against all comers in the British aristocracy, but Otis soon lost his fancy to wrestle with English statesmen. On the floor of the Massachusetts House of Representatives he was at times a wild-eyed radical, at others a strait-laced conservative. As Thomas Hutchinson said, he often seemed "more fit for a madhouse than the House of Representatives." [24]

Otis's singular conduct was the despair of patriots who, like Sam Adams, made a virtue of consistency and "picqued themselves upon their Sanctity." [25] There was always danger that when Adams was in the midst of a carefully planned coup, Otis would give the game away by a passionate harangue or spill the Whigs' secrets into their enemies' ears in a moment of repentance. Moreover, Otis did not share Adams's relish for riots and the rough-and-tumble tactics used by the Whigs against the Tories. Rather than turn loose the Boston mob, Otis much preferred "dutiful and loyal addresses to his Majesty and his Parliament, who alone under God can extricate the Colonies from the painful Scene of Tumult, Confusion, & Distress." [26] At one time he said in the Boston town meeting that no possible circumstances could justify "tumults and disorders, either to our consciences before God, or legally before men." Repeatedly, Otis's moderation saved Adams and his hot-headed followers from provoking a crisis between the mother country and colonies. Unlike Adams, Otis never thought in terms of American independence; even after Adams had become

[24] *Bernard Papers*, V, Bernard to Pownall, Nov. 5, 1765. *The Works of John Adams*, II, 179, 180. *Boston Evening Post*, June 9, 1766 (Supplement); May 19, 1766; March 31, 1766. Mass. Archives, 26, *Hutchinson Corr.*, II, 235.

[25] Peter Oliver, 57–58. *American Stamp Act Papers*, 1765, 1766, MSS. Lib. of Cong., James Otis to the Speaker of the House of Representatives for the Province of New Hampshire, Nov. 8, 1765.

[26] William Tudor, *The Life of James Otis* (1823), 178 (note).

convinced that total separation from Great Britain was the only salvation of colonial liberty, Otis believed that "were these colonies left to themselves to-morrow, America would be a mere shambles of blood and confusion, before little petty states could be settled."

Despite Sam Adams's rapid rise in politics, it should not be forgotten that he was still under a cloud as a public defaulter. Since 1764, when his defalcations had first come to light, he had made many powerful enemies among the Tories, who were eager to bring him to trial. He was lampooned as "Jet" — one of the "pack of Cur-Dogs in Boston" — by Tory journalists. "This dog is very artful, loves babbling, especially when he gets into a very large Room," it was said; "has been taught to run into houses, to pick up money and run away with it directly to his kennel." Whenever Jet's master, the people, attempted to discover where he had hid this money, "one would imagine this sagacious cur realizes his Master's intentions for the moment he sees any of them, he runs to them, fawns, licks their hands and leaps upon them with so much cunning and good humour, that they forget all about the Money, spit in his Mouth, clap him on the side; and then away goes Jet, wagging his tail, and glad enough you may be sure." [27] The Tories gave the towns-people no opportunity to forget that unless Sam Adams made good his debt to the town the money would come from their own pockets. In March 1767, the citizens of Boston, now thoroughly aroused, appointed a committee to examine the books of the town tax collectors. The committee reported that Sam Adams owed the Province Treasury some £2300 and the town treasurer over £1700 — a total of nearly £4000 after deduction of salary. Sam Adams's prospects might have been dark indeed had he not already taken steps to defend himself against the irate citizens who were hounding him for debt.

For many years, Adams had made a practice of enrolling promising young men in the Whig Party. John Adams, himself one of Sam Adams's "boys," found that his cousin made converts by cultivating the friendship of likely young Bostonians, bringing them around to the Whig Club, and warning them of

[27] *Boston Evening Post*, Nov. 23, 1767.

the "hostile designs" of Great Britain against the colonies.
Sam Adams had a keen eye for "every rising genius in the New
England seminaries" and few good prospects escaped without
a pressing invitation to attend the Whig Club, where they might
be "embodied with the Whigs, and begin to taste of their spirit
by being often in their company." Tories had a different name
for Adams's missionary labors among the young: he was, said
Peter Oliver, "ever going about seeking whom he might devour." [28] But there was no doubt of his success: Dr. Joseph
Warren, Josiah Quincy, Jr., and Dr. Benjamin Church were
among his pupils. Although Dr. Church came to a bad end
by selling Whig secrets to the British in order to maintain a
fine house and a fancy mistress, most of these young men became distinguished figures in the American Revolution. Close
to the top of Adams's class of young rebels stands that eminent
patriot, John Hancock.

In 1765, when Sam Adams first began to bring John Hancock to the patriot club, Hancock was a young man of fashion
who possessed one of the largest fortunes in America. Although
he was the son of an impoverished Congregational minister,
his uncle, Thomas Hancock, was one of the shrewdest money-
makers in the colonies. Thomas Hancock made immense
sums by smuggling and selling supplies to the British armies
that served in America during the Seven Years' War. When
he died childless in 1764, shortly before Sam Adams became
interested in John Hancock, he left the bulk of his fortune of
seventy thousand pounds to his nephew. Tory gentlemen had
no liking for Hancock, whom they considered a man whose
"brains were shallow and pockets deep"; and even the Whigs
were compelled to admit that Hancock was not one of those
"rising geniuses" of Harvard College for whom Adams was on
the watch. Nevertheless, Hancock possessed what no preco-
cious Harvard undergraduate could offer: money and prestige.
Although he was overlooked by most as a makeweight between
poor Whigs and rich Tories, Sam Adams quickly saw that his

---

[28] *The Works of John Adams*, X, 364. *Lamb Papers*, N. Y. Hist. Soc.
MSS., Thomas Young to John Lamb, Nov. 19, 1774. Joseph Galloway, 110.
Peter Oliver, 56.

eagerness for popularity and susceptibility to flattery might be
turned to advantage.   Adams was desperately in need of powerful friends; and John Hancock, the wealthiest man in New
England, gave promise of rescuing him from his embarrass-
ments.   That Adams expected to do himself a good turn at
the same time that he benefited the patriot cause can scarcely
be doubted, but it is questionable if Hancock realized that he
was expected not only to finance the Whig Party but to settle
the bills of its leader.

Tories were dismayed to find they had been napping while
Adams made a Whig of John Hancock, and they swore that he
had seduced Hancock "in the same Manner that the Devil is
represented seducing Eve, by a constant whispering at his Ear." [29]
Sam Adams did not underestimate the importance of his conquest nor was he backward in telling his close friends what use
he intended to make of Hancock.   One day, while John and
Sam Adams were strolling along the Mall, Sam stopped before
Hancock's house and said that Boston had done a wise thing
by making "that young man's fortune its own."   Hancock,
in other words, was to be made the financial godfather of the
Whig Party; or, as the Tories said, the "wretched and plun-
dered tool of the Boston rebels," the "Milch cow to the Faction,"
and the "poor plucked gawky" whom Sam Adams had stripped
bare.[30]   It was observed that shortly after Hancock fell under
Adams's influence, Hancock began to branch out into new enterprises: by constructing warehouses and wharves and engaging
in trade on a larger scale he gave employment to so many workers
that John Adams estimated that a thousand New England
families were dependent upon him for support.   It was not
likely that these laborers would offend their employer by voting
against his friend Sam Adams.   The Tories were convinced
that Adams's "serpentine Cunning" was behind Hancock's new
ventures and that a policy of giving jobs in exchange for votes
had been adopted by the patriots.   In any event, Sam Adams
determined to stand his ground in Boston and trust to Provi-

---

[29] Peter Oliver, 55.
[30] Tudor, 262. *Mass. Hist. Soc. Proceedings*, XII, Second Series (1899),
140.   *Letters to Dr. Cooper* (Boston, 1775), 105, 112.

dence and John Hancock to deliver him from his difficulties rather than to adopt the usual practice of defaulting tax collectors and skip out of the province.[31]

The story of how Adams escaped punishment for his defalcations properly belongs here. In June 1767, suit was brought in the Court of Common Pleas against him. Adams was prosecuted by his friend James Otis, attorney for the town treasurer, and although Adams won in the lower court, the appellate court gave judgment against him for the whole penalty of the bond. Execution was ordered to begin in March 1768 for £1463; and Adams was given nine months in which to raise the money.

In March 1768, Adams appeared in the Boston town meeting, not with cash, but with a petition. He asked for more time to collect his debts "that he may be enabled thereby to compleat the Obligation of his Bond." After this petition had been hotly debated in the town meeting and Adams had promised to lay a full financial statement before the people within six months, the treasurer was ordered to stay execution. This reprieve was very unpopular with many thrifty townsmen who were unable to see why Adams's patriotic services should entitle him to make away with the town's money. Twenty Bostonians, including Foster Hutchinson, the lieutenant governor's son, petitioned that a town meeting be called to reconsider the respite given Adams. For an entire day, Adams's friend and enemies debated furiously in Faneuil Hall, alternately picturing him as a patriotic servant of the people and a rascally pilferer; but by nightfall, the motion to reconsider was decisively defeated.[32]

Sam Adams spent this six months of grace in collecting small sums from delinquent taxpayers, borrowing from John Hancock, and writing another petition. In this second petition, Adams dwelt upon the obstacles that had strewn his path as a tax collector: the Boston fire of 1760, the smallpox epidemic, and the poverty of the people. If Adams's account were true, he had served as a tax collector during a singularly catas-

---

[31] *The Works of John Adams*, X, 260. Hutchinson, III, 298. Peter Oliver, 55.

[32] *Letters and Diary of John Rowe*, edited by Annie Rowe Cunningham (1903), 157. *Boston Town Records*, 16th Report of the Boston Record Commissioners, 241, 242, 243.

trophic period of Boston's history and his only crime was in
being tender-hearted to the poor. But Adams might have
spared the citizens this lengthy catalogue of his virtues and
misfortunes. By 1769, Adams and Hancock were invulnerable
in Boston. The town meeting was now chiefly composed of
Adams's friends or those who looked to Hancock for their
livelihood. Indeed, Adams found the citizens so well disposed that he urged them to accept a small sum in full payment of his debt. He prepared a list of taxpayers who were
still indebted to him and he suggested that this list be turned
over to another collector, thus absolving himself of all responsibility. There was little opposition from the Tory Party,
now at its lowest ebb, and Adams's petition was granted by
the vote of a large majority. A few grumbled that patriots
were a costly luxury to Boston and agreed with John Rowe
when he wrote that it was "a very wrong step in the Town &
what they, I am afraid will repent." [33] It was found impossible
to collect the money for which Adams was in arrears; and the
last chapter to this interlude in Adams's patriotic labors was
written in 1772 when a committee appointed to inspect the
state of the Town Treasury reported that Sam Adams still
owed fifty pounds to the Province Treasury and that there was
no hope of collecting the money owing to the town of Boston.[34]

[33] *Letters and Diary of John Rowe*, 183.
[34] *Boston Town Records*, 18th Report, 69. Hutchinson, III, 295. *Mass. Hist. Soc. Proceedings*, XX, 213, 226.

V

THE MASSACHUSETTS CIRCULAR LETTER

IN the history of the American Revolution there are many occasions when Sam Adams and the Whig Party, apparently about to suffer defeat at the hands of colonial conservatives, were rescued by the British government's timely blunder. Had Massachusetts Tories been left to fight Sam Adams alone they perhaps would have been able to stave off the Revolution for years, but they could do little against the well-intentioned interference of the British government. Whenever Adams began to founder in deep water the Ministry tossed him a life line in the form of British tyranny. After 1766, the revolutionary ferment in the colonies momentarily ceased; and radicals like Adams who had been brought to the surface by the potent yeast of the Stamp Act seemed about to slip back into obscurity. In this crisis, the British government imposed the Townshend duties upon the colonies. Instantly the cry of oppression was raised in America; the Massachusetts circular letter revived colonial unity against the mother country; and Sam Adams became one of the most powerful men in New England.

In 1766 most Americans were too busy celebrating their deliverance from British tyranny and raising statues to William Pitt to ponder the problems raised by George Grenville's plan of imperial centralization. Although the majority regarded the repeal of the Stamp Act as proof of Great Britain's benevolence toward America, Sam Adams believed George Grenville and Parliament had created such ill feeling between mother country and colonies "as it is to be fear'd will never wholly subside." [1] He believed Parliament had repealed the Stamp Act more from fear than from mercy: the colonial boycott of British manu-

[1] *The Writings of Samuel Adams*, I, 386, 387.

factures and the Stamp Act Congress had, he said, forced the mother country to give way   In his eyes, Great Britain's magnanimity toward the colonies was the result of American "firmness and resolution" rather than of Englishmen's sense of justice.   Moreover, by passing the Declaratory Act at the same time it repealed the Stamp Act, Parliament seemed to threaten future oppression of the colonies.   The Declaratory Act was a statement of the right of the British Parliament to legislate for the colonies in all matters whatsoever; and by its terms the sovereignty of the House of Commons over British America was declared as absolute as that over Ireland.   It was not difficult, therefore, for Adams to suspect the British government of harboring plans to raise a colonial revenue in spite of its defeat in the Stamp Act.   There seemed a multitude of ways by which the British government could reach its goal of a colonial revenue without awakening the colonists to their danger. "Suppose for Instance," said Adams, "that some time hereafter under the Pretext of Regulating Trade only, a revenue should be designd to be raisd out of the Colonys, would it signify anything whether it be called a Stamp Act or an Act for the Regulation of the Trade of America?" [2]   Adams's fears were well founded: within a year, the same thought was to occur to Charles Townshend, Chancellor of the Exchequer, when he took up the quest of a colonial revenue.

With fresh British tyranny in the breeze, Sam Adams was not disposed to relent in his struggle against the mother country and the New England Tories.   But until overseas oppression again became an actuality, Adams turned his attention almost wholly toward strengthening the Whig supremacy in Massachusetts Bay.   He was keenly aware that the Stamp Act was too valuable to Massachusetts patriots to be thrown aside until the last drop of propaganda had been squeezed from it.   His success in linking Hutchinson with the Stamp Act led him to accuse the entire Tory Party of being its abettor.   Adams and Otis drew up a "Black List" of Tory representatives in the General Court who, they declared, had favored the Stamp Act.   That the Boston mob might know its enemies, the "Black List" was pub-

[2] *The Writings of Samuel Adams*, I, 110.

lished in the *Boston Gazette*.   In the House of Representatives, Adams demanded that votes be cast by name; and when Tories voted against the Whigs they found their names written in the House *Journal* by Sam Adams "so as to mark the Nays for resentment."   Such measures utterly unnerved the Tory opposition: Boston's mobs kept many country Tories from taking their seats in the legislature and Sam Adams's intimidation muzzled those who had courage to come to the metropolis.   Governor Bernard attempted to rally his followers by dismissing Whigs from militia posts and offering wavering conservatives their places, but desertions continued to weaken the Tory ranks.   This browbeating of the conservative party resulted in a great Whig victory at the polls.   Nineteen blacklisted Tories were "flung out & low and ignorant Men elected in their stead." [8]

As a result of this sweeping change in the House of Representatives, James Otis was elected speaker and Sam Adams clerk of the House in 1766.   Their margin of victory was small: Otis could boast of a majority of only seven and Adams squeaked through with one vote to spare.   Sam Adams remained clerk of the House for the next decade, but James Otis was immediately negatived as speaker by Governor Bernard.   If Bernard had possessed the right of negativing the clerk of the House, he probably would have rejected Sam Adams as well.   But because the governor's privilege of refusing to accept the representatives' choice of speaker had been used only once before in the colony's history, it was regarded as a weapon of last resort. Therefore, when Bernard revived this long-disused power to keep the most popular man in New England from the speaker's chair, he brought upon himself a torrent of Whig wrath.   When it was learned that the governor had negatived James Otis's election, the Whigs rose to a man at this "signal to battle" and screamed for vengeance upon Bernard.

During a large part of the eighteenth century, the Country and Court Parties had struggled for possession of the Massachusetts Council.   It was a prize worthy of the many sieges and battles that centred about it.   The form of government

[8] *Boston Gazette*, March 31, 1766.   Mass. Archives, 26, *Hutchinson Corr.*, II, 213.

established by the Massachusetts Charter made it impossible for the royal governor to act effectively without the consent of the Council, the members of which were elected by the House of Representatives. If the Council were in opposition to the royal government, the governor's hands were tied: consequently, most Massachusetts chief executives urged the British government to alter the form of government and pack the Council with royal appointees. As long as the councilors were elected by the House of Representatives Bernard declared the government would be "like an open pleasure Boat, fit only for calm Seas & favourable Gales." After the Stamp Act, there was very little calm water or easy sailing for the royal governors of Massachusetts Bay. As long as the Council followed closely in the wake of the governor and Crown officers, the mutinous representatives below decks could be kept under control, but if the Council should begin to veer, nothing remained for the governor but to "strike his Colours" and surrender the ship to Sam Adams, who, Bernard suspected, navigated by the polestar of independency.[4]

Sam Adams nursed a deep grudge against the Council for the part it had played during the Stamp Act troubles. Instead of siding with the popular party, the Council remained loyal to the governor and planted obstacles in Otis's and Adams's path. The Council had made it possible for Governor Bernard to store the stamps in Castle William; it had opposed opening the courts without stamps; and it had kept the House of Representatives "within the Bounds of decency & moderation." Because of these sins, Otis and Adams resolved to purge the Council of Tories. Otis shrieked that the Upper House had become an "infernal Divan" and swore to take the political scalps of the sixteen Tories who paralyzed the Whig majority in the House of Representatives. The governor's negation of Otis as speaker of the House was made the signal for this purification of the Council. Four judges of the supreme court, the secretary of the province, and the King's attorney — Bernard's

---

[4] *Bernard Papers*, IV, Bernard to General Conway, Feb. 28, 1766; Bernard to the Lords of Trade, April 10, 1766; Bernard to Lord Shelburne, March 28, 1767.

staunchest supporters — were ejected from the Council and men whom Hutchinson regarded as "little better than the scum" were put in their places.[5]   Although Otis failed to clear the Council of Tories, it had not undergone such a rigorous purgation since 1741, when the aristocrats were turned out by Deacon Adams and the Land Bank Party.

Having recovered from the panic in which "mobbish Bostonians" had plunged him during the Stamp Act riots, Governor Bernard was anxious to show his courage by sparring with Sam Adams in the General Court.   After the representatives had evicted the governor's best friends from the Council, he stormed down to the House to deliver two speeches which Sam Adams said were "as infamous & irritating as ever came from a Stuart to the English parliamt." [6]   Bernard accused the representatives of "oppognation" of the King's authority by turning out of the Council the friends of royal government merely because they supported the governor in his struggles to maintain the royal prerogative and authority of Parliament.   To this outburst Adams answered that the representatives were merely destroying a pernicious system by which the same persons held legislative and executive powers.   Bernard's fury did him no good and made it easier for Sam Adams to sink the royal government deeper into disrepute.   By allying himself to Hutchinson, Bernard had proved to Adams's complete satisfaction that he had "a deeply rooted prejudice against the people"; and Adams now began to look forward to sending the governor back to England with a chain around his neck.

A system of government such as existed in colonial Massachusetts, where an appointive governor represented the Crown and an elective house represented the people, inevitably bred contention.   Moreover, Whig supremacy in Massachusetts demanded a constant quarrel between governor and people: if the province should become quiet, Sam Adams could not hope to retain the influence he had gained by means of the Stamp Act.

[5] *Bernard Papers*, V, Bernard to Pownall, June 6, 1766; Bernard to Richard Jackson, May 31, 1766; Bernard to Lord Shelburne, Dec. 22, 1766.   Mass. Archives, 26, *Hutchinson Corr.*, II, 233.   Hutchinson, III, 149, 152, 156, 157.

[6] *The Writings of Samuel Adams*, II, 165.

After getting the worst of the quarrel with the House of
Representatives in 1766, Bernard decided to avoid disputes
with Adams in the future. He attempted to put the legislators
in good humor by giving no provocation; but, no matter how
precipitately he backed away from an encounter, Sam Adams
always succeeded in bringing him into the quarrel. Whenever
Bernard addressed the General Court, Adams read into his
words such black meaning that the people were soon convinced
that the governor was their worst enemy. If Adams and Otis
could find nothing in Bernard's speech to turn into propaganda,
they "filch'd a passage" from an address the governor had
made five months before and, by distorting the meaning, "drew
from thence an insinuation which has no foundation in truth."
Finally, Bernard began to confine his speeches to bare formalities
from which even Sam Adams could not squeeze a drop of
propaganda. But Adams was revenged by fastening upon the
governor the name of "Verres" — a tyrannical Roman governor
of Sicily. It is no wonder that Bernard damned "that Adams":
"Every dip of his pen," exclaimed the unhappy governor,
"stung like a horned snake." [7]

Among those swept out of the Council by Otis's purge was
Thomas Hutchinson. Even while the quarrel between mother
country and colonies was hottest, Otis and Adams had not forgotten their feud with Hutchinson; and after the repeal of the
Stamp Act they had no intention of ceasing their efforts to pull
down the lieutenant governor and his fellow "oligarchs." Although Hutchinson had been forced to resign one of his
offices during the Stamp Act, he and his family still held all the
choice posts in the government and stood squarely in the way
of Sam Adams's ambition. Moreover, it was chiefly through
Hutchinson's efforts that the Council remained loyal to the
governor and curbed the radicalism of the House of Representatives. Several years before, when Adams attempted to dislodge Hutchinson from the Council, he argued that executive
and judicial powers should not be held by the same person.
He now pointed out not only that Hutchinson's presence in the

[7] *Boston Gazette*, June 16, 1766. *The Works of John Adams*, II, 425,
426.

Council violated the principle of the separation of powers, but that Hutchinson was one of the bitterest foes of colonial liberty. Nevertheless, Adams succeeded by only a narrow margin in evicting the lieutenant governor from his seat in the Council. A majority of three voted not to return Hutchinson to the board.

Because the Boston mob had destroyed several thousand pounds' worth of Hutchinson's property during its "frolick" in August 1765, the question of compensation became a political issue. Sam Adams had no desire to reimburse Hutchinson for a loss he did not regard out of proportion to the lieutenant governor's deserts, and Bernard's blustering attempt to browbeat the Massachusetts Assembly made Adams even more resolute in opposing the compensation bill. Although Parliament had merely recommended that the Massachusetts General Court reimburse Hutchinson, Governor Bernard declared that Parliament had made a "requisition" which Massachusetts must obey. Such bullying hardly bore out Bernard's pious hope of restoring harmony in the colony because, as easily could have been foreseen, the Massachusetts House of Representatives refused to take orders from the British House of Commons on a money bill. Even without Bernard's blundering, there were serious obstacles in the way of Hutchinson's compensation. If the lieutenant governor were reimbursed from the Province Treasury, yeomen would be compelled to share the burden with Boston. Since "Boston Banditti" had done the damage, Massachusetts farmers said that the townspeople should be obliged to pay the entire bill. Bostonians thoroughly enjoyed a good riot, but they were dismayed by the prospect of paying for the wreckage. The Boston town meeting hastened to instruct the representatives to compensate Hutchinson out of the Provincial Treasury, thus distributing the expense between town and country. These instructions made Sam Adams as ardent as any Tory to do Hutchinson justice; and, paradoxically enough, it was largely through his efforts that the lieutenant governor was reimbursed from the Province Treasury for the damage done by the Boston mob.

Sam Adams was not satisfied with having made politics an

exceedingly hazardous career for Massachusetts Tories: he wished to silence all Tories whom the conservative rural districts sent to the House of Representatives. It had occurred to Adams that before the General Court could appear in its full dignity as the Parliament of Massachusetts Bay, a public gallery should be installed after the example of the British House of Commons. The chief benefit of a gallery, however, was not that it lent a Parliamentary atmosphere to the Massachusetts House of Representatives, but that it would practically drive the Tory Party from the floor. Even when the proceedings of the House were secret, proximity to the Boston mob cooled the most headstrong Tories; but with a gallery full of Adams's "Mohawks" listening to every word spoken in the House, few Tories would invite violence by openly opposing the patriots. As the Whigs said, the gallery would permit the people to see "who and who are together." The patriot leaders wished to seat the General Court in a building "equal to the most finished playhouse," where the people could hear Adams and Otis "thunder from the Rostrum." In this "School of Political Learning," asked Dr. Thomas Young, "how many would catch the fire" and emerge ardent Sons of Liberty? [8] It was well known that Sam Adams was more violent in speech than in print and that more treason was disseminated in the Whig clubs than in the newspapers. Although the proposal to open the House of Representatives to the public and transform it to all intents and purposes into a Whig debating club meant the virtual end of freedom of speech, the motion was carried and a gallery installed. The patriots immediately put it to good use: Adams crowded it with his "Mohawks & Hawcubites, to echo the oppositional Vociferations, to the Rabble without Doors" — to the acute discomfort of the already intimidated Tories. [9]

Massachusetts patriotism could not remain at the white heat to which Sam Adams had raised it without fresh tyranny from the British government. Yet the mother country made no

---

[8] Thomas Young to ———, Nov. 23, 1766, photostat copy in possession of Mr. George P. Anderson.

[9] Peter Oliver, 157. *Bernard Papers,* VII, Bernard to Lord Hillsborough, Sept. 9, 1768. *Boston Gazette,* Feb. 17, 1766.

effort to throw fuel on the embers left by the Stamp Act: there was a change of ministry favorable to the colonies; the molasses duty imposed by the Sugar Act of 1764 was reduced; and there seemed excellent chance that Parliament would relax the laws of trade. "The repeal of the Stamp Act," said John Adams, "has hushed into silence almost every popular clamor, and composed every wave of popular disorder into a smooth and peaceful calm." The people as a whole were not alarmed by the Declaratory Act of 1766: they regarded it as a "mere naked Form" and saw none of the latent tyranny perceived by Sam Adams. It was clear that unless Adams could keep up "the Clamour and Jealousy of the People by continuing to feed them with fresh Matter" he would lose the advantage he had gained over the Tories by the Stamp Act. Both Adams and the Tories were aware that tranquillity worked in favor of the conservative party — hence the Tories' rejoicing and Adams's dejection when calm water came into view in 1766. Many Boston merchants cut their connection with the politicians and began to look fondly in the direction of the Tory Party, which, Bernard said, included "almost every Person of Fortune and Fashion throughout the Province." Such fine company exerted powerful attraction at a time when Otis's influence was on the wane and little was to be feared from Sam Adams's mobs; and for the first time since the Stamp Act, Tories confidently looked forward to regaining the ground they had lost and bringing about the downfall of Otis and Adams.[10]

There could be no doubt that the Tory revival in Massachusetts Bay had assumed menacing proportions. In spite of Adams's efforts to fill the ranks at Whig assemblies, the meetings were "very thin & insignificant" and Bernard observed with satisfaction that there were few present who had "any pretension to converse with a gentleman." Although Sam Adams attended, his presence did not raise Bernard's low opinion of the company. In the General Court, the Whig Party was so riddled by desertions in 1767 that the Tories were

<hr/>

[10] *The Works of John Adams*, II, 202. Hutchinson, III, 147. *The Writings of Samuel Adams*, I, 109, 387. Mass. Archives, 26, *Hutchinson Corr.*, II, 344.

almost an even match. Even in the Boston elections, Sam
Adams and the other Whig members of the Boston Seat had a
stormy time before their ships, "remarkable for their steady
Sailing, being well mann'd with the best of Navigators and
true Sailors, got safe into Port." When Tories came within
inches of scuttling Adams and Otis in Boston, the safest Whig
anchorage in New England, it was clear that "Otis & his Gang"
were sinking fast. Otis himself was so frightened by the prospect of being caught in the rising tide of Toryism that he attempted to patch up a truce with Governor Bernard. The Whig
leader intimated that if Bernard would give up Hutchinson, he
would have no further trouble with the patriot party. But the
governor was so certain the Whigs were beaten that he rejected their overtures. Adams and Otis might "still mutter
threats," but Bernard felt certain he was safely out of their
reach.[11]

Massachusetts Whigs had fallen upon evil days, but Sam
Adams's skill in staging patriot parades, feasts, and celebrations
served to conceal most evidence of the patriot decline. He believed men were ruled by their emotions rather than by their
reason, and he knew that a display of fireworks on the Boston
Common or parades of marching Sons of Liberty were far more
effective ways of arousing popular enthusiasm than dry constitutional arguments. Unquestionably, he was a master of
stagecraft, deeply versed in the art of swaying the popular
mind. The Sons of Liberty celebrated the repeal of the Stamp
Act with "such illuminations, bonfires, pyramids, obelisks, such
grand exhibitions and such fireworks as were never before seen
in America."[12] Effigies of popular enemies were used to inflame the people's passion; cartoons exhibiting in easily understood form the wickedness of the Tories and mother country
were passed from hand to hand; stirring phrases were coined
and spread among the common people with greater effect than
whole volumes of political reasoning; and Whig newspapers

[11] *Boston Gazette*, May 11, 1767. *Bernard Papers*, VI, Bernard to Richard
Jackson, July 29 and Aug. 30, 1767; Bernard to Lord Shelburne, March 23
and May 30, 1767.
[12] *The Works of John Adams*, II, 179.

carried the radicalism of the seaboard towns to every corner of the province.   John Adams, too, saw the importance of Whig parades, fireworks, and propaganda: "Otis and Adams are politic in promoting these festivals," he wrote, "for they tinge the minds of people; they impregnate them with the sentiments of liberty; they render the people fond of their leaders in the cause, and averse and bitter against all opposers."   The Tories, on the other hand, knew nothing of influencing the common people; instead of attempting to wean them from Sam Adams, they merely sneered at them as "the rabble" or "the scum." The fatal error made by Massachusetts conservatives during the revolutionary period was their failure to recognize the importance of the common people in the coming struggle between mother country and colonies.   They looked to Great Britain for aid against the menace of colonial radicalism just as the mercantile aristocracy of 1740 had turned to the mother country for assistance against the Land Bank Party; but had the Tories actively combated radicalism and met the Whigs upon their own ground with their own weapons, Sam Adams would have found it far more difficult to overcome Toryism in Massachusetts Bay.   After the Revolution, the Massachusetts Federalist aristocracy held its own against Sam Adams's subversive Jacobinism because it won the support of a large part of the common people; the Tories of the revolutionary period were forced into exile partly because they ignored the masses.   After the full effects of Adams's propaganda began to be seen in New England, Daniel Leonard, a Tory pamphleteer, sorrowfully confessed that his party had made an irremediable mistake.   "I will do justice to their ingenuity," he said of Sam Adams and other Whig propagandists, "they were intimately acquainted with the felings of men, & knew all the avenues of the human Heart."

The most impressive of Sam Adams's celebrations was the annual festival held on August 14 to commemorate the founding of the Sons of Liberty and the riot against Andrew Oliver, the late stamp master of Massachusetts Bay.   Here the Sons of Liberty drank bumping toasts, roared out the chorus of the Liberty Song, and were edified by such choice mimicry as

"the hunting of a bitch fox." [13]   The celebration of August 14,
1768, was typical of these Whiggish revelries.   The festivities
were opened with the Sons of Liberty massing around Liberty
Tree and singing the "American Song of Liberty" — "sublime
entertainment" that drew applause and smiles from the "fair
daughters of Liberty" who crowded all the windows around
Hanover Square to watch their heroes.   After this performance,
the wealthier Whigs climbed into their chariots and set off for
Roxbury in a cavalcade that extended for over a mile and "sur-
passed all that had ever been seen in America."   At the Grey-
hound Tavern in Roxbury, the patriots sat down to a hearty
dinner topped off with speeches and toasts.   After drinking
forty-five toasts to the principal English and American Whigs,
these stout patriots were still able to consecrate a Liberty Tree
at Roxbury, make "an agreeable excursion round Jamaica Pond,"
and parade homeward through the streets of Boston. [14]

Fortunately for Sam Adams and the Whig Party, British
squires still longed to tap the rich revenues they believed existed
in the colonies and British politicians still pondered how Americans could be made to bear a share of the expense of imperial
government and defense.   English landowners grumbled in
1767 that while they paid the war-time tax of four shillings to
the pound, the colonists shirked their duties and rioted against
the most equable form of taxation that George Grenville, the
best financier in Great Britain, could devise.   Dissatisfaction
gained such strength among the squires that the House of Commons mutinied against the party leaders and lowered the rate
of taxation from four shillings to three shillings to the pound.
Here, clearly, was an opportunity for a bright young man to save
the Ministry and appease the truculent squirearchy by forcing
the miserly colonists to make good the shilling which Englishmen had thrown over.   The hard-pressed taxpayers were not
compelled to wait long before they found their man.   Charles
Townshend, Chatham's Chancellor of the Exchequer, — known
as "Champagne Charley" in London coffeehouses, — was one
of the flashiest young politicians in England.   The revolt in

[13] *The Works of John Adams*, II, 218.
[14] Wells, I, 203.   *Boston Gazette*, Aug. 22, 1768.

Parliament against high taxes had placed him in a very painful position: Chatham blamed him for having allowed the House
of Commons to get out of hand and all parties awaited his resignation as Chancellor of the Exchequer after his defeat on a
money bill.   Rather than give up office, Townshend was prepared to risk the peace of the British Empire.   He believed the
colonies were still fair game for taxation by the British Parliament and he saved his place and hastened the Revolution by
imposing new taxes upon them.

But Charles Townshend was far too clever a young man to
send the Sons of Liberty scurrying for their muskets by repeating George Grenville's mistakes.   He chose rather to take
Americans at their word by giving them the sort of taxation
they had acknowledged to be within Parliament's power.   At
the time of the Stamp Act, the colonists had distinguished between "internal" and "external" taxes.   They had denied the
right of the House of Commons to impose an internal tax such
as the Stamp Act upon the colonies, but they agreed that port
duties — external taxes — were constitutional.   The distinction made by William Pitt was regarded in the colonies as a
final solution of the problem of imperial government: Parliament could not tax the colonies, but it exercised "sovereign and
supreme" authority over them.   Parliament, said Pitt, had the
right to restrict the colonies in their trade, navigation, and
manufactures: it was sovereign "in every thing, except that of
taking their money out of their pockets without their consent."
George Grenville habitually pointed to the colonists' ready
acceptance of this doctrine to prove his favorite argument that
Americans were rascals who clutched at any absurdity to avoid
paying taxes.   Charles Townshend treated the distinction between external and internal taxation "as ridiculous in every
body's opinion except the Americans'."   But unlike most wits
in the House of Commons, he was not content merely to jeer
at the weakness of the provincials' reasoning: he sought for
ways to take advantage of it.   Since Americans admitted that
external duties were binding, Townshend proposed to reach
by means of port duties the same goal that Grenville had hoped
to attain with the Stamp Act.   By laying taxes upon paper, paint,

tea, and lead imported from England into the colonies, Townshend told the House of Commons that at least forty thousand
pounds in additional colonial revenue would be realized and
the deficit resulting from the lowering of the tax scale in Great
Britain would be considerably decreased.   The scheme seemed
safe: it was not to be expected that Americans would rise against
port duties, the principles of which had been known in the
colonies for a century.   It was certain to raise a large revenue:
by the laws of trade the colonists were compelled to import the
dutied commodities from Great Britain alone.   Moreover, it
eased British taxpayers by shifting part of the burden of imperial government upon the colonists' shoulders.   Altogether,
the plan put forward by the Chancellor of the Exchequer
found such favor in the House of Commons that the "Townshend duties," as they came to be known in the colonies, were
promptly enacted.

Colonial patriots were not slow to see that Townshend had
forced them to seek new defenses against taxation by the British
Parliament.   Although the Townshend duties fell within the
American definition of external taxes, the colonists were not
happy that the British government had taken them at their
word.   It was the preamble to the Townshend duties which revealed to Americans that the mother country had sent another
"menacing monster" swooping down upon the colonies.   The
preamble declared that the revenue realized from the Townshend duties was to be placed at the Crown's disposal to make
governors and judges independent of the assemblies.   This
policy inevitably struck terror among Sam Adams and his followers, for all New England patriots regarded control of the
purse by the local assembly as essential to colonial liberty.   During the eighteenth century, Massachusetts had clashed with
most of its royal governors over the issue of a fixed salary and
had successfully resisted the British government's efforts to
establish a civil list in the colony.   But Charles Townshend
seemed to have succeeded where a half century of British threats
and stratagems had failed.   Americans were no longer to be
bullied into supporting a civil list: by placing taxes upon commodities which the colonists were forbidden to import from

other countries, the British government made certain of a revenue ample to place colonial governors and judges out of reach of the assemblies.   And, after having accomplished this long-sought reform in colonial administration, enough money might remain to keep up a standing army to coerce refractory colonists and prevent the Sons of Liberty from stirring up a revolt.

Charles Townshend realized that laying new port duties was not in itself sufficient to produce the colonial revenue he had promised the House of Commons.   It was clear that before any considerable sums could be looked for from America, the colonial customs system must be completely reorganized.   The customhouse did not pay its own way: smuggling was still rampant and it was notorious that most customs officers had their price.   Townshend determined to put an end to this laxity by establishing new Vice Admiralty courts, authorizing writs of assistance, and appointing five Commissioners of the Customs to oversee the collection of colonial port duties.   These Commissioners were given powers similar to those exercised by the Commissioners of the Customs in England.   They acted under the authority of the Lords of the Treasury in the mother country; and all customs officials in the colonies were made responsible to them for the suppression of illicit trade and enforcement of the laws of navigation.   As if to give the Commissioners a taste of colonial intractability at its worst, Boston was made their headquarters.   It was believed in the mother country that since Boston had taken the lead among the colonies "in trade as well as politicks," the Commissioners should begin their labors among the "Saints": if Bostonians submitted, there seemed little doubt that the rest of the continent would follow suit.   With such high hopes were the heads of the Commissioners of the Customs thrust into the lion's mouth.

Sam Adams lost no time in mobilizing hostility in New England to the Townshend duties and Commissioners of the Customs.   To alarm the people for their liberty and property, Adams produced his most "dreadful scarecrows."   He pictured the colonies drained of their hard money by British taxation; townspeople and yeomen alike ruined by commercial stagnation; and governors and judges made arbitrary "overlords" of the colonies. Evil as the Townshend duties were, Adams did not suppose the British government would be long content with the revenue they yielded. The people were told that the taxes now imposed upon them were merely a "small specimen" of what they might expect after a standing army had been established in the colonies and the provincial legislatures deprived of authority. The Townshend duties, Adams exclaimed, were merely an entering wedge for British tyranny; they were fully as menacing to colonial liberty as the Stamp Act; and the Commissioners of the Customs, who had been sent to enforce them, merited no better treatment than the stamp masters. Reports were spread by the Whig chiefs that the Commissioners had been given power by the British government to tax land in New England in order to support the bishops who were to be set over New England. Because the Commissioners had authority to appoint underofficers to assist them in enforcing the laws of trade, Adams declared they would create "an host of pensioners" in the colonies to strengthen the Tories and Crown officers. As Adams roundly said, the Commissioners of the Customs were "the greatest political curses that could have been sent amongst us." [15]

This propaganda produced immediate results in Boston. Commerce was the mainstay of the town's economic life; and if the Sugar Act of 1764 had alarmed the citizens more than the Indian massacres on the frontier, the Townshend duties and Commissioners of the Customs seemed even more ill-omened. Bostonians were "set on boiling" by Sam Adams in 1767; and the Sons of Liberty of the metropolis strengthened their alliance with the New York Liberty Boys to prepare for possible military resistance to the British government. Adams planned to fall upon the Commissioners when they landed in Boston, march them to Liberty Tree, and give them a choice between resigning office or taking their chances with the mob. But Otis refused to join in provoking a quarrel with the mother country; New York gave the Boston hotheads no hope of military aid; and the other colonies seemed "perfectly easy and satisfied with what was done by the parliament." With great reluctance, the proposed reception at Liberty Tree for the Commissioners was given up. When they reached the town on November 5, — a day usually commemorated in Boston with a rousing riot, — the mob carried twenty "Devils, Popes, & Pretenders" through the streets bearing inscriptions of "Liberty, Property, & no Commissioners." Nevertheless, the Commissioners were not touched even when they passed close to the mob's bonfires on their way through the town. Boston was ruled by a "trained mob" which obeyed Sam Adams's orders; but the Commissioners were soon to learn that the Boston cudgel-boys were sorely disappointed at losing their "frolick" and restlessly awaited permission to drive them out of town.[16]

As Sam Adams had feared, the Commissioners of the Customs vigorously enforced the laws of trade, suppressed smuggling, and began to make the American customs profitable to the British government. It was soon evident to Bostonians that the British Ministry had revived the policy that brought Randolph to New England in the seventeenth century and had replaced the easy-going customs officers who winked at evasions and drank rum with smugglers by stiff, businesslike officials who collected taxes down to the last penny. Adams was as indignant as though smuggling were one of the rights of Englishmen which the British government unjustly denied Americans; and he quickly convinced most of the citizens of the province that tyranny was again flourishing in the metropolis. In reality, the Commissioners did more good to Sam Adams's party than to King George's exchequer. As long as the Commissioners collected port duties in Boston, Adams was under no necessity of appealing to abstract rights and imaginary grievances: he now had what he most sorely needed — visible tyranny imposed by the British government. Bostonians did

---

[16] *Bernard Papers*, VI, Bernard to Lord Shelburne, Sept. 21, 1767. Mass. Archives, 25, Thomas Hutchinson to Jasper Mauduit, Nov. 13, 1767. *Boston Evening Post*, Nov. 30, 1767; Dec. 21, 1767. *Letters of a Loyalist Lady*, 8. *Mass. Hist. Soc. Proceedings*, LVI, 348.

not have to "snuff the tainted breeze" for tyranny because, in the persons of the Commissioners of the Customs and their understrappers, it made itself felt constantly. Sons of Liberty throughout the colonies drank toasts to the "speedy removal of the odious Board of Commissioners with all other vermin from America." [17]

Sam Adams's grievance against the Commissioners of the Customs was not only that they enforced unconstitutional laws, but that they undermined Boston's morals. Several of the Commissioners, being gay bloods out of England, attempted to enliven society in the metropolis, which they found insufferably dull. Their parties, balls, and concerts scandalized Sam Adams and gave Boston its first taste of real night life: at a "Turtle Feast" held at the Peacock Tavern, the Commissioners and their friends celebrated until four o'clock in the morning, when they were all carried home violently ill — which caused Hutchinson to wish that the party had been composed of Otis, Sam Adams, William Molineux, John Hancock, and "half a hundred more of the same cast." [18] The Commissioners endeavored to "mimic high life" by dressing in the height of London fashion, retaining numerous servants, and "rolling from house to house" in gilded carriages. At first their balls were unpopular, but Bostonians soon acquired a taste for these "high frolicks"; and Sam Adams had the mortification of seeing Whigs, Commissioners, army officers, and Tories drinking punch and dancing the minuet together. Although the Commissioners found to their dismay that there were no eligible "fortunes" in Boston, their assembly was so successful that the patriots were forced to establish a rival "Liberty Assembly" where Whigs might frolic without being exposed to the contaminating influence of the customhouse and royal barracks. Concerts flourished as never before in the Puritan metropolis; "grand Routs" and card parties became popular; cooks and confectioners were brought over from London to satisfy the de-

[17] *Mass. Hist. Soc. Proceedings*, XLIII, 479. Mass. Archives, 26, Hutchinson Corr., II, 318, 319, 378. *Newport Mercury*, Aug. 24, 1772. *Lamb Papers*, MSS. N. Y. Hist. Soc., Thomas Young to John Lamb, March 18, 1774. Hutchinson, III, 345.

[18] Mass. Archives, 27, *Hutchinson Corr.*, III, 249.

mand for "luxurious and costly Feasting"; and the Whigs who scorned this prodigality were awakened at night by carriages rattling through the streets carrying parties on their way from carousals in the taverns.

Like many other strait-laced patriots, Sam Adams believed it was "a bad thing for Boston to have so many gay Idle people in it" whose example might spread to the citizens. If the citizenry became infected with fashionable London vices and conceived an appetite for "Turtle Feasts," Adams was certain New England would be undone; for when Whigs loved debauchery more than liberty, despotism would make an easy conquest of the colonies. After witnessing the conduct of the Commissioners of the Customs in Boston, Adams exclaimed that the British government was making war upon New England's morals as well as upon its liberties; and, with such unholy work going on in the metropolis, it is not strange that the clergy joined him in damning the Commissioners and the government that had sent them to Massachusetts Bay. The patriots and parsons looked upon the Commissioners of the Customs as sourly as the early Puritan magistrates had regarded those accursed sprites that danced around the maypole at Merrymount a century and a half before; and Adams yearned to smite the Commissioners as old Endicott had Thomas Morton and his crew.

In 1767, the winter session of the General Court opened so quietly that Governor Bernard began to believe the country had sent down enough moderate delegates to defeat the schemes of the "great Boutefeu," James Otis. But after Otis and Adams had harangued for several days upon the state of the colonies, the iniquities of the Townshend duties and Commissioners of the Customs, and the danger of a bishop being set over New England, the representatives' amiability rapidly disappeared. Within a short time they were in a "snarling humour." Otis and Adams were elected to all the important committees and, almost overnight, they seemed to recover the ground they had lost since the repeal of the Stamp Act. The House of Representatives obediently followed their directions by dispatching a letter of protest to the King, remonstrating to the Secretary of

State, and employing a separate agent in England "as if they
were the States General of the Province, without a Governor
and King's Council." [19]   Bernard complained that the Whigs
ignored him as though there were no royal governor in the
colony: as clerk of the House, Sam Adams made no secret
among his friends of the letters the representatives were preparing to send to the King and his Ministers, but he kept their
contents hidden from the governor and the Tories.   When
the Crown officers learned that mysterious documents were being
written in the House, they immediately suspected that Otis and
Adams had some new trick up their sleeves to play against the
King's government.   It was widely believed that an effort
would be made to call another colonial Congress.   But, instead, Adams and Otis proposed that a circular letter be written
to the other British-American colonies acquainting them with
the measures adopted by Massachusetts against the Townshend duties.   This scheme struck the delegates as a first step
toward summoning a Congress; and few wished to invite
punishment from the mother country by flinging such sedition
in its face, particularly when they were uncertain of support from
the other colonies.   To the dismay of Otis and Adams, the
House rejected the circular letter by a vote of two to one.
Governor Bernard was overjoyed to see the Whigs soundly
drubbed in their own back yard and he was certain the tide had
begun to run swiftly in his favor: "The Faction has never had
so great a Defeat as this has been," he rejoiced; "nor so great a
disappointment, as it cuts off their hopes of once more inflaming the whole Continent." [20]

It was a source of great uneasiness to Massachusetts Crown
officers that the upcountry Tory representatives in the General
Court, among whom the royal government found its staunchest
supporters, began to drop out of the House early in 1768.
Believing all important business over for the session, the rural

[19] Mass. Archives, 26, *Hutchinson Corr.*, II, 284, 297. *Letters to the
Ministry* (Boston, 1768), 7.   *Papers relating to Public Events in Massa-
chusetts, The Seventy-Six Society* (Philadelphia, 1856), 52.   *Bernard Papers*,
VI, Bernard to Lord Shelburne, Jan. 21, 1768.

[20] *Bernard Papers*, VI, Bernard to Pownall, Feb. 1, 1768.   Mass. Archives,
26, *Hutchinson Corr.*, II, 287.

representatives returned to their farms, leaving the radicals in a majority.   Governor Bernard observed with alarm that "the Friends of Government are allways tired out with the extended Length of the Winter Session, which the Faction lengthen for that among other Purposes.   Hence it is that the Faction generally recovers Ground at the End of a Session."   True to form, Adams and Otis seized this opportunity to secure a reconsideration of the circular letter.   For a fortnight, they labored among the remaining delegates, convincing them of the legality of such opposition to British tyranny and quieting their fears that the circular letter would lead to a Congress.   As a result, the legislature was thrown into the "most quarrelsome humour" that Hutchinson had ever seen in a Massachusetts Assembly.   Since most of the "able Men on the Side of Government" were home congratulating themselves upon having tripped up the Whigs, Sam Adams's "private Cabals" soon whipped up a majority in favor of the circular letter.   Shortly before the end of the session, it passed the House; and, to destroy all evidence of the difficulties encountered in securing its adoption, the first vote against the circular letter was erased from the *Journal*.   Nevertheless, Tories continued to murmur that it had been "procured by surprise in 'a thin House" — a taunt which Sam Adams could not endure, probably because there was a large measure of truth in it.[21]

The Massachusetts circular letter formulated a new theory of colonial rights to combat the Townshend duties.   Since the trade duties imposed by Parliament in 1767 made it plain to Americans that the distinction they had drawn between external and internal taxes was no barrier to oppression by the British government, Otis and Adams denied Parliament's right to impose external taxes, "with the sole & express Purpose of raising a Revenue."   Although Parliament could lay taxes for the purpose of regulating colonial trade, it could not use the revenue to make governors and judges independent of the

---

[21] *Bernard Papers*, VII, Bernard to Lord Hillsborough, July 18, 1768; Bernard to Lord Shelburne, Feb. 20, 1768.   *Letters to Dennys de Berdt, Col. Soc. of Mass. Collections*, XIII, Transactions 1910–11, 336.   *The Writings of Samuel Adams*, 228, 231.

assemblies, as was contemplated by the Townshend duties, without violating natural law. Thus, against Charles Townshend and the British House of Commons, Adams and Otis set the law of God and nature which, by their interpretation, now forbade even external taxes by Parliament. Englishmen exclaimed that all Adams and Otis were saying was that Parliament could lay a small but not a large tax upon the colonies; and they rightly feared that the American Whigs would soon deny its right to impose any taxes whatever. William Knox said the powers Adams and Otis granted Parliament were similar to those the Deists gave God over mankind: "He may reward them with eternal happiness if he pleases, but he must not punish them on any account." [22]

Both Sam Adams and James Otis could take this stand against external taxes with perfect consistency. From the beginning, James Otis had ridiculed his countrymen's distinction between internal and external taxation. In 1765, he said that Parliamentary restrictions on colonial trade and manufactures were no different from internal taxes; and after the repeal of the Stamp Act, he told the Boston merchants they were fools for submitting to trade duties and restraints on manufactures because Parliament had no right to confine American commerce and manufactures. To the end of his political career, Otis kept up a steady fire against Parliamentary legislation which prevented the colonists from manufacturing iron "much beyond the making a horse shoe or a hob-nail" and swaddled intercolonial commerce so tightly that the provinces were "scarcely permitted to vend egg shells beyond their boundaries." Sam Adams had said as early as 1764 that a tax on foreign molasses laid by the British House of Commons to raise a revenue in the colonies was a direct infringement of American rights. Both Otis and Adams feared before 1767 that the British government would renew the policy of the Sugar Act of 1764 and seek a colonial revenue by means of port duties: hence they

[22] William Knox, *The Controversy between Great Britain and her Colonies Reviewed* (1769), 35, 38, 44. Hutchinson, III, 164, 165. *Remarks on the late Celebrated Oration* (London, 1766), 28. *A Plain and Seasonable Address to the Freeholders of Great Britain on the Present Posture of Affairs in America* (London, 1766), 16.

were prepared in 1767 to receive the Townshend duties with a fully developed theory of colonial rights.

Nevertheless, the Massachusetts circular letter did not go beyond the point of denying Parliament's power to raise a revenue through external taxes. Parliament was accorded the rights to regulate colonial trade and was recognized as the "supreme legislative Power over the whole Empire." The letter written in the House of Representatives by Otis and Adams to the Marquis of Rockingham in 1768 admits the "superintending power" of Parliament over the colonies, and nowhere in the extensive correspondence, petitions, and remonstrances drawn up by them in that year is there a direct attack upon Parliament's sovereignty. Its authority in the colonies was being cut away piecemeal, but the patriots were not yet aiming their blows at the root of Parliamentary jurisdiction.

John Adams was never able to understand why Sam Adams did not declare in the circular letter his conviction that Parliament had no authority whatever in America. John Adams said he himself had already reached this conclusion; yet because the circular letter admitted Parliamentary sovereignty he believed it was entirely the work of James Otis and summed it up as "the rough cast of James Otis and the polish and burnish of Samuel Adams": "Every sentence and every word," he exclaimed, seemed to spring from Otis.[23] But there is no reason to minimize Sam Adams's contribution to the circular letter merely because it acknowledged Parliament's sovereignty. No realist such as Sam Adams could close his eyes to the fact that the time was not ripe in 1768 to throw off all Parliamentary authority. Had Massachusetts taken the bold stand that John Adams favored, colonial unity would have been at an end and the Revolution set back many years. The purpose of the circular letter was to unite the colonies against British oppression; and it was clear in 1768 that the colonies could be united only on conservative ground. American political thought was dominated at this time by John Dickinson, the "Pennsylvania Farmer," who firmly believed that mobs, sedition, and ungentlemanly violence had no part in colonial resistance to the

[23] *The Works of John Adams*, 367, 374.

mother country. At the same time that Dickinson taught Americans devotion to Whig principles, he inculcated love of the mother country and reverence for King and Parliament — loyalties which did not seem incompatible in 1768. Although Dickinson denied Parliament's right to raise a revenue in the colonies by means of external taxes, he acknowledged its power to regulate colonial trade and legislate for the colonies. This doctrine, so distasteful to John Adams, became fashionable in Boston, where the town meeting in 1768 instructed the representatives in the General Court to "pursue the principles laid down by your worthy Farmer" and to state the colony's "constitutional subordination" to Parliament. As long as John Dickinson was regarded as the oracle of American political thought, no effort to throw off Parliament's sovereignty could hope for success.

John Adams ignored public opinion, frequently to his cost; Sam Adams was keenly sensitive to it. Many years after the passage of the circular letter, the latter is said to have remarked: "It is often stated that I am at the head of the Revolution, whereas a few of us merely lead the way as the people follow, and we can go no further than we are backed up by them; for, if we attempt to advance any further, we make no progress, and may lose our labor in defeat." [24] Sam Adams did not broach in 1768 so revolutionary a doctrine as complete freedom from Parliamentary authority because he knew he would isolate himself by outstripping public opinion. Had he rung the "alarm bell to a revolt" against Parliament prematurely, he would have destroyed the purpose of the circular letter and separated Massachusetts Bay from the rest of America, for not a single colony was ready to take so radical a step.

It is clear, nevertheless, that Adams believed in 1768 that Parliament had no lawful sovereignty in America. As early as 1748, in fact, Adams had regarded the Massachusetts General Court as the parliament of the colony; and he shared the conviction of the Sons of Liberty that the colonies had "no Superior upon Earth but the King." It was probably at Adams's instigation that the Massachusetts House of Represent-

[24] James Loring, *The Hundred Boston Orators* (1854), 13.

atives adopted resolves in 1765 which omit acknowledgment of the authority of Parliament.   In these resolves the Massachusetts representatives declared they "venerated" Parliament, but nowhere do they grant Parliament specific authority.[25] Although Sam Adams called Parliament that "truly august body" in 1768 and said he felt "the greatest veneration" for it, William Knox pointed out that the patriots' reverence was merely "another subterfuge for seeming to respect its authority, whilst they *mean* to disavow it."   Adams's recognition of the "superintending power" of Parliament when it was in accord with "the Enjoyment of our essential Rights as Freemen, and British Subjects," in effect stripped Parliament of most of its authority in America.   If the colonists themselves were to be judges of the constitution, their "constitutional subordination" was worthless in the eyes of British imperialists.   In every colony, Sam Adams said, the King, Council, and Assembly constituted the legislature of the province; and the British Parliament as "the Supreme Authority of the Nation" had a controlling power over the colonial legislatures so far as was consistent with the rights of Englishmen.   But, he was careful to add, no Englishman was bound by laws made by a legislature in which he was not represented: "Thus," said Hutchinson, "in the same breath they give & take away all power of Parliament over the Colonies."   Sam Adams gave a far clearer insight into his opinion of Parliamentary sovereignty when he exclaimed in the Boston town meeting in 1769: "Independent we are, and independent we will be." [26]

Hutchinson believed that Adams would soon interpret the law of nature to destroy completely Parliament's authority in the colonies: it was merely a matter of time, he said, before the cry of "no taxation without representation" would become "no legislation without representation" — an eventuality anticipated by many Englishmen as well.   After the repeal of the Stamp Act, British statesmen feared the colonists would next demand the repeal of the navigation laws — the "Palladium of the Empire."   It was hardly to be supposed that

[25] Hutchinson, III, 133–134.
[26] Mass. Archives, *Hutchinson Corr.*, II, 305.

Americans would consent long to pay 30 per cent more for highly taxed British merchandise if they could buy untaxed goods direct from the continent simply by throwing overboard the mercantilist system. "Here," exclaimed an English writer, "they are galled — *here* it is that the shoe pinches." [27]

No sooner had the Whigs pushed the circular letter through the Massachusetts House of Representatives than a new Tory menace sprang up in the colony. Thomas Hutchinson still smarted from the humiliation he had suffered in 1766 when Otis and Adams expelled him from the Massachusetts Council. Early in 1768, however, having made careful plans to recover his seat, he came within three votes of being elected to the Council on the first ballot. It seemed impossible to prevent his victory at the next vote. Adams and Otis, although they were caught napping by Hutchinson's unexpected popularity among the delegates, acted quickly. In the midst of the balloting, Sam Adams took the floor to ask the representatives if they were sure the lieutenant governor was not a pensioner of the Crown. Upon this signal, Otis leaped to his feet and exclaimed that he knew Hutchinson to be a pensioner paid by the King from the "unconstitutional" taxes collected by the Commissioners of the Customs. Otis then ran round the House "like an amazed Dæmon" furiously shouting "pensioner or no Pensioner." Hutchinson's pension consisted of a small addition to his salary as Chief Justice, which, he complained, was "scandalously mean," but nothing was more calculated to arouse the House against him than the name "pensioner" which Otis now shrieked at the top of his lungs. Otis was well rewarded for his effort. After the uproar had died down and the second ballot had been counted, it was found that enough votes had been turned away from Hutchinson at the last moment to keep him from entering the Council.[28]

The Whigs had so narrowly averted defeat at Hutchinson's hand that Sam Adams felt obliged to brace them with some

---

[27] *A Plain and Seasonable Address to the Freeholders of Great Britain, etc.*, 10, 16.

[28] *Bernard Papers*, VI, Bernard to Richard Jackson, June 6, 1768. Mass. Archives, 26, *Hutchinson Corr.*, II, 306, 308.

particularly stiff doses of propaganda.   James Otis had won
the support of the "black regiment" of Congregational ministers,
but it remained for Sam Adams to put the whole Tory Party
under suspicion of Popery.   As Adams was well aware, one of
the surest ways of arousing New Englanders was to play upon
their aversion to Roman Catholicism.   Although Puritanism
had disappeared, the hatred of Popery was still as strong as in
the days of Winthrop and Cotton: the first book school children
read was the *New England Primer,* embellished with a frontis-
piece depicting the Pope "stuck around with Darts"; and
Bostonians zealously burned "popes" on Guy Fawkes Day.   A
"papist" in eighteenth-century New England was not merely
a Roman Catholic, but a boon companion of the devil and an
abettor of all his works.

To crush the Tories, in 1768, Adams forced them to shoulder
all the obloquy which "papists" carried in New England.
Writing in the *Boston Gazette,* under the signature "A Puritan,"
he declared that Popery was abroad in Massachusetts and gaining ground so rapidly that it was more to be dreaded than British
tyranny.   He made Popery synonymous with the unwillingness shown by a large number of representatives in the General
Court to support the Boston Whigs against the royal governor
and British Parliament.   He prepared lists of "Protestant"
towns in the colony whose delegates voted with Boston, and
"popish" towns whose representatives were "Governor's Tools"
and worshipers of "graven images."   The strongholds of
Popery, by Adams's reckoning, were the Salem–Marblehead
district and the western towns in the vicinity of Hatfield: the
delegates from Salem, Hardwick, Hatfield, and Springfield
were notorious Tories and the infection had spread even to
Cambridge.   Indeed, unless Adams exaggerated the danger,
the Pope — presumably in the person of Governor Bernard —
might take possession of Massachusetts at any moment, so
alarmingly had his adherents grown; and many of those who
were not outright "papists" were so shaky in their Protestantism
that no good could be expected from them.   "A man who
Wavers," Adams exclaimed, "is but a step from a TOTAL APOS-
TACY."   Unless Massachusetts was to become the domain of

the Holy See at Westminster, the General Court must be filled with "sound Protestants" who, it was implied, feared neither the devil, the royal governor, nor the British House of Commons.[29]

Unquestionably, this skillful working with prejudice and religious intolerance had great effect in solidifying the patriot cause in the country where Tories found themselves regarded by pious rustics as secret favorers of the "Romish" faith. Tories denounced Adams for injecting religious passions into a political struggle, but Adams was never nice in his choice of methods when he believed the cause in danger. But despite Adams's success in painting the Tory Party as bigoted to the principles, if not the faith, of Roman Catholicism, there were those who whispered that Adams himself was the real papist because he insisted, with the Jesuits, that the end justifies the means.

Adams's attack upon the Tories was well timed, for, soon after his "Puritan" letters appeared, the British government formally demanded that the Massachusetts House of Representatives rescind its circular letter on pain of dissolution; and Lord Hillsborough's circular letter to the colonial assemblies ordered them to discountenance the Massachusetts letter. But when this command reached Massachusetts, the Tories were scattered and made contemptible by Adams's propaganda and the moderate Whigs had been braced by the Boston radicals. Moreover, the dictatorial tone assumed by the British government brought Massachusetts patriotism to white heat. Otis delivered a fiery oration in the Massachusetts House of Representatives against rescinding the circular letter; and the Tories maintained a discreet silence because the gallery was crowded with several hundred of Adams's "Mohawks." As a result, the representatives voted 91 to 17 to defy the British government. Most of Governor Bernard's supporters voted with the patriots, and their timeserving was fully justified by the treatment meted out to the seventeen members who voted to rescind the circular letter: their names were posted on Liberty Tree and they were branded as parricides to whom "the out done DEVIL will resign his sway." Throughout the continent, Sons of

[29] *The Writings of Samuel Adams*, I, 203, 210, 212.

Liberty drank to the damnation of "the Seventeen of Massachusetts Bay," and few of them ever sat again in the General Court.

The efforts made by the British government to compel the colonies to renounce the Massachusetts circular letter raised patriotic fervor in America to a pitch it had not reached since the Stamp Act.   Instead of rejecting the circular letter as Lord Hillsborough demanded, the colonial legislatures enthusiastically adopted it and sent promises of support to Boston.   Sam Adams believed that "no one step . . . united the colonies more" than the Massachusetts circular letter unless it was Lord Hillsborough's own.   When answers from the Virginia and Maryland legislatures reached Boston, Adams declared it the most glorious day he ever saw.   During the Stamp Act days, Massachusetts had been laggard and Virginia had first rung the "alarum bell," but there could be no question that Massachusetts had taken its proper place of leadership in resistance to the Townshend duties.

The overwhelming majority in the Massachusetts House of Representatives that voted against rescinding the circular letter gave such clear indication of the patriots' strength that the Council gave up the struggle and deserted to the Whigs.   Ever since Otis's "purge" of 1766, the Massachusetts Council had shown an alarming inclination to run with the Whigs, but until the summer of 1768 it remained under the governor's control. After the colony had hurled forthright defiance at the British government, however, the councilors seemed to stand in greater fear of the people than of the King and governor.   Several years before, Bernard had said that as soon as Otis and Adams took possession of the Council, "the Governor has nothing to do but to strike the Colours."   Therefore, when he saw the Upper House of the legislature go over to the enemy, Bernard declared the royal government was "at length subdued" and he prepared to run up the white flag.   "After a three Years' War," he wrote Lord Hillsborough, the Council — the "Citadel" of royal government — had fallen and its garrison been made "Creatures of the People." [30]

[30] *Letters to the Ministry* (1768), 65.   *Bernard Papers*, Bernard to Lord Hillsborough, July 7, 1769.

The theory of imperial government contained in the Massachusetts circular letter revealed how deep a gulf now divided British and American political thought. In Great Britain, the Massachusetts General Court was popularly supposed to be an assembly of Yankee rustics whose authority did not go much beyond making laws for the "yoking of hogs, or pounding of stray cattle." A colonial legislature seemed to Englishmen little more than "the vestry of a larger parish" or an "inferior licensed Corporation." The Massachusetts Charter, which Sam Adams believed to be "the Ark of God to New England," had little sanctity in England, where colonial charters were spoken of as "feeble Charters, these Divinities of their [the colonists'] own forming." As for the Rights of Englishmen and laws of nature upon which Adams based his arguments for colonial liberty, these seemed in the mother country to be merely "a synonymous Term for Blasphemy, Bawdy, Treason, Libels, Strong Beer, and Cyder." [31] The doctrine put forward in the circular letter that Parliament was sovereign in the colonies but could lay no taxes, internal or external, for the purpose of raising a revenue struck George Grenville, and, indeed, most Englishmen, as another proof that the colonists would swallow any absurdity. Sovereignty could not be thus parceled out, it was said; either the colonies were subject to Parliament and therefore obliged to obey its laws or they were completely beyond its jurisdiction. Even Benjamin Franklin, good American that he was, could not conceive of sovereignty divided. "I know not," he said, "what the Boston people mean by the 'subordination' they acknowledge in their Assembly to Parliament, while they deny its power to make laws for them." [32]

Unlike Sam Adams, Franklin was at this time under no necessity to conform his ideas to the slow progress of public opinion.

---

[31] John Dickinson, *Letters from a Farmer in Pennsylvania to the Inhabitants of the British Colonies* (1903), 91. *Boston Gazette*, March 17, 1766 (Britannus Americanus). *A Letter to a Member of Parliament* (London, 1765), 13, 16. Samuel Johnson, *Taxation no Tyranny* (London, 1775), 44. *Orations delivered at the Request of the Inhabitants of the town of Boston* (1807), 17.

[32] *The Writings of Benjamin Franklin*, edited by Albert Henry Smyth (1907), V, 114, 115.

Adams saw as clearly as Franklin the weakness of the principles set forth in the Massachusetts circular letter.   Nevertheless, the danger of outstripping the people upon whom he depended for support compelled Adams to stand upon this halfway ground.   As will be seen, he was merely biding his time until the people were ready to cast off all Parliamentary authority.

VI

THE MASSACHUSETTS CONVENTION OF 1768

THE frontier is not always a stronghold of political radicalism. During the revolutionary period, the spread of radical ideas in Massachusetts was from the town to the frontier, and the country was slowly brought to adopt the advanced political views that had already taken firm root in the eastern seaboard towns. Embattled farmers fought the Revolution, but Boston made it. British tyranny fell most heavily upon the commercial seaports; frequently the rural districts first learned they were oppressed when they heard the clamor raised by merchants and patriots in Boston or read Sam Adams's instructions to the representatives in the General Court. Had not Adams first brought about Boston's domination of the province, Massachusetts would not have taken the lead among the colonies against Parliament. If he had been unable to overcome the opposition of the western country which Tories regarded as "the most loyal part of the Province," a civil war might have broken out in Massachusetts with loyal western yeoman fighting for King George and the revolutionary eastern districts on the side of rebellion.[1] The battleground for which Whigs and Tories struggled was rural New England; Whigs attempted to impress Boston's ideas and spirit upon the country and Tories strove to keep it loyal to King and Parliament. Yet conservatism gave way so stubbornly that it required a decade of British misgovernment and Sam Adams's propaganda before the Tories were forced to surrender rural Massachusetts to the Whigs.

The policy of the Tory Party was to coop up sedition in Boston and to keep town and country apart. Tories recognized that it was the "fewel scattered from time to time by some of the

[1] Mass. Archives, 26, *Hutchinson Corr.*, II, 150.

Inhabitants of Boston" that kept the province in a flame: "If we could keep off the influence of Boston for one twelve month," said Thomas Hutchinson, "I think we could bring the rest of the Province to their senses." In the Tories' eyes, the metropolis seemed to "collect and ferment the ill humour of the whole body" and to discharge the poisonous product throughout New England. As "the source of all the disorders of the Government" and hatcher of "Cockatrice Eggs, which breed Serpents to poison the People," Boston was a bugbear to every well-wisher to royal government. Thomas Hutchinson declared he would willingly sacrifice all his property in the town if Boston could be separated from the rest of the province, and Tories fervently prayed, "I wish to the Lord the whole town of Boston might sink this moment." [2] The next best thing, in their opinion, to putting Boston at the bottom of the Atlantic was to see Sam Adams swing at Tyburn; but in spite of their efforts, Boston remained above high water and Sam Adams died at eighty-one in his own bed.

Tories regarded Boston as a wasps' nest because it was "an absolute Democracy" in which all real power was held by Sam Adams and the Sons of Liberty. Few gentlemen of wealth and rank were inclined to mix in its rough-and-tumble political tussles or to rub shoulders with mechanics and ropewalkers at the town meetings over which Adams presided. Although Massachusetts law required the payment of a property tax before voting in the town meetings, it was not enforced in Boston, where "any thing with the appearance of a man" was freely admitted.[3] Consequently "the lowest mechanics" swarmed into Faneuil Hall on meeting days in such "shoals" that they far outnumbered the qualified voters; and on several occasions between three and four thousand people were present, although there were not more than fifteen hundred in the whole town

[2] *Bernard Papers*, IV, Bernard to the Lords Commissioners for Trade, Jan. 18, 1766; Bernard to Thomas Hutchinson, Dec. 5, 1769. Mass. Archives, 26, *Hutchinson Corr.*, II, 377; III, 175, 538, 579, 582. *Boston Evening Post*, Jan. 25, 1773. Octavius Pickering, *The Life of Timothy Pickering* (1867–73), I, 23.

[3] Mass. Archives, 25, *Hutchinson Corr.*, I, Thomas Hutchinson to Richard Jackson, Nov. 9, 1767.

qualified to attend.   Since these citizens were highly susceptible
to Sam Adams's demagoguery, Tories complained that the town
meeting fell under the control of "a few hot and designing
men" and thus became "a constant source of sedition."   Hutchinson lamented that the Boston Sons of Liberty were so insolent
toward their betters that a gentleman did "not meet with what
used to be called common civility." [4]   Because of this hard
treatment from the Boston "rabble," "men of Property & of
the best characters" — as the Tories described themselves —
kept a safe distance from Faneuil Hall and allowed Sam Adams
free rein in running Boston.

With Adams in the saddle and the Tories bent only upon
getting safely out of his way, the Boston town meeting made
such vast encroachments upon royal authority in Massachusetts that Governor Bernard believed Adams planned to bring
"all Authority down to the level of the People."   By province
law, the authority of the towns was strictly limited, but this
barrier did not hinder Adams and his "high flying" Sons of
Liberty.   Adams called the town meeting together for whatever purpose he chose and paid no heed to illegalities.   Even
when he summoned the townspeople to consider matters in
which they had no more authority "than to declare war against
France," Hutchinson was unable to prevent the assembly.
These encroachments became so menacing that the lieutenant
governor urged Parliament to stop the spread of Boston's influence in Massachusetts Bay.   "Let the Assembly do its worst,"
he exclaimed, it could never be as troublesome as the Boston
town meeting.   Bad as were the Boston mobs, Hutchinson
considered Sam Adams and his followers who controlled the
town meeting far more dangerous because they struck deliberately at the root of royal government in the province. [5]

Had Hutchinson succeeded in keeping the Boston town meeting within its constitutional limits, Sam Adams would have
found it far more difficult to revolutionize Massachusetts Bay.

---

[4] Mass. Archives, 26, *Hutchinson Corr.*, II, 464; III, 454. *Mass. Hist.
Soc. Proceedings*, LV, 265.
[5] *Bernard Papers*, IV, Bernard to Lord Shelburne, Dec. 22, 1766.   Mass.
Archives, 27, *Hutchinson Corr.*, III, 573, 579.

Adams used the Boston town meeting to originate the measures which he hoped to see followed by the rest of the towns in the province.   After the metropolis had set an example by making a daring attack upon royal government he urged the smaller towns to come to Boston's support.   The result was that constitutional authority throughout the province was gradually undermined.   To accomplish this rape of the Crown's sovereignty by a host of petty townships, Adams struck up an intimacy with the local political leaders who, like the members of the Boston Caucus Club, ruled the "Roast" and determined their town's policy.   These men had to be handled skillfully and, in some instances, brought into the revolutionary movement against their own and their constituents' wishes.   Lest, however, rural jealousy of the metropolis upset his plan of uniting town and country against the British government, Adams took care that Boston's leadership of the province was well screened.   He seldom permitted rural New Englanders •to see that they were being dominated by Boston politicians, but there are few instances of country people meddling with affairs outside their constitutional power until after Boston had led the way.

The cornerstone of Sam Adams's policy was to put New England in leading strings to Boston and make farmers as zealous Sons of Liberty as were the North End mechanics and shipyard workers.   He knew that the metropolis could not oppose Parliament single-handed and that before Massachusetts could assume the leadership of the American colonies against Great Britain, yeomen must learn to look upon Boston as a bulwark of their liberties.   Adams hoped to see town and country sink their differences when confronted by British tyranny.   He found, however, that the long-established antagonism between town and country was not easily forgotten and was likely to reappear even in crises when Boston most needed rural support. There were many towns "principled against the Politicks of Boston" which refused to fall in line behind the metropolis. Marblehead and Salem, for example, strongholds of the Court Party, were little disposed to bow before the "Metropolis of Sedition"; and in some "remote parts of this Province which have been friends to order," Tories cultivated antagonism to Boston so successfully that the townspeople complained of the countrymen being bigoted to the doctrine of nonresistance to such an extent that they would not raise a finger against the British "when they are graciously *instructed* to cut our throats." [6]

Nevertheless, Sam Adams had much in his favor. Through the *Boston Gazette* — printed by those "Trumpeters of Sedition," Edes and Gill — he continually drenched the country with propaganda. He filled its columns with such dire prophecies of disaster and terrifying descriptions of "horred slavery" at the hands of British overlords that many yeomen were transformed into fiery Whigs. It was said of this journal that if its readers were "not in the temper of the writer at the time of publication, yet it is looked upon as the ORACLE, and they soon bring their temper to it." Furthermore, it made vastly more exciting reading than did the dull conservative newspapers that attempted to keep the country people loyal to King and Parliament; indeed, Sam Adams's journalism was so lively that the *Gazette* became practically the only newspaper read outside of Boston.[7] Although it was packed with sedition and libel, it could not be suppressed by the Crown officers; when Hutchinson attempted to induce the Suffolk Grand Jury to indict the author of a particularly "blasphemous Abuse of Kingly Government," Sam Adams brought so much pressure to bear upon the jury that the indictment was promptly quashed. During the Stamp Act, Tories had received a bitter taste of the power of the patriot press. The Stamp Act riots in Boston were so glorified by Sam Adams in the *Gazette* that rural patriots were sorely troubled because no mobs sprang up in rural New England to harry the Tories. Upcountry Whigs asked themselves "ye Reason *we* could do nothing when Such Great

[6] *Bernard Papers*, V, Bernard to Richard Jackson, Nov. 17, 1766. *Boston Gazette*, Nov. 29, 1773. *Israel Williams Papers*, MSS. Mass. Hist. Soc., II, Thomas Hutchinson to Israel Williams, Feb. 20, 1766. Peter Oliver, 59.

[7] *Copy of Letters sent to Great Britain by His Excellency Thomas Hutchinson, the Hon. Andrew Oliver, and seven other persons, born and educated among us* (Boston, 1774), 27, 30. Mass. Archives, 26, *Hutchinson Corr.*, II, 535.

Things were done at Boston." Countrymen who bore a grudge against the local squire imitated Sam Adams by threatening to get up a mob, pull down the house, and give the "aristocrat" a coat of tar and feathers. Several gangs of Sons of Liberty, with an eye toward making patriotism profitable, raided the houses of their creditors and wiped out their debts by tearing up the ledgers and account books.[8]

A second circumstance which smoothed the way for the progress of the revolutionary movement in rural New England was the ineffectiveness of the Tory opposition. Whereas Boston patriots could be called together at a few moments' notice, the ablest Tory leaders such as Timothy Ruggles of Hardwick, James Putnam and the Chandlers of Worcester, the Winslows and Thomases of Plymouth County, and John Worthington of Springfield were too remote from each other to take concerted action. They were hampered, moreover, by poor support from the mother country and by Sam Adams's practice of making them the scapegoats of British "tyranny." Between Sam Adams and the British government, New England Tories were deprived of the greater part of their rural following and the country was revolutionized in spite of the people's distrust of "Boston Politicks."

In 1768, a sudden emergency made the country's aid vital to Boston. Before the metropolis was fully entrenched in its position of leadership, Adams's incompleted work was forced to withstand a severe attack. To punish Boston for its riots, the British government ordered several regiments of British regulars to the town. The question which Sam Adams anxiously asked himself during the summer of 1768 was whether the country would stand by quietly if British troops overran the metropolis. Would the people *"away back* in the province" who were ill-disposed toward Boston and Whig principles make no resistance while the townspeople were forced to surrender their freedom at the bayonet's point? If Bostonians determined to fight the troops, would New Englanders answer a call to arms against the mother country? Adams found a conclusive

---

[8] Mass. Archives, 25, *Hutchinson Corr.*, John Cushing to Thomas Hutchinson, Dec. 29, 1765. *Bernard Papers*, V, Bernard to Pownall, March 31, 1766.

answer to his questions in the Massachusetts Convention of
1768.

It was the rioting that broke out in Boston early in 1768
against the Commissioners of the Customs that brought royal
troops to the metropolis.   After a hard winter, with unemploy-
ment rife and prices high, Hutchinson found Bostonians looking
more "sowre and discontented" than he had ever seen them.[9]
Since the people had been fully convinced by Sam Adams that
their hardships were owing to acts of Parliament and the Commissioners of the Customs, the mob was spoiling to run the
Commissioners out of Boston and stop the collection of "unconstitutional" taxes.   When it was rumored that the mob
would rise on March 18, 1768, the anniversary of the repeal
of the Stamp Act which was celebrated in Boston as a "Day of
Triumph over Great Britain," the Commissioners confidently
expected to be attacked.   But much to the mob's disappointment, the leading Sons of Liberty refused to permit a riot and
even removed the effigies of the Commissioners that had been
hung on Liberty Tree in anticipation of the evening's sport.
The "great Opposers of Parliamentary Authority" came out
strongly against terrorism and Sam Adams astonished his followers by declaring that there were to be "NO MOBS — NO CON-
FUSIONS — NO TUMULTS" in Boston.   Adams was well aware
that an uprising in Boston would defeat the purpose of the circular letter by turning the Southern colonies against "mobbish"
Boston; as long as Massachusetts was attempting to unite
America in protest against the Townshend duties, Adams put
Boston strictly on its best behavior.   He took the edge off the
Liberty Boys' chagrin, however, by promising them speedy satisfaction against the Tories: "We know *WHO* have abus'd us," he
said, ". . . but let not the hair of their scalps be touch'd: The
time is coming, when they shall lick the dust and melt away."[10]
Tories suspected that Adams meant that the patriots would have
the pleasure of loading the governor and Commissioners aboard
the next brig for England.   By means of such promises, the mob

---

[9] Mass. Archives, 26, *Hutchinson Corr.*, II, 297.

[10] *Mass. Hist. Soc. Proceedings*, LV, 269.   Mass. Archives, 26, *Hutchinson
Corr.*, II, 296.   *Boston Gazette*, March 14, 1768.

was held in leash; instead of riding out of Boston tarred and feathered on a rail, the Commissioners were untouched during the celebration and the evening passed with no greater disturbance than usually took place on a holiday.

Although both Hutchinson and Bernard, who had seen the Boston mob at close quarters in its ugliest moments, declared that no damage had been done, the Commissioners of the Customs were not disposed to take the matter so lightly. Sam Adams and his "Mohawks" had made the Commissioners feel that as long as they remained in Boston they were sitting on a volcano. At night, their houses were frequently surrounded by a mob of Liberty Boys lustily beating drums, blowing horns, and emitting the "most hideous howlings as the Indians, when they attack an enemy." [11]   The Commissioners were unaccustomed to Boston mobs, which they found singularly lacking in the good humor of English rioters, and they firmly expected to be roughly handled before they had remained long among the "Saints." They saw that it was only because Adams held the mob in check that they were permitted to collect His Majesty's customs in Boston. They found living at the mercy of such a notorious riot lover as Sam Adams extremely uncomfortable; yet it was clear that if he gave the mob "the least hint" that the Commissioners were fair game, Boston would become too hot to hold them. The threatened assault of March 18 convinced them that they could not remain in Boston unless British regulars were sent to their protection. But garrisoning Boston with royal troops promised to be ticklish business: no soldiers had been stationed in the metropolis since the close of the Seven Years' War; the citizens were accustomed to having the nearest "Serjeant's Guard of real Soldiers" two hundred miles away; and it could easily be foreseen that Sam Adams would use British military tyranny to touch off an explosion. Nevertheless, two regiments of British regulars were ordered to proceed from Halifax to Boston. In the light of later events, it is important to remember that the British government first sent troops to the Puritan metropolis in consequence of a disturbance which Sam Adams himself had prevented from being

[11] *Letters to a Loyalist Lady*, II.

more serious than "a few disorderly boys hollooing before Mr.
Inspector Williams' door." [12]

The riot of June 10, 1768, which led the Ministry to send
two more regiments to Boston from Ireland, was an affair of
more serious character.   This outbreak occurred when the Commissioners of the Customs seized John Hancock's sloop *Liberty*
and put it under the guns of *H.M.S. Romney* for running a
contraband wine cargo into Boston.   A mob of "sturdy boys &
negroes" thereupon made its long-delayed attack upon the
Commissioners, several of whom fled to Castle William for
refuge.   The morning after the "Liberty Riot" — so called
from the name of Hancock's sloop — signs were hung on Liberty Tree urging the citizens to rise against the Commissioners
if they again attempted to collect unconstitutional taxes.   The
metropolis was clearly no longer tenable and the Commissioners
refused to return unless they were given a bodyguard of redcoats.   "The Security of the Revenue, the Safety of its Officers,
and the Honor of Government," they said, made imperative
the speedy dispatch of men-of-war and British regulars.   Governor Bernard, who, too, had had his fill of Boston and was
preparing to get to England out of harm's way, urged the Ministry to send troops "to rescue the Government out of the hands
of a trained mob."   It seemed very unlikely that the British
government would let slip an opportunity to rid itself of such
a thorn in its side as Boston.   Besides driving the Commissioners out of town, the Whigs had smartly rapped Lord Hillsborough's knuckles and defied the British government by refusing to rescind the circular letter.   After such open bearding of
the British lion, Sam Adams began to look forward to an attempt on the part of the Ministry to even the score with Boston.   With the Commissioners screaming they were at the mercy
of the Boston mob, it seemed probable that the British government would dispatch an army to tame the "Saints."

It was no secret to Sam Adams and his fellow patriots that
the governor and Commissioners were outdoing each other in
calling for British soldiers and men-of-war.   With fear of

[12] *Boston Gazette*, Sept. 19, 1768.   *Bernard Papers*, IV, Bernard to Richard Jackson, Aug. 31, 1767.   *Mass. Hist. Soc. Proceedings*, LVI, 348.

military despotism as a spur, radicalism increased by leaps and bounds through the summer of 1768.   During the debate on rescinding the circular letter in the Massachusetts House of Representatives, James Otis made "the most violent insolent abusive treasonable Declaration that perhaps was ever delivered."   Otis declared that Lord Hillsborough's ultimatum to Massachusetts was written in such wretched style that in Massachusetts Bay it would pass for the "performance of School Boy" — which was to be expected from a member of an aristocracy who went to Oxford and Cambridge merely to learn the fine arts of "Whoring, Smoking and Drinking."   There was not a man in England, Otis exclaimed, who was capable of writing "so elegant so pure & so nervous a Writing as the Petition to the King" which had been penned by Sam Adams and Otis himself.   In his opinion, King George appointed "none but Boys for his Ministers" to administer the colonies; virtuous American statesmen could do nothing to restore harmony within the Empire as long as they were compelled to deal with such striplings and dullards in the British Colonial Office.   Otis gave the British House of Commons — "those mighty Men that effect to give Law to the Colonies" — an even more severe tongue-lashing.   He upbraided the members as "a parcel of Buttonmakers, Pin-makers, Horse Jockeys, Gamesters, Pensioners, Pimps and Whore Masters" — no doubt to the great joy of Adams's "Mohawks" in the galleries, who took democratic delight in seeing the whole British aristocracy dragged through the mud.   After having shown up the scandalous illiteracy and immorality among the British peers, Otis turned the tables on Parliament and warned it to rescind *its* measures or be "lost for ever," and then passed "an Encomium upon Oliver Cromwell & extolled the Times preceeding his Advancement & particularly the Murther of the King."   At the Boston town meeting in the Reverend Mr. Sewall's meetinghouse on July 14, 1768, Otis made a "Harangue from the Pulpit" in which he launched another violent attack upon British policy.   If American grievances were not speedily redressed "and we were called on to defend our liberties and Privileges," Otis declared "he hoped and believed we should one and all resist even unto

Blood; but, at the same time, prayed almighty God it might never so happen." Should England use redcoats against the colonies, Otis believed there was "nothing more to do, but to gird the Sword to the Thigh and Shoulder the Musquet." [13]

The threat of British troops threw Sam Adams into a frame of mind even more warlike than James Otis's. The dissolution of the Massachusetts General Court after its refusal to obey Lord Hillsborough's "mandate" to rescind the circular letter convinced Adams that the British government was determined to leave the colony only a "vain semblance of liberty"; and when British regiments were reported on their way to Boston, he did not doubt that military law would be fastened upon the metropolis. The caution and reserve which Adams usually displayed in transforming American discontent into revolutionary fervor were characteristics acquired through many years of self-discipline. By nature, Adams was passionate, excitable, and violent, but he rarely allowed these qualities to appear in public. Bostonians usually saw him as a dignified, patient patriot who strove to keep the controversy with the mother country upon lofty constitutional grounds rather than as a hot-tempered revolutionist who spirited up mobs and longed to disrupt the British Empire. But the crisis of 1768 caused him to throw off the "serpentine cunning" which Tories dreaded more than the fire-eating of other patriot leaders, and to make a rash appeal to arms. Rather than allow a standing army to garrison Boston, Adams revived the plan which the Sons of Liberty had adopted during the Stamp Act of fighting off the British troops before they could gain a foothold in the colonies.

The morning after the Liberty Riot, Adams was seen in the South End of Boston "trembling and in great agitation" while he harangued a crowd of listeners to make a bold attack upon the royal government. "If you are Men," he exclaimed, "behave like Men; let us take up arms immediately and be free and Seize all the King's Officers: we shall have thirty thousand Men to join us from the Country." Boston was filled with "many wild and violent proposals" to prevent the landing of British troops, but Sam Adams's plan meant nothing less than

[13] *Chalmers Papers*, II, Speech of Otis, June 1768. *Bernard Papers*, VI, Bernard to Lord Hillsborough, June 25, 1768.

war with Great Britain. Rather than pay the Townshend duties and submit to military rule, Adams declared, "We will take up arms and spend our last drop of blood." To stir up Bostonians' war enthusiasm, he promised that thousands of embattled farmers "with their knapsacks and bayonets fixed" would swarm down from the country and cut off the British force to a man. Adams had no more hesitation in fighting King George's soldiers than Louis XV's "papists"; George III, he said, had no right to send troops to dragoon New Englanders and they should be regarded as foreign enemies.[14] Once before, Adams had prepared for war with the mother country, but no British army had been sent in 1766 to determine whether or not the Sons of Liberty were merely bluffing. In 1768, however, it seemed probable that the Massachusetts patriots would have ample opportunity to show their mettle.

With Sam Adams preaching war and sedition on Boston street corners, the Crown officers saw the metropolis becoming a hotbed of military fervor. While the country as a whole remained calm, Boston was caught up in the full stride of this radical movement. Instead of frightening Bostonians with threats of armed coercion, the British Ministry seemed to have stirred up a hornets' nest. Tories who observed the swift growth of the war spirit in Boston during the summer of 1768 expected to see England and Massachusetts at blows when the royal transports and men-of-war entered Boston Harbor. "The Promoters of the present Evils," wrote one particularly apprehensive conservative, "are ready to unmask and openly discover their long and latent Design to Rebel." [15]

Sam Adams had little fear of punishment from Great Britain even if Massachusetts patriots massacred the British troops sent to keep order in Boston. In the eyes of Boston Sons of Liberty, the British Empire was so "tottering" and rotten that it was almost beyond human aid; only John Wilkes seemed able to keep "the Great System from dashing to Pieces." [16] Because Englishmen were "degenerate" and the British Empire on the verge

[14] *Chalmers Papers*, III, Information of Richard Silvester of Boston taken before Thomas Hutchinson, Jan. 23, 1769.

[15] *Letters to the Ministry*, 104.

[16] Boston Sons of Liberty to John Wilkes, June 6, 1768, MS. Mass. Hist. Soc., Gay Transcripts, *Miscellaneous Papers*, III.

of destruction, Adams believed he had little to fear from a government that was busy with both hands in keeping itself afloat. Since the Stamp Act had first revealed the weakness of British colonial administration, the debility of government in England, the rioting and turbulence of the London mobs, and the corruption of English political life had been spread before New Englanders by Sam Adams in the *Boston Gazette*. This steady disparagement of British power led many colonists to believe America was more than a match for the mother country. It was difficult to respect the long arm of government which appeared "to totter on the brink of destruction from the unbounded licentiousness of the people" and which was unable to suppress "the great tumults and risings of the people all over England and Ireland." To encourage New Englanders to resist British demands, Sam Adams pointed out that the English government was harassed by "the Weavers mob, the Seamens mob, the Taylors mob, the Coal miners mob, and some say, the Clergys mob; and in short it is to be feared the whole kingdom . . . will unite in one general scene of tumult." If, as Sam Adams said, the ministry could not put down riots "at the very gates of the palace, and even in the royal presence," how could it deal, at a distance of three thousand miles, with the stout cudgel-boys of Boston after they had driven off the troops? Moreover, Adams believed that when the British government attempted to coerce America with military force, the mob would rise in England and paralyze its hands. He expected that the nonimportation agreement which Boston and New York had formed against British manufactures would lead to new working-class riots in England and cause serious embarrassment to the government. Boston patriots put great store in the laborers of the manufacturing towns, whom they hoped would "commit Riots and Tumults in their Favor." [17] After the American nonimportation agreement had begun to close English factories

---

[17] *Boston Gazette*, Jan. 27, 1766 (Supplement); Aug. 4, 1768. *Pennsylvania Journal*, Aug. 4, 1768. *Massachusetts State Papers: Speeches of the Governors of Massachusetts, from 1765 to 1775*, edited by Alden Bradford (1818), 170. Public Record Office: Colonial Office, Class or Series 5, LXXXVI, 266. General Gage to Lord Hillsborough, Sept. 26, 1768, Lib. Cong. Transcript.

and throw thousands of artisans out of employment, Sam Adams and his followers believed themselves well out of reach of reprisals.   Thus, as seen through the eyes of the Boston Sons of Liberty in 1768, England appeared so torn with dissension and the government so preoccupied with political squabbles and mob uprisings that American patriots felt free to settle affairs in the colonies to their own taste without risk of punishment.

With Bostonians in this highly inflammable state, Governor Bernard feared an explosion if definite news of the troops' coming were made public.   When he received information from General Gage in New York that two regiments had been ordered from Halifax to Boston, he held it back from the Council and people lest an insurrection should break out against the Crown officers before the troops arrived.   The governor preferred to let the bad news leak out gradually in order that the "*Heads* of the *Faction* might have time to consider well what they were about, and prudent men opportunity to interpose their advise." Accordingly, on September 3, Bernard told one of the councilors that he had private information that troops would soon reach Boston, but insisted that he had not received public orders.

Before night, all the citizens had learned that British regulars were coming to Boston and "nothing was to be heard among them but declarations that the troops should not enter the Town."   The Sons of Liberty declared that unless the people immediately took up arms there would be a bloody purge of Boston Whigs by the British: "some were to be pilloried, some whipped, some to lose their ears and others their heads." Adams pictured the troops as "dragoons and executioners" who had been sent out by the Ministry to cram unconstitutional acts of Parliament down the colonists' throats and bring them to "the very borders of slavery."   The citizens were told that their alternative was to resist the troops or tamely submit to a military despotism which would deprive them of all liberty. Confronted with this dilemma, the political temperature in Boston rapidly climbed to the bursting point.   The general expression among the people was "sullen Discontent on almost every Brow except where a panic fear seemed fix'd."   But what most alarmed the Crown officers and Tories was the report that

two secret meetings had been held in Boston by the Sons of
Liberty.   At the first and larger of these meetings, it was believed that the patriots had laid a plan to raise the country against
the troops and that at a smaller and more secret "meeting of
the most violent" a plot had been hatched to surprise Castle
William and garrison it with Sons of Liberty.[18]

As the key to Boston Harbor, Castle William must necessarily
have played an important part in any attempt to prevent the
landing of British troops.   If the Castle should fall into the
hands of the Sons of Liberty, it was believed there would be
a good chance of beating off the British fleet when it attempted
to enter the harbor, for "the Gunners could sink every ship that
attempted the Castle" and force the men-of-war into the open
sea.   Moreover, the castle was not garrisoned by royal troops:
Massachusetts soldiers were in possession, and Adams believed
they would deliver up the stronghold with little, if any, resistance.   Because this strategic point was in such vulnerable state,
Governor Bernard was kept in a flutter of anxiety lest he should
suddenly find the Liberty Flag run up over Castle William and
the ramparts bristling with armed Liberty Boys.   Bernard did
his utmost to have the few royal ships in the harbor stationed
in position to guard it from a surprise by the Boston Patriots.
Therefore, when it was learned that the Boston town meeting
of September 12, 1768, had brought forth such "inflaming
Speeches" and "Treasonable Resolves" that there seemed real
danger of an attack, Captain Corner of the *Romney* placed the
Magdalen between Castle William and Boston — a precaution
which he believed "disconcerted the Mobilities scheme" and
prevented an assault by the Sons of Liberty.

Sam Adams had determined to call a town meeting when
Governor Bernard first let it be known that British troops were
expected.   As in most Boston town meetings of the revolutionary period, the proceedings had been carefully prearranged by
a small group of politicians who met secretly several days before

---

[18] *Boston Gazette*, Sept. 19, 1768 (Supplement).   Public Record Office,
Administrative Secretary, Letters, 483: *Diary of Captain Corner*, 215, Lib.
Cong. Transcripts, 25.   *State of Disorder . . . in Massachusetts Bay*, Mass.
Hist. Soc., Gay Transcripts, *State Papers*, XIII.

the townspeople assembled. It was well known that Sam Adams, James Otis, and Joseph Warren gathered at Warren's house on September 10, where they "drew up the Resolves, Debates and other matter" for the town meeting which met on September 12.[19] By following the plans made by Sam Adams in this "caucus," the Boston town meeting came within a "hair's breadth" of treason and forced the British government to prepare for war with Massachusetts.

On the day of the town meeting, Adams and Otis came down to Faneuil Hall surrounded by the "Mohawks." No attempt was made to confine the meeting to lawful voters — there were "very few Gentlemen there," said Bernard, and "such as were, appeared only as curious, and perhaps anxious spectators." [20] So many Sons of Liberty had turned out, however, that, with James Otis in the moderator's chair, Sam Adams pushed through his schemes without difficulty. His first step was to demand that Governor Bernard summon the General Court immediately. Bernard knew from painful experience that the General Court planted thorns in the governor's chair at every opportunity, but rather than face the rising indignation in the province he would have risked even that acute discomfort had not royal instructions tied his hands. Bostonians had tried every means from petitions to threats to open the General Court; but even when the Boston town meeting in July 1768 put Hancock, Adams, and a score of other prominent patriots in chariots and sent them out of Roxbury to lay a petition before the governor that the legislature be called, Bernard refused to violate Lord Hillsborough's instructions. When the town meeting learned, on September 11, that Bernard had again rejected their demands, they adopted the doctrine formulated by Adams and Otis in the caucus, that the King could not impose a standing army upon Massachusetts without first securing the consent of the General Court, the parliament of the colony. The pressing danger of British regulars led Sam Adams to exalt acts of Parliament and to attack the prerogative, — a reversal

[19] *Diary of Captain Corner*, 217.
[20] *Papers Relating to Public Events in Massachusetts, the Seventy-Six Society* (1856), 102.

of his practice in 1765, — but few Whigs believed that constitutional arguments would prevent the troops from landing.
Sam Adams and his followers had sharper weapons with which
to keep Boston clear of redcoats.

When Sam Adams preached battle against the King's soldiers,
he did not entirely throw his habitual caution to the winds. He
was keenly aware of the danger of attempting to stir up an
armed insurrection when troops were already on their way to
crush the revolt. Adams never neglected to leave loopholes
behind through which he might beat a quick retreat; and when
advocating such barefaced sedition as taking up arms against
British troops, he kept a watchful eye to the rear. By employing the fictitious danger of a French invasion of New England, he hit upon a stratagem which permitted the Boston patriots to denounce King, Parliament, and Ministry and threaten
to rise against the British "invaders," yet at the same time preserve the appearance of loyal, obedient subjects. The Boston
town meeting adopted a resolution urging every householder
to carry out that "good and wholesome law of this Province"
which required that they should possess themselves of "a well
fixed Firelock Musket Accoutrement and Ammunition." [21]
Although everyone knew that these muskets and balls were to
be used against the British, the town meeting saved itself from
outright treason by declaring that the citizens should prepare
for war because "there is at this Time a prevailing apprehension,
in the minds of many, of an approaching War with France."
This pretext was put to good purpose by patriot orators who
used it to make their meaning clear without going to the length
of treasonable words. When the Sons of Liberty in the Boston
town meeting enthusiastically approved these preparations for
war, the town arms, which had been removed from the store-
rooms for cleaning, stood ominously before the Whig speakers.
These weapons, it was said, were to be used against *their enemies;*
the motion to distribute the muskets among the people, which
was voted down as too radical a measure, was put in the form
of a resolve to oppose *the enemy.* Occasionally, however, as
the patriot haranguers became more heated in their denuncia-

[21] *Boston Town Records*, 16th Report, 264.

tions of British tyranny, the "flimsy veil" was thrown off, and the true motive behind this military preparation exposed. One speaker forgot discretion so far as to exclaim that New Englanders "had a right to oppose with Arms military Force which had been sent to oblige them to submit to unconstitutional laws." In a crucial point of the debate, Otis is said to have declared that "they understood one another very well," and, pointing to the town arms, added, "There are the Arms, when an attempt is made against your Liberties they will be delivered, our declaration wants no explanation." In spite of this effort at dissimulation, not a Boston Son of Liberty expected to waste his powder on French "papists"; British regulars were the real enemy and it was against them that the citizens were urged to arm. This "disingenuous, canting, Jesuitical pretence" deceived no one, but it served as a convenient loophole through which the patriots later wriggled to escape treason trials. Indeed, it was so successful that Sam Adams used it as a blind to cover military preparations down to the eve of the Revolution.[22]

Because it was clear that Governor Bernard would not call the General Court before the troops reached Boston, Sam Adams proposed to summon the representatives of the people of Massachusetts Bay without the consent of the royal governor. Two years before, Otis and Adams had attempted to bring the legislature together over the governor's protest and had failed to shake the rural delegates from their conservative distrust of unconstitutional institutions and suspicion of the designs of Boston patriots. In 1768, however, Adams hoped for better things from New England farmers. There was no more effective way of sounding the country's disposition toward military resistance than to assemble delegates from the entire colony in Boston. If Sam Adams and his followers were given an opportunity to influence the country representatives, there was excellent prospect of sending them home with highly contagious cases of war fever which would spread over the entire colony. This meeting of popularly elected "committees" intended to

[22] *Boston Evening Post*, Oct. 31, 1768. *Papers Relating to Public Events*, 103.

fill the place of the dissolved General Court Adams suggested
should be known as the "Convention."

Before inviting the Boston town meeting to touch off this
train of explosives, the patriot leaders believed the townspeople
needed to be spurred by new provocations against the Crown
officers. There were few men more likely to arouse the citizens'
wrath than the Commissioners of the Customs. Could some
fresh outrage be laid at their doors, the patriots anticipated little
opposition in pushing their plans through the town meeting.
Unfortunately, however, the Commissioners were still in Castle
William and showed no inclination to return to Boston until
escorted by British regulars. Despite this obstacle, the patriot
leaders contrived to manufacture an incident which set Boston
in an uproar against the Commissioners and silenced all opposition to the Convention. The night before the Convention was
proposed in the Boston town meeting, it was reported that an
attempt had been made to cut down the flagstaff on the sacred
Liberty Tree. The Sons of Liberty claimed to have caught the
culprit, who, after a sound cudgeling, confessed that the Commissioners of the Customs had bribed him "and was to present
him with a suit of Cloaths for that purpose." It is not likely
that the Commissioners would have gone deliberately out of
their way to make themselves more hated in Boston at a time
when they were without the protection of British soldiers and
rumors were abroad of a patriot plot to capture Castle William.
It is more probable that Adams himself had fabricated the story,
for it was by such means that Adams brought the people to approve his schemes and pulled the wires that set the Boston town
meeting in motion against royal government in Massachusetts.[23]

But no Sons of Liberty doubted the Commissioners' guilt,
and the town meeting obediently adopted Adams's proposal to
call representatives to Boston. The selectmen were directed
to send a circular letter to all the towns in the colony acquainting them with the dangers that threatened the metropolis and
with the military preparations that had been made to prevent

[23] *Boston Gazette*, Sept. 19, 1768 (Supplement). Public Record Office,
Colonial Office, Class or Series 5, LXXXVI, 276. *Diary of Captain Corner*,
218.

the impending French invasion.   In order that "such Measures may be consulted and Advised as his Majestys service, and the peace and safety of his Subjects in this Province may require," it was urged that the towns elect delegates or committees to meet in Boston on September 22.   This recitation of the innocent purposes behind the Convention did not allay the fears of the Crown officers.   Governor Bernard believed that it was to be the signal for resuming the first charter, which Massachusetts republicans loved because it had "no ingredient of Royalty in it."   He was certain that the real motive in calling this province-wide meeting was to make "an intended Insurrection more general."   In the Boston selectmen's circular letter, the governor observed a sentence which quickened his apprehensions.   The selectmen asserted that the proposed Convention "may happily prevent any sudden and unconnected Measures" which the people might take.   "What," asked Bernard, "can *unconnected* be applied to, but to forcible Opposition to the King's Government?" [24]

Sam Adams certainly expected more from the country than appeared in the selectmen's circular letter.   He had led the town artisans and laborers, from whom the war party drew its chief support, to believe that the country stood solidly behind the metropolis and would rush to arms at its call.   The common people of Boston, who "were in a frenzy and talked of dying in defence of their liberties," did not intend to fight the British alone: they put up a bold front because they expected to be reënforced by thousands of yeomen.   Sam Adams made every effort to extend the war spirit over New England and the neighboring colonies: emissaries were sent throughout Massachusetts Bay to rouse the country people to a fighting pitch and other provinces were sounded for military support against the British troops.   It was never decided upon whom the command of this patchwork army of farmers and townsmen was to devolve.   New England boasted many veteran Indian fighters, but the Boston Sons of Liberty exclaimed that the crisis called for another Cromwell.   But there was no New England Crom-

[24] *Boston Town Records*, 16th Report, 263.   *Bernard Papers*, VII, Bernard to Lord Hillsborough, Jan. 24, 1769.

well to fall upon the King's soldiers and the Boston patriots
were left to lament that "Oliver Cromwell was a glorious fellow and what a pitty it was that they had no such another to
espouse their Cause at present." [25]   Although lacking a commander, the Sons of Liberty continued to make preparations for
war.   In order that the town and country might be kept in
close communication, a beacon consisting of an empty turpentine
barrel was put on the pole on Beacon Hill, which, when fired,
was expected to send a host of armed farmers hurrying to the
town.   Tories believed that the beacon would be lighted the
moment the British transports and men-of-war were sighted off
the Boston lighthouse.   The Boston selectmen, who took their
orders from Sam Adams, refused to take down the beacon even
after being directed to do so by the Council, and it was not
until September 15 that the sheriff summoned up enough courage to remove it.

On September 19, however, when Governor Bernard finally
made public orders for dispatching troops to Boston from Halifax and Ireland, a large number of Adams's partisans began
to drop out of sight.   There could now be no question that
nearly one thousand redcoats would soon be in Boston Harbor
and that Adams would have to fight or eat his threats.   As
long as it was doubtful whether troops would actually come
to Boston the Liberty Boys boasted of their military prowess
and promised to make short work of the "invaders," but when
they learned that the regiments were within a few days' sail,
many lost heart.   One wing of the patriot party still favored
calling in the country and fighting the British, but the conservative Whigs fell back upon the plan of letting the troops land
unopposed and then devising means of getting rid of them.
Thomas Cushing, speaker of the House of Representatives
and one of the members of the "Boston seat," now said that he
had "always been for moderate Measures" and was in favor of
nothing more radical than putting Bernard and Hutchinson
out of the way.   This backsliding outraged the radical group

[25] Mass. Archives, 25, *Hutchinson Corr.*, I, Oct. 5, 1768.   *Chalmers Papers*, III, Sentiments of the Sons of Liberty.   *Bernard Papers*, VII, Bernard
to Lord Hillsborough, Sept. 9, 1768.

and Otis wrathfully told Cushing that "he was as great an Enemy to his own party as Frank Bernard, Thom Hutchinson, or the Commissioners." [26]   Nevertheless, Otis himself had begun to waver.   In spite of his war talk, Otis was unable to believe that the King would really send troops to Boston; and as their coming became increasingly certain he shrank from the prospect of conflict with the mother country.   However, a large number of Bostonians were still eager for resistance, and although Sam Adams was losing ground he retained enough influence to make Boston's line of action uncertain when the British fleet should appear in the harbor.   The decisive factor, however, in determining whether the metropolis would fight the troops or submit peaceably seemed to lie in the manner in which the country responded to Sam Adams's appeal to arms.

In England the Boston news became so alarming that stocks tumbled on the London Exchange.   Rumors spread that Massachusetts was in arms and ready to pounce upon the British if they attempted to disembark.   Although most Englishmen believed that British regulars would easily rout the Sons of Liberty, there were some who foresaw a hot battle on the Boston water front.   Lord Hillsborough was said to be questioning closely every ship captain and passenger out of Boston, but their portentous accounts of New England's military preparations brought him small comfort.   Excitement mounted when it was reported that the militia had been called out to fight the British "invaders."   After long skirting the borders of treason, Massachusetts seemed finally to have slipped over into outright rebellion.   War appeared certain, and the Ministry prepared to settle an old score with the New England "Saints."   "It was justly esteemed a dreadful and destructive conflict which they were about to engage in, yet they were determined to undertake it at all hazards, and to rely upon the superiority of their arms for the support of their authority in America."   Yet there was some trepidation in embarking upon this coercive policy because it was believed that the New England militia, one hundred and fifty thousand strong, were such expert marksmen

[26] *Chalmers Papers*, III, Nathaniel Coffin's Declaration to Governor Bernard, Feb. 6, 1769.

that they could shoot "a pimple off a man's nose without hurting him." [27]

But these sharpshooting New Englanders were far less eager than Sam Adams had imagined to test their marksmanship on British redcoats. Indeed, the country in general seemed strongly inclined to cool the Boston hotheads with dashes of cold water. "We are not to act like Rebels," said the *New Hampshire Gazette.* "Scorn the Thought — we have a good King and his royal Ear is not wilfully shut against us . . . we are represented as Rebels against his Crown and Dignity — But let us convince him by a dutiful Submission to his Government, and the British Constitution, that we are oppressed, and that we have a Right to Petition him thereon." In every town, Tories and lukewarm Whigs attempted to prevent participation in the Convention. Even in Cambridge, usually under the thumb of Boston politicians, the Tories mustered sufficient strength at the town meeting to carry, "with the aid of a *veering Whig*," an adjournment that kept Cambridge from taking part in the Convention. But the principal opposition to the metropolis came from the town of Hatfield, located in the heart of western rural Toryism. Here the proposed Convention was not only rejected, but denounced as a snare laid by Bostonians to involve the country in their quarrel with the mother country. The Hatfield voters declared that Boston's acts were "unconstitutional, illegal, and wholly unjustifiable, and what will give the enemies of our constitution the greatest joy; subversive of government, destructive of that peace and good order which is the cement of Society, and have a direct tendency to rivet our chains, and deprive us of our charter rights and privileges." Hatfield lectured Boston on the constitutional rights of towns in the province and gave Sam Adams instructions on how the metropolis should behave toward its smaller neighbors. In particular the townsmen ridiculed the pretense of a French war as a call to arms; if there was real

---

[27] *The Grenville Papers*, edited by William J. Smith (London, 1852–53), IV, 395; Knox to Grenville, Nov. 1, 1768. *Mass. Hist. Soc. Collections*, 5th Series, IX, *Trumbull Papers*, I, 300; William Samuel Johnson to William Pitkin, Nov. 18, 1768.

danger of a French invasion, why did not Sam Adams and his fellow townsmen welcome the prospect of British troops being sent to their protection? It was singular, they said, that Boston should meddle with military matters before war had been declared against France and when the arrival of British regulars was expected at any moment.[28] Instead of promising to follow Boston dutifully, Hatfield urged that the metropolis be left to take its punishment alone, which, the Hatfield voters intimated, it richly deserved. If Boston had brought this storm upon its head by allowing the mob to run wild, its citizens should humble themselves in repentance before the throne and by "loyalty and quiet behaviour soon convince his Majesty and the world" that troops were unnecessary because all Bostonians were not rioters.

By hurling this defiant broadside at Boston, Hatfield made itself the chief opponent in western Massachusetts of the capital's domination of the colony, until the spread of Sam Adams's committees of correspondence forced out the ruling Tory clique in 1773. Not all the towns took a course so disconcerting to Sam Adams as that of Hatfield: in eastern Connecticut particularly, the citizens were zealous in Boston's cause and sent instructions to their representatives in the Connecticut General Court which, had they been followed by the Massachusetts towns, might have led to some lively fighting when the British fleet hove to in Boston Harbor. Sam Adams regarded the resolves of Lebanon, Connecticut, as a model which all towns should follow when the metropolis called upon the country for aid. Although the Lebanon townspeople found it convenient to threaten war upon the royal troops in the same cryptic language that had suddenly become fashionable in Boston, they made a forthright promise ·to "assist and support our American brethren at the expense of our lives and fortunes." [29] Norwich, Connecticut, was not content merely to approve the Boston Liberty Boys' war preparations, but called for a muster and review of the Connecticut troops "in order that the Militia be at all Times properly furnished" and ready to withstand an

[28] *Massachusetts Gazette*, Oct. 6, 1768.
[29] *Boston Gazette*, Oct. 10, 1768 (Supplement).

enemy attack.   Such pledges of aid were meat and drink to the
Boston war party.   But outside eastern Connecticut Sam Adams
found little to nourish his hopes that a yeoman army would
rush to arms for Boston's support.

The Massachusetts Convention met in Faneuil Hall on September 22, 1768, with about seventy delegates present.   Adams
had given such short notice in calling the meeting that some
towns had not had time to elect representatives and many strag-
glers were still on their way when the Convention opened.
Within a few days, however, the empty seats were filled by late-
comers and the Convention began to assume a striking resemblance to the dissolved House of Representatives whose meetings
had been forbidden by the British government.   Adams seemed
to have called into being a close counterpart of the Lower House
of the General Court, but would he be able to persuade it to
usurp governmental authority and summon the country to fight
the British troops?

The temper of the delegates who had been sent to the Convention from rural Massachusetts gave Adams no encouragement.   Most of them had been representatives in the last General Court who had little desire to add the fighting of British
troops to the offense they had already given the mother country
by refusing to rescind the circular letter.   "Some of the
best men in the province" were sent down to Boston, and there
was little likelihood of their being swept off their feet by town
demagoguery.   Their attitude was that "waters not a bellows"
ought to be used on fiery Bostonians.[30]   Even had they caught
the war fever that raged in the metropolis, most of the country
members were committed by their constituents' instructions not
to join the town radicals.   These instructions were generally
of the kind given Jedidiah Preble, who represented Falmouth
in the Convention.   Preble was ordered to do nothing rash or
unconstitutional; only a cautious and legitimate resistance was
to be resorted to.   Such instructions made the outcome of the
Convention a foregone conclusion and completely crippled the
radicals' war plans.   Instead of rushing to Boston the thirty

[30] *Arthur Lee Papers*, Sparks MSS., Harvard College Library, I, 41; Peter
Livius to his brother in London, Oct. 18, 1768.

thousand armed men Sam Adams hoped for, the country sent only a handful of conservative politicians who made it clear that they would do nothing more rash than write another petition to the King.

The open rift that began to appear among Boston patriot leaders gave great encouragement to these rural moderates. Thomas Cushing, the speaker of the Convention, committed himself to the conservatives by declaring that its purpose was to "bring together some prudent people who would be able to check the violent designs of Others." During the first three days, James Otis did not appear at the Convention. Nothing could be done without him, and the delegates sat in Faneuil Hall with open doors for three days while he played truant in the country. These desertions dismayed Adams, for he was unable to hold the radical fort alone; when, after being elected clerk of the Convention, he "attempted to launch out in the language used in the House of Representatives," he was silenced and compelled to give way to the opposition. But it is not probable that even Otis, with his great influence over the country members, could have made headway against the flood of conservatism that swept down from rural Massachusetts. He made no attempt to breast this current, for when he finally took his seat in the Convention, he was "perfectly tame" and content to let the country delegates have full sway.[31]

This unexpected moderation displayed by the Boston patriot leaders was partly owing to the refusal of the New York Sons of Liberty to join the struggle against the British government. At first, news that war was brewing in Boston aroused great enthusiasm in New York. "Peoples' Eyes here," wrote General Gage, "are now turned upon Boston and its feared too many rejoice at the Proceedings there, and encourage those People to proceed to every Extremity, tho' they might not chuse to venture so far themselves." But the New Yorkers never permitted their ardor for their hard-pressed Boston brethren

---

[31] *New England Historical and Genealogical Register*, XXII, 412. *Chalmers Papers*, III, Nathaniel Coffin's declaration. Thomas Cushing to Stephen Sayre, Oct. 7, 1768, MS. Mass. Hist. Soc. *Bernard Papers*, VII, Bernard to Lord Hillsborough, Oct. 3, 1768.

to carry them to the point of beating up recruits for the expected
hostilities at Boston.   And, after a report reached the colonies
that "measures were taking at home, to bring the Bostoners to
Reason," they were even less inclined to take a plunge with
the "Saints" into rebellion.[32]   Because it was clear that the
British government intended to reason with redcoats and men-
of-war, New York patriots left Boston to its fate.

Since New York and rural Massachusetts were overwhelmingly opposed to radical measures, the Convention surprised
the Tories by acting "with more caution decency and order
than could have been reasonably expected considering in what
an extraordinary manner this famous Committee of Safety was
called together." [33]   After Sam Adams was satisfied that the
popular pulse beat feverishly only in Boston, he made no further effort to uphold the radical cause; he abruptly threw in his
lot with the majority and became such a wholehearted conservative overnight that his draught of a letter to the Colony agent
stating the purposes of the Convention was accepted by the
delegates.   As a result, the Convention's public utterances fell
far short of the seditious blasts that Governor Bernard had expected; and he remarked that they revealed a moderation "very
different from the Tempers of those who called this Meeting." [34]
Instead of opening a fresh controversy with the British government, the Convention merely sent the King another copy of the
petition drawn up by the House of Representatives in Febru-
ary 1768.   The delegates scrupulously avoided raking the
coals left by the Boston town meeting of September 12, 1768,
and dissociated themselves from the metropolis's warlike menaces by declaring they were "plain honest men, humbly consulting peace and order," whose purpose was to prevent "all
tumults and disorders into which our present calamities may
betray us."   They asserted that the Convention was not a
revolutionary body created at Boston's behest to deal a blow

[32] Public Record Office, Colonial Office Class or Series 5, LXXXVI, 263,
Lib. Cong. Transcripts.

[33] *Arthur Lee Papers*, I, 41.

[34] *Bernard Papers*, VII, Bernard to Lord Hillsborough, Oct. 3, 1768.
Andrew Oliver, *Letter Book*, Gay Transcripts, MSS. Mass. Hist. Soc., I,
Andrew Oliver to Thomas Pownall, March 1, 1769.

at the prerogative; on the contrary, Sam Adams said that George III should regard it as "a fresh token of the loyalty of our respective towns to his Majesty, their attachment to his government, and love of peace and good order." [35]   Nevertheless, King George and his ministers always suspected that Sam Adams had called the Convention to fight the King's troops rather than to enhance the royal prerogative and demonstrate New Englanders' loyalty to the Crown.

No sooner had the Convention been called to order than Governor Bernard issued orders to disperse on pain of feeling the full weight of the royal prerogative.   He warned the delegates that juggling names did not conceal the fact that the Convention was an assault upon the Crown's constitutional authority: it was an illegal assembly of the people's representatives "and it is not the Calling it a Committee of Convention that will alter the Nature of the Thing."   Bernard greatly prided himself upon the boldness of tone he took in this counterblast to the Convention and he believed it kept the rural delegates in awe and "frightened them not a little."   But although there was a large party that was "fearful of the legality of their proceedings and would gladly break up without doing anything," the Convention did not scatter because of Bernard's bluster.[36]   The majority were determined to sit until the troops arrived in order to prevent the town hotheads from taking some reckless step that would involve the whole province in a quarrel with the mother country.   Yet all the delegates had one eye cocked on Boston Harbor lest they be found in session when the British fleet appeared.   None were disposed to run the risk of being dispersed at the point of bayonets: therefore, when British men-of-war were reported off the Massachusetts coast the Convention broke up without more ado and the representatives "rushed out of town like a herd of scalded hogs," swearing that "they were sent to keep the rest from doing mischief." [37] They separated none too soon: that afternoon the British regi-

[35] *Boston Chronicle*, Oct. 3, 1768.

[36] *Bernard Papers*, VII, Bernard to Lord Hillsborough, Oct. 3, 1768. *Mass. Hist. Soc. Collections*, Fourth Series, IV, 428.

[37] *Mass. Hist. Soc. Collections*, Fourth Series, IV, 432.   Mass. Archives, 26, *Hutchinson Corr.*, II, 333.

ments from Halifax reached Boston Harbor and a few days later two more regiments from Ireland arrived in the metropolis.

On September 11, 1768, orders had been received in Halifax for two regiments and an artillery company "to embark with the utmost Expedition for Boston." A strict embargo was immediately clapped upon the port and preparations were pushed ahead with "more Caution used than in War Time, when they were fixing out for to take Louisbourg." The British were taking no chances with the Boston Sons of Liberty and came prepared to fight their way into the town, if need be. When the fleet entered the harbor, it approached the town with as much caution as though Boston were an enemy port. Keeping their guns trained upon the town, the ships "ranged themselves on the North East Side of the Metropolis, as if intended for a formal siege," while the Commissioners of the Customs set off skyrockets and roared the chorus of "Yankee-Doodle" behind the walls of Castle William. The troops were landed in Boston under the guns of the men-of-war and marched unopposed with drums beating and flags flying to Faneuil Hall, "the School of Liberty," where they took up their quarters. Not a Son of Liberty raised his finger against them.[38]

When it was learned that British troops had taken possession of Boston without so much as seeing a rebel musket, the Boston Sons of Liberty became the laughingstock of the "sticklers for prerogative doctrines" throughout the colonies. In New York, news that redcoats were in the Puritan metropolis was received with "Glee and Triumph" by the Tories, who immediately began to "decry the behaviour of our oppressed brethren of Boston, and maliciously and invidiously sneer at their not having opposed the landing of the troops." Even to some New York Sons of Liberty, the quick collapse of the Boston war party seemed to be an example of "the ridiculous Puff and Bombast for which our Eastern brethren have always been but too famous."[39] But the backsliding of the Boston Sons of Liberty

---

[38] *Boston Gazette*, Oct. 10, 1768. Thomas Cushing to Stephen Sayre, Oct. 7, 1768, MS. Mass. Hist. Soc. *Boston Evening Post*, Oct. 3, 1768.

[39] *New York Journal*, Oct. 20, 1768; quoted in the *Boston Evening Post*, Oct. 31, 1768.

was no surprise to His Majesty's military officers stationed in New York. "I am very much of Opinion," said General Gage before the outcome of the Massachusetts Convention was known, "they will shrink on the Day of Trial. . . . They are a People, who have ever been very bold in Council, but never remarkable for their Feats in Action." [40]

To English politicians, as well, the war scare of 1768 was proof that New Englanders' threats need not be taken seriously. The collapse of the Boston war party showed that Sam Adams was unsupported by the bulk of the people; and as long as the memory of the Massachusetts Convention remained fresh, Englishmen had no difficulty in believing that the opposition party in New England was confined to a small clique of blustering Boston politicians whom a few redcoats could easily drive to cover. The Boston patriots were regarded in England "as having made a vain bluster and parade to no purpose," and the Convention was contemptuously spoken of as "that thing of Straw, which at last was afraid of its own shadow." [41] After Boston had been brought to its knees by two regiments of redcoats, it was difficult to believe the townsmen would really fight, no matter how much they clamored for redress of grievances and boasted of their readiness to die for American freedom. Many Englishmen considered the military occupation of Boston "as a trial of strength and courage between this kingdom and the Colonies," and the decision seemed to reveal that the mother country had little to fear from American courage. The conviction deepened among English politicians that all that was necessary to make a New Englander wilt was to show him a loaded musket in the hands of a British regular.

For England, however, the triumph at Boston was dearly bought. Never before had Great Britain seemed so much a "step-mother" to her colonies as when royal troops and men-of-war trained their guns on Boston to batter down the Sons of Liberty. Boston's recent riots had strengthened many

[40] *The Correspondence of General Thomas Gage . . . 1763–1775*, edited by Clarence E. Carter (1933), II, 488.
[41] *Trumbull Papers*, I, 301. *Bernard Papers*, XII, Thomas Pownall to Francis Bernard, Nov. 19, 1768.

Southern patriots' prejudice against "mobbish" New Englanders, but the British government's policy of military coercion
made Americans forget Boston's mobs and think only of its
martyrdom at the hands of royal troops. New Hampshire
patriots looked upon "the calm and serene Regions, once the
Seats of Ease and Contentment . . . now transformed into
gloomy and dismal Scenes." The threat of military despotism
hung heavy over America. "Instead of the Civil," warned
the patriots, "we all see a military Government forming . . .
the Lives, Liberties and Fortunes of several Millions of his Majesty's most loyal and useful Subjects are in Danger." [42] "We
are no longer strangers to the measures Great Britain is determined to use in treating with her loyal colonies in America,"
exclaimed a "British Carolinian." "Already New England is
marked out as the place upon which she intends to lavish her
maternal affection in an extraordinary manner, by sending out
of Troops to bring them to compliance with all her measures
whether right or wrong." [43] The taunt which the colonists
believed common in England that "Americans cannot endure
the smell of gunpowder" rankled among the patriots and
made them long for another opportunity to prove to British
regulars that American Whigs could stand their ground in the
hottest fire. Several years before, Benjamin Franklin had
told the House of Commons how to cause uprisings in the colonies: if British troops were sent to America, Franklin warned,
they would not find a rebellion, but they probably would make
one. Franklin's recipe was closely followed by the Ministry,
which, by throwing British soldiers into the same town with
Sam Adams, stirred together two of the principal ingredients
for producing a smacking rebellion.

The Massachusetts Convention of 1768 is an important mile-
stone in the history of Boston's gradual domination of New
England. The metropolis alone, acting under Sam Adams's
direction, had called into being a representative body which, to
all intents and purposes, was the dissolved Massachusetts House
of Representatives masquerading under a new name. The

[42] *New Hampshire Gazette*, Oct. 7, 1768.
[43] *Essex Gazette*, Nov. 23, 1768.

Convention was one of the first and most significant of those extra-legal institutions which Sam Adams was to bring forth with bewildering rapidity later in the Revolution. It was the precursor of the Massachusetts Provincial Congress and paved the way for linking together the towns of the colony under Boston's guidance and committees of correspondence. Thomas Hutchinson declared that in summoning the Convention, Boston had revealed "a greater tendency towards a revolution in government, than any preceeding measures in any of the colonies." [44] Governor Bernard believed that "so daring an assumption of the Royal Authority was never practiced by any city or town in the British Dominions, even in the times of greatest disorder, not even by the City of London when the great Rebellion was at the highest." [45] The crisis produced by the sending of British troops to Boston had brought forward the boldest and most radical of the patriots, who looked upon the Convention as a steppingstone to a later usurpation of governmental power. The curtain was drawn aside momentarily to reveal the existence of a formidable party headed by Sam Adams that was ready to take up arms against the mother country in defense of American liberties. Although Adams failed to find support for his plans in 1768, it was, wrote Hutchinson, "a bold attempt, and carried strong marks of that venturous spirit which has appeared in many stages of the American revolution." [46]

[44] Hutchinson, III, 205.
[45] *Papers Relating to Public Events*, 105.
[46] Hutchinson, III, 206.

VII

THE BOSTON MASSACRE

BRITISH troops had marched into Boston unopposed, but Sam Adams did not propose to allow them to enjoy long the hospitality of the Puritan metropolis. Rather than provide barracks for the soldiers, Adams was resolved to let them freeze in their encampment on the Boston Common. Whigs were told to show redcoats the same courtesy they did "Serpents and Panthers," and Sam Adams felt that even the Common in the dead of winter was too good for them. Adams insisted that, since the General Court had not consented to receive the troops, they had no right whatever to be in Massachusetts; and he construed the Mutiny Act, by which Parliament had provided the manner and place of billeting royal troops in the colonies, to rule them out of Boston and station them in Castle William, three miles out to sea. Boston selectmen and the Massachusetts Council supported Adams in refusing to quarter the soldiers in Boston, but the British military authorities were determined to post them in the heart of town until the citizens had been thoroughly cured of their weakness for rioting. If the regiments were put in Castle William, Boston Sons of Liberty might tar and feather Tories and Commissioners at will before order could be restored. Consequently, Boston warehouses were converted into barracks and the metropolis was garrisoned with redcoats whose "spirit-stirring drum and ear-piercing fife" grated discordantly with the "sweet songs, violins, and flutes, of the serenading Sons of Liberty" until the Boston Massacre.[1]

With four regiments of British regulars in Boston, many of the Sons of Liberty began to cover up their attempts to incite resistance with a less stiff-necked bearing toward the "invaders."

[1] *The Works of John Adams*, II, 213; X, 199. *The Writings of Samuel Adams*, I, 249–250; II, 48, 49, 392.

After patriotically preventing the soldiers from being housed elsewhere in Boston, William Molineux tried to rent out for a garrison a warehouse on Wheelwright's wharf in which he had an interest; and James Otis sent General Gage his card and an invitation to dinner which the general firmly declined. Parliament almost threw these uneasy patriots into a panic by reviving a statute of Henry VIII to transport Americans suspected of treason to England for trial. Adams felt safe with a Boston jury which was certain to be loaded with Sons of Liberty, but he knew that English jurors would show him small mercy. Tories and Crown officers hopefully awaited the "Doom of Boston"; and Thomas Hutchinson began taking depositions to speed Adams and his crew on their way to Tyburn. Wagers were offered in Boston that Adams, Hancock, and Otis would swing from the gallows, and it was whispered among Tories that Adams "shuddered at the sight of hemp." In London, the King's friends remarked "with a snear" that James Otis, the mad Bostonian, would soon have an opportunity to "defend the assumed rights of the New World at the bar of the House of Commons." [2] But a rude disappointment was in store for the British Tories who promised themselves huge diversion from this cargo of transported American Whigs. The Massachusetts patriots had been too cautious to run their necks into a noose. No treason could be proved against them, although the attorney-general found that they had come "within an hair's breadth of it." By this slim margin, Otis and Adams were spared the Tower. The Whigs quickly recovered from their fright and, when they saw that the Ministry intended to pocket the affront, they became "more assuming and tyrannical than before." [3] After the Massachusetts Convention, bluffing

[2] Andrew Oliver, *op. cit.*, Andrew Oliver to John Spooner, Oct. 28, 1768. *Chalmers Papers*, III, Sparks MSS., Harvard College Library; Thomas Hutchinson to Lord Hillsborough, April 27, 1770. *The Correspondence of Thomas Gage, 1763–1775*, edited by Clarence E. Carter (1933), II, 501. *Hess-Wendell Papers*, MSS. Mass. Hist. Soc., Edmund Quincy to John Wendell, Jan. 17, 1769. *Boston Gazette*, Jan. 23, 1769.

[3] *Debates in the House of Commons, Reports of Sir Henry Cavendish* (1841), I, 196. *Chalmers Papers*, III, Thomas Hutchinson to Lord Hillsborough, April 27, 1770.

was thought to be a besetting sin of Bostonians, but when the British government let the patriot leaders go scot-free after having threatened them with being drawn and quartered on Tyburn, it was clear that British Tories were as mighty bluster-ers as the Boston Whigs. By this unexpected change of policy, American patriots were encouraged to regard the menaces of the British government as empty gestures which would never be carried out.

As Sam Adams feared, the British "invasion" of Boston proved to be a thoroughgoing military occupation. Faneuil Hall — that "celebrated school for Catalines & Sedition" — remained in the troops' hands, and, until the middle of No-vember, they overran the Town House. Guards were stationed at Boston Neck to challenge all who entered or left the town, and patrolling companies hovered near every ferry to Boston. So closely was the metropolis guarded that even the carriage of a member of the Massachusetts Council was stopped at the lines on Boston Neck. But the crowning indignity, in Adams's eyes, was the stationing of the main guard opposite the Boston Town House and the setting up of cannon whose muzzles pointed directly at the door of the legislative chambers. When Adams and other Massachusetts representatives left the Gen-eral Court they found themselves looking squarely into the mouths of British guns. It would have needed only a well-aimed whiff of grape to put Sam Adams and several score of Massachusetts Whigs out of the way of Tories and Crown officers. And all this severity was owing to two riots, one of which Adams insisted was a parade and the other a justifiable demonstration against customhouse officers who had made an illegal seizure! [4]

No Bostonian smarted under these humiliations more deeply than did Sam Adams. Like his cousin John, he believed that when British troops took possession of Boston, the mother country had proved beyond doubt that its determination "to subjugate us was too deep and inveterate ever to be altered by

[4] *Boston Evening Post*, Jan. 9 and 23, 1769; Feb. 11, 1769. *New York Gazette and Weekly Mercury*, Nov. 7, 1768. *The Writings of Samuel Adams*, II, 239, 241.

us." John Adams dated Sam's determination to make America independent of Great Britain from the period of the military occupation of Boston. Unquestionably, he began to look forward to a speedy separation from the mother country after the failure of the Massachusetts Convention. He regretted bitterly that his plan of fighting the redcoats had been upset by rural conservatism. Even after having watched the regulars manœuvre and parade on the Boston Common, he was still convinced that New Englanders could have driven them back to their ships with "the greatest ease, for what was an handful of troops to subdue a large country?" [5] In his eyes, when New England farmers failed to march to Boston to meet the British, they merely postponed an inevitable crisis. Now that the troops were in Boston, the problem was to get rid of them before they could establish the rule of tyranny which Adams did not doubt was the real reason of their coming. He expected to find military law riveted upon the province, and Thomas Hutchinson and Governor Bernard with an "army of placemen and pensioners" kept in power by British arms. Although the troops had received strict orders from the Ministry to remain subordinate to the Massachusetts civil government and to act only at the command of magistrates, Sam Adams looked forward to an outright despotism and a "bloody career of the military." "Where," he exclaimed, "is the bill of rights, magna charta and the blood of our venerable forefathers?" [6] And how would New Englanders defend themselves against this new "menacing monster" — a British army? Although Adams did not receive his answer until 1775, he determined in the meantime to clear the Puritan metropolis of redcoats before they could gain a foothold.

Massachusetts Tories paid a heavy price for the luxury of British military protection. Although the "hideous Sound of Conch Shells" which warned Boston householders that the Sons of Liberty were abroad was no longer heard, and Hutchinson

[5] *The Works of John Adams*, II, 214; IX, 596. *The Writings of Samuel Adams*, I, 393.
[6] *The Writings of Samuel Adams*, I, 252, 253, 256, 258, 259, 392; II, 48–49.

and his friends slept for the first time in years without dread of being turned out by a mob, few Tories could regard the troops as an unmixed blessing. It was clear that peace would endure only as long as the soldiers kept order; the moment this "Interval or Truce procur'd from the dread of a Bayonet" was over, Liberty Boys would fall to terrorizing Tories as never before. Temporary security from mobs was no compensation for the rapid strides in power which Sam Adams made as a consequence of the troops' presence in Boston. Adams almost ruined the Massachusetts Tory Party by linking it with British military aggression. Not ten men were left in the Massachusetts House of Representatives to oppose him, and the Council was almost cleared of the governor's friends. Adams dominated the Council so completely through his friend James Bowdoin that he wrote its answer to the governor's speech; although this paper purported to have come from the councilors themselves, Bernard recognized Adams's hand in the "barefaced Chicanery & Falsity of this Writing as well as the stile." He exercised similar influence over the Boston selectmen and wrote their address to Governor Bernard, which the selectmen presented as their own. With his hands tied by the Council's defection and with the House of Representatives swarming with Whigs, Governor Bernard was guilty of only slight exaggeration in saying that Otis and Adams were "in full Possession of the Government." [7] When Sam Adams declared that the House of Representatives would do no business until the troops were removed from Boston, the few Tories who still sat in the House made no opposition. In spite of the protection of British bayonets which made Boston safer for country Tories than it had been for many years, the governor's friends continued resolutely to remain at home and no amount of pleading could bring them to face Adams and Otis in the General Court. When Thomas Hutchinson pressed the stay-at-home squires to come to Boston and give Adams a drubbing, they

[7] Andrew Oliver, *op. cit.*, Andrew Oliver to John Spooner, Oct. 28, 1788; Andrew Oliver to Israel Mauduit, July 10, 1769. *Bernard Papers*, VII, Bernard to Pownall, March 5 and June 1, 1769; Bernard to Lord Hillsborough, July 7, 1769; Bernard to Lord Barrington, May 30, 1769.

answered that it was "to no purpose — the whole Province must give way" to Sam Adams and the Boston Whigs.[8]

The security afforded by British soldiers and men-of-war did not tempt Governor Bernard to tarry in Massachusetts Bay. During the last years of his administration he held one fixed purpose — to escape from the colony before the Sons of Liberty put him through the "ordeal" at Liberty Tree. Bernard had been in mortal terror of "mobbish Bostonians" ever since the Stamp Act riots, and he felt certain each time the mob broke loose that he would never see England alive unless he made a quick getaway. He had not forgotten that the Liberty Boys had sworn to put to death all who were concerned in bringing troops to Boston, and he knew that Sam Adams held him, Hutchinson, and the Commissioners responsible for their presence. When the heart was cut out of his picture in Harvard College, Bernard's homesickness became more acute. He had so completely lost the popularity he enjoyed during the first five years of his administration that most New Englanders were as anxious to be rid of him as he was to be safe in England. By picking quarrels with the Assembly and writing alarmist letters to the British government, he brought the governorship into low repute and gave Sam Adams an opportunity to put royal government in bad odor throughout the colonies. British officials hoped for better things from Massachusetts Bay when Bernard should be removed: "His doubles and turnings have been so many," wrote Commodore Hood, commander of the British squadron in Boston Harbor, "that he has altogether lost his road, and brought himself into great contempt." [9] Yet Bernard might well have protested that he was being made the scapegoat of an unworkable system and the mistakes of the British Ministry and Parliament. After the Stamp Act, there was no middle course for a royal governor of Massachusetts: he must either favor the people, which would have brought him a prompt dismissal from the Crown, or defend the royal government, which meant endless conflict with the popular branch of the legislature. The difficulties faced by a royal

---

[8] Mass. Archives, 26, *Hutchinson Corr.*, II, 471.
[9] *Grenville Papers*, IV, 378.

governor of Massachusetts, always formidable, had become staggering after 1765, when he became the embodiment of the new policy of centralization attempted by British imperialists. In reality, revolutionary forces were at work in the colony and Bernard's successor had no better fortune in averting the crisis which Sam Adams was doing his utmost to hasten.

Before Bernard could leave Massachusetts he felt the smart of the shots with which Sam Adams usually sped a departing royal governor on his travels. The Massachusetts colony agent sent copies to Boston of a large number of letters written by Governor Bernard, General Gage, and the Commissioners of the Customs. There was little in this correspondence that the Whigs did not already know and much less incriminating matter than they had long since charged to Bernard, but Sam Adams skillfully used it to convict the governor of plotting against that "sacred ark," the Massachusetts charter. Bernard's letters were published in the *Boston Gazette* and sent to most of the newspapers on the continent to put Americans on their guard against all royal governors and to raise such a storm in rural Massachusetts that the handful of Tories still in the General Court would be blown out of their seats and replaced by Sons of Liberty. In the Boston town meeting, Sam Adams declared that "if all Records were to be Searched, no Instance could be found of so much Malice and falsehood collected to Injure as Loyal and Religious People, who were at that Time really oppress'd, and under a Tyranny," as was to be found in Bernard's correspondence. But when William Cooper, the town clerk, began reading the governor's letters to the citizens, interspersing Bernard's words with asides and cracking jokes which "generally occasion'd a Grin of applause," Adams stopped him before he had read halfway through because "so many plain matters of Fact appear'd against them in the Course of the Perusal." [10] Indeed, Bernard's account of the patriots' activities proved so embarrassing that Sam Adams was directed by the town to write an "Appeal to the World" to whitewash Boston's reputation of all the governor's "slanderous *Chit-chat*." The

[10] *Chalmers Papers*, III, The Proceedings of a Town Meeting held at Faneuil Hall the 4th October, 1769.

Suffolk Grand Jury indicted the governor, General Gage, and the Commissioners for libeling the inhabitants of the province; and Adams succeeded in persuading the General Court to petition the Crown for Bernard's removal on the ground that he had proved himself hostile to the liberties of His Majesty's loyal subjects in Massachusetts Bay.

So eager was Bernard to return to England that he left Lady Bernard behind in Massachusetts; but even this dispatch did not spare the governor the humiliation of witnessing the Sons of Liberty celebrate his departure. His ship lay becalmed outside the harbor, from where he could see the Union Flag run up Liberty Tree and Saint George's banner flying from Hancock's wharf and hear the bells and cannon that sounded throughout the day. That evening, while Bernard's vessel was still unable to get under way, huge bonfires were lighted on Fort Hill and in Charlestown to show the luckless governor how Massachusetts rejoiced to be free of "a Scourge to this Province, a Curse to North America, and a Plague on the whole Empire." [11] Massachusetts patriots had added another governor's scalp to their collection and had carried out to the full every threat they had made against him when he first came into the colony. As Bernard impatiently awaited a favorable wind and listened to the whooping Liberty Boys ashore, he well knew why he had been warned when he first arrived in Massachusetts Bay against Sam Adams, a "noted writer in the newspapers" and the terror of royal governors. But after his safe arrival in England Bernard had no difficulty in dismissing the impeachment proceedings of the Massachusetts House of Representatives as "Groundless, Vexatious & Scandalous." Instead of sending Bernard to the Tower, as Adams devoutly hoped, the persecution of the Massachusetts patriots so endeared him to King George that he was created a Baronet. [12]

Having turned out the royal governor, Sam Adams could give his undivided attention to ridding Boston of the royal troops. The British had scarcely landed in New England before Adams was at work drumming up hatred against them

[11] *Boston Gazette*, Aug. 7, 1769.
[12] *Collections Col. Soc. of Mass.* (1910–11), XIII, 386, 410.

throughout the length and breadth of the American colonies.
Boston patriots had connections with influential newspaper printers throughout the continent, and Sam Adams's political articles
not infrequently appeared in New York or Philadelphia papers
weeks before New Englanders saw them.   The patriots' purpose
was to educate Americans in "Boston politics" or to lead New
Englanders themselves to believe that the Southern colonies
were warm in their behalf and that Southern Whigs were
busily engaged in turning out political tracts which reëchoed
Adams's principles.   After the Massachusetts Convention had
failed to approve his war plans, Adams set out to make the British military occupation of Boston an intercolonial issue.   He
hoped to see the entire continent support Massachusetts in demanding the withdrawal of the troops and to raise such a storm
against "military tyranny" throughout the colonies that the
British government would be forced to hand Boston back to
the Sons of Liberty.   This undertaking required the aid of every
colonial printer on good terms with the Boston patriots.   Shortly
after the arrival of the British fleet in Boston Harbor, New
York printers received from Boston the first installment of
Adams's raciest propaganda, the "Journal of the Times" or
"Journal of Events."   From New York, the "Journal" was
sent to most newspapers on the American continent and even
to England, where it appeared in the *Gentleman's Magazine*
and was put to good purpose by the opposition in Parliament.
Probably none of Adams's work had a wider circulation or had
greater influence in laying the foundation for the intercolonial
support given Boston, "the antient Capital of North America,"
during the Port Bill days of 1774.

In the "Journal of Events," Sam Adams served colonial
Whigs with piping-hot "British atrocities" committed by the
soldiery in Boston.   It made a spicy dish indeed for countryfolk accustomed to a steady diet of almanacs and scripture.   The
"Journal" consisted of bloodcurdling descriptions of British
regulars brutally beating small boys on Boston streets; violating the Sabbath with gunfire, carousing, and horse racing; and,
above all, raping Boston matrons and young girls.   If Adams
and his fellow journalists were to be believed, scarcely a day

passed without a British soldier assaulting a woman; none were safe from these "bloody-backed rascals," and even the worthiest families were apt to share the grief of that venerable patriot who "the other morning discovered a soldier in bed with a favourite grand daughter." [13]   That royal troops were the monsters Sam Adams painted was indignantly denied by the Crown officers.   Thomas Hutchinson, who believed that Adams first published the "Journal" away from Boston because there was no one to contradict his "Infamous falsehoods," assured his friends that nine tenths of it was untrue and Governor Bernard said that "if the Devil himself were of the Party, as he virtually is, there would not have been got together a greater collection of impudent virulent & Seditious Lies, Perversions of Truth & Misrepresentations than are to be found in this Publication."   The soldiers themselves swore there was no need to use force, since women of easy virtue were so plentiful in Boston that there was not an officer or private "down to a drummer, that cannot have his bedfellow for the winter; so that the Yankey war, contrary to all others, will produce more births than burials." [14]

Thomas Hutchinson was alarmed to find that Adams's propaganda was turning Americans against Crown officers and British troops in most of the colonies and making New Yorkers and Philadelphians, who "for some time past seem to have been cool," into fire-eating patriots.   For, in spite of all denials, colonists eagerly swallowed the atrocities Sam Adams spread before them every week in the newspapers.   He left unmentioned, of course, the riots that originally caused soldiers to be sent: Boston was overrun with "foreign invaders" who made the Iroquois seem tame in comparison, solely because the citizens had asserted the "just rights of Americans" in the teeth of the British government.

But it was in Boston itself that the "Journal of Events" raised

---

[13] *Boston Evening Post*, July 24 and 31, 1769.

[14] *Israel Williams Papers*, MSS. Mass. Hist. Soc., II, Thomas Hutchinson to Israel Williams, Jan. 26, 1769. *Bernard Papers*, VII, Bernard to Lord Hillsborough, Feb. 25, 1769. *New York Journal or General Advertiser*, May 4, 1769.

the most turbulent storm. By fanning Bostonians' hatred of
the British troops, Adams set the stage for the Boston Massacre, and his lurid descriptions of imaginary rapes, quarrels,
and insults led directly to real bloodshed.

In this highly charged atmosphere, it would have been
strange if the sparks Sam Adams struck off in the "Journal of
Events" had not quickly produced an explosion. The Sons
of Liberty rankled under the sneer that they lost their appetite for fighting as soon as they smelled gunpowder, and some
of the British troops who had been bitterly disappointed at not
finding the Boston Sons of Liberty in arms in 1768 were eager
to give them a trouncing. At the outset of the military occupation of Boston, the patriots had aroused the soldiers' resentment by their "low and spiteful devise" of attempting to freeze
the troops out of Boston by forcing them to remain on the Common all winter. Before the troops had settled themselves in
the town, a near battle was fought at the Manufactory House,
where the town paupers and Sons of Liberty prevented the
British from turning the building into a barracks. Unquestionably many of Adams's choice stories in the "Journal" were
true: a large number of British soldiers made a practice of jab-
bing patriots in the ribs with bayonets and hustling them off the
sidewalks, but the patriots in turn haled the soldiers into court
on every pretext and made their lives as miserable as creditors
can. Eighteenth-century British armies were composed in
large measure of scourings and scrapings, but the Twenty-ninth
Regiment, which the Ministry had sent to tame the Bostonians,
seems to have had more than its share of gallows birds. "They
are in general, such bad fellows, in that Regiment," said Thomas
Hutchinson, "that it seems impossible to restrain them from
firing upon an insult or provocation given them." Since the
Boston ropewalk workers were equally aggressive, a hot feud
sprang up between them and the "bloody-backed rascals" in
which both parties enthusiastically cracked each other's pates.
With such riotous allies, Adams had little difficulty in kindling
an "immortal hatred" between soldiers and his "Psalmsinging
Myrmidons." Thomas Young remarked that New Englanders needed "but a spark to set them all in flames," and Sam

Adams was sending out a shower of sparks every week in his "Journal of Events."[15]

In the summer of 1769 the British government planned to withdraw two of the four regiments of British regulars from Boston — to the great consternation of many Crown officers, who feared that the remaining troops would be unable to hold the Sons of Liberty in check. Governor Bernard believed that what was really required was "a Reinforcement of the King's Forces at Boston [rather] than a weakening of them." When Sam Adams learned that it was proposed to reduce the Boston garrison he immediately presented a set of resolves to the House of Representatives so seditious that Commodore Hood declared they were "of a more extraordinary nature, than any that have yet passed an American Assembly." Just as the Sixty-fourth Regiment was about to embark for Halifax, Adams published these resolves — which, in effect, denied all Parliamentary authority over the colony — in the *Boston Gazette,* although they had not yet passed the House of Representatives. This "alarm bell to revolt" so frightened the Crown officers that the embarkation was suspended and the troops were ordered back to their barracks lest the townspeople attempt to throw off British sovereignty and drive the remaining troops out of town. It was only after Adams's resolves had been repudiated by the House of Representatives that this alarm was allayed. When the town had quieted down, two regiments boarded the transports for Halifax, leaving less than five hundred effective regulars in Boston to keep order. The patriots were now more than a match for the troops and Hutchinson's misgivings deepened that there would soon be bloodshed in the metropolis.[16]

[15] Mass. Archives, 26, *Hutchinson Corr.,* II, 525. *Bernard Papers,* VII, Bernard to Lord Hillsborough, Dec. 26, 1768. *The Works of John Adams,* II, 230. *Chalmers Papers,* III, Thomas Hutchinson to Lord Hillsborough, March 12, 1770. *Mass. Hist. Soc. Proceedings,* XLVII, 202.

[16] *Bernard Papers,* VII, Bernard to Lord Hillsborough, July 7, 1769. Public Record Office, Admiralty Secretary, In Letters, 483, Lib. Cong., 25, Commodore Hood to Philip Stevens, July 10, 1769. Letters of Samuel Cooper to Pownall and Franklin, 1770–74, Bancroft Transcripts, New York Public Library, Samuel Cooper to Thomas Pownall, July 12, 1769. *Bernard Papers,* VII, Bernard to Lord Hillsborough, July 7, 1769. Hutchinson, III, 242.

Early in the spring of 1770 the situation in Boston passed entirely out of the control of the peace officers. Sam Adams's "Mohawks" brawled with redcoats in taverns and back alleys while the ropewalkers picked quarrels with the Twenty-ninth Regiment — those guardians of law and order whose bad tempers were the terror of sober citizens whether Whig or Tory. Then, in March 1770, an incident occurred which led directly to the Boston Massacre. Samuel Gray, one of the hardiest brawlers employed at Gray's ropewalk in Boston, asked a soldier of the Twenty-ninth Regiment if he wanted a job. When the man answered that he did, Gray said he had a privy that needed cleaning. This insult provoked an immediate fight between the soldiers and ropewalkers, but no serious clash took place until their pent-up animosity burst forth on March 5, 1770.

One morning shortly before that day, the citizens of Boston awoke to find the streets plastered with notices, signed by many of the soldiers garrisoned in the town, that the troops intended to attack the townspeople. This startling news threw the town into a ferment, for apparently few citizens doubted the genuineness of these papers. It is singular, nevertheless, that the soldiers should have given their plans away in this manner if they really contemplated an attack and that they signed their names to documents that might be used as damning evidence against them. These notices were doubtless forgeries made by Adams and his followers and posted during the night by the "Loyall Nine" to produce an explosion that would sweep Boston clear of redcoats; for during the Massacre trials it is significant that the prosecution did not enter them as evidence of the soldiers' guilt. The events of the night of March 5 bear out this explanation of their origin. That evening a crowd of small boys began to snowball the British sentry in King's Street. Pelting the redcoats had become a recognized pastime among the Whigs, but it was soon apparent that this was to be no ordinary evening in Boston, for both soldiers and civilians had been convinced by Adams's propaganda that they were in danger of massacre from their enemies. After the sentry had sent his tormentors scampering, crowds of townspeople began to gather and head for King's Street. The square before the customhouse was soon filled with a swearing, turbulent mass of men, many of whom were armed with clubs, staves, and formidable pieces of jagged ice. Although Sam Adams and other patriots carefully avoided calling this crowd a mob, John Adams declared the name too good for it — a "motley rabble of saucy boys, negroes and mulattoes, Irish teagues and outlandish jack tars," he said, had turned out to fight the troops. Among them were Samuel Gray, the ropewalker who had started a free-for-all a few days before by inviting a soldier to clean his outhouse; Crispus Attucks, a huge mulatto noted for his prowess with the cudgel; James Caldwell, a ship's mate; and Patrick Carr, a seasoned Irish rioter. These stout cudgel-boys had beaten up so many redcoats that the sentry hastily summoned the main guard, which, led by Captain Preston of the Twenty-ninth Regiment, tumbled out eagerly for a fight. Consequently, the mob found itself face to face with its worst enemies; pellets of ice, sticks, and cudgels flew fast; and a large body of citizens who had gathered in Dock Square, where a mysterious gentleman in a red cloak and red wig harangued them to make a concerted attack upon the troops, rushed to join the brisk work that was going on before the customhouse. It was a wild scene even to Bostonians hardened to "Pope Day" riots and patriotic demonstrations; as John Adams later described it, "the multitude was shouting and huzzaing, and threatening life, the bells ringing, the mob whistling, screaming and rending like an Indian yell, the people from all quarters throwing every species of rubbish they could pick up in the streets." [17] Meanwhile, the ringing of bells all over Boston and the near-by towns was bringing hundreds of reënforcements to the mob in King's Street. Thus far, the soldiers had used their bayonets to keep the mob at bay and no patriot had suffered worse casualty than a smart rap on the shins. In spite of the hail of missiles, the soldiers withheld their fire until the mob screamed that the "bloody-backed rascals" did not dare to shoot. The troops restrained themselves with difficulty from giving Adams's "Mohawks" a taste of powder and ball, but when one of them was

[17] Frederick Kidder, *The Boston Massacre* (1870), 255–257.

sent sprawling by a patriot brickbat he recovered his gun and
fired directly into the mob.   Most of the soldiers likewise
opened fire, — at Captain Preston's order, many of the town's
witnesses later testified, — and after they had emptied their guns
five civilians had been killed or mortally wounded.

The victims were typical members of the Boston mob: Samuel Gray, Crispus Attucks, James Caldwell, and Patrick Carr
all fell in the British fire.   Samuel Maverick, the fifth victim,
was an apprentice who had taken no part in the riot.   John
Adams said that those killed in the Massacre were "the most
obscure and inconsiderable that could have been found upon
the continent," but Sam Adams made them pure and holy
martyrs to liberty.[18]   Crispus Attucks, the Framingham mulatto, a veteran of a score of riots, was exalted with the rest,
although it was common knowledge that he had led an army
of thirty sailors armed with clubs in Cornhill on the night of
March 5 and that it was chiefly his violent assault upon the
troops that had caused bloodshed.   Only one of the victims,
Patrick Carr, was denied the sweets of martyrdom by Sam
Adams, because his deathbed confession absolved the soldiers of
all blame for the Massacre.

Sam Adams lost no time in making the most of the "Bloody
Work in King's Street."   The day after the Massacre, the
town meeting was called in Faneuil Hall, where Adams made
such a rousing speech from the rostrum that his hearers declared it was "enough to fire any heart with a desire to become
a patriot." [19]   Having thrown the citizens into this bristling
frame of mind, Adams demanded the immediate withdrawal
of the British troops from Boston.   This, the townspeople
agreed, was the only way to prevent further "blood and carnage."   Adams thereupon placed himself and Hancock at the
head of a town committee and marched to the Town House
overlooking the scene of the Massacre, where, in the Council
chamber hung with the portraits of Charles II and James II and
"little miserable likenesses" of the Puritan magistrates, Adams
laid his demands before the Council.   At the head of the Coun-

[18] *The Works of John Adams*, IX, 352.
[19] *New York Journal or General Advertiser*, March 29, 1770.

"The Bloody Massacre"

PERPETRATED IN KING STREET, BOSTON, ON MARCH 5, 1770,
BY A PARTY OF THE 29TH REGIMENT

(*From the well-known engraving by Paul Revere*)

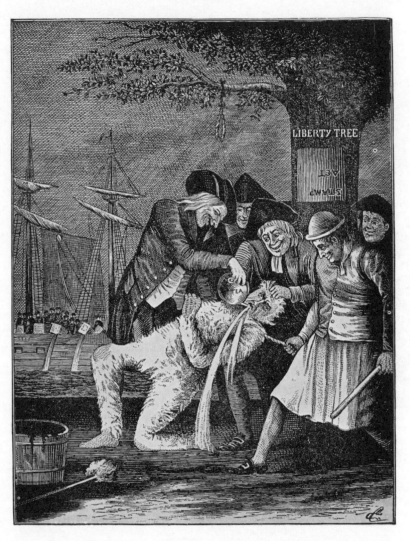

BOSTONIANS PAYING THE EXCISEMAN

cil table sat Lieutenant Governor Hutchinson; at his right, Colonel Dalrymple, commander in chief of His Majesty's forces in Boston; and around the table were seated twenty-eight councilors wearing "large white wigs, English scarlet cloth cloaks." [20] Standing before these dignitaries as spokesman for the citizens of Boston, Adams described the "dangerous, ruinous, and fatal effects of standing armies in populous cities in time of peace," the hatred of New Englanders toward the troops who had spilled patriot blood, and repeated the resolves of the Boston town meeting demanding the immediate removal of the soldiers from the metropolis.   Hutchinson answered that since he had no authority over the King's troops nothing could be done until he had consulted the home government.   But Adams was not to be put off so easily; he instantly appealed to the Massachusetts charter by which Hutchinson was constituted commander in chief of all the military and naval forces within the province.   When Hutchinson and Dalrymple saw that Adams was determined to force their hand, they laid their heads together and, after much whispering, offered to remove the Twenty-ninth Regiment, which alone had fired upon the citizens, to Castle William and to keep the other regiment confined to quarters in Boston.   But here again Hutchinson played into Adams's hands.   "In his venerable grey locks, and with his hands trembling under a nervous complaint," Adams told Hutchinson and Dalrymple that if they had "authority to remove one regiment they had authority to remove two," and that nothing short of a complete evacuation of the town by all the troops would preserve the peace of the province.[21]   Unless the metropolis were cleared of redcoats, Adams warned, there would be more bloody work in Boston — this time with the King's troops as the victims.   Fifteen thousand fighting men, he exclaimed, were ready to pour into Boston to take revenge upon the soldiers.   Dalrymple needed little persuasion: he was well aware that he could not defend his position against the New England militia with the four hundred men he could bring into the field; and he had no desire to risk a disgraceful

---

[20] *The Works of John Adams*, X, 250.
[21] *Ibid.*, X, 252.

rout at the hands of farmers and Boston Sons of Liberty. When
Adams made these threats he believed he saw Hutchinson's
legs tremble and his face grow pale — "and," added Adams,
"I enjoyd the Sight." For a few hours, Hutchinson planned
to resist the townspeople, but when he saw "how artfully it was
steered" by Adams, whose strategy had placed the entire responsibility of keeping the troops in Boston upon his shoulders,
he acknowledged that he must either yield or leave the province. The Council assured Hutchinson that New England
would soon be in arms against the troops and that "the night
which was coming on would be the most terrible that was ever
seen in America." The danger of defying the people was too
great; before nightfall, Hutchinson struck his colors and Bostonians were promised the speedy removal of both regiments.[22]

The army of New Englanders with which Adams threatened
Hutchinson and Dalrymple was no empty menace. Had the
crisis been protracted, the metropolis would probably have
seen those embattled farmers that Adams had vainly looked
for during the Massachusetts Convention. The country people
were led to believe that Boston was to be given over to a general massacre and they were "on Tip toe" to rush in and save
the townsmen; "forty thousand men could have been brot
into the gates of this city at 48 hours warning," boasted a
patriot. The "Bloody Work in Boston calls loud for VENGE-
ANCE," exclaimed the Portsmouth Sons of Liberty, who talked
of marching ten thousand strong to help drive the redcoats
into Boston Bay; and the Salem Liberty Boys, not to be outdone, promised that thousands of Essex yeomen would turn
out to help Boston destroy a "licentious and blood-thirsty
Soldiery." Never before had Boston stood higher in the
estimation of New Englanders: the metropolis was now hailed
by countrymen as "the capital of British America," pledges of

---

[22] But the troops were not immediately removed from Boston. The delay
greatly alarmed the Whigs, who continued to threaten Hutchinson and other
Crown officers with an attack upon the troops. When the soldiers finally
marched out of their barracks to the wharf from which they took ship to
Castle William, it was necessary for William Molineux to march beside them
to protect them from the hooting citizens. *The Works of John Adams*, X,
252, 253.

support poured in from every side, and military fervor spread so rapidly over the country that Sam Adams began to believe his countrymen were in fact "Old Romans."

Adams's first thought was to convince the world that Boston was innocent of any blame for the Massacre.   There was need of quick action, because immediately after the bloodshed, Robinson, the Commissioner of the Customs, who had been most active in counterworking the Whigs, secretly left Boston for England with papers which the patriots suspected were to be used to prove Boston's guilt.   To offset this Tory propaganda, Adams had himself, Hancock, and the Boston selectmen appointed a committee by the citizens to take *ex parte* testimony from witnesses and draw up an account of the Massacre for public consumption.   Adams and his followers fell to work with such enthusiasm that they were soon attempting to prove that the Commissioners of the Customs had fired upon the citizens the night of the Massacre and were as guilty as the soldiers of murdering unarmed Whigs.   The patriots were eager to pin some fresh atrocity upon the Commissioners to render them more hateful to the people: therefore Adams proclaimed that he had ferreted out a conspiracy between the military officers and Commissioners of the Customs to slaughter Bostonians.   "Some of the Banditti," remarked a Tory, referring to Adams and his fellow committeemen, "prevailed on a little French Boy belonging to Mainwaring [a customhouse officer] to swear he actually fired three Guns from the Custom House window under his Master's Directions."   Moreover, Adams's examination of the witnesses seemed to prove conclusively that the soldiers and Commissioners were the sole aggressors and that the townspeople had been treated with "unexampled Barbarity"; but Tories said that Adams was forced to stoop to perjury and falsehood to save Boston's reputation.   Had Hutchinson possessed authority to enforce his orders, he would have stopped Adams and the selectmen from taking testimony because he believed they were attempting to fasten the witnesses to signed affidavits before the trial took place — a procedure which would put the soldier's defense under a serious disadvantage.   But before Hutchinson could act, the damage was done: the evidence was turned over to Adams and Bowdoin to be put into literary form.   Robinson was already on his way to England, but Boston chartered a speedy vessel to carry its "Narrative" to the mother country; and although Robinson won the race, the patriots were not far behind with a cargo of red-hot propaganda with which to avert punishment by the British government.

Sam Adams was keenly aware of the necessity of bringing the soldiers to trial while the memory of the Massacre was still fresh.   He bent every effort therefore to secure an early trial; and when it was reported that the illness of two judges would force a postponement until June, he headed a town committee to demand that Hutchinson appoint special judges immediately. At court, Adams made a "very *pathetic* Speech" in which he used such strong language that the Tories perceived that "the plain design of this Speech was, that gentlemen, you must comply with our demand." [23]   The spectacle of Massachusetts royal judges "overawed and insulted" by such a raw plebeian as Sam Adams spurred Hutchinson to action.   The governor knew that by opposing Adams he was risking another explosion in Boston: popular hostility toward the troops still blazed so fiercely that the patriot leaders themselves had difficulty in preventing another mob attack upon the soldiers before their final removal to Castle William, and there was constant danger that Preston would be dragged from prison for a lynching party at Liberty Tree. [24]   Nevertheless, Hutchinson encouraged the judges to resist the patriots and, as a consequence, the trials were delayed until October 1770, over six months after the Massacre. Yet, even with this respite, it seemed unlikely that anything short of a royal pardon would save Preston and his men from a gibbet on the Boston Common. [25]

Despite Adams's eagerness to see the soldiers declared guilty, he urged John Adams and Josiah Quincy, two of the best

[23] *Chalmers Papers*, III, Narrative of Events in Boston.   Peter Oliver, 123. *Boston Gazette*, March 19, 1770.

[24] *The Works of John Adams*, X, 252, 253.   Mass. Archives, 26, *Hutchinson Corr.*, II, 497, 525.

[25] Thomas Gage to Thomas Hutchinson, April 30, 1770, MS. Mass. Hist. Soc.

lawyers in the patriot party, to undertake their defense.   Preston's friends advised him to "stick at no reasonable fee" to secure the services of lawyers friendly to the Whig leaders, but it was Sam Adams's persuasion and John Adams's high sense of duty rather than the prospect of a fat fee that brought Josiah Quincy and John Adams to Preston's aid.   Since 1768, when John Adams had yielded to Sam's importunities and entered Boston politics, he had risen high in the patriot party.   His law partner, Josiah Quincy, was a promising young patriot who many Whigs believed would eventually step into James Otis's place at the head of the Massachusetts Country Party.   It is singular that Sam Adams, who was never known to give his enemies an advantage, should have bestowed this array of legal talent upon men he hoped to convict of murder.   Certainly, Adams had lost none of his rancor toward the "bloody-backed rascals" who had shed patriot blood in King's Street, nor had he failed to perceive that an acquittal would be a disastrous blow to the Boston Whigs.   Adams's action sprang from his conviction that if patriot lawyers defended Preston and his men, the town's witnesses would not be cross-examined so closely as to bring to light evidence which proved Bostonians responsible for the Massacre.   In John Adams, Sam did not mistake his man.

The younger Adams saw as clearly as did his cousin that Boston's reputation was at stake and that the town's witnesses should not be pressed too warmly: when Josiah Quincy's ardor for his clients caused him to interrogate sharply the prosecution's witnesses, John Adams quickly stopped him by declaring that unless Quincy ceased he would resign as counsel.   Although John Adams encountered a "torrent of unpopularity" from the rank and file of the patriot party for defending the soldiers, it is significant that Sam Adams, far from bearing him resentment, praised him in the Boston newspapers for his conduct during the trial.[26]

Undoubtedly Sam Adams had much to conceal.   The Tories' suspicions were early aroused by the readiness of the country towns about Boston to march to the aid of the metropolis im-

[26] Gordon, I, 291.   *Boston Gazette*, Jan. 7, 1771, Harbottle Dorr Files, Mass. Hist. Soc.

mediately after the Massacre. It was observed that the bells had been set ringing simultaneously at Boston, Charlestown, and Roxbury to call out the patriots the night of the Massacre, and that the next day expresses were sent to Boston from Marblehead, Dedham, Milton, and other near-by towns promising armed assistance at a moment's warning. This preparedness seemed to point to a well-laid scheme to rouse the country when the Boston Sons of Liberty struck at the British troops. Andrew Oliver, later lieutenant governor of Massachusetts Bay, said that one of the Massachusetts councilors had declared in Council that a plot had been made by "men of estates, and men of religion" to drive the British out of Boston; and Hutchinson wrote that "you cannot find one Man in fifty who makes any doubt of ye determined design to remove the Troops." John Adams was convinced that the Massacre was an "explosion which had been intentionally wrought up by designing men, who knew what they were aiming at better than the instruments employed." [27] Of these "designing men," Sam Adams was probably the chief and the instruments he used to bring about the Massacre were his "Mohawks" from North Boston. Lord North made no mistake when he dubbed the regiments forced out of Boston by the patriots "Sam Adams' Regiments."

The six months' delay in bringing Preston and his men to trial worked greatly to the disadvantage of the Boston patriots, who had counted upon a jury passionately determined to take revenge upon the murderers of their countrymen. When the trials finally took place, the people were dispirited and fearful they had already gone too far, and Boston Harbor was filled with royal ships and troops to remind them that the "long arm" of the mother country still extended to New England. Sam Adams complained that the long postponement made conviction difficult because many of the town's key witnesses were no longer within reach, but his anxiety was chiefly caused by the character

---

[27] *Chalmers Papers*, III, Narrative of Proceedings in Boston, 1770. Francis Maseres, *A Fair Account of the Late Unhappy Disturbance at Boston* (London, 1770), Appendix, 26, Deposition of Andrew Oliver. Mass. Archives, 25, Thomas Hutchinson to Francis Bernard, March 12, 1770. *The Works of John Adams*, II, 230.

of the jury that had been chosen to decide the soldiers' fate. The prosecution was lukewarm — the Crown officers in Boston had no wish to convict Preston and thereby throw him to the mercy of the Boston Liberty Boys — and the defense was quick to seize every straw that promised an acquittal. As a result, John Adams and Josiah Quincy were permitted to pick a jury which consisted entirely of countrymen — every Bostonian was carefully weeded out by challenge. Sam Adams's dismay was great when he found that not a single town Son of Liberty was to try Preston and his men. He had hoped for a jury of townsmen who knew at first hand the evils of military despotism, yet he now found himself forced to cope with rustics who had not yet learned to hate the sight of a British uniform. With good reason, Adams believed that the outcome of the trials was decided when the defense was allowed to load the jury with countrymen.

In spite of John Adams's care not to probe too deeply into Whig activities, evidence was brought out at the trial which raised serious doubt in New England whether the Boston Massacre had not been precipitated by Sam Adams and the Sons of Liberty in a desperate effort to turn the troops out of the metropolis. Thirty-eight witnesses testified that there had been a civilian plot to attack the soldiers, and the defense put forward evidence proving the townspeople were the aggressors. From the beginning, the case began to turn against the patriots and, with a jury so little to Sam Adams's taste, the result was not long in doubt. The proceedings proved so painful to the patriot leaders that few of them attended the trials and the people behaved "remarkably decent" for Bostonians. Judge Lynde's speech to the jury clinched the case for the defense: "I feel myself deeply affected," said the judge, "that this affair turns out so much to the disgrace of every person concerned against him [Preston], and so much to the shame of the town in general." [28] Preston was promptly acquitted on the ground that there was not sufficient evidence that he had given orders to fire. Of the soldiers who had fired upon the mob, only two were found guilty of manslaughter, and their punish-

[28] Mass. Archives, 27, *Hutchinson Corr.*, III, 47. Gordon, I, 291.

ment was mitigated to burning on the hand when they pleaded with their clergy.   The trial of Mainwaring, the customhouse officer who was accused of firing upon the people from the windows of the customhouse the night of the Massacre, blew up when the jury acquitted him without leaving the courtroom. All the Commissioners of the Customs were proved to have been miles away from King's Street on the evening of March 5, and the "little French boy" — the patriots' star witness in proving the Commissioners and soldiers had hatched a plot to murder civilians — was shown to be a perjurer whose falsehood had been encouraged by divers high Whigs, William Molineux among them.

Adams and his followers felt themselves cheated by the court: was this, they exclaimed, to be the only punishment for men who had butchered Whigs until the very dogs were seen "greedily licking human Blood in King-Street"?   The townspeople grumbled that no one had been condemned to death and it was common to hear lamentations that a slight burning on the hand was "ye only satisfaction the Public has got for the Murder of 5 Men." [29]   Judges and jury were exceedingly unpopular in Boston, where the people spoke of the judges with "atrocious impudence" and where even the pulpits "rung their Peals of Malice against the Courts of Justice."   The patriot leaders had difficulty in keeping their resentful followers within bounds: one of Sam Adams's admirers posted a notice on the door of the House of Representatives urging the people to assassinate the judges who had betrayed them.   This rousing bit of sedition was not carried out because the people as a whole were thoroughly weary of bloodshed.   No explosion followed the soldiers' acquittal and Hutchinson observed with satisfaction that the Whig leaders were rapidly falling out of public favor.[30]

Sam Adams attempted to save Boston's reputation by trying the soldiers over again in the *Gazette* under the signature "Vindex."   He set out to convince New Englanders that, re-

---

[29] *Boston Gazette*, Nov. 26, 1770; Dec. 10 and 17, 1770.
[30] *Boston Evening Post*, May 11, 1772.   Peter Oliver, 129, 130.   Mass. Archives, 27, *Hutchinson Corr.*, III, 73.

gardless of the jury's verdict, the soldiers were murderers of innocent Whigs. It did not trouble Adams that he was forced to sidestep all the evidence that had been brought forward at the trial and rely entirely upon the testimony gathered by himself and the Boston selectmen. Between the two sets of evidence there was enough discrepancy to convict or acquit the soldiers, for even the testimony of the same witnesses differed materially when they were examined *ex parte* by Adams and the selectmen and when they were cross-examined in the witness box by John Adams or Josiah Quincy. Adams explained the soldiers' acquittal not by the evidence brought forward in the trial, but by the shortcomings of the jury. A jury of countrymen, he said, was unable to judge the credibility of witnesses who were almost all townsmen; had a jury of Boston mechanics been impaneled, he did not doubt the citizens would have gotten satisfaction. To open New Englanders' eyes to the miscarriage of justice that had taken place in Boston, Adams conjured up all the horrors of the Massacre: redcoats firing wantonly into a throng of peaceably disposed Whigs; the dogs lapping the patriot blood in King's Street; and the soldier Kilroi brutally attacking the ropewalker Gray, who, by Adams's account, stood with his arms "folded in his bosom," although the evidence produced at the trial showed that Gray was wielding his cudgel with great effect until he was stopped short by a bullet. British atrocities alone, however, were not sufficient to convince the people that murder had been done on the night of March 5: there was the deathbed confession of Patrick Carr, that the townspeople had been the aggressors and that the soldiers had fired in self-defense. This unlooked-for recantation from one of the martyrs who was dying in the odor of sanctity with which Sam Adams had invested them sent a wave of alarm through the patriot ranks. But Adams blasted Carr's testimony in the eyes of all pious New Englanders by pointing out that he was an Irish "papist" who had probably died in the confession of the Roman Catholic Church. After Sam Adams had finished with Patrick Carr even Tories did not dare to quote him to prove Bostonians were responsible for the Massacre.

Sam Adams's "Vindex" articles contributed to stamp the

fray of March 5, 1770, as the "horred Massacre" in the minds
of nearly all New Englanders in spite of the jury's verdict and
the weight of evidence.   Better to remind the people of British
atrocities, a Boston town committee of which Adams was a
member proposed that an annual oration and celebration be held
every year on March 5 to commemorate the Massacre.   This
annual observance gave Whig orators an opportunity to vent
their wrath against the mother country and keep the memory
fresh of the "bloody work in King Street"; "The wan tenants
of the grave," shrilled one patriot, "still shriek for vengeance
on their remorseless butchers." [31]   On Massacre days, bells
tolled mournfully in Boston until far into the night; lighted
pictures of dead and dying patriots were exhibited from a window in the North End of town; and portraits of Hutchinson
and Oliver were shown in the select company of Empson and
Dudley.   Neither of the Adamses ever gave a Massacre oration: John Adams because he believed that by defending the
soldiers he had made it impossible for him to denounce the
"bloody-backed rascals" in the true Whig style; Sam Adams
because he distrusted his oratorical powers.   Still, Sam Adams
undoubtedly wrote a large part of the oration John Hancock
delivered on March 5, 1774, to a "crowded audience of Narragansett Indians" fresh from the second Boston Tea Party.
Hancock was quite incapable of writing that "hash of abusive,
treasonable stuff" which so delighted the redskins who swarmed
into Faneuil Hall on that occasion; it was really Adams speaking when Hancock called upon every father in New England to
gather his children about his knees and tell them the story of the
Massacre "till tears of pity glisten in their eyes, and boiling
passion shakes their tender frames." [32]

Sam Adams used the Boston Massacre not only to embitter
Americans toward Great Britain but to prove the necessity of
fighting British troops before they had opportunity to gain a

---

[31] *Orations, delivered at the Request of the Inhabitants of the town of
Boston* (Boston, 1807), 37.   *Boston Town Records*, 18th Report (1887),
47, 48.
[32] *Orations, etc.*, 43.   Gordon, I, 300.   Lorenzo Sears, *John Hancock,
the Picturesque Patriot*, 143.

foothold in the country. The Massacre seemed to bear out Adams's contention that the King's soldiers should have been resisted when they reached Boston. It was futile, he preached in 1770, to look to the courts for redress; the militia, not judges and juries, must save New Englanders from military despotism. After the Massacre, Adams was joined by a host of amateur generals who proposed to save New England by bringing the militia to full fighting strength and replacing the "ancient methods of bushing fighting" with modern strategy and formations. The seat of danger was no longer the frontier and redskins but the seaboard and redcoats; military tactics which were effective against Indians would be useless against British regulars — therefore, New Englanders must henceforth practise manœuvres in open fields and train themselves to meet large bodies of troops fighting in European fashion. The fiction of an impending French war that had proved so useful during the Massachusetts Convention was again employed to screen these preparations to wage war against British troops; and Sam Adams and his followers still talked of grappling with France while they prepared to fight England.[33]

Like other Whig leaders after the Boston Massacre, Sam Adams painted war as glorious and fostered those "generous and manly Sentiments, which usually attend a true Military Spirit." He was overjoyed to see how eagerly New Englanders cleaned their muskets and drilled in militia companies to prepare for the day when they should be compelled to fight for their liberties. Boston led the movement to build up a militia capable of holding its own against British regulars, and plans were laid to give the next army of British "invaders" a warm reception. When it was rumored that troops would be sent from England to punish Boston for attacking British soldiers on the night of the Massacre, the Sons of Liberty held a meeting in William Molineux's house to decide whether to oppose their landing; and Hutchinson did not doubt that if the force sent out from England were small, the patriots would fight. To set an example for New Englanders, Bostonians went through their

---

[33] *Boston Evening Post*, April 30, 1770; June 11, 1770. *Boston Gazette*, Jan. 27, 1771; Feb. 24, 1772. *The Writings of Samuel Adams*, II, 68, 69.

military exercises every evening on the Common and declared
openly that no royal troops would ever again land in the
metropolis. "Innocence is no longer safe," exclaimed Adams
and his followers, "we are now obliged to appeal to GOD and to
our ARMS for defense." [34]

[34] *Boston Gazette*, April 12, 1770.

VIII

THE NONIMPORTATION AGREEMENT

THE Townshend duties brought about the riots in Boston which compelled the British government to send troops to preserve order in the metropolis; and the presence of royal soldiers, in turn, led to the Boston Massacre. It is now necessary to turn to other consequences of the Townshend duties: the colonial nonimportation agreement and the growth of American unity.

Almost a decade before Americans began to think of political separation from the mother country, the idea of economic independence had become widespread in the colonies. While the colonists still remained subjects of the mother country they began to cut the economic ties that bound them to the Old World. Stimulated by Charles Townshend's scheme of taxation, the colonists were seized with a fervor for economic self-sufficiency that matches present-day nationalistic aspirations. This spirit manifested itself in an intercolonial boycott of British manufactures and the establishment of home industries designed to free America of dependence upon Great Britain. Although the immediate origin of the nonimportation agreement of 1768 was Parliament's attempt to tax the colonies, in a deeper sense it was the first concerted attempt made by the colonists to escape from the swaddling clothes which British colonial policy had fastened upon them. It was a step toward the fulfillment of America's "manifest destiny" as a "Great Empire" politically and economically independent of Great Britain.

Although it has been supposed that Sam Adams originated the idea of coercing Great Britain by boycotting her manufactures, he actually played small part in its early develop-

ment.[1]   During the height of the Stamp Act excitement, while
the Sons of Liberty were tightening their military alliances and
cleaning their muskets for use against the King's troops, New
York merchants were taking surer means of procuring the repeal
of the Stamp Act.   One of Great Britain's most profitable
branches of trade was with the American colonies, and British
merchants had extended them credit to the tune of four million
pounds.   Provincial patriots regarded this bumping commerce
and immense debt as levers with which to pry concessions from
the mother country, but the New York merchants were the first
to demonstrate their true value in a controversy with Great
Britain.   By canceling orders for goods and refusing to make
further purchases until the Stamp Act was repealed, the New
Yorkers began in October 1765 the first of three colonial boycotts of the mother country's manufactures designed to redress
American grievances.   Early in November, Philadelphia followed New York's example, but it was not until December 9,
1765, that Boston belatedly joined the movement.[2]   The result
was a complete victory for the American merchants.   British
traders were panic-stricken at the prospect of seeing colonial
trade and debts slip through their fingers and they lobbied so
vigorously in Parliament that the Stamp Act was repealed in
1766, largely through their efforts.

This easy success set the fashion for every subsequent attempt
by the colonies to force the mother country to grant their demands.   Having found the Englishmen's weakness, American
patriots hammered it until the outbreak of the Revolutionary
War, confidently expecting to see the mother country give way as
it had done in 1766.   Sam Adams, in particular, became convinced that the only way to reason with Englishmen was to
pinch them in their pocketbooks, and he believed that American
boycotts would so terrify Great Britain that everything the colonies asked would be given them.   When the Townshend duties

---

[1] Wells, I, 82, 149.
[2] *Publications Col. Soc. of Mass.*, Transactions 1919, 159–179. *Lamb
Papers*, MSS. N. Y. Hist. Soc., New York Sons of Liberty to the Providence
Sons of Liberty, April 2, 1766. *Boston Gazette*, Dec. 6, 1765; May 5, 1766
(Supplement). *Bernard Papers*, VI, Bernard to Lord Shelburne, Aug. 31,
1767. Gordon, I, 194.

were imposed upon America, Adams remembered how the excited merchants had stormed Parliament during the Stamp Act and he began to urge that pressure again be brought against the mother country.   It is as the instigator of the second colonial boycott rather than as the originator of the scheme that Sam Adams should be remembered.

Adams particularly relished a boycott of British manufactures because he regarded it as a step towards Puritanism.   He believed the nonimportation agreement was a double-barreled gun which would mow down luxury and high living in New England at the same time that it made Great Britain smart for its "tyranny" over the colonies.   The first move, in Adams's opinion, to clear the ground for Puritanism was to stop the importation of British "Baubles" which he believed Cotton and Winthrop would have cast out as snares of Satan.   Adams looked sourly upon the homes of rich Boston merchants with their expensive "Decorations of the Parlor, the shining Side Boards of Plate, the costly Piles of China," and compared their ostentation with the simple frugality of the founders.[3]   He saw a grain of good even in British oppression because he expected it to hasten the return of puritanic simplicity in New England; after the Sugar Act had pricked the bubble of war prosperity, Adams and his friends declared that "Nothing but FRUGALITY can now save the distress'd northern colonies from impending ruin."[4]   The heavier the taxes with which the British government loaded New Englanders, the more like Puritans the people were forced to become in order to survive.   Probably George Grenville and Charles Townshend would have been the last to suspect that they were making the rowdy New England Saints "old Puritans" once more.   Nevertheless, Sam Adams hoped to use the colonial revenue acts to put the people on the highroad to Puritanism.

In characteristic fashion, Sam Adams set the nonimportation agreement in motion.   After the passage of the Townshend duties, the Boston town meeting was called and the citizens were persuaded to forgo an elaborate list of British imports

[3] *Boston Gazette,* Oct. 1, 1764.
[4] *Ibid.,* Oct. 8, 1764.   *Massachusetts Gazette,* Oct. 29, 1767.

which Sam Adams had decided were unfit for Whigs and "Old
Puritans." To secure signatures to this pledge, a subscription
paper was carried from house to house in Boston. At first,
signing was entirely voluntary, but the names came in so slowly
and the scheme was so firmly "rejected & discountenanced by
the Principal Gentlemen of the Town," that Tories began to
believe Adams had overshot the mark. Governor Bernard suspected that the agreement was another piece of patriot bluff;
and conservatives ridiculed the Whigs, who in their eagerness to
add names to the subscription paper induced "Porters & Washing
Women" to sign a promise not to buy silks, velvets, coaches,
and chariots. In spite of this unpromising beginning, the proceedings of the Boston town meeting were sent to every important town on the continent and Adams began to demand that
the Boston merchants set the colonies an example of a boycott
against British goods to repeal the Townshend Act.[5]

As has been seen, opposition to the Townshend duties was
primarily political; in contrast to the Sugar and Stamp Acts,
they did not immediately menace the well-being of colonial
merchants. When Sam Adams began to agitate a boycott of
British imports among Boston merchants he found them deeply
alarmed by the political consequences of the Townshend duties
but little concerned with economic grievances against the mother
country: money and credit were abundant in the metropolis
and there had never been "a more apparent Ballance of Trade"
in favor of Massachusetts Bay.[6] Rather than permit the merchants to enjoy this prosperity, Adams proposed to throw them
into the thick of the political struggle that was raging around
the Townshend duties. If they proved unwilling allies, Adams
had a whip to crack about their ears. After patriot spell-
binders and newspapers had aroused the common people's enthusiasm for a boycott, the merchants were told that if they
wished to remain in the citizens' good graces they must cease
to import; and those who displayed obstinacy were reminded

---

[5] Peter Oliver, 84. *Mass. Hist. Soc. Proceedings* (1923), LV, 266.
[6] *Bernard Papers*, VI, Bernard to Lord Shelburne, Oct. 8, 1767; March 21,
1768. *Boston Evening Post*, Nov. 9, 1767. *Letters to the Ministry* (1768),
16.

of the unpleasant consequences of attempting to oppose "the Stream of the People." With the threat of Adams's "Mohawks" hanging above their heads, Whig principles rose remarkably in the favor of "gentlemen in trade" and converts to nonimportation began to appear on every side.[7]

But even without the aid of such forceful persuasion, Adams had many friends among the smaller merchants who were ready to carry out his plans. Those who were considered merchants in pre-revolutionary Boston were not usually wealthy aristocrats who looked down upon Sam Adams with the patrician disdain of Thomas Hutchinson; on the contrary, it was said that seven eighths of the Boston merchants were "more properly forestallers, retailers, pedlars, milliners, hawkers, squeezers, and grinders." Every shopkeeper in Boston was regarded as a merchant because the London traders dealt directly with them rather than through a middleman. As a result, whenever the merchants held their meetings in Faneuil Hall, it was difficult to distinguish them from the attendants of the Boston town meetings because "every master of a Sloop & broken Shopkeeper or Huckster" was admitted as freely as were the rich merchants and had an equal voice "in ordering the Property of the first Trader in the Province."[8] Hancock carried in his train many small traders who, when joined with Adams's supporters, could easily outvote the "mercantile overlords" who opposed the patriots' schemes. Thus, when the Boston merchants finally adopted a nonimportation agreement in March 1768, Thomas Hutchinson remarked that two thirds of those who voted in favor of the boycott were small shopkeepers who imported little or nothing from Great Britain.[9]

It was a more difficult matter to induce other colonies to erect a barrier against British commodities. Philadelphia refused to join Boston in April 1768 and for several months Adams's scheme seemed stillborn. But in August 1768, the New York

---

[7] *Letters to the Ministry* (1768), 16. *Bernard Papers,* VI, Bernard to Lord Shelburne, March 21, 1768.

[8] *Boston Evening Post,* Dec. 14, 1767. Peter Oliver, 101. Mass. Archives, 26, *Hutchinson Corr.,* II, 361.

[9] Mass. Archives, 26, *Hutchinson Corr.,* II, 322, 514.

merchants, hotly pressed by the Sons of Liberty, united with Boston in prohibiting the importation of British and European goods, with the exception of certain "enumerated" articles, to force the repeal of the Townshend duties. Committees of inspection were appointed by the merchants to oversee all imports; refractory merchants were threatened with the loss of customers and credit; and the colonists consoled themselves for the loss of British manufactures with the hope that this "bloodless" war with the mother country would quickly redress all American grievances.

At the outset of the nonimportation agreement, Sam Adams saw that the colonies could not go on indefinitely without British and European commodities unless home industries were established. Therefore Adams became one of the most enthusiastic promoters of colonial manufacturing in America. He believed that nothing would be more alarming to the British merchants than the sight of colonists trooping to factories and producing all their necessities — Adams never envisaged them turning their hands to luxuries — by their own efforts. He dreamed of America as a "Great Empire" permanently freed of dependence upon Great Britain for both political and economic guidance. He set the clergy to work "to preach up Manufactures instead of Gospel"; and under his inspiration Boston Whigs nursed tea leaves and mulberry trees in their gardens and hopefully looked forward to the day when the course of trade would be reversed and Massachusetts Bay would export tea, silk, linen, and iron to Great Britain. Thomas Young, that redoubtable freethinker and right-hand man of Sam Adams, exhorted New England farmers to turn their oak plains into sheep pastures and produce enough wool to clothe every American colonist. To be clad in homespun became the mark of an American patriot; and Harvard and Princeton seniors delighted the Sons of Liberty by taking their degrees at commencement in clothing manufactured in the colonies. "Female Patriots" spun and drank home-grown "Labradore" tea instead of wasting their time in "idle conversation" over cups of British bohea. Public-spirited Whigs attempted to establish factories to supply colonial needs, particularly in com-

modities taxed by the British government; and optimistic patriots believed that America would soon be able to manufacture all its necessities while "superfluities will be wholly given
up." [10]

Few Crown officers were frightened by Adams's efforts to
create colonial manufacturing.   "For New England to threaten
the Mother Country with Manufactures," said Governor Bernard, "is the Idlest Bully that ever was attempted to be imposed upon sensible People." [11]   Tories who attempted to run
down the stories in patriot newspapers of the rapid strides being made toward economic self-sufficiency remarked that the
Whigs had given their imaginations free rein.   Even James
Otis ridiculed Adams's plan: "I can never hear American manufactures seriously talked of," he remarked, "without being
dispos'd to a violent fit of laughter."   Otis pointed out that
the high price of labor and scarcity of raw materials in America
were insuperable obstacles.   Although Massachusetts had more
sheep than any other colony, Otis showed that it could not produce enough wool to keep New Englanders even in stockings,
much less supply all British America with woolen clothing;
and he damped his followers' enthusiasm for economic independence by demonstrating that unless New Englanders
bought British or European hose they would be compelled to go
barefoot.[12]   In fact, colonial manufactures were to play little
part in bringing about the repeal of the Townshend duties and
Adams did not live to see America reach the goal of economic
freedom of Europe.   It was not until after the War of 1812
that New England began to take its place in the industrial world
and shut out those "British Baubles" which Adams exclaimed
against in 1768.   But Adams did not foresee that Americans
would promptly begin to manufacture the same "Baubles" for
themselves.

Nevertheless, the attempt to foster American manufactures

[10] *Chalmers Papers*, III, Information of Richard Silvester.   Peter Oliver,
87.   *Boston Gazette*, April 3, 10, 23, 1770; June 27, 1768; Jan. 4, 1768.
Boston Evening Post, Nov. 16 and 23, 1767.

[11] *Bernard Papers*, VI, Bernard to Lord Shelburne, March 21, 1768.

[12] *Boston Evening Post*, Nov. 23, 1767.   *Boston Gazette*, Aug. 12, 1765.
Otis, *Brief Remarks on the Defence of the Halifax Libel, etc.*, II, 170, 171.

behind the protection of a boycott brought to light significant differences between Sam Adams and other leading colonial Whigs. John Dickinson, the foremost patriot of the Southern colonies, looked upon the nonimportation agreement as a mixed blessing because he feared that it might succeed in producing such a powerful "spirit of manufactory & Oeconomy" in America that the mother country would be seriously injured. "My Heart bleeds at the Prospect of our Success," Dickinson wrote; "How mournful a Reflection is it, that a just Regard for ourselves, must wound Great Britain, the Mother of brave, generous, humane Spirits, the chief Bulwark of Liberty on this Globe, and the blessed Seat of unspotted Religion." [13] Sam Adams, on the other hand, never showed concern for the suffering he might be bringing upon England — his attitude was that the mother country richly deserved to be punished for attempting to enslave the colonies. Unlike James Otis and John Dickinson, Adams felt little loyalty toward the mother country; in his eyes, America must become a "Great Empire" regardless of the well-being of Great Britain.

At the outset, Sam Adams added an ominous note to the nonimportation agreement which might well have disturbed English Whigs who believed that Americans would not go beyond constitutional opposition to the mother country. The Boston Sons of Liberty declared the boycott was "the only *pacifick* method of recovering our lost Liberties" — if defeated in their economic war with the mother country, Americans must fight in earnest for their liberties. Sam Adams said the nonimportation agreement was the only means outside of a "deluge of blood" by which the colonists could gain redress of grievances; and declared that the fate of *"Unborn Millions"* hung in the balance between peace and war.[14] Had Englishmen taken the Boston Liberty Boys' threats seriously in 1768 they would have seen they must do one of two things: either concede the colonists'

[13] *Arthur Lee Papers*, Sparks MSS., Harvard College Library, I, John Dickinson to Arthur Lee, June 26, 1769. *Chalmers Papers*, III, Information of Richard Silvester.
[14] *Lamb Papers*, New York Sons of Liberty to the Philadelphia Sons of Liberty, May 11, 1770. *Boston Gazette*, Oct. 9, 1769; Feb. 5, 1770. *The Writings of Samuel Adams*, II, 7.

demands or prepare for war.   Unfortunately for the British Empire, they chose to do neither.

Even without this menacing chorus from Sam Adams and the Boston Whigs, the nonimportation agreement was a manifestation of colonial unrest which augured ill for the peace of the empire.   By 1769, almost all the colonies had joined the boycott and a wall had been raised from Massachusetts to Georgia against a large number of proscribed British manufactures. The movement toward colonial unity which had produced the Stamp Act Congress and the corresponding committees of the Sons of Liberty appeared to have culminated in the nonimportation agreement.   "One spirit," Sam Adams exclaimed, "animates all America . . . to *quench* the spirit, all the colonies must be absolutely *destroyed*." [15]   By 1769, Adams believed the provinces had fully learned the importance of concerted action — an achievement he called "a pleasing *omen* in favor of the great American cause" and the most hopeful sign of eventual success against the mother country.   Never before had American affairs appeared more rosy in his eyes.   While Tories groaned that the "Dementation" that had first seized Massachusetts Bay had now spread to all the colonies, Adams exulted that "the *tighter* the cord of unconstitutional power is drawn round this bundle of arrows, the *firmer* it will be." [16]   The New York and Boston Sons of Liberty were in as close communication as during the Stamp Act period: when Nathaniel Rogers, a Boston importer, attempted to escape from the mob in Boston, the Sons of Liberty sent an express to their New York brethren to give him a warm reception if he came their way.   When Rogers reached New York he was hunted down by the Liberty Boys and barely got out of town in time to escape a coat of tar and feathers. [17]

When the Boston Sons of Liberty found themselves sup-

---

[15] *Boston Evening Post*, April 10, 1769; April 25, 1769 (Supplement). *Boston Gazette*, Jan. 29, 1770.

[16] *Miscellaneous Papers*, MS. Mass. Hist. Soc., Letter from ——— to ———, Aug. 10, 1770, p. 76.

[17] *Boston Gazette*, May 21, 1770.   Mass. Archives, 26, *Hutchinson Corr.*, II, 488, 491.   *Lamb Papers*, New York Sons of Liberty to Philadelphia Sons of Liberty, May 11, 1770.

ported by most of British America they became almost as warlike as in 1768 before British troops entered Boston.   Indeed,
they grew so bumptious that some Tories feared they were
"ripe for Rebellion" in 1769 and ready to fight Great Britain
single-handed.[18]   If the patriots were to be taken at their word
there was good reason for apprehension.   Whig newspapers
stiffened the patriots' courage by declaring that as long as the
colonies remained united "it is not in the power of all the world
to enslave us."   At the Boston town meeting, William Molineux
assured the citizens that the entire British army and navy could
not compel them "to act against their Wills"; and it became a
common saying in the metropolis that "no Act of Parl[iament]
against the mind of the people shall ever be executed here." [19]
Just as in 1768, when Sam Adams attempted to stir up resistance
to the British troops, the degeneracy, debt, riots, and political
disorders of the mother country were contrasted with the vigor,
purity, and courage of the colonies.   It was said that Great
Britain was so corrupt that the moment "their high mightinesses
the manufacturers" saw their precious pounds and shillings
jeopardized by the nonimportation agreement they would storm
Parliament and buy back American business with offers of
political freedom.   Those who feared punishment from Great
Britain were told they were out of the reach of Parliament.[20]
Undoubtedly, the success of the nonimportation agreement
was heady wine to many patriots who, like Sam Adams, took
such deep draughts that they began to think America invincible.

The Whigs' high spirits were dashed, however, by the opposition to the boycott which started to spring up in the colonies.
The success of the nonimportation agreement required support
from all importers of British goods, yet there was in every seaport a clique of Tory merchants who continued to trade with

[18] *Chalmers Papers*, III, George Mason to Joseph Harrison, Oct. 20, 1769.
[19] *Boston Gazette*, March 27, 1769; July 19, 1770.   Mass. Archives, 26,
Hutchinson Corr., II, 389, 465, 492.   *Bernard Papers*, VI, Bernard to Lord
Shelburne, March 21, 1768.   *Grenville Papers* (edited by W. J. Smith, 1853),
IV, 439.
[20] *Chalmers Papers*, III, Narrative of the Events in Boston, 1770.   Mass.
Archives, 25, Thomas Hutchinson to Francis Bernard, May 3, 1770.

the mother country.   Much to the patriots' consternation, these British manufactures found a ready market in the colonies. It was clear that if the boycott was observed only by Whig merchants, the Tories would gobble up fat profits and put their self-sacrificing competitors out of business.   This circumstance alone was sufficient to arouse the Whigs against violators of the boycott: but in Boston hatred of importers was particularly strong because most of them were relatives or close friends of Thomas Hutchinson.   The lieutenant governor and his sons were themselves prominent merchants, and their refusal to sign the nonimportation agreement encouraged others to resist the Whigs.   It was widely believed that Hutchinson was the backbone of Tory opposition to the nonimportation agreement; and certainly, at every turn, the patriots found themselves face to face with the lieutenant governor, who, instead of yielding to mobs and threats, rallied his followers and undermined the boycott with imported British merchandise.   As long as Hutchinson encouraged the Tories, the nonimportation agreement was in danger of collapse.   It is no wonder, therefore, that Sam Adams railed at Hutchinson in the Boston town meeting with "peculiar pleasure" and became one of the most relentless hounders of importers in the colonies.[21]   At the town meeting held in Faneuil Hall in October 1769, Adams produced a list of violators of the nonimportation agreement who, he said, should be "Stigmatiz'd & declar'd Enemys of the Country, and to be recorded in the Town Books as such to the latest posterity." When it was learned that several importers were ready to sign the agreement, Adams refused to allow any last-minute recantations: it was too late, he declared, for them to make peace because by resisting the people they had committed an unpardonable sin — "no atonement could be made on this Side the Grave; God perhaps might possibly forgive them, but He and the rest of the People never could."   This intractable policy endeared Adams to the common people of Boston, who enthusiastically resolved in the town meeting to denounce the

---

[21] Mass. Archives, 26, *Hutchinson Corr.*, II, 384, 528.   *Chalmers Papers,* III, Journal of Transactions at Boston; Proceedings of the Town Meeting, Oct. 4, 1769.   *The Writings of Samuel Adams,* I, 395.

Tory merchants as "obstinate and inveterate Enemies to their Country" who had severed themselves from the commonwealth and the protection of its laws. Every importer, declared the citizens, was to be regarded as a public enemy to whom the people were forbidden to show any "Act and Office of common Civility . . . *for ever* hereafter" on pain of similar ostracism.[22] The offending merchants, it was clear, were now fair game for the mob.

With the exception of Thomas Hutchinson, no Massachusetts Tory was more feared by the Whigs than was John Mein, printer of the *Boston Chronicle*. Unlike most New England conservatives, Mein was not afraid to beard Sam Adams in his own den. He deliberately set out to wreck the nonimportation agreement by spreading suspicion throughout the colonies of Boston's good faith in enforcing the boycott. Mein secured copies of the manifests of all vessels that had entered Boston since the beginning of the agreement and discovered that a number of Boston merchants, John Hancock among them, were secretly importing British commodities which were retailed to the people at a large profit. These manifests were printed in the *Boston Chronicle* and in a pamphlet entitled, *Account of the late Importations &c in the port of Boston*. Mein scattered hundreds of copies over the colonies with the result that an uproar was produced not only "in the very heart of the Boston Faction, but between that Faction and the other combining colonies."[23] Even while exposing the "trickery" of the New England "Saints," Mein continued to remain in Boston openly defying Sam Adams and the "Mohawks," although he was given ample warning of what was in store if he persisted in his efforts to break up the boycott. Sam Adams said that Mein had "set himself in Opposition to an *awakened*, an *enlightened*, and a DETERMINED Continent," and so many threats were made by the Sons of Liberty that he was compelled to arm himself with

[22] Mass. Archives, 26, *Hutchinson Corr.*, II, 384.   *Boston Gazette*, Jan. 29. 1770.

[23] *Chalmers Papers*, III, Extract of a Letter from Mr. Fleeming, Printer at Boston, to his Partner, Mr. John Mein, now in London, July 1, 1770. *Publications Col. Soc. of Mass.*, Transactions 1916–17, XIX, 229.

pistols when he walked the streets of Boston.   It was evident
that Mein had sunk his shafts into too many prominent Boston
patriots to remain long unmolested.   As the "common enemy
of America," he was in daily danger from the mob; and one day
he was attacked on the Boston Exchange by twenty Liberty
Boys "armed with Spades, Canes & Clubs."   Through rare
luck, Mein escaped into the near-by guardhouse where the
soldiers kept the mob at bay.   The magistrates immediately
swore out warrants for Mein's arrest; and Adams and Molineux
personally assisted the peace officer in searching for him.   But
even Adams and Molineux, expert as they were in ferreting
out Tories, could not find Mein.   The disgruntled patriots were
compelled to admit that "the Bird was flown" to England.[24]
Thus, with the aid of the mob, Sam Adams removed a serious
menace to the success of the nonimportation agreement, but, as
he was soon to learn, it was far easier to hustle Mein out of
Boston than to heal the wounds his sharp pen had inflicted upon
the reputation of the Puritan metropolis.

Even more destructive than John Mein's pamphleteering was
the conciliatory policy adopted by the British government.
Thoroughly alarmed by the formidable league against British
manufactures created in the colonies by the Townshend duties,
the Ministry quickly took steps to redress American grievances.
In 1769, Lord Hillsborough announced in a circular letter to
the American colonies that, for "commercial reasons," the
Ministry proposed to repeal all the Townshend duties with
the exception of the tax on tea and to renounce all plans of drawing a large revenue from the colonies.

In Boston, the British government's tempting "Sugar Plum"
had disastrous effect upon the nonimportation agreement: the
Whig merchants became lukewarm; the committees of inspection stopped work; and even the Sons of Liberty began to grow
dispirited.   It was now apparent that Adams must delve deep
into his bag of tricks if the boycott was to be saved and Hutchinson and the Tories crushed.   Adams met this emergency by

[24] *Boston Gazette*, Aug. 28, 1769; Jan. 15, 1770.   *John Hancock Papers*,
MSS. Mass. Hist. Soc., John Longman to John Mein.   *Chalmers Papers*, III,
George Mason to Joseph Harrison, Oct. 20, 1769.

making sweeping changes in the nonimportation agreement. Although from the beginning the guiding spirits of the boycott were Boston politicians, it was nominally in the hands of the merchants, who, by holding meetings separate from the people's and enforcing the agreement by means of committees of inspection chosen from among themselves, made its success or failure dependent upon their efforts.   By 1770, these "gentlemen in trade" had proved to Adams's satisfaction their unfitness to play a leading part in the commercial war against Great Britain.   They were slow to harass importers; they were jealous of interference by the Sons of Liberty; and, after Lord Hillsborough's circular letter of 1769, many were eager to call a truce in their quarrel with the mother country.   Moreover, they were utterly unable to cope with Hutchinson and his friends. Startling proof of the merchants' laxity came to light early in 1770, just before the Boston Massacre, when it was shown that Hutchinson's sons had secretly removed and sold some of the tea they had been compelled to store for safekeeping with the committee of inspection.   There was no longer any doubt that the Whig traders lacked the vigilance and zeal necessary for the success of the nonimportation agreement.   New vigor was required, and Adams undertook to supply it by throwing out the merchants and putting the politicians and common people in direct command.

Immediately after the Hutchinsons' double-dealing had been discovered, Boston was plastered with notices urging the merchants "and all others who are concerned in or *connected* with trade" to meet in Faneuil Hall.   This meant that, for the first time, the people as a whole were to control the nonimportation agreement, because, as the patriots pointed out, Boston lived by trade and every person in town could be regarded as "*connected* with trade." [25]   To make sure of a thumping majority over those who favored halfway measures against the importers, Sam Adams and other patriot leaders went about Boston "trotting from house to house, to engage the master workmen, to suffer their journeymen and apprentices to attend at Faneuil Hall, and to make what they called a respectable ap-

[25] *Boston Gazette*, Jan. 22, 1770.

pearance." [26] The meetings were henceforth open to all citizens regardless of legal requirements for voting: when a motion was made to exclude unpropertied townspeople the speaker was shouted down with cries from the floor that "if they had no property they had Liberty, and their posterity might have property." [27] Such staunch democrats might be expected to show small mercy to importers and to disregard the interests of the wealthy merchants whose lukewarmness had brought the nonimportation agreement to the verge of ruin.

Adams had long been clamoring for "spirited" measures to enforce the boycott and, after the people had displaced the merchants, he lost no time in giving the Tories a taste of true Whig spirit. For several years, Tories had feared that Adams would use the mob to beat down opposition to the boycott: when the agreement was first proposed in Boston, Governor Bernard declared it could not be carried out without the aid of Sam Adams's "Mohawks." [28] In 1770, these apprehensions were fully realized. To prepare the citizens for violence, Adams raised the cry that Boston's inactivity was undermining its reputation as a patriot stronghold: "Our brethren in the other Governments Complain'd of our want of Spirit," he said, "that our measures were too lax & in short began to grow very jealous of us." New Englanders whose fame extended "not only throughout the Colonies but throughout the world" were in danger, the Boston Sons of Liberty warned, of making their names "for ever detested & abhorred." [29] There was no more certain way of arousing Bostonians than reproaching them as laggards in the struggle for liberty, and the mob soon gave Americans convincing proof that there was still life in the Puritan metropolis. Adams's "Mohawks" fell upon the Tory merchants with such good will that Boston soon became the most uncomfortable spot on the continent for violators of the nonimportation agreement. At night, their houses were surrounded by "the most diabolical crew that are upon the face of the earth," bawling

[26] *Boston Chronicle*, Feb. 5, 1770.

[27] Mass. Archives, 26, *Hutchinson Corr.*, II, 492.

[28] *Bernard Papers*, VI, Bernard to Lord Shelburne, March 21, 1768.

[29] *Massachusetts Papers*, MSS. Mass. Hist. Soc., Committee of Merchants to Dennys De Berdt, Jan. 30, 1770. *Boston Gazette*, Feb. 5, 1770.

threats and "calling out with a Loud Voice kill that dog . . .
he is a Governours man a Bastard of Liberty." [30]   The patriots
stationed small boys before the importers' shops to pelt the
owners and customers with filth.   McMasters, a prominent
Tory merchant, was carted out of town to a gallows, where he
was forced to swear never to return to Boston on pain of hanging; and the "lawless banditti" of the metropolis who acted
on Sam Adams's orders gained such strength that terror-
stricken Tories expected "to hear of Blood and Murder every
hour."   Many of Adams's enemies fled to Castle William for
refuge or slept with loaded pistols beside their pillows in anticipation of a visit from the "Mohawks."   Yet, in spite of the
Tories' groans that the patriots had begun a reign of terror,
Adams believed the Boston Sons of Liberty displayed great
restraint in their treatment of the importers.   "Good God!"
he exclaimed.   "How much longer is it expected that the
patience of this injured Country shall hold out!" [31]

Another of Sam Adams's "spirited" measures to terrorize the
importers was to marshal hundreds of Bostonians into ranks and
files and march at their head to the merchants' shops.   As soon
as the people had been called into the merchants' meeting, the
whole body, one thousand strong, — composed, Tories said,
"of the very refuse of the town," — marched out of the town
hall up King's Street to the importers' shops and demanded
that they deliver their goods into the hands of the committee of
inspection. [32]   But even the forbidding spectacle of a thousand
Sons of Liberty outside their doors and the threat of the
"ordeal" at Liberty Tree failed to shake the merchants as long
as they believed themselves supported by Hutchinson.   It was
clear that the lieutenant governor must first be terrified into
submission before his followers would give way to the Whigs.
But when Sam Adams and William Molineux proposed in the

[30] *Chalmers Papers*, III, Journal of Transactions at Boston; and Extract of
a Letter from Mr. Fleeming, Printer at Boston, to his Partner Mr. John Mein,
now in London, July 1, 1770.   Mass. Archives, 25, *Hutchinson Corr.*, I,
Robert Jamieson to Thomas Hutchinson, May 30, 1770.

[31] *The Writings of Samuel Adams*, I, 395.

[32] *Chalmers Papers*, III, Journal of Transactions at Boston.   *Boston Gazette*,
Jan. 22, 1770.

town meeting that the people be led to Hutchinson's house to demand that he order his sons to surrender their goods to the committee, they brought a hornets' nest about their ears. Josiah Quincy, Jr., the young Whig lawyer who was shortly to defend the soldiers in the Massacre trials, declared the procedure illegal and called upon James Otis to confirm his opinion. But poor "Muddlehead" Otis spoke so unintelligibly that no one could tell whether he opposed or favored Adams's plan.[33] Sam Adams, however, made very clear his belief that there was nothing illegal in the step; and he spoke so plausibly that he soon had the people clamoring to be led to the lieutenant governor's. Nevertheless, when Hancock, Otis, and William Phillips were nominated to serve on the committee that was to march at the people's head, they declined the honor. A wave of consternation passed over the patriot ranks. Adams and Molineux were dismayed to find themselves deserted by most of their friends. "It would be impossible, sir," wrote a Tory spectator, "to describe the looks of Mollineaux . . . he drew his hand across his Throat, and declar'd he was ready to Die that Minute, that for his part he scorn'd to have any thing more to do with them," and, jumping down from the platform, began to walk out of the hall. Dr. Thomas Young caught him before he had reached the door and begged him "for God's sake to stay" unless he wished to ruin the patriot party. After "much perswasion and a great deal of pulling," Molineux was brought back to his seat. Otis and Phillips then consented to join the committee and Otis was "Clapp'd by the People universally." [34]

With Otis once more among the radicals, the people streamed out of Faneuil Hall, formed their ranks in the market place, and marched two thousand strong to Hutchinson's house. But, to the patriots' chagrin, Hutchinson faced the crowd without wavering. He warned the people that they were acting illegally, that "Mr. Otis as a Lawyer knew it," and'that they must go back instantly to their homes. Hutchinson's firmness disconcerted Sam Adams and his followers, and when they

[33] *Chalmers Papers*, III, Journal of Transactions at Boston; A Key to a certain publication.

[34] *Ibid.*, III, George Mason to ——, Jan. 24, 1770.

returned to Faneuil Hall they were "considerably non plus'd." [35]
Yet in reality the lieutenant governor was on the point of surrender: he had made a brave show before the crowd, but he
was rapidly becoming convinced that he could no longer withstand Sam Adams and the "Faneuil Hall patriots."   He had
failed to form any party capable of opposing the Whigs: in spite
of their eagerness to free themselves from mob rule, the Tories
were made helpless by fear "for their fine Houses."   Conservatives thought only of getting out of the way of the patriot steam
roller.   "Few among us," they lamented, "are hardy enough to
dare assert their just rights, but timidly submit and tacitly be-
wail their hard fate." [36]   Instead of setting out to destroy the
Whig "courts of inquisition" they sought to keep in the good
graces of the Liberty Boys lest the mob be turned against them.
Hutchinson could do nothing to break up the meetings in
Faneuil Hall where the patriots made such deep inroads upon
royal authority that he feared the time would come when "every
town every Parish & every particular club will meet & Vote &
carry their votes into execution just as they please." [37]   The
Boston patriots' usurpation of constitutional power was, in the
lieutenant governor's eyes, far more menacing than riots and
tumult because it blotted out all notion of subordination from
the people's minds.   Nevertheless, the Council refused to support him in defending imperial authority in Massachusetts Bay;
his entreaties failed to rouse the Tories; and his commands were
disregarded by the Sons of Liberty.   Undoubtedly, further
opposition would merely provoke greater violence from the
patriots' "trained mob": therefore, early in 1770, Hutchinson
ordered his sons to surrender their merchandise to the committee of inspection.   And after the lieutenant governor had
given way, the importers quickly made terms with the patriots
rather than risk an attack by the "Mohawks."
Although Sam Adams seemed to have won a crushing victory
over the Tories and the British government, there were many

[35] *Chalmers Papers*, III, George Mason to ——, Jan. 24, 1770.
[36] Mass. Archives, 26, *Hutchinson Corr.*, II, 385, 492, 495. *Boston
Chronicle*, Jan. 15, 1770.
[37] Mass. Archives, 26, *Hutchinson Corr.*, II, 391.

disintegrating forces at work that threatened to destroy the nonimportation agreement.   There was no uniformity among the colonies with regard to the number of British commodities boycotted: some imported almost without restraint, while others shut out practically all manufactures from the mother country. Consequently, sectional jealousies were inflamed and each colony suspected it was being overreached by the sharp practices of its neighbors.   John Mein had succeeded in putting most of the continent on its guard against the secret importations of the New England "Saints."   Moreover, with the exception of a few Whig leaders, there were few in the colonies who realized that firm union was essential to the American cause.   Even in Boston, the hotbed of the movement toward colonial union, the people dreaded incorporation in a large government because they believed that New York "being near the center & having other natural advantages would be the Capital." [38]   The American union which Adams believed invulnerable in 1769 was really exposed on every side and in imminent danger of falling apart before the purposes of the nonimportation agreement had been achieved.

Moreover, the British Ministry's promise of a partial repeal of the Townshend duties drove a wedge between the colonies and brought the boycott to a premature end.   New York was the first to respond to Lord Hillsborough's circular letter of 1769.   The New York merchants, thoroughly weary of the bullying of Sons of Liberty who had nothing to lose by economic war with Great Britain, threw off their control in the spring of 1770 — a step which Bernard said the Boston merchants might have taken long before had they not been guilty of "extreme Pusillanamity." [39]   After having freed themselves from the radicals, the New York traders proposed that a congress of merchants be held at Norwalk, Connecticut, where the nonimportation agreement might be revised and the British government met halfway in conciliation.

Instead of inclining Sam Adams toward reconciliation with

[38] Mass. Archives, 26, *Hutchinson Corr.*, II, 442.   *New York Gazette and Weekly Mercury*, Aug. 6, 1770.

[39] *Bernard Papers*, VII, Bernard to Thomas Hutchinson, Aug. 20, 1770.

the mother country, Lord Hillsborough's peace offering of 1769 led him to raise his demands. The original purpose of the non-importation agreement was to repeal the Townshend duties, but when Sam Adams believed he had put the British government in retreat, he began to regard the boycott as a means of redressing all colonial grievances. As Hutchinson said, "Gaining one point makes them [the Boston Whigs] more sure of another & more restless until they obtain it." [40] Besides the repeal of the Townshend Act, Adams now demanded that the mother country remove the Admiralty Courts, clear Boston of redcoats and Commissioners of the Customs, and put the colonies back in the situation they occupied "before the late extraordinary Measures of Administration took Place." [41] Adams hinted that the boycott should be prolonged until Parliament had repealed all commercially oppressive acts from the reign of Charles II to George III, but most Whigs were not disposed to drive such a hard bargain with the mother country: the redress of grievances imposed since 1760 was in their eyes a sufficient price for ending the boycott. Still, all of Sam Adams's followers agreed that Lord Hillsborough's offer of a partial repeal of the Townshend Act was merely a sop cast to unwary Americans to break up the nonimportation agreement and destroy colonial unity.

Sam Adams saw that the British government's conciliatory offer left untouched the principles that lay at the root of the struggle between mother country and colonies. Although the American cause was based upon the doctrine of "no taxation without representation," Lord Hillsborough's circular letter of 1769 made clear that the mother country had no intention of receding from its claims. Parliament still held fast to its right to tax the colonies — "and it is the right," exclaimed the Boston patriots, "we contend against." Sam Adams believed the real purpose of the nonimportation agreement political rather than economic: it was intended not merely to remove a few taxes but

[40] Mass. Archives, 26, *Hutchinson Corr.*, II, 397, 487.
[41] *The Writings of Samuel Adams*, I, 441. British Museum, King's MSS. 203, Lib. Cong. Transcript, Samuel Cooper to Thomas Pownall, Jan. 30, 1770. *Grenville Papers*, edited by W. J. Smith (1853), IV, 456.

to establish the principle that all taxation of the colonies by the British House of Commons was illegal. Until the Declaratory Act of 1766 was repealed Adams believed "we acquire nothing, and all our labour is in vain." In proposing to abrogate part of the Townshend duties on the ground of commercial expediency, the British government revealed to Sam Adams how little it understood the causes of colonial discontent: while "even a Pepper Corn" was taken by Parliament from the colonists without their consent, there could be no hope of peace between mother country and provinces. "It is not the Quantum of the Duty, nor the Number of the Articles taxed," exclaimed the Boston Whigs, but the tax itself that kept the Empire in discord.[42]

Even without recourse to these "higher Principles" which Sam Adams kept always in view, there was good reason to believe the Ministry's "Sugar Plum" contained a bitter core. Lord Hillsborough let it be understood in his circular letter that the tea duty, which alone of the taxes laid by Charles Townshend yielded a considerable revenue, would not be repealed. In revoking the duties upon glass, paint, and paper, the British government was really surrendering nothing of value because these taxes brought only small sums into the Exchequer. The tea duty, on the other hand, was so profitable that if the price of tea were reduced to half what it brought in England, there would still remain a revenue larger than the sum of the salaries of all the Crown officers which were intended to be paid from it.[43] And, because the preamble to the Townshend duties was left intact by the Ministry in its "conciliation gesture" of 1769, the tea duty continued to be a tax laid expressly for revenue purposes. Its proceeds might be used to support armies in the colonies and make governors and judges independent of the legislatures. Therefore it was said that every pound of British tea purchased in the colonies would further enable the Ministry to take American money and property and "daub them in gold lace on every dirty rascal, who has a scullion wench of a sister, inviting enough to make

---

[42] *New York Gazette and Weekly Mercury*, July 30, 1770.
[43] *Boston Gazette*, Aug. 15, 1768. Hutchinson, III, 351.

a whore to a commissioner." [44]   Even more harrowing to apprehensive colonists was the fear that the tea duty would be
regarded by the British government as a precedent for taxation
of the colonies and would be extended to "the necessaries of life
among us, and the very land that produces them."

As a result, Sam Adams flatly rejected the New York merchants' proposal of a congress at Norwalk. "The least altera-
tion in the present agreement," he declared, ". . . might shew
a levity of disposition probably injurious to the common cause." [45]
Whereas the New Yorkers saw a favorable opportunity in Hillsborough's circular letter to make terms with the mother country,
Adams and his followers considered it "the most unlucky Sea-
son" to talk compromise because they believed the Ministry
would soon be forced to give way completely to American demands. Moreover, Adams thoroughly distrusted the merchants whose lukewarmness had caused him to put into the
common people's hands the enforcement of the nonimportation
agreement. Rather than risk "so dangerous an Experiment"
as "committing the whole State of American Freedom, to a small
Deputation of Merchants," the Boston radicals intended to uphold the patriot cause by their own efforts. [46]   If a deputation of
merchants were given ambassadorial power and packed off to
Norwalk, it seemed likely to Adams that the "gentlemen in
trade" would sell out American liberty for the first mess of
pottage offered by the British government.

But despite Sam Adams's determination "firmly [to] ad-
here to the nonimportation agreement," the New York merchants began to import all British merchandise with the exception of tea, after a house-to-house canvass of the metropolis had
revealed that a majority of the people favored breaking the
boycott. Although this method of ascertaining public opinion
was recommended by the New Yorkers for trial in Boston, Sam
Adams preferred to settle the question in Faneuil Hall, where
his power was overwhelming and no Tory dared raise his voice.

[44] *Massachusetts Spy*, May 23, 1771. *New York Gazette and Weekly
Mercury*, July 30, 1770.

[45] *Boston Gazette*, June 11, 1770.

[46] *New York Gazette and Weekly Mercury*, July 30, 1770. *New York
Gazette or Weekly Post Boy*, June 25, 1770.

Boston town meetings had an unsavory reputation among New York gentry, who said that even a child would laugh if told that these "doughty Meetings" really expressed popular opinion.   Certainly, the citizens who assembled in Faneuil Hall left no doubt of their sentiments.   When the letter from the New York merchants announcing the end of the boycott was read in the Boston town meeting, the people were so enraged they tore the letter to pieces and threw it "to the Winds as unworthy of the least Notice." [47]

New York's desertion of the nonimportation agreement did not immediately dishearten Sam Adams.   He hoped to see the New York mechanics force the merchants to resume the boycott; and as long as Philadelphia, Boston, and Charleston remained firm, there was a prospect that New York could be brought back into the movement.   Adams and his followers urged Bostonians to forget the "fancied Miseries" for which they held the nonimportation agreement responsible and to think only of the hardships endured by their ancestors to establish a government based upon "the generous Plan of Liberty." Adams still promised that the boycott would reëstablish colonial liberty "without the Risque of Blood" and warned the Boston merchants that, regardless of what had happened in New York, it was not yet safe in Boston to anger "the BODY of the people" by importing prohibited British merchandise. [48]   Popular enthusiasm was kept warm with rosy pictures of the miracles the nonimportation agreement was to work.   Those who protested it was taking an unconscionable long time to bring relief were met with the answer that "one year more will do the business & bring Parliament to what terms we please."   In the Boston town meeting, Sam Adams exclaimed that if the boycott were continued for another twelve months a storm would be raised in England such "as would endanger the heads and necks" of the British Ministry. [49]

[47] *New York Gazette and Weekly Mercury*, Aug. 27, 1770.   *Boston Evening Post*, July 30, 1770.
[48] *New York Gazette and Weekly Mercury*, July 30, 1770.   *Boston Gazette*, July 23, 1770; Aug. 6, 1770.
[49] Mass. Archives, 26, *Hutchinson Corr.*, II, 492.   *Chalmers Papers*, III, Narrative of Events in Boston, 1770.

One of Sam Adams's most persistent errors was his conviction that Englishmen would sacrifice their political principles for the sake of preserving the wealth they drew from the colonies. On the contrary, instead of frightening the mother country into surrendering to the colonists' demands, the nonimportation agreement solidified public sentiment in Great Britain against Americans and stiffened the people's determination to see the quarrel through to the bitter end. When news reached the mother country that the Boston town meeting had declared a boycott of British manufactures it was said that "the Bostonites could not by any other means have so forcibly inculcated upon their countrymen, that the essence of American virtue consists in distressing, affronting and starving Britain." The New Englanders seemed disposed to turn "this island into a desart"; and it was whispered that "those who would starve us would cut our throats, if they could effect that carnage." [50] Never before had Bostonians appeared in Englishmen's eyes so much like scoundrelly republicans who wished to strip the mother country of all sovereignty over the colonies except the privilege of protecting them at British taxpayers' expense.

But after the New York merchants threw the Sons of Liberty overboard and opened the port to British merchandise, Sam Adams and his crew of "Mohawks" struck rough water in Boston. When the common people were put in control of the boycott, the merchants, smarting from their humiliation by the politicians, went over to the opposition. After the separate merchants' meetings had been swallowed up in the gatherings of the townspeople, few prominent Whig merchants, with the exception of John Hancock and William Phillips, attended the "mob meetings" where patriot policy was decided. Most of the wealthy traders of the metropolis were eager to "shake off their Faneuil Hall friends" and to follow New York's example in coming to terms with the mother country: they were weary of protracting the boycott until the British government should recognize the principle of no taxation without representation, and they were fearful of the growing power of the mob. Whig

[50] *New York Journal or General Advertiser*, July 7, 1768 (Supplement).

merchants had no more love for mobs and riots than had Tory
gentlemen once it had become clear that the "Mohawks" were
ready to turn upon them.   But, as Hutchinson said, the merchants had raised the Devil and now they could not lay him.

The outbreak of open hostility between Boston merchants and
politicians was hastened by Sam Adams's efforts to crush all
signs of opposition to his policies.   In 1770, when the Philadelphia merchants proposed to revise the nonimportation agreement, a number of Boston traders called a meeting at the British
Coffee House and voted to import all British goods except tea
if the Philadelphians did likewise.   No sooner had Adams
gotten wind of this mutiny than the bells were set ringing for
a meeting of the townspeople and Dr. Thomas Young was sent
with orders to the merchants to disperse immediately.   While
Young was delivering this command he was asked how he presumed to dictate to gentlemen in trade since he himself was no
merchant.   Young replied that, though he was no merchant,
"he was one that the Merchts had called in to their assistance
& he would not leave them." [51]   Meanwhile, at Faneuil Hall,
Molineux and Adams were damning the merchants as "Rebels &
Usurpers" so forcefully that had they not obeyed Young's orders and broken up their meeting they probably would have
found a mob of Sons of Liberty at their doors.   Swallowing their
humiliation, the merchants gave way to the politicians; their
meetings were forbidden by Sam Adams, the sovereign of Faneuil Hall; and "Tom, Dick & Harry" compelled the traders
to maintain the boycott of British merchandise.

In order to prove Boston's loyalty to the nonimportation
agreement in spite of "Sugar Plums" from Great Britain and
treachery from New York, Sam Adams demanded that the British goods stored in Boston by the committee of inspection should
be shipped back to England.   By this gesture, Adams hoped
to whitewash Boston's reputation of the blots left by John
Mein's pen and to set the colonies an example that would, if

---

[51] Mass. Archives, 25, *Hutchinson Corr.*, I, Thomas Hutchinson to ———,
May 3, 1770; Mass. Archives, 26, II, 492, 494.   *Chalmers Papers*, III,
Narrative of Events in Boston, 1770.

followed throughout the continent, greatly increase the distress felt in England from the boycott. It was apparent, however, that this expedient, although pleasing to the politicians, was highly distasteful to the merchants. But "the lower Sort of People who were called in as Servants" were now masters and they insisted that the merchants reship the goods or risk "a meeting in the evening" from the Sons of Liberty. The citizens exclaimed that "if a Ship was to bring in the plague nobody would doubt what is necessary to be done with her," and there were few who disagreed with Sam Adams that British manufactures were a plague to New England. When Hancock offered the free use of one of his ships to carry the merchandise to England, his offer was immediately accepted and a cargo placed aboard. "Our Zealots have no bowels," cried the merchants; and Hutchinson compared the position of people and merchants to that of a highwayman who had his pistol pressed against the ribs of a defenseless traveler.[52]

By resorting to such rough methods, Sam Adams alienated the conservative patriots and split the Whig Party. By 1770, the left wing of the patriot party, of which Sam Adams and William Molineux were the guiding spirits, had taken command of the nonimportation agreement. Only the most violent Whigs held influence among the people: Molineux raised himself in popular favor by declaring that he had no scruple in putting to death with his own hands every violator of the nonimportation agreement; and Sam Adams won applause by relentlessly hunting down importers and refusing to temporize with the British government until all colonial grievances had been redressed.[53] And when Sam Adams vaulted into the leadership of the patriot party, he brushed aside all conservative Whigs who stood in his path. Among the first to fall was James Otis, the "American Hampden" of the earlier revolutionary movement.

In 1769 Otis had been severely clubbed in a Boston tavern by John Robinson, one of the Commissioners of the Customs.

[52] *Chalmers Papers*, III, Thomas Hutchinson to Lord Hillsborough, April 27, 1770; May 18, 1770; Narrative of Events in Boston.
[53] *Ibid.*, III, Journal of Transactions at Boston.

Sam Adams manufactured rare propaganda from this brawl by screaming that the Commissioners had deliberately attempted to assassinate Otis, but Hutchinson said it was a "very pretty drubbing." [54]   In any event, Otis never entirely recovered from his encounter with Robinson.   The eccentricity and mental instability which his enemies had ridiculed earlier in his career now flared into outright insanity.   At the Whig Club, his conversation degenerated into such a steady stream of "trash, obsceneness, profaneness, nonsense, and distraction," that no other member could get a word in edgewise — a hardship that seems to have been particularly distressing to John Adams.[55] He became so talkative that he could not be trusted with secrets lest Hutchinson learn of them; and, in frequent fits of repentance, he lamented his incendiarism and blamed himself for all the evils of the day.   "I meant well," he exclaimed to Hutchinson, "but am now convinced I was mistaken.   Cursed be the day I was born." [56]   Such behavior cost Otis the last shreds of influence with the Whigs.   He was left out of the Boston seat in the elections of 1770 and Sam Adams stepped into his place as leader of the Whig Party.

Otis took his dismissal hard.   When he learned that Sam Adams had dished him, Otis told John Adams that he was "a d——d Fool for not taking Warning by his Fate" — advice which may have had something to do with Lawyer Adams's decision to wash his hands of Boston politics and beat a retreat to Braintree.[57]   Harassed by doubts, tortured with the realization that revolutionary movement had passed beyond his control, and nagged by a Tory wife whose "curtain lectures" probably hastened his insanity, Otis became the most pathetic figure in the Whig Party.   In the spring of 1770, he was seized with a "mad freak" in which he fired guns from his windows and broke the windows in the Town House.   He drank himself into a frenzy, although, as Hutchinson said, "the partition was al-

---

[54] *The Writings of Samuel Adams*, I, 380–386.

[55] *The Works of John Adams*, II, 227.

[56] *Bernard Papers*, XII, Thomas Hutchinson to Francis Bernard, Nov. 27, 1769.

[57] Peter Oliver, 117.   Hutchinson, III, 339.

ways very thin." The man whose writings and oratory had
set fire to the colonies now became a local nuisance whose
"drunken distracted frolicks" scandalized his neighbors. He
was the sport of young Tory lawyers; and his own practice
steadily dwindled until finally he was bound hand and foot,
loaded into a chaise, and carted out of Boston, an apparently
hopeless maniac. Hutchinson, believing he had seen the last
of Otis, wrote an epitaph: "He has been as good as his Word,"
said the governor, "set the Province in a flame and perished in
the attempt." [58]

Many of Otis's former followers were not sorry to see him
out of the way. The revolutionary movement in Massachusetts had long since swept past him and left him far in its wake:
by 1770, his views were considered so conservative that Tories
used his writings to support their arguments. "I shall rely
solely on him [Otis]," declared a Tory partisan. "He avows
the right of Parliament, full as extensively as I would carry it,
and that an imperium in imperio is a solycism in politics." As
Hutchinson said, James Otis had always opposed "in his calm
Moments" schemes to separate the colonies from the mother
country, and even "in his ravings . . . stopped when any thing
was said like denying the authority of an Act of Parliament &
pronounced it High Treason." [59]   Otis had begun the revolutionary movement, but, as the struggle against the mother
country became fiercer, he clearly showed that he was not of
the stuff of which revolutionists are made. Among such company as Sam Adams, William Molineux, and Dr. Thomas
Young, Otis's reverence for the mother country and insistence
upon orderly, constitutional change seemed the voice of an earlier
generation. Had Otis continued sane, he might have played
the part of a Mirabeau in the American Revolution; but after
his banishment there was no patriot leader in New England
capable of opposing Sam Adams and preserving the people's
loyalty toward the mother country. And whatever satisfaction Tories derived from Otis's fall was turned to gall and

---

[58] Mass. Archives, 27, *Hutchinson Corr.*, III, 231, 260. *Bernard Papers*,
XII, Andrew Oliver to Francis Bernard, Dec. 3, 1769.

[59] *Boston Chronicle*, March 5, 1770. Hutchinson, III, 339.

wormwood by the rise of "that more pernicious Devil Adams." [60]

Shortly after Otis disappeared from Boston, rumors began to spread of wholesale desertions of the nonimportation agreement by New England seaports. From the beginning of the boycott, Portsmouth, New Hampshire, and "the little, filthy, nasty, dirty colony of Rhode-Island" had been thorns in Sam Adams's flesh.[61] In Portsmouth, a "swarm of stupid Tories" kept the port open to British merchandise, thereby gaining a large part of Boston's trade in western Massachusetts. In Newport and Providence, Jews and Tories made huge profits by openly flouting the nonimportation agreement.[62] To dam these gaps through which British goods poured into the colonies, Sam Adams proposed that Boston break off all commercial intercourse with Portsmouth, Newport, and Providence until importations from the mother country ceased. The citizens quickly adopted his plan and so watchful were the Boston patriots that commerce stopped as completely as though the plague were raging in New Hampshire and Rhode Island. Nevertheless, the recalcitrant merchants continued to make inroads upon Boston's trade by selling British manufactures to rural New Englanders. In 1770, to Adams's consternation, it was reported that Salem, Marblehead, and Newburyport were likewise secretly importing prohibited British commodities. Because the embargo against New Hampshire and Rhode Island had failed to achieve its purpose and was regarded as the "meer impotent malice" of the Boston patriots, Sam Adams saw that he must use sharper weapons against the mutinous Massachusetts merchants.[63] At a meeting in Faneuil Hall it was voted to send a committee of inspection headed by William Molineux to visit all the suspected seaports and drive out the importers. By this stroke, Sam Adams hoped to strike terror among the Tories and put Boston in control of the nonimportation agreement throughout New England.

[60] *Chalmers Papers*, III, Extract of a Letter from Boston, Dec. 30, 1769.
[61] *Boston Gazette*, May 7, 1770.
[62] *Samuel Adams Papers*, Joseph Ward to William Cooper, July 13, 1770. *Boston Gazette*, Dec. 11, 1769.
[63] Mass. Archives, 26, *Hutchinson Corr.*, II, 484.

But the results of Molineux's inquisitorial tour of New England were a bitter disappointment to Sam Adams.   In Salem, Molineux and his party were awakened in the dead of night with news that a mob was assembling at the Long Wharf with enough tar and feathers for the entire Boston delegation.   Although the mob failed to attack, Salem was obviously not a healthy spot for the Bostonians, who resolved to move on to Newport to inspect the warehouses and throw out the "infernal cabal" that made the town a Tory stronghold.   But Molineux was given no opportunity to ferret out the guilty Rhode Islanders: the citizens of Newport were prepared to give him a warmer welcome than he had expected and "nothing was heard talk'd of but tarring and feathering of Molineux and his Party." [64] Indeed, Molineux thought himself fortunate to escape from Newport unscathed on the first boat to Providence.   After these rebuffs, it could no longer be doubted that nonimportation was a lost cause; and the unhappy Molineux admitted to the Providence Sons of Liberty that unless Boston was supported by other seaports, the boycott was doomed.   Boston alone could not hold out against Great Britain, yet New Englanders seemed so little disposed to aid the metropolis that they brought out for the visiting Boston committee of inspection the tar and feathers they usually reserved for Tories and customhouse officers.

Even the most uncompromising boycotter could now see that Boston was doing itself an injury by carrying on after New York and other seaports had been opened to British trade. Whigs as well as Tories began to raise the cry that Boston's folly was driving commerce to other towns.   Thanks to the politicians' obstinacy, the merchants lamented, the "antient channels of Commerce" were being diverted to enrich smaller ports at the metropolis's expense.   "Providence, which was the other day but a straggling village," they said, "does now bid fair to rival this town in greatness." [65]   The boycott had brought privation and distress to the common people of Boston: hundreds of workmen were unemployed and so restive that Tory gentlemen feared they would soon begin to "plunder the Rich"

[64] *Boston Gazette,* May 7, 1770; Aug. 20, 1770; Sept. 3, 1770.
[65] *Boston Chronicle,* Feb. 5, 1770.

and cut their throats.[66] Though Sam Adams said business was good and the suffering in Boston trifling, the depression created by the boycott was steadily undermining his power. The small shopkeepers whose loyalty to Adams had made possible the nonimportation agreement were the greatest sufferers: the wealthy merchants had laid in such large supplies of goods before the agreement went into effect that they made large profits from the boycott and drove their smaller competitors out of business. In the eyes of an increasingly large number of Bostonians, the town was "tottering on the brink of ruin" and Sam Adams and his fellow politicians were solely to blame.

Nevertheless, Adams made a last effort to continue the boycott by proposing to the Philadelphia merchants that a congress be held to form a new nonimportation agreement. The Philadelphians' refusal to take part in a congress was the deathblow to the boycott: the Boston merchants met at the British Coffee House and, without interference from Sam Adams, voted to import all British commodities except tea. Thus the agreement came to an end before any of the purposes Sam Adams prized most highly had been attained: Parliament had made no renunciation of its right to tax the colonies; the Commissioners of the Customs still collected "unconstitutional" taxes; and the tea duty remained a precedent for future taxation by the mother country. Throughout the colonies, Crown officers exulted over Sam Adams's discomfiture: "The Pride of the Bostonians is lowered," said General Gage. ". . . After a fair Struggle between Patriotism and Interest, the latter seems to have gained a compleat Victory." [67] Here was more proof for His Majesty's Ministers of State that the disturbances in the colonies were the work of a few blustering politicians and that the mass of the people were unalterably loyal to the mother country.

Englishmen might well believe they had little further to fear from American patriots. The union of the colonies was

[66] Mass. Archives, 26, *Hutchinson Corr.*, II, 359, 500. *Letters of James Murray Loyalist*, edited by N. M. Tiffany (1901), 132. *Boston Chronicle*, Feb. 5, 1770. Andrew Oliver, *op. cit.*, I, Andrew Oliver to Francis Bernard, Nov. 21, 1769.

[67] *The Correspondence of General Thomas Gage*, edited by C. E. Carter (1931), II, 561.

completely at an end. At no time since the Stamp Act had
Sam Adams's dream of a united America appeared more remote than in 1770 when the provinces fell to quarreling among
themselves over the blame for the failure of the nonimportation
agreement. The Philadelphia Sons of Liberty upbraided New
York's "abandoned Perfidy and Parricide" in importing British
merchandise and voted to break off all commercial intercourse
with New York and avoid the town "as they would a poisoned
City, lest they should be scabb'd with their Principles, as well
as corrupted with their Goods." [68] At a huge meeting under
their Liberty Tree, the Charleston, South Carolina, patriots
declared they would not trade with New York until the citizens
atoned "for their treacherous Separation from their Countrymen." [69] The quarrel between New York and Boston was
particularly bitter: as Hutchinson said, "our People are in a
perfect Rage against New York." [70] Bostonians railed against
the "perfidious Yorkers" who, in turn, denounced the "vile
and scandalous Behaviour of the Town of Boston . . . the
Common Sewer of America." [71] Each town accused the other
of secretly breaking the agreement and making profits behind
a screen of patriotism and self-sacrifice: when it was shown that
over five thousand packs of playing cards had been imported
into Boston during the nonimportation agreement, New Yorkers asked "whether ALL those VIRTUOUS PLAYTHINGS were imported for the *sole* Use of the few CHURCHMEN who are in that
Colony?" John Mein had sown suspicion throughout the
colonies that the "saintish, canting, puritanical, grace-pouring-
down countenanced" New Englanders were pious rogues. Sam
Adams failed to convince Americans of Bostonians' honesty by
shipping the merchants' goods back to England, for it was
widely believed that Hancock's ship had been loaded with
"billets of wood, shavings and brick bats." In spite of Adams's
efforts to clear his fellow townsmen's skirts, it was said that the
"Boston way" of storing prohibited British merchandise was to

---

[68] *Boston Gazette,* July 30, 1770.
[69] *New York Gazette and Weekly Mercury,* Oct. 1, 1770.
[70] Mass. Archives, 26, *Hutchinson Corr.,* II, 523.
[71] *New York Gazette and Weekly Mercury,* Aug. 27, 1770.

place the goods in a warehouse with a convenient back door that might be opened unobserved in the small hours of the night.[72]

For this calamitous ending of the nonimportation agreement, Sam Adams blamed the merchants — those recreants who, "like a Spaniel meanly cringed & kiss'd the rod that whip'd them." [73] The lesson Adams learned from his failure in 1770 was that no trust could be placed in merchants whose eyes were fixed upon the profit-and-loss columns of their ledgers rather than upon colonial liberty, and who fell easy victims to "Court Influence." Adams now said he had expected the agreement to fail from the beginning because the merchants were guided by self-interest; it had, indeed, lasted longer than he hoped. But its results were so disastrous that he wished to forget the colonies had ever entered upon an economic war with Great Britain: Americans, he said, must again turn their attention to "our first grand object" — the union of the colonies — in order to repair the damage done by the merchants. Adams was wary of the trap in which he had once been caught: the merchants, he declared, had shown themselves "unworthy of any future Confidence" from colonial patriots.[74] He saw that the only way to make nonimportation effective was to place it entirely in the hands of yeomen and townspeople who, by refusing to buy from merchants handling prohibited British merchandise, would quickly put all importers out of business. "We can live without the baubles of Britain," said the Whigs. "If there are no purchasers there can not long be Importers; we shall save our money, and save our Country." Henceforth, Adams said, the "Edge of Resentment" against Great Britain must be kept sharp in order to encourage Americans to establish colonial manufactures and live as frugally as Old Romans. Thus, as early as 1770, Sam Adams outlined the plan of nonimportation adopted in 1774 after the passage of the Boston Port Bill. From 1770 until the end of the Revolution, Adams acted upon

---

[72] *New York Journal or General Advertiser*, July 19, 1770. *Massachusetts Gazette*, Jan. 11, 1776. *Boston Gazette*, Sept. 3, 1770.

[73] *Publications Col. Soc. of Mass.*, Transactions, XIX, 255.

[74] *The Writings of Samuel Adams*, II, 65, 307. William Pepperell to Arthur Lee, MS. Mass. Hist. Soc., Nov. 21, 1770.

the principle that it was the common people "who must, under GOD, finally save us." [75]

In reality, Sam Adams had no one but himself to blame for the plight in which the colonies found themselves in 1770. Nonimportation was an effective weapon against the mother country, but it could not work the miracles Adams demanded of it. It could not bring Parliament to abandon its claim of right to tax the colonies, nor could it procure the repeal of all Parliamentary legislation distasteful to the Whigs. Had the nonimportation agreement been confined merely to the removal of economic disabilities it might well have succeeded in its purpose, but Adams and his fellow politicians added so many political demands that failure was inevitable. Moreover, by hanging out the sign "No Compromise," Adams exposed himself to certain defeat and made it impossible for the colonists to withdraw with honor from the economic struggle with the mother country.

[75] *Boston Gazette*, Sept. 11, 1769; Oct. 15, 1770. *The Writings of Samuel Adams*, II, 58, 65.

IX

THE DECLINE OF THE PATRIOT PARTY

THE collapse of the nonimportation agreement and the acquittal of the British soldiers in the Massacre trials were the sharpest defeats yet suffered by the Massachusetts Whigs. For the first time in many years, Tories could toast Sam Adams's downfall with prospects of speedy success. An era of good feelings succeeded the five years of turbulence ushered in by the Stamp Act, and the revolutionary movement was brought to an almost complete standstill in the colonies. America was more peaceful than at any time since George Grenville first prodded the hornets' nest, and, although Sam Adams continued to shriek "oppression" and "tyranny" as lustily as ever, there were few to heed him. The Whig man-of-war, rigged for stiff gales, became becalmed in this unwonted tranquillity. Adams and his crew of "Mohawks" kept their eyes glued hopefully to the barometer for signs of storm, but the mass of colonists were content to drift with the tide and enjoy the calm. Adams was compelled to wait so long for a breeze — for fully two years the American colonies were not so much as mentioned in debates in the House of Commons — that mutiny broke out among the crew and skipper Adams came perilously near being thrown off the quarter-deck. And while the Whig leaders wrangled for the command and Whig principles went out of favor among the countrypeople, the Tories began to regain the ground they had lost since 1764. Even in Boston, Adams narrowly averted defeat at the hands of the revived Tory Party. But just when Sam Adams and the Whig Party seemed to have reached the lowest point of their fortunes, the British government again came to the rescue with a timely blunder.

In 1770 there was still a strong conservative spirit in New

England which the British government would have done well
to cultivate. The greater part of the people were thoroughly
weary of quarreling with the mother country and their demands
were so moderate that most of the generation that fought the
Revolution to establish American independence would have
been satisfied in 1770 if Great Britain had returned to the
colonial system in force before the Sugar and Stamp Acts. They
were overwhelmingly in favor of "recurring to first Principles
— the old Establishment upon which they have grown & flourish'd," rather than following Sam Adams along a slippery path
that led no one knew where.[1] "We wish nothing remov'd but
Innovations," they exclaimed: the Commissioners of the Customs should be withdrawn; the revenue acts should be repealed;
and the money collected from port duties for the regulation of
trade should not be used to make judges and governors independent of colonial legislatures. The charter of William and
Mary was regarded as the basis of a permanent union between
mother country and colony because it gave "ev'ry reasonable
Security to ye Nation & Government, for our Subordination."[2]
Although Sam Adams reëchoed his countrymen's longings to
return to the old colonial system, his sincerity is open to question. Because Adams always strove to be the spokesman of
the common man, he was forced to adjust himself to the slow
pace at which public opinion moved. The mass of the people
wished nothing more in 1770 than the "good old days" of
Pownall; hence, Adams took the stand that if Great Britain
reverted to its former imperial policy, the mother country
would "lose Nothing which she ought to retain" and Americans
would again become loyal, obedient subjects of King George.[3]
Yet it is probable that Adams would have been dismayed had
the British government taken him at his word. In spite of
his insistence that he wished to go back, not forward, Adams

---

[1] British Museum, King's MSS. 203, Lib. Cong. Transcript, Original Letters from the Rev. Dr. Cooper and Dr. Franklin, Samuel Cooper to Thomas
Pownall, Jan. 1, 1770. Letters of Thomas Cushing, *Mass. Hist. Soc. Collections* (1858), IV, Fourth Series, 357.

[2] British Museum, King's MSS. 203, Samuel Cooper to Thomas Pownall,
Jan. 1, 1770.

[3] *The Writings of Samuel Adams*, II, 57, 58.

already had visions of a new political and social order.   Since
the landing of British troops in Boston in 1768 he had regarded
independence as the only escape from British "tyranny."   Because he supposed "degenerate" Great Britain on the point of
slipping into the worst vices of the declining Roman Empire,
he was anxious to sever the ties between colonies and mother
country before the contagion spread to America.   Furthermore,
a return to the old colonial system would not settle the domestic
quarrels of Massachusetts or bring the high-flying Hutchinsons
and Olivers down to the dust where Adams hoped to see them.
Adams was far too astute a politician to believe his struggle
against Hutchinson would be made easier if the discord with
the mother country was brought to an end: tranquillity always works in favor of the conservative party and strengthens
the grip of "oligarchs."   His pious hankering for the "good
old days" of good will between colonies and mother country
was merely a pose struck to win public support.   To veil his
real aggressions upon British authority in the colonies, Adams
pretended to be a peace-loving colonist, desiring nothing so
much as peace and quiet, reluctantly driven by intolerable grievances into rebellion.   Adams's true element was rough water
— not the calm seas he professed to seek — and at heart he was
a revolutionist who longed to overthrow the Tories and sever
the bonds between mother country and colonies.

Perhaps the bitterest draught Sam Adams was forced to swallow after the failure of the nonimportation agreement and the
acquittal of the British soldiers was the appointment of Thomas
Hutchinson as royal governor of Massachusetts Bay.   Many
years before, James Otis had said that Hutchinson's elevation to
the governorship would be "as terrible to the honest part of
this Province as a Volcano or an Earthquake," and, since Otis
had made this dire prophecy, Hutchinson had made himself
even more feared by the Whigs.[4]   None of the Massachusetts
patriots seriously believed that the British government would
force their worst enemy upon them as governor.   But whoever
the Massachusetts Whigs opposed in Boston was certain to have

[4] Mauduit, LXXIV (1918), 76, 77.   *Boston Gazette,* June 18, 1770.
Peter Oliver, 133.

his fortune made at Westminster: Bernard had been made a baronet for the persecution he suffered at Sam Adams's hands and Hutchinson was appointed governor of the colony because it was recognized that for two decades he had been a bulwark of the royal government against Adams.   Furthermore, Hutchinson had been well seasoned as lieutenant governor for the part he was expected to play in restoring order in the province.   He was deeply ambitious of succeeding Bernard in the governor's chair and he had undertaken a vigorous campaign among his English friends to procure him the post.   But after the Boston Massacre and its ominous foreshadowing of conflict between Great Britain and the colonies, Hutchinson abruptly changed his mind and wrote to England to withdraw his name from consideration.   He was reluctant to enter the arena against Sam Adams and his "Mohawks" without even the support of a loyal Council.   Rather than undertake what he feared might prove a hopeless task, Hutchinson preferred to remain as Chief Justice — a comparatively safe haven against the storm he saw brewing in the colonies.   But before his letter expressing this decision reached England his commission as governor had already been dispatched.   Unable to flinch publicly by resigning, Hutchinson accepted the office and the quarrel with Sam Adams that had by 1771 become an inescapable part of its responsibilities.[5]

As Hutchinson had foreseen, his assumption of the governorship raised a tempest in the Whig teapot.   It availed him nothing to say that he had attempted to avoid the office: John Adams said in public that Hutchinson, far from declining, had schemed deliberately for the prize; and Sam Adams ridiculed the notion that he could have rejected an office "which his Soul is every day panting after & without the Possession of which his Ambition & Lust of Power will perpetually torment him."[6] The cause of the Adamses' alarm was the healthy respect they entertained for Hutchinson's ability as an "oligarch" and tyrant. Unlike most royal governors of Massachusetts Bay, Hutchinson

---

[5] Hutchinson, III, 257.

[6] *Israel Williams Papers*, MSS. Mass. Hist. Soc., Thomas Hutchinson to Israel Williams, Jan. 10, 1771.

had been born in the colony and, outside Boston, was popular among the people as a "native son" who had made good.   It touched the pride of many yeomen that the King had appointed one of their countrymen as governor.   Pious rustics who could not forget that Bernard had been a member of the Church of England were endeared to Hutchinson because of his strict Congregationalism.   Indeed, Hutchinson enjoyed the reputation in the colony of being an "eminent saint." [7]   Like Sam Adams, the "Saint" of the Whig Party, Hutchinson gained his ends by tact and subtlety.   He would have none of the forthright methods Bernard had unsuccessfully used in Massachusetts Bay; unlike that blunt English country gentleman who imagined that New Englanders could be bulldozed into loyalty to the Crown, Hutchinson knew how to handle the "Saints."

No sooner had Hutchinson taken the governor's chair than Sam Adams set out to prove he was the worst tyrant since the fall of the Roman Empire.   For the benefit of country people who were well disposed toward Hutchinson because he had been born in the province, Adams raked up "horrible examples" from Roman history calculated to terrify the most complacent; natives of Rome, Adams demonstrated, had always shown themselves to be the worst tyrants of their home town.   It was understandable that a "foreigner" like Bernard should join heartily in the British government's plan to snuff out colonial liberty, but when a man who was "bone of our Bone, & flesh of our flesh" aided the unholy work, he was a double-dyed villain. [8]   For colonists who believed Hutchinson a staunch friend to the Massachusetts charter there was, exclaimed Adams, a sharp awakening in store: the charter had no more dangerous enemy than Thomas Hutchinson, who was ready to undertake any oppression "for the sake of rising a single step higher," and who had already given notable proof of his real intentions by plotting the Stamp Act. [9]   There was no difference, Adams believed, be-

---

[7] *The Works of John Adams*, II, 189, 361, 362.   *The Writings of Samuel Adams*, II, 276.

[8] *Ibid.*, II, 67, 175, 207.

[9] *Ibid.*, II, 67, 201.   *The Works of John Adams*, II, 361, 362.

tween Hutchinson and Bernard except that they worked with different methods: where Bernard blustered and fumed, the "soft
& oily tongu'd" Hutchinson attempted to persuade New Englanders to do what they "would not be *driven* into by fleets &
armies." Of the two, Adams much preferred to deal with a
swaggering tyrant whose arbitrary acts kept the people sweating
for their liberties rather than with a despotically-minded "oligarch," such as Hutchinson, who worked in the dark with
gloves. In comparison with Hutchinson, Bernard was a blessing: "Happy indeed it was for the Province," Adams cried, that
Bernard had been governor, because his bullying had aroused
"such a Jealousy & Watchfulness in the people as prevented
their immediate & total Ruin." Instead of being a flattering
concession to New England, Hutchinson's appointment was
simply a step forward in the British government's new scheme
to tax the colonies: Hutchinson was expected to keep the people
calm and lull them "into that *quietude* and *sleep* by which
slavery is always preceeded." [10] Adams did not even spare
Hutchinson's repute as a Congregational saint. Because the
governor was present at an Episcopal christening, Adams in-
sinuated that he was about to go over to the Church of England; and, with a characteristic play upon New Englanders' religious prejudices, he said that Hutchinson venerated royal
instructions "as ever a poor deluded Catholic reverenc'd the
decree of Holy Father at Rome." [11]

But despite this abuse heaped upon the new governor, Sam
Adams was sorely disappointed to find how unshaken Hutchinson's "unbounded popularity" in the country remained.[12] In
the House of Representatives Adams was able to win a majority
of only one vote in preventing a congratulatory address being
sent to the governor; but the Convocation of Congregational
clergy — the "black regiment" that had done Otis and Adams
good service in spreading patriotic fervor over New England

---

[10] *Boston Gazette*, Sept. 13, 1773.   *The Writings of Samuel Adams*, II, 58,
165, 203, 245.
[11] *The Writings of Samuel Adams*, II, 41, 188.   *Boston Gazette*, April 1,
1771.
[12] *The Works of John Adams*, II, 295.

— outraged the Whigs by publicly complimenting Hutchinson upon his accession to the governorship. Adams was at first at a loss to explain the divines' backsliding, but he finally concluded that a few Tories had crept into the Ministry, where they were up to their old tricks of counterworking the Whigs. Because only a small minority of the Congregational clergy attended the convocation that voted to send its well-wishes to Hutchinson, Adams declared their address was nothing more than "the foul breath of sycophants and hirelings" which, had the whole body of clergy been present, would have been easily voted down. Nevertheless, Adams was dismayed to find the ministry riddled with Toryism and he urged that those who were responsible for the convocation's work be regarded in the same light as were the seventeen Tories who had voted to rescind the Massachusetts circular letter in 1768. It was not until 1773, when Benjamin Franklin put into Sam Adams's hands the means of destroying Hutchinson's popularity in New England, that the governor ceased to be a constant threat to the Whigs' power.

At the beginning of his administration, Hutchinson succeeded in putting a British garrison into Castle William behind the patriots' backs. Castle William, as has been seen, was held by Massachusetts troops whose questionable loyalty to Great Britain during such crises as the Massachusetts Convention of 1768 kept the Crown officers in chronic uneasiness. Late in 1770, Hutchinson received instructions from the British government which, he realized, could they be carried out without producing an explosion in the colony, would regain much of the ground lost when Boston Whigs had hustled British regulars out of the metropolis in the previous March. The governor was ordered in these instructions to exchange the colonial garrison at Castle William for British regulars. Hutchinson worked with such caution that, before Adams knew what had happened, the Massachusetts soldiers had been discharged and the fortress put in possession of redcoats. Moreover, as a further precaution, the British Ministry designated Boston as the headquarters of the royal men-of-war in North American waters. Thus, a permanent British garrison was placed within striking

distance of Boston, and the Sons of Liberty, who hoped to see
no redcoats or men-of-war closer than New York and Halifax,
found themselves within range of British cannon and bayonets.[13]

Because Castle William had been built by Massachusetts,
Adams regarded it as the colony's property to be used by the
Crown only after permission had been secured from the General
Court.   Yet Hutchinson had seized it for the King by distinctly
underhand methods: no pretense whatever had been made of
consulting the General Court.   With Boston "environ'd with
ships of war" and the fort surrendered to "foreign" troops who
had recently shed patriot blood, Adams again lost his self-com-
mand as he had when British soldiers were reported on the way
to Boston in 1768.   At a merchants' meeting in Boston, Adams
interrupted the proceedings with a fiery speech in which he accused Hutchinson of breaking the Massachusetts charter by
handing over the castle to the British government, but the merchants cut him short by protesting that this "was not the business
of the Meeting and repeatedly stopped him from going on."
This rebuff so little discouraged Adams that he was soon going
about Boston urging that twenty thousand men be raised in the
country to retake the fort.[14]   Had the need for such action
arisen shortly after the Massacre when Boston was regarded in
the country as a martyred town, Adams might have found embattled farmers pouring into the metropolis from every side;
but by November 1770, when Hutchinson tricked the colonial
garrison into surrendering Castle William and Sam Adams began
to talk war, New England yeomen were in no mood to follow
Boston into hostilities with the mother country.

The evidence unearthed at the Massacre trials gave New
England countryfolk a glimpse of "mobbish Bostonians" at
work — a spectacle that Adams always took great pains to conceal.   Proof of the mob's eagerness to scuffle with the soldiers,
the serious provocation given by Gray's ropewalkers, and the
suspicion that Sam Adams had deliberately planned an attack
upon the soldiers put the Massacre in very different light from

[13] Mass. Archives, 27, *Hutchinson Corr.*, III, 10, 14, 24, 392, 393.
[14] *Ibid.*, III, 3, 60.   *Massachusetts Spy*, June 13, 1771; Nov. 26, 1773.

that shed by Adams's *Narrative*.   To counteract these damaging disclosures, Adams wrote his "Vindex" articles in the *Boston Gazette* and sent copies of the *Narrative* to New England innkeepers in order that their guests might be provided with racy literature — "And bitter reading they were," said a Tory, "for they were wrote with a Pen dipped in the Gall of Asps." [15]

Despite Adams's energetic whitewashing, country people began to suspect that Boston was not as pure and holy as the Whigs painted it; and the Tories were at their ears whispering that "the Town has by its rashness bro't all this Mischief upon us." [16] It became common to hear yeomen openly declare that Bostonians were to blame for the Massacre; and in most parts of New England the bitterness that had been heaped upon the soldiers was now turned against the townspeople.   "From the Borders of Connecticut all the Way to Boston," countrymen denounced the metropolis for their misfortunes and threatened to throw off its leadership.[17]   John Mein's exposure of Boston's secret importations during the boycott deepened rural distrust: "I hate them [Bostonians] from my very soul," exclaimed a countryman to John Adams.   "Great patriots! were for non-importation, while their old rags lasted; and, as soon as they were sold at enormous prices, they were for importing; no more to be heard about manufactures, and now, there is a greater flood of goods than ever were known."   Once Boston's spell over the country was broken, the delighted Tories found the old reverence for government reappearing and the people beginning to "look round them with astonishment and . . . willing to hear with both Ears."   Many feared to plunge into the "savage state" toward which the patriots seemed headed; unless the colony was to feel the "terrible effects of a state of Anarchy," it was said, royal authority could no longer be treated with contempt.   Hutchinson reported to the British ministry that there was more "general appearance of Contentment" in Massachu-

---

[15] Peter Oliver, 100.

[16] *Boston Gazette*, Sept. 24, 1770.

[17] Mass. Archives, 25, *Hutchinson Corr.*, I, Henry Young Brown to Thomas Hutchinson, Nov. 28, 1770, III, 72.

setts Bay than at any time since the Stamp Act.[18]   The tide ran
so strongly against Boston that Hutchinson had hope of dam-
ming up Whiggery in the metropolis and making Tories of New
England farmers; the time had come, he believed, to strengthen
royal government in Massachusetts by changing the Massachusetts charter and abolishing Boston's "pestilential" town meetings for a corporate form of government such as New York's.[19]

The Tories' strategy was to stir up antagonism between Boston and the interior by painting the metropolis as a hotbed of
irreligion and the patriots themselves as blasphemous free-
thinkers.   Boston put men in power not because of their morals
or religion but because they bawled loudest for liberty, cried
Tory partisans; the only standard in the metropolis was whether
candidates hated King and Parliament.   Had Massachusetts
Bay preserved the high ideals of the Puritans, conservatives
believed, Boston would be at "the tail instead of the head of
the province."   They were at a loss to explain how New Englanders, the descendants of Puritans, came to be guided by such
"thorough-paced infidels, and virulent opposers of Our holy
RELIGION" as Dr. Thomas Young and William "Paoli" Molineux.   Pious yeomen were frequently reminded that Molineux
"ridicules and sets at nought" all religion and that Dr. Young
was a notorious scoffer; indeed, the doctor was raked over the
coals so frequently for infidelity that he complained the Tories'
inquisitorial methods were more fit for "the meridian of Madrid
than Roxbury or Boston." [20]   Sam Adams rushed into print
with a rousing defense of Dr. Young, proving by illustrations
from Greece and Rome that pagans could be as great statesmen
as Christians.   Dr. Young, Adams exclaimed, was an "un-
wearied assertor of the rights of his countrymen" who should

[18] *Boston Gazette*, Dec. 24, 1770.   *The Works of John Adams*, II, 265,
266.   Mass. Archives, 25, *Hutchinson Corr.*, I, Henry Young Brown to
Thomas Hutchinson, Nov. 28, 1770.   *Boston Evening Post*, June 3, 1771;
April 6, 1772.   *Mass. Hist. Soc. Proceedings* (1882), XIX, 132.   *Chalmers
Papers*, III, Thomas Hutchinson to Lord Hillsborough, Jan. 24, 1772.
[19] Public Record Office, Colonial Office, Class or Series 5, 245, Lib. Cong.
Transcript, Thomas Hutchinson to ——, Jan. 22, 1771.   Mass. Archives,
27, *Hutchinson Corr.*, III, 150.
[20] *Boston Evening Post*, March 16, 1772.   *Boston News Letter*, Nov. 26,
1772.   *Boston Chronicle*, Feb. 19, 1770.

be judged by his patriotism, not by his religious opinions.[21]   Sam Adams himself was too pious to be open to attack on the score of irreligion, but Tories made the most of his shady record as a tax collector.

While painting Boston in the blackest colors, Tories pictured Massachusetts Bay as a prosperous, thriving colony, disturbed only by a "few gloomy discontented mortals" who croaked dismally of tyranny and oppression.   Whereas Adams summed up the grievances of Massachusetts, Tories weighed its blessings: the low indebtedness of the province; the light taxes; the flourishing state of commerce; and the roads crowded with "Coaches, Chariots and Chaises" whose well-to-do occupants had no desire to reopen the controversy with the mother country.   Conservatives pointed out that the mother country had dropped its quarrel with the colonies: Parliament seemed to have forgotten their existence and the Ministry had promised not to attempt to raise a large revenue from America.   At no time since the Stamp Act had Great Britain appeared more inclined to use leniency towards the colonies; and many loyal provincials believed that Parliament kept up its claim to the right of taxation solely to prevent Americans from making good their demand that they be exempt from Parliamentary taxation.[22]   Tea was cheaper in Massachusetts than in England, and the clamor raised by Boston merchants and patriots against the Sugar Act of 1764 had been silenced by reducing the duty on molasses to one penny per gallon.   As for those Boston Whigs who still continued to groan of British tyranny, Tories declared that they would be satisfied only when Massachusetts had been made "totally democratical" and independent of Parliamentary sovereignty.[23] Hutchinson and his friends appealed to all supporters of royal government to muzzle these grumblers who disturbed Massachusetts' honeymoon with George III; conservatives, they claimed, should go to the polls with the slogan, "All 's Well in Massachusetts Bay" and sweep Adams and his crew out of office because they were kindling discontent at a time when all

[21] *The Writings of Samuel Adams*, II, 376, 378.
[22] *Massachusetts Gazette*, Jan. 2, 1772.   Hutchinson, III, 332.
[23] *Boston Evening Post*, May 27, 1771.

good citizens should be quietly enjoying the prosperity brought them by King George's benevolent rule.

But when the Tories congratulated themselves upon the end of the Whig "tyranny" and the "expiring efforts" of Sam Adams's party, they rejoiced too soon.   However peaceable the country, in the seaport towns where the revenue acts and the Commissioners of the Customs were standing grievances, Sam Adams still held his own.   Hutchinson said that if the patriot party was dying, it was dying hard; and it took such an unconscionable long time that he began to suspect that what he had at first thought was good will toward royal government was in reality merely "sullen discontent." [24]   Even the cessation of intercolonial correspondence between the Sons of Liberty did not make all Tories feel safe: Hutchinson said there could never be real security because the provinces were not distinct islands and Boston was not placed far out in the Atlantic.[25] Adams and other Whig chiefs had escaped unscathed for their work in the Massachusetts Convention and the nonimportation agreement in spite of the Tories' warnings that there would be no lasting peace in Massachusetts until the patriot party had been forcibly broken up.   "If Parliament dont give us a flogging," said a conservative, "we shall be as rampant as ever." Most disquieting of all to the Tories was the fact that there was no sign of weakening in Sam Adams: he kept on dealing out "malicious Strokes" in the newspapers, and passers-by who saw a light burning late at night in his room knew that he was writing against the Tories.   "If it was not for 2 or 3 Adamses," said Hutchinson, "we should do well enough."   Although the governor was unable to understand John Adams's obstinacy because he seemed "when he began life to promise well," there was nothing surprising in Sam Adams's stubbornness.   "He never appear'd different from what he does at present," Hutchinson said, and added grimly, "I fear never will."   It was useless to tempt Sam Adams with bribes and there was no office at the governor's disposal which seemed likely to purchase his silence.   Yet it was clear that he must be quickly put out of the

[24] Mass. Archives, 27, *Hutchinson Corr.*, III, 172 236.
[25] *Ibid.*, 243.

way. "I doubt," said Thomas Hutchinson, "whether there
is a greater Incendiary in the King's dominions or a man of
greater malignity of heart, or who less scruples any measure
ever so criminal to accomplish his purposes; and I think I do
him no injustice when I suppose he wishes the destruction of
every Friend to Government in America." [26]

Sam Adams could not remain idle while Tories sowed suspicion of Boston in the country and bottled up Whig principles in
the metropolis. "That Fiend Hutchinson" might attempt to
separate town and country, but Adams believed that New England yeomen were too wise "to be catch'd in such a snare." [27]
Nevertheless, Adams saw that the country was rapidly cooling
and that farmers were becoming "too unconcern'd Spectators"
of the British government's attacks upon colonial liberty. [28]
Before rural New England was entirely weaned away from
the metropolis by the "contemptible wretches" who were busy
with their "old Tricks to divide the Country from the town,"
Adams proposed to administer some particularly stiff doses of
counter-propaganda. He and his assistants in the *Boston Gazette* attempted to convince the country people that Bostonians
were orderly, long-suffering patriots who mobbed only when
their oppressions became intolerable; who were zealous for the
rights of New England, not merely of Boston alone; and who
were on *"one bottom"* with their rural supporters. [29] But it was
apparent that if yeomen were to become as fiery Whigs as were
the Boston Sons of Liberty it was necessary to bring the menace
of tyranny to their very doors. Bostonians had borne the brunt
of the British government's severities: while Commissioners of
the Customs and British army officers enforced acts of Parliament
in the metropolis, the rural population derived most of its ideas
of tyranny from reading the Boston newspapers. The townspeople really tasted British despotism over the colonies: it was
the countryfolk who, inspired by Sam Adams, "snuffed tyranny
in every tainted breeze." Adams set out to arouse the farmers

[26] Mass. Archives, III, 102, 104, 437.
[27] *The Writings of Samuel Adams*, II, 111.
[28] *Ibid.*, II, 334.
[29] *Boston Gazette*, Sept. 24, 1771; March 23, 1772. *Massachusetts Spy*,
Sept. 3, 1772.

by predicting that their lands would be heavily taxed or forcibly taken from them by the British government and handed over
to court favorites and "King's Friends." If Great Britain
could take money out of the pockets of colonial merchants, it
could dispossess farmers of their land — and Adams had no
doubt that the Ministry would do so the moment it saw an
opportunity. The stage properties with which Adams usually
terrified his countrymen were the clanking chains and groans
of slavery to British "tyranny," but to convince New Englanders that their homesteads were in danger of confiscation or
ruinous taxation he was forced to turn on his horrors full blast.
He declared that as soon as port duties had been saddled upon
the colonists quitrents would follow: "If the breath of a british
house of commons can originate an act for taking away all our
money, our lands will go next or be subject to rack rents from
haughty and relentless landlords who will ride at ease, while
we are trodden in the dirt." [30] A British minister might seize
colonial lands to give huge estates to hangers-on at the court,
and New England yeomen be compelled to choose between serf-
dom or the repurchase of their farms from royal favorites.
Those who remained in possession of their estates would find
themselves in worse plight than those who gave up the struggle: such a plague of taxes would descend upon them that
they would soon be degraded into "mere Hewers of Wood and
Drawers of Water" to English landlords. There would be
window taxes, hearth taxes, land taxes, poll taxes, and these
oppressions were simply a prelude "for reducing the country
to lordships." [31]

Although this "perpetual incantation" brewed in Boston by
Sam Adams was one of the most powerful means of transforming rural conservatism into rebellion against Great Britain, the
patriots had little proof to support their fears of crushing taxation and colonial baronies. They attempted to raise an alarm
over the activities of Governor Tryon of New York in ejecting

[30] *The Writings of Samuel Adams*, II, 359. *Boston Gazette*, Dec. 23,
1771; Aug. 17, 1772. Hutchinson, III, 351.
[31] *Independency the Object of the Congress in America* (London, 1776),
18.

settlers in the New Hampshire grants, but the situation there was unique and could hardly be regarded as an instance of British land grabbing that endangered the security of Massachusetts farmers. Adams emphasized the grievances that still existed in Massachusetts Bay to expose the pitfalls in British policy. He pointed out that the Massachusetts charter was still unrecognized by the British government as a "Sacred Ark" of liberty; Admiralty Courts and Commissioners of the Customs continued to enforce "unconstitutional" laws; a fleet and army were stationed in the province without the consent of the House of Representatives; and Parliament kept up its claim to the right of taxation.[32] The root of all colonial grievances, in Adams's eyes, was Parliamentary taxes — "as arbitrary a tribute as ever the Romans laid upon the Jews" — which made the colonists' property insecure.[33] But the tea duty was the only considerable source of revenue that remained of the revenue acts, and Parliament showed little inclination to make further experiments in colonial taxation. Furthermore, however dangerous in tendency, the tea duty was deprived of most of its sting by the smugglers who swarmed in every colonial seaport and supplied the market with Dutch contraband. Indeed, Adams was hard pressed to discover evidence of British oppression with which to arouse the apprehensions of his readers in the *Boston Gazette*. He was forced to go back as far as the Stamp Act in search of padding for those "dreadful scarecrows" which had made Americans tremble for their liberties. Tories rejoiced to see how low Adams was running in propaganda: he was, said Hutchinson, dusting off his old bugbears and "raking the Ashes of Old Newspapers" in quest of a fresh supply of "Chaff & stubble" for his followers.[34] Unquestionably, he needed new tyranny and violent aggression from the mother country before he could hope to regain the ground lost by the nonimportation fiasco and the acquittal of the soldiers. But in only one significant instance did the British government

[32] *Massachusetts Spy*, June 4, 1772. *The Writings of Samuel Adams*, II, 33, 53, 76, 184, 312, 313, 316, 317.

[33] *The Writings of Samuel Adams*, II, 184.

[34] Mass. Archives, 27, *Hutchinson Corr.*, III, 126. *Massachusetts Gazette*, June 4, 1772.

oblige Adams by giving him a burning grievance with which to keep warm the controversy between mother country and colonies.

By means of royal instructions, the Massachusetts General Court was moved from Boston to Cambridge. Massachusetts Crown officers had urged for many years that the legislators be bundled out of the metropolis to some quieter spot where mobs and Sons of Liberty were rarely seen. Although both Hutchinson and Bernard preferred Salem or Concord to Cambridge as being farther away from Boston, the British Ministry designated Cambridge as a meeting place for the General Court. Its removal promised a real-estate boom to Cambridge, but Harvard College authorities did not welcome the Massachusetts legislators with open arms: they were reluctant to turn the college into an arena for Adams's and Hutchinson's squabbles and to make politicians of a student body "already enough taken up with politics." [35] Adams himself regarded the removal to Cambridge as bitterly as though the General Court had been banished to the wilderness. He declared that the Legislature had been torn out of its "ancient, established and only convenient Seat in Boston" and sent to Harvard College "to the great Inconvenience of the Members, and Injury of the People, as well as Detriment to that Seminary of Learning." When the General Court sat in Boston, the country delegates were so lavishly "dinnered & supper'd" by the town Whigs that Tories complained they were lured into the radical ranks, and Hutchinson at one time even considered having the influential members of the House of Representatives at his table every day in order to give them an antidote to the "Poison" Adams and Hancock dished out.[36] In Cambridge, however, the patriots were unable to regale the rural delegates; and the countrymen were disgruntled to find themselves prevented from transacting their usual trading business in the metropolis and saving living expenses by being "treated & caressed" by

[35] Letters from Andrew Eliot to Thomas Hollis, *Mass. Hist. Soc. Collections*, Fourth Series, IV, 447. *Chalmers Papers*, III, Thomas Hutchinson to Lord Hillsborough, April 9, 1770.

[36] Thomas Cushing to Benjamin Franklin, Nov. 6, 1770, MS. Mass. Hist. Soc. Peter Oliver, 140. Mass. Archives, 27, *Hutchinson Corr.*, III, 340.

the Boston Whigs. Adams complained that the representatives lost the benefit in Cambridge of listening to "the Reasonings of the People without Doors," but Tories suspected that his discomfiture was principally owing to the fact that he had lost the aid of his "Mohawks" in influencing the voting. But few delegates, whether townsmen or countrymen, relished exchanging their snug quarters in the Boston Town House for the cold, fireless Harvard chapel.[37]

In protesting against the removal of the General Court to Cambridge, Sam Adams struck the shrewdest blow against royal authority that had ever been delivered in the colonies. Because Hutchinson acted under royal instructions in calling the assembly to Cambridge, Adams put forward the doctrine that the royal prerogative could be used only for the good of the community and that whenever it injured the people it was not binding. What stiffened conservatives with alarm was that the community itself, in Adams's eyes, was to judge whether the exercise of the prerogative was beneficial or harmful and to support or nullify as it saw fit. Clearly, Adams argued, the King as well as Parliament was bound by natural laws "antecedent & paramount to all positive Laws of Men." [38] Without the aid of natural law, Adams would have been unable to justify his theory of a prerogative limited by popular consent. Positive law yielded him nothing because royal instructions, in the eighteenth-century British Empire, were regarded as the constitutions of the American provinces and paramount to colonial charters. Hence Adams was compelled to appeal directly to natural law without even a preliminary effort to argue from positive law. He declared that the vast distance between the colonies and mother country had made it impossible for statesmen at Westminster to judge provincial matters: such exercise of the prerogative as proroguing or removing the Massachusetts General Court should be decided by the Massachusetts governor on the spot, not by Lord Hillsborough, who knew

[37] Peter Oliver, 140. *The Writings of Samuel Adams*, II, 27. *Bernard Papers*, VIII, Bernard to Thomas Hutchinson, Oct. 7, 1770. British Museum, King's MSS. 203, Lib. Cong. Transcript, Samuel Cooper to Thomas Pownall, March 26, 1770.

[38] *The Writings of Samuel Adams*, II, 23, 24, 26.

nothing of local conditions and who acted upon stale second-hand information. Adams feared that if instructions were to be made "rules of administration," binding upon colonial legislatures, America would be under a despotism fully as oppressive as Parliament's: between the tyranny of the Crown and the House of Commons there was little to choose.[39]   Once royal instructions were recognized as laws, Adams's theory that the constitution must be permanent and fixed was overthrown quite as effectively as though Parliament's enactments were accepted as the supreme law of the colonies: the constitution would be "as vague as the Will of a Minister" and the Massachusetts charter would be little better than a scrap of parchment.   The General Court would be put in "a more humiliating state than even the parliaments of France" and the governor of the province would be a puppet moved by the Ministry at Westminster.[40]

Like other Sons of Liberty, Sam Adams was a staunch supporter of royal authority only as long as the King did not exercise his prerogative in the colonies.   When the trial came, Adams showed no more reluctance in attacking the Crown's "unconstitutional" powers than Parliament's; and he spoke as early as 1770 of making an "Appeal to Heaven" against George III.[41]   It is clear that Adams had little reverence for kingly power: when Parliament threatened colonial liberties, Adams exalted the Crown as the sovereign power, but when the royal prerogative in turn endangered American rights, he was prepared to destroy its jurisdiction.   If George III wished to be "King of America" and remain on good terms with Sam Adams, he would have to keep his hands strictly out of colonial affairs and be content to remain a figurehead at the pleasure of Sons of Liberty who were ready to reach for their muskets the moment they believed he had overstepped his powers. After Sam Adams had whittled away the prerogative, George III would have had a slender rod indeed with which to rule his

[39] *The Writings of Samuel Adams*, II, 3, 31, 166, 167, 227.
[40] *Boston Gazette*, Nov. 5, 1770; June 17, 1771; March 4, 1772; March 23, 1772.
[41] *The Writings of Samuel Adams*, II, 22, 23.

American subjects. George soon made it clear that instead of
the fragile birch proffered him by Sam Adams, he would be
satisfied with nothing less than a stout club to beat loyalty
into his seditious overseas subjects.

At the same time that Adams vigorously pared the royal prerogative he was careful not to touch the person of the King.
The patriots still kept up the fiction that "good King George"
dearly loved Americans and would set matters right in the colonies the moment he got out of the clutches of his ministers.
Even Sam Adams solemnly declared that the instructions which
sent the General Court to Cambridge were the "subtle Machi-
nations, and daring Encroachments of wicked Ministers" to
which the King was an innocent bystander.[42] The people were
not yet ready to hear George III denounced as a scoundrel: had
Sam Adams openly assailed the King in 1771, he would have
alienated the greater part of his followers and convinced English Whigs who supported the colonies in the House of Commons that American Whigs were a set of rebellious republicans
bent upon setting up an independent commonwealth. In throwing off Parliament's sovereignty, popular conservatism forced
the Whig leaders to move so slowly that it was not until the
eve of the Declaration of Independence that Parliament was
denied all authority over the colonies. In the difficult operation of slicing away George III's sovereignty over the colonies,
even greater delicacy was required. Popular veneration for
the Crown compelled Sam Adams to handle George gently
and to join in the cry raised by the Sons of Liberty: "We are
rebels against parliament; — we adore the king."[43] Nevertheless, some Sons of Liberty had already begun to suspect that
George III was the greatest rascal in the kingdom. As early
as the Stamp Act days, Thomas Chase, a Son of Liberty and
Boston brewer, had expressed the opinion that George was no
better than Charles I and deserved the same end. There is
no reason to suppose that Sam Adams entertained a much higher

[42] *The Writings of Samuel Adams*, II, 33, 34. *Boston Evening Post*,
Aug. 20, 1770. *Boston Gazette*, April 27, 1772.
[43] *Orations, delivered at the request of the Inhabitants of the Town of
Boston to commemorate the evening of the Fifth of March, 1770* (1807), 7.

regard for the King, in spite of his efforts to make the Crown the sole sovereign of America.   Adams was in close touch with correspondents in England who gave him good grounds for believing that King George was no righteous monarch led astray by his ministers, but a despotical-minded young man who had the Ministry securely in his own pocket.[44]

By denying the King's right to move the General Court about the province at will, Adams startled Hutchinson, who began to fear that royal authority in the colonies would go the way of Parliament's.   It seemed evident that men who denied the King's right to instruct his governors would soon begrudge him the right of appointing them.   Hutchinson was convinced that the struggle between himself and Adams had reached its crisis: if Adams succeeded in blunting the edge of royal preroga-tive, no Crown officer could stand against the Whigs.   Conse-quently, the governor was resolved to keep the legislature in Cambridge until the King's right to fix its place of meeting had been positively acknowledged by the General Court.   Sam Adams, on the other hand, was equally determined to march the assembly back to Boston and to take up the cudgels with King George after his successful bouts against George Grenville and Charles Townshend.

Unfortunately for Hutchinson's plans, the Tory revival in Massachusetts had not succeeded in wresting control of the House of Representatives from the Whigs.   Tories recognized that until Sam Adams's hold on the General Court was broken, Massachusetts Bay would not be "as decent & polite" as its neighbors, but few of them showed any eagerness to meet the patriot leader upon his own ground.[45]   Even Ruggles, Wor-thington, and Murray — redoubtable figures in the "Tory County" of Worcester — remained at a comfortable distance from the House of Representatives.[46]   Hutchinson declared

---

[44] *Chalmers Papers*, III, Information of Richard Silvester. *Samuel Adams Papers*, Arthur Lee to Sam Adams, Dec. 22, 1773. *Boston Gazette*, Aug. 31, 1772.

[45] Mass. Archives, 27, *Hutchinson Corr.*, III, 319. *Israel Williams Papers*, MSS. Mass. Hist. Soc., II, 167.

[46] *Massachusetts Spy*, June 25, 1772. Mass. Archives, 26, *Hutchinson Corr.*, II, 514; *Ibid.*, 27, III, 332.

that so many of his supporters stayed away that the meetings of the General Court resembled a "rump," but his pleas failed to arouse any considerable number of Tories who were capable of bearding Adams in such a Whig den as the House of Representatives. On almost every question, the patriots were in a majority; the Massachusetts state papers were still filled with the same "seditious spirit" that Adams exhibited in the Boston newspapers; and conservatives continued to be driven out of public life and compelled to "quit the helm to the bold Adventurers." Hutchinson could not even regain possession of the Council, which remained under the control of James Bowdoin, who carried out the orders sent him by that "pale, lean Cassius," Sam Adams.[47]

Sam Adams endangered this Whig supremacy in the House of Representatives by his uncompromising demand that the royal governor return the General Court to Boston regardless of royal instructions. Because Hutchinson stubbornly refused to give way until the Crown's right to move the Assembly had been explicitly recognized, a deadlock was created which sorely tried the patience of the Whig rank and file, many of whom were eager to patch up a compromise which would leave the principle of royal prerogative untouched yet bring the legislature back to Boston. The legislators were anxious to leave their cheerless quarters in Cambridge, and the attack upon the King's authority did not prove as popular in Massachusetts Bay as had the struggle against Parliament. All these circumstances caused murmurings in the Whig Party against Sam Adams's leadership, but the first serious opposition sprang up in an unexpected quarter.

It was James Otis — the erstwhile "American Hampden" — who led the mutiny against Sam Adams. Otis had been carried out of Boston in 1770 in a strait-jacket, but early the next year he popped up again in the metropolis, apparently cured of his insanity, and was promptly elected to the House of Representatives. Otis's reverence for the British Crown had not been

[47] Mass. Archives, 26, *Hutchinson Corr.*, II, 522, 532, 547; III, 6, 164, 330. Andrew Eliot, *op. cit.*, II, Andrew Eliot to Francis Bernard, July 20, 1771.

swept away by the mounting revolutionary fervor in Massachusetts Bay: indeed, his quarrel with John Robinson, the Commissioner of the Customs who had clubbed him in a Boston tavern, was caused by Otis's indignation upon learning that Robinson was picturing him to the British government as an enemy to the King. Such loyalty to the Crown made a break inevitable between Adams and Otis. In 1771, when Adams moved in the House of Representatives that no business be done except in Boston and launched into a bitter tirade against Hutchinson, the patriot benches were startled to see Otis rise in the governor's defense and declare that the Massachusetts General Court could be moved anywhere the Crown pleased — even to "Houssatonick" if it saw fit. Adams's motion was lost, and although Otis was unable to bring the General Court to end the quarrel and return to Boston, for a time it seemed that he might lead a conservative reaction against his former lieutenant. But the Tories soon saw that Otis was no great catch. Recurrent fits of insanity drove him permanently from politics within a few years. In 1772, he became chairman of the Boston committee of correspondence, but the days when the "great Leviathan" of the Whig Party swayed New England were forever ended.

Otis's revolt, however, was far less menacing to Sam Adams's leadership than was John Hancock's flirtation with the Tories. Hancock, as has been seen, was the financial backer of the patriot party. But patriotism had proved expensive to him — putting Adams's affairs to rights had been in itself a costly matter — and he was anxious to recoup his losses by minding his business, which, in his preoccupation with politics, he had permitted to run down. He had come out of the nonimportation fiasco with a badly battered reputation — for which he might thank Sam Adams and other politicians who had egged him on. Hancock's vanity was hurt and he began to feel that it was not proper for a gentleman of his wealth and importance to be on too close terms with politicians who had scarcely a shilling to lose and who were willing to ruin every merchant in Boston, himself not excepted, to gain their ends. Then, too, Adams seemed to be losing ground and Hancock was ambitious of seiz-

ing the Whig command: in 1771, Ezekiel Goldthwait, a Tory,
received more than double the number of votes cast for Sam
Adams in the election for registrar of deeds for Suffolk County.
Tories crowed "like dung-hill cocks" over this victory and
Adams's lieutenants began to murmur that his attack upon the
royal prerogative was breaking up the Whig Party.[48]   Early
in 1771, Hutchinson learned that Hancock and other "heroes
of liberty" were ready to turn against Adams and make terms
behind his back to return the legislature to the metropolis by
acknowledging the King's right.   But Hancock was too good a
pupil of Sam Adams's to burn his bridges behind him and rush
blindly into Hutchinson's hands: he chose rather to make alliances with both parties and sit safely on the fence as long as
it remained doubtful which was to be the winning side.   Nevertheless, Hancock's actions aroused great anxiety among the
Whigs: he broke with James Otis; took his legal affairs out of
John Adams's hands; was "very civil" to Hutchinson and accepted from him the appointment of colonel of cadets; stayed
away from the Whig Club for months at a time and got himself
an entirely "new set of acquaintances"; and seemed on the
verge of joining the Tory Club.   Still, Hancock did not go
so far as to cause a total breach between himself and Sam
Adams: even though he voted against Adams in the House
of Representatives, he continued to give him occasional lifts
in his chariot and left the door open for a future reconciliation.[49]

Hutchinson saw that Hancock was such a rare catch that it
would require all his skill in angling to land the Whig leader
safely in the Tory basket.   The governor had little hope of
making Hancock a whole-hearted Tory because he knew Hancock to be too fond of popularity to choose the forlorn and thorny
path trod by Massachusetts Tories.   His plan was rather to
lead Hancock on until his reputation as a patriot had been

[48] *The Works of John Adams*, II, 259.
[49] *Israel Williams Papers*, II, Thomas Hutchinson to Israel Williams,
Jan. 23, 1771.   Andrew Oliver, *op. cit.*, Andrew Oliver to James Gambier,
May 8, 1772.   *The Writings of Samuel Adams*, II, 296.   *The Works of
John Adams*, II, 306.   Mass. Archives, 27, *Hutchinson Corr.*, III, 286.
Gordon, III, 20.   *Mass. Hist. Soc. Proceedings*, XIX, 139.

so utterly ruined that it would be impossible for him to join
forces again with Sam Adams.[50]

Hancock probably did not suspect to what use he was to be
put by Hutchinson. His only thought was for personal popularity; and in the widespread uneasiness over the deadlock
between Adams and Hutchinson at Cambridge he saw his opportunity to make his reputation as a popular leader. He introduced a motion in the House of Representatives that the governor be petitioned to remove the General Court to Boston solely
on the ground that Cambridge was inconvenient — thus surrendering the principle at stake between Sam Adams and the
governor. Although Adams mustered a small majority to
defeat this proposal, Hancock resolved to make another effort.
Early in 1772, he and Cushing sounded Hutchinson on his terms
for returning the legislature to Boston. They were bluntly
told that if they still claimed the right to dictate to His Majesty
where the legislature should meet, they would not sit in Boston
while Hutchinson was governor of Massachusetts Bay. The
governor then warned Hancock and Cushing to beware of Sam
Adams's "art and insidiousness," which they would find pitted
against them if they attempted to compromise the quarrel.[51]
The two Whigs followed Hutchinson's advice, undermined
Adams's following in the House of Representatives, and
brought the General Court back to Boston in spite of Adams's
insistence that it remain in Cambridge without doing business
until the home government had acknowledged it had no right
to move the legislature from the Boston Town House. Although the victory was not as clear-cut as Hutchinson had
hoped for, it was unquestionable that the governor, with the
support of the conservative Whigs, had won a two years' struggle against Sam Adams and the radicals.[52]

The radicals were dismayed by this defeat and many hastened
to abandon the sinking ship. When it was rumored that the
Boston Sons of Liberty were to be punished by the British gov-

---

[50] Mass. Archives, 27, *Hutchinson Corr.*, III, 260, 286, 340.

[51] *Mass. Hist. Soc. Proceedings*, XIX, 138. Mass. Archives, *Hutchinson
Corr.*, III, 342.

[52] Hutchinson, III, 357.

ernment, some of the patriots were heard whispering among themselves that they had indeed gone too far.   The growing antagonism to the metropolis in rural New England disheartened many others: Dr. Thomas Young took passage for North Carolina and Dr. Benjamin Church, another of Adams's trusted disciples, secretly switched to the Tories and began parodying in the Tory newspapers the patriotic songs and political tracts he wrote for the Whigs.   There were "a Languor and feebleness" in Massachusetts, said John Adams, which "discouraged almost every good man in it"; and John Adams himself bid politics farewell, and retired to "still, calm, happy Braintree," thoroughly disillusioned with public life and resolved to mind his farm and office rather than listen again to that siren, Sam Adams, who still attempted to lure him back to Boston politics.[53] Other patriots were so "flattened away" by adversity that they talked more like Tories than Whigs.   As Governor Bernard had said many years before, the Boston Whigs seemed to be an "expiring Faction."

The decline of the Whig Party in Massachusetts was merely a reflection of what was occurring everywhere in the colonies. The New York Sons of Liberty were humbled by the conservatives in 1770; and the Philadelphia patriots, notorious in Boston for their lukewarmness, were unable to breast the current that set in against them after the collapse of the nonimportation agreement.   Even in Virginia, little was heard from the Whigs. Sam Adams was dismayed to find that the Southern newspapers which formerly inculcated Whig doctrines upon the people now contained little more than "Advertisements of the Baubles of Britain for sale."[54]   When Adams urged John Dickinson, the "Pennsylvania Farmer," to rouse the people from "dozing upon the Brink of Ruin," Dickinson politely declined.[55] In attempting to define the limits of Parliamentary authority over the colonies, Adams found that "the Silence of the other Assemblies of late upon every Subject that concerns the joynt

[53] Mass. Archives, 27, *Hutchinson Corr.*, III, 102, 173.   *The Works of John Adams*, II, 256, 257, 260, 305.   *Warren-Adams Letters*, II, 399 (Appendix).
[54] *The Writings of Samuel Adams*, II, 267.
[55] *Ibid.*, II, 392; III, 14.

Interest of the Colonies" made it impossible to determine what principles they held in common. Colonial jealousy again made itself felt, and many Massachusetts patriots suspected that the other colonies were more inclined to take advantage of them than to join with them in defending American liberty. With greater truth than Sam Adams cared to acknowledge, Tories warned New Englanders that if they took a radical step against the mother country they would be deserted by the other colonies, every one of which had made its peace with the British government.[56]

Still, Sam Adams gave no sign that he believed himself to be upholding a lost cause. Even after many of his firmest supporters had begun to give way and rural Massachusetts had turned against the Boston Whigs, he continued to talk as boldly as though he had all British America behind him. "All of them except Adams abate of their virulence," said Hutchinson, but as long as he continued to hold the fort the Tories could not free themselves from the fear that a bombshell would explode unexpectedly in their midst.[57] Adams had already resolved to be the last defender of popular liberty to give up the struggle: the prospect of being outnumbered by his enemies had no terrors for him because he believed it "no Dishonor to be in a minority in the Cause of Liberty and Virtue." "Where there is a Spark of patriotick fire," he exclaimed, "we will enkindle it."[58] Years later, when King George III asked Thomas Hutchinson to what he ascribed Sam Adams's power in New England, Hutchinson replied: "A great pretended zeal for liberty, and a most inflexible natural temper."[59] Tories might doubt the sincerity of Adams's patriotism, but they could not question his tenacity of purpose when he doggedly kept fighting long after the greater part of his followers had found safe seats along the side lines.

Because there was no guarantee of peace while Sam Adams remained in politics, the Tories determined to drive him from the

---

[56] *The Writings of Samuel Adams*, III, 13. *Massachusetts Gazette*, Feb. 6, 1772.

[57] Mass. Archives, 27, *Hutchinson Corr.*, III, 246.

[58] *Warren-Adams Letters*, I, 9, 14.

[59] *The Diary and Letters of Thomas Hutchinson*, edited by Peter Orlando Hutchinson, I, 167.

House of Representatives.   His failure to poll votes in recent
elections encouraged them to hope that a full-fledged mutiny
might be begun against him in Boston.   Their first step was to
turn upon Bostonians a deluge of propaganda that matched
Sam Adams's best efforts.   He was ironically hailed as the
"*truly patriotic* DICTATOR" of Boston whose predatory raids
upon the public treasury had resulted in the "insupportable
Town Tax" that had been laid upon the townspeople.[60]   Tory
partisans reminded the citizens of Sam Adams's readiness to
sacrifice the town's commercial prosperity during the nonimportation agreement in order to compel Parliament to grant
his impossible demands.   "Remember, my beloved Fellow-
Citizens," said one of Adams's enemies, "the commercial Trade
hath been violently expelled for four Years' past from this
Metropolis" and diverted to other seaports by Adams's folly —
which should teach the townspeople to be on guard against
men who did not have Boston's mercantile prosperity closest
to their hearts.   Yet, while Boston's trade was sinking and its
taxes mounting, Sam Adams, a public defaulter, was permitted
to go scot-free, and his henchman, William Molineux, made
off with more of the people's money.   The rise to power of
Adams and his satellites was, in the Tories' eyes, "the most
extraordinary phaenomenon that hath appeared in this city,
from its foundation"; even Andros and Randolph seemed
benevolent in comparison with this "unrelenting Tyrant" who,
with his "gang," would "monopolize every town office, suck its
vital blood and churn its gore to satiate their unbounded ambition." [61]

Conservatives marched to the polls in 1772 resolved to
oust Adams from his seat in the House of Representatives.
They failed to achieve this long-desired purge, but they
showed alarming strength against Adams.   Almost one third
of the total votes cast were against Adams, and he received
nearly two hundred less votes than the other successful candidates.   Thomas Cushing, the conservative patriot who had

[60] *Massachusetts Gazette*, Jan. 2, 1772; March 19, 1772.   *Boston Evening
Post*, March 23, 1772.
[61] *Massachusetts Gazette*, Feb. 6, 1772; April 19, 1772.   *Boston Evening
Post*, March 23, 1772.

opposed the war party in the Massachusetts Convention and had
joined Hancock in bringing the General Court to Boston, received 699 votes, whereas Adams polled only 505.[62]   It could
no longer be doubted that there was still life in "the *court* end
of the town" and that Boston was not past saving by the Tories.
Heartened by this promising beginning, the conservatives began
to form themselves into a "firm, compact body" — a "Phalanx"
that seemed likely to become increasingly formidable to the dis-
organized Whigs.[63]

But, in fact, the Tory Party had reached its high-water mark
and a swift ebbing followed this effort to swamp Adams in the
Boston elections.   The Tory menace now appeared so threatening that a cry was raised among the rank and file of the Whig
Party that Hancock and Adams make peace and present a
united front to their enemies.   After some persuasion, the two
Whig chiefs were brought together; and to prove that the reconciliation was complete, Hancock commissioned John Copley
to paint his and Adams's portraits.   As a final proof of friendship, Hancock hung the pictures side by side in his drawing-
room.

Sam Adams blamed the Tories' "scurvy trick of lying" for
his quarrel with Hancock.[64]   But Adams always saw Tories at
the bottom of any mischief and he held them responsible for
evils in which they had no hand.   It is clear that Tories had
done no more in 1772 than "blow the coals" that smouldered
between Hancock and Adams and hasten a disruption of the
Whig Party that had already begun.[65]   As Adams was to learn,
the differences between himself and Hancock had not been settled when Hancock hung their pictures together; for fourteen
years after the Tories had been exiled and the colonies made independent of the mother country, the two men were to be the

[62] *Massachusetts Gazette*, May 7, 1772. *Boston Town Records*, 18th
Report of the Record Commissioners (1887), 78.

[63] Andrew Oliver, *op. cit.*, II, Andrew Oliver to James Gambier, May 8,
1772. *Boston Gazette*, Nov. 18, 1771. Hutchinson, III, 356. *Otis
Papers*, MSS. Mass. Hist. Soc., Samuel Allyne Otis to Joseph Otis, April 15,
1771.

[64] *The Writings of Samuel Adams*, III, 23.

[65] Mass. Archives, 27, *Hutchinson Corr.*, III, 260.

bitterest political enemies in New England.   Actually there was little real friendship between Adams and Hancock: Hancock was eager to snatch the leadership of the patriot party from a man whom he secretly regarded as a plebeian wire-puller; and Adams, although he prized Hancock as a figurehead and financial godfather to the Whigs, distrusted him for a flighty young man of fashion whose life and ideals were decidedly un-Puritan. The two leaders had very different goals: Adams's purpose was to resurrect old-fashioned manners and morals and found a Puritan republic, whereas Hancock's dominant motive was to make himself popular and place himself at the head of a fashionable aristocracy.   So divergent were Adams's and Hancock's aspirations that, after the Revolution, they were to pursue each other as relentlessly as they had once hounded Tories together.

X

THE COMMITTEES OF CORRESPONDENCE

HANCOCK was once more back in the patriot fold after his flirtation with the Tories, but the Whig Party was still in the grip of depression. British tyranny was essential to the prosperity of Adams and the Whigs, yet the mother country seemed to have buried its dispute with the colonies. It would have been fortunate for the British Empire had this policy of "let sleeping dogs lie" been continued in the colonies. Since 1768, significant changes had taken place in Adams's attitude toward Great Britain which boded ill for the peace of the British Empire if the schemes of Grenville and Townshend were again revived by British imperialists.

After Lord North and the Tory Party came into power in England in 1770, Adams lost all faith in the British government and people. With Tory squires and placemen swarming in the House of Commons and edging Whigs out of high office, Adams considered that England was well on the way to a "total Depravation of principles & manners," if not already "irrecoverably undone." He no longer believed, as he had in 1766, that the colonists should pin their faith to British parliamentarians who had "distinguished themselves as the Guardians, under his Majesty, of the Rights of British American Subjects."[1] Instead of urging Americans to trust to the Whigs at Westminster, Adams now deplored the state of mind which manifested itself in "anxiously waiting for some happy Event" in England, after it had become clear that no good could be expected from the mother country. If Americans were to wait for justice from England, Adams exclaimed, they would wait until doomsday or until they had become "so accustomed to bondage, as to forget

[1] *The Writings of Samuel Adams,* I, 178; II, 230–233.

they were ever free." He regarded the House of Commons, traditionally the guardian of English liberty, as a tool in the Ministry's hands, bought and paid for by King George. Rather than lean upon the broken reed of English Whiggery, Adams declared that "America herself under God must finally work out her own Salvation" and fight her battle for liberty unassisted by English liberals.[2]

The regularity with which the colonies' petitions to King and Parliament reached the wastebasket of the Colonial Secretary soured Adams toward further petitioning for redress of grievances. "For God's sake," he asked, "what are we to expect from petitioning?" When the matter of an appointment of an agent to represent Massachusetts in London came before the General Court in 1770, Adams favored dropping the colonial agent altogether and waiting the British government's moves "with a Sullen Silence" until the ministers should find themselves "*at the end* of their Tether." It was not merely "ye Inutility of all remonstrances & Negotiations" that prompted Adams to throw over colonial agents, but the character of the man Massachusetts wished to make its London representative.[3] Benjamin Franklin was always disliked by the Adamses: John Adams believed him to be a scandalous old rake and Sam Adams distrusted him as a Tory at heart. Franklin was suspected by Massachusetts radicals of being a tool of Lord Hillsborough or, at best, one of those lukewarm Whigs whom Sam Adams feared more than outright Tories. They exclaimed that he was "not for their turn" and published such violent squibs against him in the *Boston Gazette* that Thomas Hutchinson, whose friendship with Franklin dated back to the Albany Congress of 1754, became convinced that his old friend would find serving as Massachusetts agent very painful "unless he will go all their lengths."[4]

Adams soon saw that the Massachusetts House of Representa-

---

[2] *The Writings of Samuel Adams*, II, 190, 267.
[3] *The Writings of Samuel Adams*, II, 283. *Letters of Samuel Cooper to Pownall and Franklin* (1770–1774), Bancroft Collection, N. Y. Public Library, Samuel Cooper to Thomas Pownall, Oct. 12 and Nov. 5, 1770. *Samuel Adams Papers*, Samuel Cooper to Thomas Pownall, Sept. 8, 1769.
[4] Mass. Archives, 27, *Hutchinson Corr.*, III, 240, 241, 246.

tives could not be persuaded to sever itself completely from
English affairs. Since the legislators wished to keep an agent
in the mother country, Adams's choice fell upon Arthur Lee,
a young Virginian resident in London who had convinced Massachusetts Whigs of his sterling patriotism by making virulent
attacks in the newspapers under the signature "Junius Americanus" upon British and American Tories. Adams and his
followers pushed Lee for office as "the only Man for he will
go through with it." Franklin, in their opinion, would only
go halfway. But in spite of their opposition, Franklin's friends
in the House of Representatives were able to secure his appointment as agent with Lee as substitute in case of Franklin's death
or absence. Sam Adams always preferred to correspond with
the substitute rather than with the regular agent, and Lee soon
became his most trusted adviser on English affairs. Lee possessed certain faults of temperament which made him an un-
trustworthy correspondent. He was a highly excitable young
man, whose fiery Whiggish outlook distorted his view of British politics. His judgments of men were frequently at fault;
he was constantly engaged in bitter quarrels; and he was suspicious of everyone's integrity except his own. His lively
fancy pictured all British Tories, from the King down, as
plotting deliberately to make the American colonists slaves.
His letters put such black construction upon the acts of the
British government that Sam Adams was kept constantly in
alarm for colonial liberty and was convinced that nothing but
oppression could be expected from the mother country. Adams
paid no heed to the more reasoned judgments of cooler men;
Arthur Lee appeared to him to be an "able and stanch Advocate
for the Rights of America & Mankind" and he never ceased
to place implicit reliance on Lee's opinion of British colonial
policy.[5]

The British government was eager to believe that the Massachusetts Whig Party was an "expiring Faction," and Hutchinson's letters describing the steady progress of Toryism in the
colony encouraged British imperialists to try fresh experiments.
In 1771, the Ministry determined to make Governor Hutchin-

[5] *Boston Gazette*, April 6, 1772.

son financially independent of the colonial legislature by paying his salary as governor from the revenue collected by the Commissioners of the Customs.   From the standpoint of imperial efficiency, this was a highly desirable cure for the ills that beset colonial administration, but it touched New Englanders in a sore spot and raised again the spectre of centralization of the Empire.   Throughout the eighteenth century, successive British ministers had attempted to change the system in force in Massachusetts Bay, where an appointed governor and elected house wrangled almost without intermission for whole administrations.   In relieving Governor Hutchinson of financial dependence upon the Massachusetts legislature, Lord Hillsborough accomplished what most of his predecessors had attempted to do.   But even a smattering of Massachusetts history would have told Hillsborough that the power of the purse was one of the most jealously prized of colonial rights and that every effort to seize it immediately put the most radical colonial leaders in power.   With Sam Adams and his "Mohawks" famishing for want of grievances, Hillsborough's interference in Massachusetts Bay was uncommonly ill-timed.   Nothing was more certain to keep the revolutionary pots boiling than an independent governor paid by the Crown out of "unconstitutional" taxes collected by the hated Commissioners of the Customs.

When Adams learned that the power of the purse had been taken from the Massachusetts House of Representatives he exclaimed that Massachusetts was in the grip of a "perfect Despotism" and began to beat the old alarm that had made generations of New Englanders quake for their liberties.   If Hutchinson were permitted to draw his salary from Westminster instead of from the Commons at Boston, Adams warned, the checks and balances of the Massachusetts constitution would be utterly destroyed and the governor freed from all control by the people: the only thing that would then prevent Hutchinson from becoming the Cæsar of Massachusetts Bay was that Cæsar, "to do him justice, had learning, courage, and great abilities."   Adams was fully vindicated as a prophet of English oppression: the governor of New York was given a royal salary, and Benjamin Franklin wrote that there was no longer doubt of the intention

of the British government to make all colonial governors independent of the legislatures as soon as the expense could be
met from the American revenue.   Adams's fancy pictured the
American colonies plunged into "abject slavery," ruled by
petty despots who looked to George III as satraps to an "Asiat-
ick Monarch." [6]   The prospect was so dire that Adams could
find a parallel only in his favorite "dreadful example," the
Roman Catholic Church: the payment of royal governors by the
Crown was similar to the Pope's giving the King of England
an annual gift provided he turned "papist."   Adams's apprehensions were not altogether groundless, for it seemed likely
that in putting the governors beyond popular control, the British government was merely taking the first step in a policy that
would eventually make judges, armies, fleets, and a host of petty
officials dependent only upon the Crown; and they, in turn,
would pave the way for such abominations as "episcopates &
their numerous ecclesiastic retinue; pensioners, placemen and
other jobbers, for an abandon'd and shameless ministry; hirelings, pimps, parasites, panders, prostitutes and whores."   After
the colonies were swarming with this "vermin," the House of
Commons would begin in earnest to enforce acts of Parliament
in the colonies, "where they have no more Just Authority than
they have in Jerusalem." [7]

Adams gave Hutchinson little opportunity to enjoy the fruits
of royal bounty.   He made the governor known the length and
breadth of the province as King George's "first American Pensioner" — with the result that even thrifty New England farmers who thought it would be a good thing for taxpayers if the
Crown paid the governor's salary were thoroughly frightened.
Hutchinson felt Adams's sting even in his own home.   Better
to attend his official duties, Hutchinson moved from his Milton
house to the Province House in Boston, which had fallen into
a bad state of disrepair.   At Hutchinson's request, the House of
Representatives appointed a committee to view the house to de-

---

[6] *The Writings of Samuel Adams*, II, 135, 252, 278, 280.   *Boston
Gazette*, April 15, 1771.
[7] *The Writings of Samuel Adams*, II, 247, 280.   *Boston Gazette*, Dec. 21,
1772.

termine what repairs were necessary, but unfortunately for Hutchinson Adams was made a member of the committee of inspection.   Adams prevented the committee from handing in its report and forestalled every later effort to have the governor's house repaired in spite of Hutchinson's wails that it was "a dishonour to His Majesty's Commission that the Governor lives in it in its present state."   Adams justified this treatment on the ground that, by accepting a salary from the Crown, Hutchinson ceased to be the constitutional governor of the province and merited no favors from the legislature.   But, he let it be understood, Hutchinson had only to refuse the royal salary in order to enjoy a house "not barely tenantable, but elegant," at the expense of the Commons of Massachusetts Bay.[8]

In 1772, while Adams was making political capital out of Hutchinson's pension, a rumor reached Boston that the judges of the Massachusetts superior court were likewise to be made independent of the legislature for their support.   The judges, like other public officers whose salaries were set by the General Court, were grievously underpaid: their wages, said one, were like "the Wages of Sin, for no Man could get a living by them."[9] The combined stipends of Hutchinson's three offices scarcely enabled him to maintain his household, but the judges of the superior court were so meanly paid that they got little more than a bare living.   Peter Oliver's salary as judge of the superior court was inadequate to support his family, yet the Massachusetts House of Representatives ignored or denied his pleas for higher pay.   Because of this niggardly aid from the General Court, the Massachusetts judges were overjoyed when it was reported they were to receive a fixed salary from the customhouse revenue.

The rumor that the Crown was about to pay the salaries of the Massachusetts judges gave Adams the opportunity he had long been waiting.   It was true that he had only a rumor to work upon, but Adams had the gift of dressing hearsay and tavern gossip into fact in the pages of the Boston Gazette.   His

[8] Mass. Archives, 27, Hutchinson Corr., III, 60, 363.   The Writings of Samuel Adams, II, 331, 332.

[9] Peter Oliver, 46.

strong inclination to believe the worst of the British government's intentions toward the colonies wiped away any doubt that the judges were to share in the revenue collected by the Commissioners of the Customs. Adams was not disposed to wait for confirmation of this latest tyranny, for it gave him fresh supply of propaganda after the wearisome diet of "Chaff & stubble" and hashed-over grievances he had been compelled to foist upon his followers. For the first time since the Boston Massacre he had a stirring issue with which to reinvigorate the Whig Party. Since 1768, Adams had waved the bugbear before New Englanders of an independent, and therefore presumably arbitrary, judiciary. The Massachusetts judges did not hold office during good behavior as did English judges — they were removable only at the Crown's pleasure. But an even more disquieting circumstance was that the Massachusetts judiciary was filled with Hutchinson's relations: the Lyndes, Olivers, Cottons, and Hutchinson himself occupied the most important offices. If such "oligarchs" were made independent of the legislature, Sam Adams confidently looked forward to seeing another Jeffreys riding a "bloody circuit" in New England. It was no wonder, then, that the rumor of royal salaries for the judges became a call to arms to Massachusetts patriots: Boston Sons of Liberty raised the cry that the British government had aimed a "FINISHING STROKE" at American liberty which would make the colonists "as complete slaves as the inhabitants of Turkey or Japan." The Ministry appeared to have created an emergency that made the do-nothing policy of the "half-way Whigs" as dangerous as that of the Tories: Sam Adams must again take command and "NOW strike a home blow, or sit down under the yoke of Tyranny." [10]

Sam Adams's home thrust at British tyranny was the establishment of the committees of correspondence. Corresponding committees had been used by American patriots from the beginning of the controversy with the mother country: merchants' corresponding committees had organized resistance to the Sugar

[10] *The Writings of Samuel Adams*, III, 30. *Boston Gazette*, May 5, 1771; Oct. 19, 1772; Nov. 2, 1772.

Act of 1764 and the Sons of Liberty had covered the colonies
with a network of societies whose circular letters and secret correspondence were one of the most striking manifestations of
colonial unity during the Stamp Act period. In 1770, Sam
Adams had broached to confidential friends a plan of committees of correspondence which would embrace England as well
as America, but his loss of confidence in English Whigs led him
to drop the British connection in favor of a purely colonial in-
stitution which, originating in Massachusetts, would extend
over all British America. The first step in this ambitious undertaking was to link the towns of Massachusetts Bay together so
closely that they would present a solid "phalanx" to the British
government — "a band of brothers, which no force can break,
no enemy destroy." [11] Once Adams's radical followers — under the name of committees of correspondence — were in
power in every Massachusetts town, the whole colony would
act in concert with Boston and the rural representatives would
be sent down to the General Court with instructions to join the
metropolis in whatever measures it took to oppose the mother
country. With committees of correspondence ruling the province there would be little danger of the country deserting Boston in an emergency. Such union between town and country
would exhilarate the Whig morale, which, since the failure of
patriot policies after the Massacre, had reached a low ebb.
Those "timid sort of people" who made the country's antagonism to Boston a justification for inactivity would be silenced
by proof that New England yeomen were ready to support the
metropolis, and the radical Whigs promised themselves that
a "plan of Opposition will be easily formed, & executed with
Spirit." [12] Bernard's taunt that the Massachusetts patriot party
was an "expiring faction" still rankled Adams and he was eager
to show Americans that Massachusetts Whigs were still as
fiery patriots as in the days of the Massachusetts circular letter.
Lastly, Adams hoped to rout the Tories by means of the committees of correspondence. When they saw "the flame burst-

[11] *Boston Gazette*, Oct. 19, 1772.
[12] *The Writings of Samuel Adams*, II, 347.

ing in different parts of the Country" simultaneously, they could do nothing to check its spread.[13]

Yet few Whigs agreed with Sam Adams that the iron was sufficiently hot to strike such a heavy blow at British authority in Massachusetts. Almost single-handed, and against the opposition of most of his lieutenants, Adams brought forth the Boston committee of correspondence and thereby hatched the "foulest, subtlest, and most venomous serpent ever issued from the egg of sedition."[14] Most Boston Whigs regarded Sam Adams's plan of appointing a committee of correspondence "to state the rights of the colonists, and of this province in particular, as men and Christians, and as subjects," as political dynamite that was likely to explode in their own hands before they could plant it under the Tories; if the country failed to follow Boston's example in appointing a committee of correspondence, the patriot cause would suffer a setback that might permanently cripple it.[15] The more cautious patriots protested against risking the future of the Whig Party on a rumor that might well prove to be false: no one knew for certain that the judges were to be paid by the Crown, yet Adams was ready to gamble everything on the chance that the report was true. These arguments satisfied the majority of Sons of Liberty, and when Adams petitioned for a town meeting to establish the committee of correspondence, the Boston selectmen, John Hancock among them, flatly refused to consent to call the townspeople together for so seditious a purpose. Even after the town meeting had been summoned, Adams failed twice to win a favorable vote. At the third adjournment, Adams saw his opportunity: only a handful of citizens now remained in Faneuil Hall, and this rump consisted of a majority of his followers. While Adams held this momentary advantage the motion to appoint a committee of correspondence was rushed through the town meeting — an instance of how an aggressive minority triumphs over an unorganized majority. Nevertheless, throughout its existence,

[13] *The Writings of Samuel Adams*, II, 350; III, 43.
[14] *Massachusetts Gazette*, Jan. 2, 1775. Mass. Archives, 27, *Hutchinson Corr.*, III, 461.
[15] Gordon, I, 312–313.

the Boston committee of correspondence bore the stigma of having been midwifed into the world by Sam Adams while most of the townspeople had their backs turned.[16]

Even this victory did not remove all obstacles from Adams's path. There remained the knotty problem of finding men to serve on the committee of correspondence. So few wished for the honor that for a time it seemed not unlikely that only Adams would accept. Cushing, Phillips, and Hancock declined their elections by pleading business — a lame excuse that failed to conceal their real fears that the committee would come to a bad end. But Adams — the "grand Incendiary of the Province" who had carried the scheme to the verge of success on his own shoulders — was not to be turned back by a few timorous Whigs: a meeting of the leading patriots was hurriedly called, the courage of the faint-hearted was screwed up by Sam Adams, and a list of those willing to run the risk of serving on the committee of correspondence was sent down to the town meeting.

Twenty-one patriots, with James Otis as chairman, were elected by the townspeople to serve upon the committee of correspondence. From the beginning, James Otis took little part in the committee's work and most of the other members delegated their authority to sub committees of radical Whigs dominated by Sam Adams, William Cooper, and Thomas Young. Hutchinson declared that this clique boasted "as black-hearted fellows as any upon the Globe"; and he resolved to stay out of dark alleys when members of the committee of correspondence were abroad.[17] These Whigs who struck such terror among the Tories met in the Boston selectmen's chambers or at William Molineux's house. Their meetings usually lasted from six to nine-thirty in the evening; and, no matter how urgent the occasion, the committee scrupulously observed the New England custom of ceasing work from Saturday until an hour after sundown on the Lord's Day. All committeemen were sworn to such strict secrecy that the citizens were kept completely in the dark as to their doings. By hedging itself behind this mystery the committee laid itself open to suspicion that it was

[16] *Boston Gazette*, Nov. 9, 1772.
[17] Mass. Archives, 27, *Hutchinson Corr.*, III, 412.

making away with large sums of money belonging to the town
of Boston, as Sam Adams had done a decade before. Stung by
this accusation, the committee voted to charge the town only
for "ye Candles & Firing" used during the meetings and
to tax the members a dollar apiece for the purchase of "Some
Rhode Island Beer." As final proof of good faith, the clerk
was directed to bring in the account "of the Expence already incurred for Liquours." [18] Having thus fortified themselves for
the business of combating tyranny, Adams and his friends proceeded to make the committee of correspondence the most formidable revolutionary machine that was created during the
American Revolution.

Sam Adams's first move was to draw up a declaration of colonial rights and grievances which, in his hands, swelled to such
a "great twelve-penny book" that Solicitor General Wedderburn said Adams told New Englanders of "a hundred rights,
of which they never had heard before, and a hundred grievances which they never before had felt." [19] Had Wedderburn
been a Bostonian he would have found most of the grievances
familiar, but even a Bostonian might well have been startled
by Adams's boldness of tone in stating colonial rights. As
Wedderburn said, Adams had produced "a set of ready drawn
heads of a declaration for any one colony in America, or any
one distant county in the kingdom, which shall chuse to revolt
from the British Empire, and say that they will not be governed
by the King and Parliament at Westminster." Adams now
brushed aside all arguments from positive law and placed his
claim squarely upon natural rights "exclusive of all charters
from the Crown." Conservatives had always dreaded the doctrine of natural law as a great cornucopia of revolutionary principles, but it remained for Sam Adams, delving far deeper than
had James Otis, to draw from it a full justification of American
rebellion. It was indeed disquieting for British imperialists to
hear Sam Adams shouting in the colonies that by a law of
nature "all Men have a Right to remain in a State of Nature

[18] *Committee of Correspondence Papers,* Jan. 12, 1773; Feb. 1, 1773.
[19] *Letters of Governor Hutchinson and Lieutenant Governor Oliver*
(London, 1774), 113.

as long as they please: And in case of intollerable Oppression, Civil or Religious, to leave the Society they belong to, and enter into another." [20]   Sam Adams had already made an "Appeal to Heaven" against the British government and it was clear that if he were to judge when "intollerable Oppression" justified rebellion, an upheaval in the colonies was not far distant.

Sam Adams was keenly aware that rural New England was the battleground on which the fate of the committees of correspondence would be decided.   Far from sharing Adams's confidence that the committees would sweep the country, many Boston Whigs expected the scheme to meet with a resounding defeat at the hands of Massachusetts farmers because rural patriotism was dead "and the Dead cant be raised without a Miracle." [21]   As these cautious patriots feared, Tory squires did not give way to the committees of correspondence without a struggle.   "New made Colonels," stiff in fresh militia regimentals, came to town to persuade the farmers not to be dragged into rebellion by holding to Boston's skirts.   They swore that country people had been "too often imposed upon by Boston," where a few pushing Whigs were perpetually bearding King George and Parliament and were now trying to snare unwary New Englanders in a plan that had been approved by only a handful of the Boston "rabble." [22]   Edward Bacon, the Tory representative from Barnstable in the General Court, made a particularly bitter attack upon Boston patriots which promptly brought him into hot water with the Boston committee of correspondence.   Bacon said that William Molineux and Thomas Young were "men of no Principles and Infamous Characters" and urged that Barnstable refuse to correspond with "the Vilest of men." [23]   Bacon later remarked that he preferred to have his master three thousand miles away than in Boston and sneered

[20] Letters of Hutchinson and Oliver, 113.   The Writings of Samuel Adams, II, 351.
[21] Warren-Adams Letters, Mass. Hist. Soc. Collections, LXXIII (1925); II, 401 (Appendix).
[22] Boston Evening Post, Jan. 18, 1773; Feb. 8, 1883.   Mass. Archives, 25, Hutchinson Corr., I, Peter Oliver to Thomas Hutchinson, Dec. 12, 1772.
[23] Committee of Correspondence Papers, James Otis to William Molineux, March 11, 1773.

that "Adams was worth but little if his Debt was paid and that it was for his interest to contend with them in this way in order to get a Living." [24] After having thus taken most of the leading Boston Whigs through the mud, Bacon incautiously came up to the metropolis. The Boston committee of correspondence was waiting for him to show himself in town and he was immediately haled before it. Behind the closed doors of the committee's chamber, Adams and Molineux procured from Bacon a written denial that he had ever slandered the high-ranking Whigs of the metropolis. This retraction was printed and sent to the districts where it was expected to do the most good, but its beneficial effect was largely nullified by a persistent rumor that it was either a forgery or had been bludgeoned out of Bacon while he was detained in the committee's chamber. [25]

Hutchinson had no better success than Tory squires in stopping the spread of committees of correspondence over New England. When he denounced the Boston committee for seizing authority that belonged rightfully to the Crown, Sam Adams quoted natural law to justify the usurpation: that "great and perpetual Law of Self preservation to which every Person or corporate Body hath an inherent Right" gave the people authority to establish committees of correspondence and adopt all other measures necessary to oppose tyranny. [26] Although at first the committees spread so slowly in rural New England that Hutchinson believed Adams had lured the Whigs into "such a foolish scheme that they must necessarily make themselves ridiculous," the governor soon realized his error. The propaganda with which Adams had steadily drenched New Englanders since the Stamp Act now brought forth a bumping crop. Plymouth was the first town outside of Boston to appoint a committee of correspondence, and it was followed by Cambridge, Marblehead, Charlestown, Newburyport, and a host of smaller towns throughout New England. By 1774, the Boston com-

[24] *Publications Col. Soc. of Mass.* (1894), XXV, 312.

[25] *Committee of Correspondence Papers*, James Greenleaf to James Otis, June 22, 1773; Bacon's Certificate, June 1, 1773. *Publications Col. Soc. of Mass.*, XXV, 265–348.

[26] *The Writings of Samuel Adams*, III, 5, 6, *Chalmers Papers*, VI, Thomas Hutchinson to Lord Dartmouth, Oct. 23, 1772.

mittee of correspondence was in communication with more than three hundred towns in Massachusetts alone, besides carrying on an intercolonial correspondence with Sons of Liberty as far south as Charleston, South Carolina. Thus, lamented Hutchinson, "was the Contagion which began in Boston" diffused over the continent. "All on a sudden," he exclaimed, "from a state of peace, order, and general contentment . . . the province, more or less from one end to the other, was brought into a state of contention, disorder, and general dissatisfaction." [27]

The committees of correspondence mark the rejuvenation of the Whig Party in the American colonies and the reappearance of Sam Adams as a serious menace to the stability of the British Empire. As Adams himself said, the committees diverted the people's attention from "picking up pins, and directed their Views to great objects" — with the result that politics again became the besetting passion of New Englanders and "the Genius of Liberty" was once more "Roused after a Languor if not a profound Sleep." [28] Sam Adams was once more regarded as the watchdog of New England's liberties, alert to all British "Schemes to Subvert our happy Constitution." With Adams on the lookout, the Boston committee never lacked alarming rumors of impending British tyranny which, when sent over the network of corresponding committees, kept New Englanders constantly on edge for their liberties. As soon as the local committee received word from Boston of the plots being hatched by British ministers against colonial freedom, the town meeting was called and instructions were rushed to the representatives in the General Court to uphold Sam Adams's policies against the mother country. For the benefit of backward towns, the Boston committee sent out circular letters containing political doctrines which Adams judged proper for rural patriots. The answers that poured into Boston from the interior were highly gratifying to Sam Adams, who had gambled everything on the hope that the rural districts would again become a hotbed of

[27] Mass. Archives, *Hutchinson Corr.*, III, 412, 431, 465. Hutchinson, III, 370 (note).

[28] *Warren-Adams Letters*, I, 245. *Committee of Correspondence Papers*, Boston Committee to the Sandwich Committee, March 9, 1774: Plymouth Committee to the Boston Committee, April 8, 1773.

Whiggery; but Wedderburn found the resolves of the country towns "full of the most extravagant absurdities, Such as the enthusiastic rant of the wildest of my countrymen in Charles the 2d's days cannot equal." [29]   In particular, the resolves of the town of Pembroke horrified Wedderburn and delighted Sam Adams.   "This people are warranted," the Pembroke citizens declared, "by the laws of God and nature, in the use of every rightful art and energy of *Policy, Stratagem,* and *Force*." [30]

But while Adams thus educated New Englanders in "Boston principles" he was careful to lead the country people to believe that instead of being led by Boston they themselves were in reality the leaders.   Bostonians had no wish, said Adams, to "obtrude ·*their* Opinions upon their Fellow-Countrymen," and he flattered the village Hampdens by assuring them that their "resolution to oppose Tyranny in all its forms is worthy the Imitation of this Metropolis."   In his letters to rural patriots he skillfully soothed their distrust of the metropolis and overcame their unwillingness to be led by town folk into a quarrel with the mother country.   He always spoke of back-country Whigs as his "sensible Brethren in the Country" or as his "worthy & much esteemed Brethren." [31]   Indeed, if Sam Adams were to be believed, the Boston Sons of Liberty were merely responding to pressure from the country people in provoking controversy with Great Britain.

As has been said, Sam Adams hoped to extend committees of correspondence throughout the colonies if the experiment succeeded in Massachusetts Bay.   At the first opportunity, he planned to introduce a resolution in the General Court that a circular letter be sent to all the provincial assemblies urging that committees of correspondence be appointed. [32]   But here Adams was anticipated by the Virginia patriots.   As early as 1768, Richard Henry Lee of Virginia had suggested that the colonies ought to establish committees for intercolonial correspondence. Adams's success in Massachusetts convinced Lee, Patrick Henry,

---

[29] *Letters of Hutchinson and Oliver,* 113.
[30] *Ibid.,* 114.
[31] *The Writings of Samuel Adams,* III, 16, 17, 32.
[32] *Ibid.,* II, 380.   Mass. Archives, 27, *Hutchinson Corr.,* III, 437.

and Thomas Jefferson that the time was ripe to carry out this plan.   Early in 1773, therefore, they introduced resolutions in the Virginia House of Burgesses establishing a committee of correspondence and inviting the other provincial legislatures to do likewise.   This proposal met with instant favor throughout the continent and almost every colonial assembly appointed corresponding committees.[33]

The action of the Virginia House of Burgesses in initiating intercolonial committees of correspondence has provoked controversy between historians of the Old Dominion and the Bay State as to whether Virginia or Massachusetts can lay best claim to having created the mainspring which later pushed the colonies into revolution.   Sam Adams supposed that Massachusetts had inspired Virginia, but there is good reason to believe that the Virginia patriots were acting upon ideas that had been clearly formulated in their minds many years before.   But the matter is of slight importance.   The colonies were not revolutionized by the committees of correspondence that were created by the colonial legislatures acting upon the suggestion of the Virginia House of Burgesses: they corresponded little and most of the letters they interchanged are formal in nature and of relatively small interest.   The committees of correspondence that made the American Revolution possible were the town committees dominated by local "Sam Adamses" who were in close touch with Boston and other centres of radicalism.   These committees owed their origin to Sam Adams rather than to the Virginia Whigs.   Without their aid it is doubtful if the first Continental Congress would have been held in 1774 and the revolutionary movement in the colonies brought to its fruition in the Declaration of Independence.   They made possible the domination of a great part of British America by cliques of radical patriots who looked to Sam Adams for leadership against the mother country.   These committees were a direct outgrowth of the intercolonial unity that had been seen in the military alliances and corresponding committees of the Sons of Liberty during the Stamp Act.   After 1774, the colonies fairly bristled

[33] *Dictionary of American Biography*, Richard Henry Lee (1933), XI, 117–120.

with hot-tempered Liberty Boys, who, instead of calling themselves Sons of Liberty, were now known as the committees of correspondence. But under whatever name these patriots worked, their purpose remained the same: to defend colonial liberty with arms rather than submit to British "tyranny."

The creation by provincial assemblies of committees of correspondence upon the Virginia model encouraged Adams to take a bold step in political radicalism. The resolves of the Virginia House of Burgesses in 1773 were the first sign given Adams for several years that patriotism was reviving in the Southern colonies. Instead of finding nothing but advertisements for British "Baubles" in Southern newspapers, he was now overjoyed to see Whig political principles coming back into favor. Once more he looked forward to colonial unity against the British government: "There is now," he wrote after learning of the Virginia resolves, "a fairer prospect than ever of an Union among the Colonies." [84] Virginia gave him new hope that "the Fire of true Patriotism" would sweep the colonies as in the days of the Stamp Act, and he took the opportunity to level a particularly aggressive attack upon the British government. It has been seen that as early as 1765 the Sons of Liberty regarded the King as the only bond between mother country and colonies and that only the slowness of public opinion prevented Sam Adams from openly declaring that Parliament had no authority whatever in the colonies. But in 1773, after the committees of correspondence had begun to sow political radicalism in the colonial mind, Adams judged the hour had struck to speak frankly. He now declared that the King was the sole sovereign of America and that each colonial legislature was a parliament completely independent of the Lords and Commons at Westminster. Indeed, Adams insisted that Parliament had never had any rightful authority in the colonies: if Americans had submitted to its laws it was "rather from inconsideration, or a reluctance at the idea of contending with the parent state, than from a conviction or acknowledgment of the Supreme Legislative authority of Parliament." He denied that the dissolution by Parliament in 1741 of the Massachusetts

[84] *The Writings of Samuel Adams*, III, 21.

Land Bank formed a precedent for Parliament's jurisdiction over the colonies: the Massachusetts House of Representatives had not carried out in its full severity Parliament's Bubble Act, but had passed an act of its own which, Adams insisted, was directly contrary to the intentions of the British government.[35] Had not Adams been so intent upon making out a case against Parliamentary authority, perhaps he would have remembered that the Massachusetts Land Bank had been destroyed solely by Parliamentary legislation and that, even after the Massachusetts House of Representatives had mitigated the Bubble Act, the Adamses had been harassed for two decades by the Land Bank Commissioners. In keeping with the Massachusetts General Court's dignity as the "Parliament" of the province, Adams now called the House of Representatives "his majesty's commons"; the debates he styled "parliamentary debates"; acts of Parliament became "acts of the British Parliament"; and the province laws were termed "the laws of the land."[36] By means of the committees of correspondence, Adams made the watchword in Massachusetts Bay: "Freedom from every legislature on Earth but that of the province." "Equal liberty" with Great Britain now meant that the power of the British Parliament be confined to the realm and its claim of authority in the colonies surrendered to a dozen or more provincial assemblies which exercised with the King full sovereignty within their borders. Unless the mother country recognized this principle, Adams said that Americans ought to feel themselves treated "as bastards and not Sons."[37] He had no doubt, however, that if Great Britain adopted his ideas of how colonies should be governed, the mother country and provinces would "live happily in that connection, and mutually support and protect each other."[38] But before this Utopia could be attained, Parliament must repeal the Declaratory Act, acknowledge it had no authority over the colonies, and recognize King George as "King of America."

[35] *The Writings of Samuel Adams*, II, 423, 424, 451.
[36] Hutchinson, III, 413 (note).
[37] *The Writings of Samuel Adams*, II, 55.
[38] *Ibid.*, II, 424.

Adams's conception of the relationship between mother country and colonies foreshadowed the connection between Great Britain and the Dominions in the modern British Empire; but England was not prepared in 1773 to adopt Adams's revolutionary ideas of imperial government. The mercantilist system under which Great Britain had developed her colonial empire was based upon the principle that colonies were worth only what the mother country received from them; and Englishmen had not yet given up hope that a considerable revenue could be extracted from the colonies. The problem, as Englishmen saw it, was not to join hands with Sam Adams and leap into untried schemes of government, but to keep closely to the beaten path and devise means of compelling the miserly colonists to disgorge some of their wealth. Moreover, George III was not flattered by his American subjects' devotion to the Crown and anxiety to make him sole sovereign of the colonies. George III had not bought and paid for part of the House of Commons and put himself at the head of the "King's Friends" to see Americans declare themselves independent of Parliamentary authority. He preferred to rule through Parliament because its venality enabled him to "be a king" and yet remain within constitutional limits. British Whigs were as determined as King George to preserve Parliament's authority over the colonies. The traditional purpose of the Whig Party was to debase the power of the Crown — not to enhance it, as Sam Adams proposed. Thus, when Adams laid his axe at the root of Parliamentary jurisdiction over the provinces, he cut the last tie between British and American Whigs.

Unquestionably, Sam Adams had greater faith in American independence as a barrier to British tyranny than in preserving the connection with Great Britain through King George III. He was well aware that George was not the man Americans supposed him to be when they toasted him as the "Patron" of colonial liberty. Adams was warned by his friends in England that the King "hates most cordially every American because he thinks they have an attachment to their Liberty." Arthur Lee told Adams that "the Heart of the King is hardened,

like that of Pharoah," against the colonists.[39]   These disquieting reports of King George's villainy convinced Adams that he
was not fit to be "King of America": and rather than see such
a hard master set over the colonies, Adams hoped to make
America completely independent of Great Britain.   In 1772
it was said in Boston that the colonies ought to form a separate
commonwealth upon the model of the Dutch provinces and open
their trade to all nations.   "How shall the Colonies force their
Oppressors to proper Terms?" asked Adams in 1773, and he
replied to his own question by saying that only the formation
of a separate state — an "American Commonwealth" — would
"answer the great Purpose of preserving our Liberties."   He
told the people that Great Britain had no more right to their
money than had France or Spain and that there was no reason
why "robbers from one nation should have more indulgence
than from another."   Nevertheless, Adams still accompanied
his most rousing pieces of sedition with professions of loyalty
to the British government, and even when he appealed to the
"Law of Heaven" he hastened to disclaim any intention of
carrying out his threats.   But Adams's solemn assertions that
he was an obedient, peace-loving subject of King George III
carried no conviction with the Tories, who knew him far too
well to believe he reverenced either the King or the Empire.
And, indeed, their judgment of Sam Adams was not far wrong.
As the next two years were to show, Adams steered his course
not with George III, the "King of America," but with American
independence as a polestar.   "This country shall be independent," Adams said, "and we will be satisfied with nothing short
of it"; Great Britain might crumble, but America would "rise
full plumed and glorious from her Mothers Ashes." [40]

[39] *Samuel Adams Papers*, Mentor (William Lee) to Sam Adams, May 14,
1774; Arthur Lee to Sam Adams, Dec. 22, 1773.

[40] *Boston Gazette*, Nov. 2, 1772; Oct. 11, 1773.   Gordon, I, 347.   *The
Writings of Samuel Adams*, III, 21.

XI

THE BOSTON TEA PARTY

BECAUSE Sam Adams and other leaders of the American Revolution have handed down to posterity self-portraits in which they exhibit themselves as patient, peace-loving men driven to rebellion by intolerable British tyranny, the fact that they themselves made repeated aggressions upon the British government and did much to precipitate the Revolution is often overlooked. After the Massachusetts Convention of 1768, Sam Adams deliberately set out to provoke crises that would lead to the separation of mother country and colonies. He had scored his most notable success in the Boston Massacre, but, as has been seen, the consequences of the "bloody work in King's street" were not altogether happy for Adams or the Massachusetts Whig Party. A far greater triumph was the Boston Tea Party, which, by precipitating the American Revolution, deserves to rank as the masterpiece of Sam Adams's efforts to create an unbridgeable gap between Great Britain and her American provinces.

Intercolonial rivalry for leadership against Great Britain was one of the strongest forces that pushed the colonies, slowly but inexorably, into revolution. Many colonies hoped to distinguish themselves in the struggle against British "tyranny" by putting forward the most radical political doctrines or making the most violent resistance; and provincial patriots longed to make themselves the reigning toast among Sons of Liberty, whether as "the freedom loving Virginians," "the brave Carolinians," or "the patriotic Bostonians." In particular, Virginia and Massachusetts ran a hot race for colonial leadership and thereby hastened the eventual crisis between the mother country and colonies. If one colony took a step upon the slippery path to revolution, the Sons of Liberty in the other provinces immediately prepared to follow lest they be suspected of back-wardness in the "sacred cause of Liberty." Sam Adams and other patriots never ceased to urge that "every colony still astern in the glorious cause, should advance close up to the foremost, that there may be no ground to suspect a disparity of sentiment upon any point of importance." By 1773, it had become apparent to the Crown officers in America that "every new advance upon government in any colony excites an emulation in the next," and that one "leading province" such as Massachusetts Bay could alone throw all British America into turmoil by "blowing up the general flame." [1]

Sam Adams's policy was to make Massachusetts the spearhead of American opposition to Great Britain and to weld the provinces into a solid phalanx behind the leadership of the Bay Colony. He believed that American liberty was safe only when Massachusetts was in the forefront of battle; it was as essential, in his eyes, that Massachusetts lead the American colonies as it was that Boston lead Massachusetts. Adams and the Boston Whigs never doubted that their boldness would serve as an example to Sons of Liberty elsewhere in the colonies and that, if they plunged Massachusetts into a quarrel with the mother country, the rest of British America would rush to their support: however deeply Dr. Thomas Young of Boston might lament the decline "of the noble spirit of the Yorkers," he was certain they could be depended upon to act vigorously if "a hard emergency" arose and New England called upon them for aid.[2] And, as the nonimportation agreement had shown, there was no surer way of producing quick action in Boston than to convince the citizens that they were being outstripped in patriotism by other colonies. Whenever Sam Adams wished to deal a particularly violent blow at British authority, he first aroused the townspeople's apprehensions that the Sons of Liberty in New York, Philadelphia, or Charleston were about to take into their own hands the leadership of the American col-

[1] Mass. Archives, 26, *Hutchinson Corr.* II, 184, 189.
[2] Thomas Young to Hugh Hughes, Aug. 31, 1772, MS. through courtesy of Mr. G. P. Anderson. *Boston Gazette*, Nov. 2, 1772. *Bernard Papers*, VI, Bernard to Richard Jackson, Aug. 24, 1765.

onies against Great Britain. Having once excited this fear,
Adams usually found the Boston Whigs eager to atone for their
backsliding with a riot or an attack upon royal government.
The Boston Tea Party — "the boldest stroke which had yet
been struck in America" — was a direct outgrowth of this intercolonial rivalry.[3]

Hutchinson's popularity in rural New England still remained a serious stumblingblock to Sam Adams's revolutionary
propaganda. The committees of correspondence had revived
Whig principles in the country, but rural patriotism had not
yet been highly spiced with hostility against Hutchinson and the
"oligarchs" — in great contrast to that of Boston, where Sam
Adams waged war on two fronts against local and overseas tyrants. Adams had waited many years to ruin Hutchinson,
but it probably had never occurred to him that the means of
achieving this ambition would come from Benjamin Franklin,
the "lukewarm Whig" whom Adams opposed in 1770 as the
colony's London agent. Since 1770, Franklin had strengthened the suspicions of Massachusetts Whigs that he was no
friend to colonial liberty by hobnobbing with Lord Hillsborough and running over to Ireland to visit that noble lord in his
Irish castle. Such intimacy with British ministers shocked
Adams and his radical friends, and they were about to write
Franklin down as a renegade Tory when he unexpectedly proved
himself a true patriot. Franklin was perhaps aware that his
conduct had raised misgivings in Massachusetts Bay and that
it was necessary to act quickly lest he be cast utterly out of
Adams's graces. He knew certainly that the surest way to pla-
cate Sam Adams was to put into his hands the power of pulling
down Thomas Hutchinson. By means he never explained,
Franklin got possession of a large number of letters Hutchinson
had written Thomas Whately, a former member of Parliament, and sent this "cargo" of private letters to Massachusetts
Bay in care of John and Sam Adams, James Bowdoin, Thomas
Cushing, Charles Chauncy, and Samuel Cooper. To protect
his own reputation, Franklin attached strings to his gift: no
copies of the letters were to be made; they were to be shown

[3] Hutchinson, III, 439.

only to a few confidential friends; and they were to be returned
to England.[4]

Although Franklin settled all doubts of his patriotism in
Massachusetts Bay by sending Hutchinson's letters to the province, it cost him much of his popularity in England and the
office of postmaster general for the colonies.   Franklin's misfortunes were caused by Sam Adams, who, by breaking all the
instructions which had accompanied the letters, revealed Franklin's part in the affair.   When Adams saw the governor's letters
he immediately realized that he had in his hands a weapon
which would infallibly work Hutchinson's downfall; and from
that moment Adams determined to violate Franklin's orders.
His first step was to announce that "a most shocking scene would
soon open" in which it would be shown how certain "great persons" in the colony had attempted to destroy the Massachusetts
charter and dragoon the citizens with British troops.[5]   He hinted
that incriminating letters had come to light which proved beyond question who was responsible for burdening the colony
with taxes, soldiers, customhouse officers, and all other such
"vermin." [6]   By this means, the people were thrown into such
excitement that Hutchinson declared if Adams "had bro't Chevy
Chase into the House & proved it had been sent to England by
the Governor they would have found some latent treasonable
meaning against the Constitution & a Vote wou'd have passed
accordingly." [7]

After having raised the citizens' apprehensions to this pitch,
it was suddenly moved in the House of Representatives that the
galleries be cleared and the doors barred to all messages from
the governor.   Sam Adams then informed the members that
a number of letters written by "persons of rank in America"
to gentlemen in England had reached his hands.   These letters,
Adams explained, were to be used only upon certain conditions
to which the representatives must agree before they could be

[4] *Israel Williams Papers*, MSS. Mass. Hist. Soc., II, Thomas Hutchinson to
Israel Williams, April 12, 1774.   *The Works of Benjamin Franklin*, edited by
E. D. Smyth, VI, 195.
[5] Mass. Archives, 27, *Hutchinson Corr.*, III, 514.
[6] *The Works of John Adams*, II, 319.
[7] Mass. Archives, 27, *Hutchinson Corr.*, III, 514.   Hutchinson, III, 402.

read. The House quickly consented to be bound by these terms and Adams read the letters. But merely reading Hutchinson's correspondence to the Massachusetts legislators was not sufficient for Adams's purpose: the letters must be printed and scattered over the length and breadth of the province. Franklin had clearly stipulated that no copies were to be printed, but Adams overreached him with a trick that shocked even Hutchinson, hardened as he was to Adams's "knavery." "It was not in the power of Human Wisdom," exclaimed the governor, "to guard against this last Villainy." [8]   Acting upon Adams's directions, Hancock rose in the House to say that "some body in the Common" had given him a manuscript which appeared to be a copy of Hutchinson's letters which the representatives were considering.[9]   It was then moved that these letters be compared with the originals in Sam Adams's possession and, if identical, the clerk of the House (Sam Adams) should attest them and prepare them for publication. Everyone in the House knew that the letters which Hancock swore had been handed him on the Common were merely copies of the correspondence sent by Franklin. Despite its barefacedness, this stratagem enabled Sam Adams to print hundreds of copies of Hutchinson's correspondence without violating the letter of Franklin's instructions. As Hutchinson said, Sam Adams, the "Master of the Puppets," directed the business "with very great Art, as well as by sticking at no Falsehood, ever so glaring," and with "such baseness as no civilized people have ever countenanced." To the governor, it was clear that Adams was acting upon the principle which always guided his policy: "In political matters the Publick good is above all other considerations & every rule of morality when in competition with it may very well be dispensed with." [10]

Hutchinson was unable to understand how "a dozen harmless letters" written many years before when he was lieutenant

[8] Public Record Office, Colonial Office, Class or Series 5, 246, Lib. Cong. Transcripts, Thomas Hutchinson to Thomas Pownall, July 3, 1773.

[9] Mass. Archives, 27, *Hutchinson Corr.*, III, 509.

[10] Public Record Office, Colonial Office, Class 5, 246, Lib. Cong. Transcripts, Thomas Hutchinson to Thomas Pownall, July 3, 1773. Mass. Archives, 27, *Hutchinson Corr.* III, 516, 550.

governor of the province and addressed to an Englishman who held no political office could shatter the esteem in which he was held by rural New Englanders. Hutchinson had written little that might be used to incriminate him as an enemy to colonial liberty, but in one letter to Whately he had expressed his opinion that "there must be an abridgment of what is called English Liberty" and he had repeatedly urged that Parliament take vigorous measures to assert its sovereignty over the colonies before Sam Adams swept away all respect for government. But Hutchinson was convicted of plotting against colonial freedom not so much by his own words as by Sam Adams's interpretation of them. "It was not possible," grieved the governor, "for greater art to be made use of to inflame the people." [11] It had long since been observed that Sam Adams had only to accuse Hutchinson of bad faith to convict him in Bostonians' eyes; and it required merely the flimsiest of evidence to convince the people as a whole that the governor was secretly their enemy. By dint of frequently repeating that Hutchinson's correspondence revealed the "principal movers, in all the disturbance, misery, and bloodshed" in Massachusetts, and the governor's "Avarice & a Lust of power," Adams persuaded the people that there was more in these letters than met the eye.[12] Moreover, as Hutchinson said, in printing the letters Adams twisted their meaning by lifting passages from the text and omitting what preceded or followed. Another trick he used to expose Hutchinson's villainy was to jumble together his own and the governor's words in such a manner that readers were unable to distinguish whether it was Sam Adams or Hutchinson speaking. For example, Hutchinson was made to say in the *Boston Gazette:* "Nothing yet remains to compleat my wishes and *designs* but the arrival of the troops," and exult that his efforts had "at length prevailed on administration to conclude that all is in *anarchy* here." In reality, these words were put into Hutchinson's mouth by Sam Adams, but it was done so cunningly that the audience did not detect the deception. Adams seemed to have produced overwhelming proof that Hutchinson was re-

[11] *The Diary and Letters of Thomas Hutchinson*, I, 82.
[12] *The Writings of Samuel Adams*, III, 41, 42, 44.

sponsible for the Stamp Act, the Townshend duties, the Boston Massacre, and the "plan of slavery" for the colonies which the Ministry had been attempting to put in force for a decade.   He even convinced the people that Hutchinson was responsible for bringing the troops to Boston in 1768, although it was clear that his letters describing the crisis in the colony could not have been received in England until long after orders had been sent for the troops to embark for Massachusetts.[13]

Printed copies of Hutchinson's letters were sent by the Boston committee of correspondence to all the towns in the province and to the Sons of Liberty outside New England.   Everywhere it was emphasized that Hutchinson had urged the restriction of colonial liberty.   The Boston committee of correspondence exclaimed that God, who had protected New England from its earliest settlement, had brought to light a plot laid by its most "malicious and invidious Enemies."[14]   Having thus revealed himself an instrument of the Deity, Sam Adams began to urge in the House of Representatives that the King be petitioned to remove Hutchinson as governor.   The time had come, Adams believed, to send Hutchinson on his travels because he had shown himself to be one of the worst enemies of colonial liberty in America.   During the debate that followed this motion, Adams was asked what evidence he could present to support his allegations.   He replied that he and his followers "did not trouble themselves about supporting them.   the people of the province would give credit to them.   this would make the Governor and Lieutenant Governor odious and the King would always remove such a Governor.   they had succeeded in this way against Sir Francis Bernard" and Hutchinson would be removed "as was the case with Governor Bernard & would be with all Governors who would not keep on good terms with the people."[15]   Adams's arguments carried conviction and a petition to the King was drawn up in which Governor Hutchinson and Lieutenant Governor Oliver were pronounced the "chiefe

---

[13] *Boston Gazette*, June 21, 1773; Aug. 2, 1773.   Hutchinson, III, 407.

[14] *Committee of Correspondence Papers*, MS. N. Y. Public Library, Circular Letter, June 22, 1773.

[15] Mass. Archives, 27, *Hutchinson Corr.*, III, 495, 522.

Instruments" in bringing a fleet and army to Massachusetts and therefore responsible for "all that Corruption of Morals in this Province, and all that Confusion Misery and Bloodshed" which followed.[16]   But if Adams really expected that the King would remove Hutchinson on the strength of this arraignment, he was grievously disappointed.   The Lords of the Committee of Council for Plantation Affairs declared that the Massachusetts petition was "groundless, vexatious, and scandalous, and calculated only for the seditious purposes of keeping up a spirit of clamour and discontent in the said province." [17]   No evidence had been put forward by the colony, said the Lords, which in any way impeached the integrity of either Hutchinson or Oliver.

Although this attack failed to tumble Hutchinson out of the governor's chair, his reputation in New England was seriously undermined.   Country people began to look upon him askance and to listen to Sam Adams's warnings that the worst tyrants were local boys who had made good by truckling to the British government.   This sharp decline of Hutchinson's prestige in New England is especially important because it coincided with the appearance of another "menacing monster" in the colonies — the East India Tea Act.

Having seen what Sam Adams had done with a rumor that the Crown was to pay the judges' salaries, it might be expected that the British government would have avoided giving him fresh grievances.   But Englishmen had not yet learned the folly of taxing Americans and the Ministry still hoped to appease the tax-ridden squires by means of an American revenue. Moreover, the financial muddle in which the East India Company had become mired made it essential that the British government take action in the colonies.   The East India Company was heavily indebted to the government and immense quantities of its tea lay rotting in London warehouses.   At the same time, the British American colonies, one of the principal tea markets of the world, smuggled in huge quantities of Dutch

---

[16] *The Writings of Samuel Adams*, III, 47.
[17] *The Letters of Hutchinson and Oliver*, 141.   Mass. Archives, 27, *Hutchinson Corr.*, III, 564.

tea rather than pay the tax on British bohea. Thus, the most obvious course open to the British government was to unload the East India tea upon the colonies, lower the price, and take the profit out of smuggling by underselling Dutch contraband.

To British statesmen, there seemed an excellent chance that the colonists, thin-skinned as they were to British tyranny, would leap at the opportunity to buy tea at half the price it brought in London. At first, it is true, Americans were disposed to rejoice at the prospect of slaking their thirst with prime British bohea at low cost, but their joy was quickly damped by Sam Adams and other patriot leaders.[18] The British government had made East India tea cheap in the colonies, but it had not repealed the tax paid in colonial ports upon every pound of tea imported from the mother country. The tea duty, it will be remembered, was the only tax left untouched by Parliament in 1770 when it repealed the remaining Townshend duties in order to break up the nonimportation agreement in the colonies. As Sam Adams had then pointed out, the tea duty brought in a larger revenue than all the taxes combined that had been imposed by Charles Townshend. It was the sums collected by the Commissioners of the Customs from tea that permitted the British government to carry forward its policy of making colonial governors and judges independent of the legislatures: and if East India tea were permitted to pour into the colonies from the overstocked British warehouses, this revenue would be enormously increased. And, with the advantage of low price, the East India Company would possess a virtual monopoly of the American market because it would undersell the smugglers and cut out the colonial middlemen who had formerly bought their tea through London agents. When viewed in this light, the Tea Act was "more insidious than the Stamp Act" because, under the pretense of good will toward the colonies, it led directly to *"parliamentary despotism."* Instead of being compelled to pay unconstitutional stamp duties, the colonists were now to be tempted to drink themselves out of their liberties with cheap tea. Every time an American sat

[18] Hutchinson, III, 422.

down to breakfast, it was said, he would pay a duty to the British government.[19]

Although most colonists had patriotically patronized their local tea smugglers after the downfall of the nonimportation agreement in 1770, New Englanders continued to import British tea and pay the tax to the Commissioners of the Customs. Tea was not drunk merely by the upper classes of the towns: its use was general among all classes and far more was consumed in the country than in Boston. Sam Adams and other patriot propagandists vainly attempted to wean the people from tea. Because it was taxed by the British government, tea was said to be infected with a plague which destroyed colonial liberties, weakened the "tone of the stomach, and therefore of the whole system, inducing *tremors and spasmodic affections*," and turned strong men into "weak, effeminate and creeping valetudinarians." Nevertheless, "luxurious and enervating" tea continued to be so popular in New England that James Otis declared his countrymen would "part with all their liberties, and religion too, rather than renounce it." New Englanders gagged at home-grown "Labradore" tea — "that nauseous weed" — and were contented only with genuine British bohea.[20] To satisfy this thirst, — "the bane of New England," — John Hancock and other Whig merchants joined with the rankest Tories in importing British tea and paying the tax.[21] With good reason, the Boston Whigs believed that, in the matter of tea, New England was guilty of backsliding which called for atonement in the form of a particularly vigorous blow at British authority.

The loudest outcry against the East India Act came from Philadelphia and New York, where the Dutch smugglers were more numerous and the merchants better organized than in Boston. The Philadelphia citizens resolved on October 8,

---

[19] *Newport Mercury*, Nov. 22, 1773. *Boston Gazette*, Aug. 15, 1768; Oct. 25, 1773.

[20] *Essex Gazette*, May 19, 1772; Jan. 4, 1774. *Pennsylvania Chronicle*, Nov. 28, 1768. *Boston Gazette*, Aug. 15, 1768. *Pennsylvania Packet*, Dec. 13, 1773. *Rivington's New York Gazetteer*, Dec. 22, 1773. Mass. Archives, 27, *Hutchinson Corr.*, III, 610.

[21] *The Works of John Adams*, II, 381.

1773, that all who aided in the sale of East India tea were to be treated as public enemies. It was not until a month later that the Boston town meeting voted to follow Philadelphia's example in outlawing abettors of the East India Company. The Philadelphia and New York Sons of Liberty also took the lead in demanding that the company's consignees in the colonies resign and publicly promise not to handle the tea when it arrived — a measure which Boston belatedly followed. But there were obstacles in the way of the Boston Sons of Liberty which did not hamper the New York and Philadelphia patriots. In the Southern colonies, the tea consignees hastened to resign and treat the Whigs "in a soothing manner"; but the Boston consignees were of a tougher breed and refused to be frightened by the patriots' threats.[22] The Boston Liberty Boys summoned the tea importers to Liberty Tree and made elaborate preparations to receive their resignations: the flag was run up Liberty pole; bells were rung in the meetinghouses; and a huge crowd assembled in Hanover Square — but the show had to be called off because the importers ignored the summons and refused to appear. This unexpected resistance was owing to Thomas Hutchinson, who, for a brief period, seemed about to worst Sam Adams in one of the most crucial encounters of their long quarrel.

Although his own popularity had been shattered by the publication of his letters, Hutchinson resolved to rally the Tories and make a desperate effort to enforce the Tea Act in Massachusetts Bay. Besides, he himself was a merchant and the tea destined for Massachusetts had been consigned by the East India Company to his sons and friends. Because of the close connection between the governor and the tea, Sam Adams exclaimed that Hutchinson had persuaded the British government to pass the East India Act in order that he might "finger the profits" of the monopoly.[23] But, in reality, the unlucky job of selling the tea had been wished upon the Hutchinsons

[22] Hutchinson, III, 423. *Boston Gazette*, Nov. 15, 1772. *Letters of Samuel Cooper to Pownall and Franklin, 1770–1774* (Bancroft Collection), N. Y. Public Library, Samuel Cooper to Benjamin Franklin, Dec. 17, 1773.
[23] *Boston Gazette*, Dec. 13, 1773.

and their Tory friends by their English acquaintances, who mistakenly supposed they were making the enforcement of the Tea Act easier by giving a handful of Tory merchants a virtual monopoly of the trade, freezing out both honest tea merchants and smugglers. Moreover, Hutchinson had had nothing to do with the scheme conceived by the British Ministry of saving the government's investment in the East India Company and drawing a revenue from the colonies. Like Benjamin Franklin, Hutchinson had regarded the government's refusal to repeal the tea tax when the other Townshend duties were revoked in 1770 as poor surgery which left a splinter in an unhealed wound. He warned the British Ministry that in keeping up the tea duty it had left a powder keg in full view of colonial radicals who might kick it over at any moment. Hutchinson believed the East India Act of 1773 was an ill-timed and futile measure, but, because the British government had begun a new quarrel with the colonies, he saw that he must bear the brunt of the attack Sam Adams and the radical Whigs were certain to make upon royal government in the colonies.

Because Hutchinson encouraged the Boston tea consignees to resist the Whigs, Sam Adams and his "Mohawks" encountered an unexpected obstacle. They had anticipated no more difficulty in compelling the tea merchants to resign than they had experienced with the stamp masters, but in spite of menaces and mobs, the Hutchinsons and their friends would do no more than promise to store the tea when it landed and await word from England before taking further action.[24] Because of the failure of the Boston Sons of Liberty to bring the tea consignees to their knees, the reputation of the Puritan metropolis as a patriot stronghold began to sink rapidly throughout the colonies. "There are many fears respecting Boston," wrote a Philadelphian; "some even going to the length of asserting that tea was being imported and the duty paid; while in Philadelphia not an ounce of tea had paid duty." New Yorkers remembered that the "Saints" had imported dutied British tea

---

[24] Mass. Archives, 27, *Hutchinson Corr.*, III, 12, 14. *The Diary and Letters of Thomas Hutchinson*, I, 100. *Israel Williams Papers*, II, Thomas Hutchinson to Israel Williams, Dec. 23, 1773.

while the other colonists had patriotically drunk Dutch contraband; and the successful resistance of the Boston tea merchants was sneeringly contrasted with the speedy downfall of the New York and Philadelphia consignees.[25] In New York, the "Mohawks" were already threatening to destroy the tea when it arrived and the Philadelphia Sons of Liberty were laying plans to set the tea ships on fire with burning rafts when they appeared in the Delaware. "What think you, Captain," the Liberty Boys asked the Delaware pilots who were expected to guide the East India Company's vessels to Philadelphia, "of a Halter around your Neck — ten Gallons of liquid Tar decanted on your Pate — with the Feathers of a dozen wild Geese laid over to enliven your Appearance?"[26] If the Boston patriots hoped to keep pace with these fire-eating Sons of Liberty in the Southern provinces, it was clear that they must strike an audacious blow directly at the British government.

Thus, in 1773, to kindle an explosion which would prove to the Southern colonists that Boston Whigs were still fervent patriots, Sam Adams began to beat the alarm he had sounded during the nonimportation agreement. "Our credit is at stake," he told the people; "we must venture, and unless we do, we shall be discarded by the sons of liberty in the other colonies." Boston Sons of Liberty, he exclaimed, must "wipe off the score" of irresolution by striking another home blow at British tyranny.[27] How Sam Adams intended to make amends for Boston's backsliding was not long in doubt.

Adams did not believe that New Englanders would be able to resist the East India tea if it were offered for sale in the country: its low price was an almost "invincible temptation" to thrifty yeomen addicted to bohea.[28] Although he declared the Ministry had infected the tea with a plague by laying taxes upon it, he feared that New Englanders would shut their eyes

[25] *Boston Gazette*, Nov. 15, 1773; Dec. 13, 1773. Mass. Archives, 27, *Hutchinson Corr.*, III, 610. *Connecticut Courant*, Dec. 21, 1773.

[26] *Rivington's New York Gazetteer*, Dec. 2, 1773. Broadside, Lib. Cong., To the Delaware Pilots, Philadelphia, Nov. 27, 1773.

[27] Gordon, I, 336. *Massachusetts Gazette*, Dec. 20, 1773.

[28] *Mass. Hist. Soc. Collections*, IV, Fourth Series, 374. Hutchinson, III, 430, 433.

to the danger and swallow the bait. For this reason, he determined not to permit the tea to be landed and stored in warehouses from which it might be smuggled into the country. He insisted, instead, that the tea be sent back in the same ships in which it had arrived, before there was an opportunity to pay the duty or import it secretly into the country. But in making this demand Adams came in conflict with British law. By act of Parliament, no dutiable merchandise could be returned to Great Britain in the same bottom without a pass from the governor. The governor, in turn, could not issue such a pass without a receipt from the customhouse that the duty had been paid. Thus, if the tea were shipped back to England without payment of duty, the vessels that carried the tea would be liable to confiscation by the British government — but this objection carried little weight with Sam Adams because it was based upon acts of Parliament which New Englanders "had nothing to do with," since they "owed no Sybjection to yt Power & that thr Transactions might be carried on witht paying any Regard to It." [29] In this manner, a deadlock was created between the patriots and tea consignees in Boston: the merchants offering to store the tea, which Adams regarded as a complete victory for the East India Company and the British government; the patriots demanding that when the tea arrived it be immediately returned, which the merchants knew would result in their financial ruin.[30]

Yet there was an escape from this dilemma which, had Sam Adams permitted it to be utilized, would have made unnecessary the Boston Tea Party. If the tea ships anchored below Castle William instead of entering the port of Boston, they could return to England without a pass from the governor, payment of duty, or observance of any of the formalities required by Parliamentary law. But if the ships came beyond Castle William, they could not again put to sea until the tea had been landed or the duty paid. Hutchinson planned to avert the

[29] British Museum, Additional MSS. 35912, Hardwicke, Lib. Cong. Transcript, Extracts of Private Letters from Boston, Mr. H. to Mr. M., Jan. 6, 1774.

[30] Mass. Archives, 27, *Hutchinson Corr.*, III, 605. *The Works of John Adams*, II, 324. *Mass. Hist. Soc. Collections*, IV, Fourth Series, 374.

crisis he saw gathering in Boston by ordering the tea ships to anchor below the Castle so that, if it appeared that the tea could not be landed, they could set sail for the mother country.[31] But Sam Adams had very different plans for the "plagued" East India tea.

Adams had long hoped to produce an emergency that would force Bostonians to show their mettle. Hutchinson saw that Adams and the radical Whigs were eager "to engage the people in some desperate measure" to clear Boston's skirts of all suspicion of remissness and bring the colonies nearer separation from the mother country.[32] Sam Adams seldom let slip an opportunity to plunge the colonies deeper into controversy with Great Britain; and he soon showed that he had no intention of allowing the crisis brought on by the East India Tea Act to pass quietly. When the first tea ship anchored below Castle William, its captain was summoned before the Boston committee of correspondence, where he was ordered by Adams and other committeemen to bring his ship up to the Boston wharves and land all the cargo except the tea on pain of being tarred and feathered by the Liberty Boys. The captains of the two tea ships which shortly after arrived in Boston Bay were given the same alternative. In Philadelphia, where there was no Sam Adams to evolve a desperate scheme to destroy the tea, the ships were ordered by the Sons of Liberty to anchor below the port in order that their cargo might not become liable to port duties.[33] In Boston, on the other hand, three vessels laden with East India tea were made fast at Griffin's wharf on a water front that swarmed with Sons of Liberty. Sam Adams might well have rejoiced in having created a dilemma which only his "Mohawks" could solve.

If Sam Adams was planning, as the Tories suspected, to push the metropolis headlong into a quarrel with Great Britain, he did not intend that Boston should act alone. The reaction in rural New England against Boston after the Massacre had shown

---

[31] *The Diary and Letters of Thomas Hutchinson*, I, 100.

[32] Hutchinson, III, 439. Mass. Archives, *Hutchinson Corr.*, III, 609.

[33] *The Diary and Letters of Thomas Hutchinson*, I, 100–101. Hutchinson, III, 425, 430. *Pennsylvania Gazette*, Dec. 29, 1773.

the Sons of Liberty the importance of country support, and they proceeded in 1773 to put the lesson to profit.   The country, as well as the town, was to be involved in resisting the East India tea.   Whenever a tea ship appeared in the harbor, the bells were set ringing for a "general muster" and handbills were posted throughout the country calling upon "Friends! Citizens! Countrymen!" to aid the metropolis.   The Boston committee of correspondence dispatched circular letters to the Massachusetts country towns to inform them of the emergency in Boston; and rural committees of correspondence were summoned to the metropolis, where they sat as "a little senate" deliberating upon the disposition of the tea.   When a tea ship was seen off the coast, Adams rushed expresses to the neighboring towns to meet the Boston committee in Faneuil Hall the next day to assist the townspeople in warding off British tyranny.   He urged the country people to attend the meetings of "town and country" in Boston, and hundreds of the rural patriots flocked to Faneuil Hall to hear Adams thunder against the British government and the tea importers.   Hutchinson remarked that the yeomen were brought to the metropolis "by the Artifices of Boston expecting them to share in the criminality to lessen their own share."   At these gatherings of Boston mechanics and country farmers, Adams "never was in greater glory," and Tories observed with dismay that many country people were becoming more and more inclined toward violence as they rubbed shoulders with Boston Sons of Liberty in Faneuil Hall.[34]

The menace of East India tea revealed what a powerful revolutionary machine Sam Adams had created in the Boston committee of correspondence.   The committee took complete charge in Boston and directed the patriots' activities, which culminated in the destruction of the tea.   By means of the committees of correspondence, Adams kept the people in a state of feverish excitement: if the tea were landed, he told New Eng-

[34] *Mass. Hist. Soc. Proceedings* (1866), VIII, 324.   *Committee of Correspondence Papers*, Boston Committee to Dorchester, Brookline, Cambridge and Charlestown Committees, Nov. 28, 1773.   Mass. Archives, 27, *Hutchinson Corr.*, III, 581, 587, 605.

landers in his circular letters, taxes would be imposed upon all necessities imported from Great Britain, and even the land "purchased and cultivated by our hard laboring Ancestors" would be taxed to support miscreants in office "whose vileness ought to banish them from the Society of Men." [35] As a result, royal authority in the province became daily more powerless: when Hutchinson attempted to disperse the meetings in Faneuil Hall his proclamations met with "infinite Contempt" and a "loud and very generall hiss." [36] Indeed, many of the patriots were so infuriated that the Boston committee of correspondence was forced to appoint a military watch along the water front to guard the tea against an attack.

There seemed, indeed, no alternative to destroying the tea or experiencing the appalling taxes and wholesale confiscation of colonial lands by British "overlords" which Sam Adams prophesied would follow payment of the tea duty.   Governor Hutchinson refused to give the ships permission to return to England until the Commissioners of the Customs gave him a receipt; the Commissioners declined to give the governor a receipt until the duty had been paid; and the tea consignees refused to court financial ruin by sending back the tea without a pass from the governor and receipt from the customhouse.   Rather than trust themselves further with the Boston mob, the tea merchants took refuge in Castle William.   Their flight smoothed the way for Sam Adams's plans.   Whatever now happened in Boston, he could hold Hutchinson responsible.   The governor's obstinacy in withholding a pass for the ships, Adams exclaimed, had made desperate measures necessary.

The destruction of the tea struck Boston patriot leaders as the only effective solution of the deadlock that Sam Adams had created by ordering the ships to come beyond Castle William. If the tea were thrown into the harbor, there would be no longer danger of its being smuggled into the country to tempt the patriotism of rural Whigs.   There was in Boston a large body of men ready for any violence: several hundred "veteran Sons

---

[35] *Committee of Correspondence Papers*, Circular Letter, Nov. 22, 1773.
[36] *Mass. Hist. Soc. Proceedings*, IV (1860), 218.   Mass. Archives, 27, *Hutchinson Corr.*, III, 601.

of Liberty," it was said, were enrolled in the metropolis to destroy the tea or "perish in the Attempt." [37] Moreover, the British force in the vicinity was not likely to give trouble: only one regiment of royal troops was in Castle William, and the townspeople had no fears of the British fleet in the harbor because they believed that the admiral "might as well hang himself, as burn the town." [38]

If the tea were to be destroyed, the dead line for the business was December 17, 1773, when it would become liable to seizure by the customhouse officers for nonpayment of duty. After the tea had fallen into their hands and been stored in Castle William, Sam Adams had no doubt it would be either secretly imported into the country or left untouched until a British army could be sent to cram it down the colonists' throats. It was essential, therefore, that the Sons of Liberty strike before December 17. As this momentous day approached, it became clear that the Whig leaders were preparing for rough work: guns suddenly disappeared from all the shops in Boston. " 'T would puzzle any person to purchase a pair of p[isto]les in town," said John Andrews, "as they are all bought up, with a full determination to repell force by force." [39] The destruction of the tea had been agreed upon many days before the Tea Party; and on the morning of December 16, 1773, Sam Adams received a last-minute appeal from a Whig friend to spare the tea lest a rash attack "give yr Enemys a thousand Opportunitys against this Town." [40] But Boston's reputation as a patriot stronghold was in need of saving and Adams was not to be swerved from his scheme by the risk of retaliation from Great Britain. On the afternoon of December 16, several thousand people crowded into the Old South Meetinghouse to demand that Rotch, one of the owners of the tea ships, make a last effort to secure a clearance from Hutchinson. The candles were being lighted when Rotch returned to the Old South with

[37] *Boston Gazette*, Jan. 10, 1774. *Massachusetts Gazette*, Dec. 20, 1773.
[38] *Ibid.*, Dec. 20, 1773.
[39] *Mass. Hist. Soc. Proceedings*, VIII, 325. *Pennsylvania Packet*, Dec. 13, 1773.
[40] *Samuel Adams Papers*, Letter in old style handwriting, signed "W.T." to "Mr. Addams," Dec. 16 (1773).

Hutchinson's refusal.   In the gathering dusk, Sam Adams arose
and solemnly declared that "this meeting can do nothing further to save the country."   His words were the signal for a
wild war whoop from the galleries and the street outside the
meetinghouse where several hundred "Mohawks," who had
been fortifying themselves with punch and putting the finishing touches on their Indian make-up at Edes and Gill's printing
shop, broke from the crowd and headed for the water front
closely followed by a mob of spectators.   As this howling procession approached the water front there was such an uproar
that "you 'd thought the inhabitants of the infernal regions had
broke loose." [41]   Most of these "Narragansett Indians" were
Adams's followers from the North End — shipyard workers,
artisans, and ship masters — decked out in war paint and feathers.[42]   Once aboard the tea ships, the braves worked quickly,
and within a few moments three hundred and forty-two chests
of the finest tea that ever tempted New Englanders' palates,
pocketbooks, and patriotism were at the bottom of Boston Harbor.

After the Tea Party, Sam Adams and the Boston Whigs were
in "a perfect Jubillee."   For, as Hutchinson said, it was "the
boldest stroke which had yet been struck in America" and fully
restored Boston to the leadership of the American colonies.[43]
The Puritan metropolis again stood forth as a citadel of patriotism: in New York, Philadelphia, and Baltimore, Bostonians were
"highly extolled" by the Sons of Liberty, although the Tories
railed against "ye wicked Bostonians, who have given it to the
fishes!" [44]   But most New Englanders were charmed, as was
John Adams, by the "Sublimity" of the Tea Party; and in Massachusetts, the town and country were more firmly united than
at any time since the Stamp Act.   It now became a patriotic
duty to follow Boston's leadership.   "Many thought they

[41] *Mass. Hist. Soc. Proceedings,* VIII, 325; Wells, II, 122.

[42] Gordon, I, 341.

[43] *Essex Gazette,* Dec. 28, 1773.   Hutchinson, III, 439.

[44] *Boston Gazette,* Jan. 3, 1774.   *Essex Gazette,* April 5, 1774.   *Pennsylvania Gazette,* Dec. 29, 1773.   *Rivington's New York Gazetteer,* Jan. 27,
1774.

could not be Friends to their Country," lamented the Tories, "unless they trod in the same Steps, and imitated the Example of the Bostonians." [45]

Had British statesmen realized the strength of this determination in the colonies to stand by Boston — the "antient capital of America" — they might have been less ready to single out the metropolis for punishment. In England, news of the Tea Party provoked an immediate outburst against "the licentious Bostonians" who, it was believed, were making ready to rebel.[46] Englishmen were unable to see any cause for the destruction of the tea other than the zeal of the "Boston Fanatics" to pick quarrels with the mother country upon every occasion.[47] They regarded the Tea Party as "a downright thrashing from our own subjects" — an indignity which, it was pointed out, no European power would dare offer the victor of the Seven Years' War. If we can swallow this affront, Englishmen exclaimed, let the seat of Empire be moved from Westminster to Boston, since the New England "Saints" had shown themselves to be "the only people on earth who could trample on our once boasted spirit with impunity." Sam Adams and his "Mohawks" seemed to have brought the dispute between the mother country and colonies to a sudden head; the issue was now clearly defined: "Whether the Colonies shall give laws to England, or England to the Colonies?" The day of halfway measures had passed: the "Boston mutineers" must be deprived of their charter, "the spring and source of all their insolent and unjustifiable acts," and taught to respect the might of England before they rose in outright rebellion.[48]

Thus, by its achievement in forcing the British government's hand in the colonies and rallying colonial radicals to Boston's defense, the Tea Party might well be regarded as a crossing of

---

[45] *Warren-Adams Letters*, II, 403 (Appendix). *Letters of Samuel Cooper to Pownall and Franklin*, Samuel Cooper to Benjamin Franklin, Dec. 17, 1773.

[46] *New York Gazette and Weekly Mercury*, May 9, 1774. *Rivington's New York Gazetteer*, May 12, 1774.

[47] *Independency the Object of the Congress in America* (London, 1774), 2.

[48] *New York Gazette and Weekly Mercury*, May 9, 1774. *Rivington's New York Gazetteer*, May 12, 1774.

the Rubicon which left Sam Adams the desperate alternative of "Neck or Nothing." [49] It was a headlong plunge toward revolt which set free the forces, long gathering in America, that led to war between the mother country and colonies. The British government could not overlook the insult it had received at the hands of Sam Adams and his "Mohawks"; but British statesmen were utterly unaware of the true strength of the revolutionary movement in America. And it was clear that upon their decision hung "the FATE OF A GREAT EMPIRE." [50]

[49] Peter Oliver, 146.
[50] *Rivington's New York Gazetteer*, May 12, 1774.

XII

SAM ADAMS AND THE SOLEMN LEAGUE
AND COVENANT

SAM ADAMS was well aware that by serving the British government a dish of tea brewed with salt water, Boston was certain to be punished. It was widely believed in the colonies that Lord North was eager for an opportunity to send a fleet to America and blow the Sons of Liberty out of Faneuil Hall; indeed, it was said that American liberty had only to be mentioned to the Prime Minister to have him fall into a fit: "foaming at the mouth, and with eyes starting from their sockets," he would "vomit forth" horrid threats against the rascally American republicans. Rumors spread that he had ordered troops and men-of-war to Boston to collect damages for the tea and enforce a new stamp act; and Arthur Lee put Adams on his guard against a "particular stroke of revenge" from the British Ministry.[1] Sam Adams and his "Mohawks" seemed indeed to have brought a hornets' nest about their ears.

While the Boston Liberty Boys dug themselves in for the expected blow from England they proceeded to sweep away the last vestiges of Parliamentary authority in the colonies. For many years, Tories had pointed to the American post office as an example of Parliamentary authority which refuted the Whig argument that the British Parliament had no precedents for the internal taxation of the colonies. The American post office had been established by an act of Parliament, but it was so vital to the colonies that the patriots were reluctant to forgo

---

[1] *Newport Mercury*, Aug. 8, 1773 (Supplement). *New York Gazette and Weekly Mercury*, April 4, 1774. *Rivington's New York Gazetteer*, May 12, 1774. *Essex Gazette*, April 5, 1774. R. H. Lee, *The Life of Arthur Lee* (1829), I, 242.

its benefits by attacking it along with the Stamp Act.   By 1774,
however, Sam Adams believed the time had come to discard all
Parliamentary authority; and when William Goddard, a Pennsylvania newspaper printer, popped up in Boston with a scheme
for an independent colonial post office, he was warmly welcomed
by Adams and the committee of correspondence.   Adams was
eager to make a fresh assault upon British authority, for he
knew it would be fatal for the revolutionary movement in the
colonies to appear to stand still after the Tea Party.   Moreover,
he foresaw that if matters came to the worst between the mother
country and colonies, America would require a separate system
of postriders to prevent a stoppage of intercolonial correspondence; hence his denunciations of the constitutional post office as
"an usurpation of the Parliament no longer to be borne." [2]

At the same time that British statesmen watched colonial
Whigs pulling up Parliamentary jurisdiction root and branch,
Hutchinson exclaimed that Sam Adams was stripping the governor and Council of Massachusetts of all authority and setting up
a new constitution by the "grossest falsities and misrepresentations." [3]   By impeaching Chief Justice Oliver in the Massachusetts General Court, Adams took a long stride toward making the provincial legislature the complete "Parliament" of
the colony.   No Crown officer had ever before been impeached
by the General Court, but lack of precedent was never an obstacle to Sam Adams: Oliver had accepted the salary proffered
by King George and therefore he must be removed from office.
From Thomas Hutchinson, however, Sam Adams encountered
serious opposition.   When Adams brought forward Chief Justice Oliver's impeachment in the House of Representatives,
using the form and words of the British House of Commons, the
governor attempted to stop the proceedings by refusing to attend the Council meeting before which Adams, as chairman of
the House committee, was compelled to bring the articles of
impeachment.   As long as Hutchinson remained absent from
the Council, the Chief Justice seemed out of reach of his enemies

[2] *Committee of Correspondence Papers*, Boston Committee to the Salem,
Marblehead, etc., Committee, March 24, 1774; Boston Committee to the
Newport and Providence Committees, March 29, 1774. *Lamb Papers*,
MSS. N. Y. Hist. Soc., William Goddard to John Lamb, March 23, 1774.
[3] *The Diary and Letters of Thomas Hutchinson*, I, 140.

and the case against him was brought to a standstill. The Whigs exclaimed that not even the most arbitrary English King would have dared to protect his favorite from the House of Commons with such brazenness.[4] Hutchinson congratulated himself upon having tripped up the Whigs and exposed the Massachusetts House of Representatives as a mere "Mock Parliament," but he did not take into account Adams's resource. When it became evident that no persuasion or threats could bring Hutchinson to the Council, Adams declared the governor was "presumed" to be present and ordered the impeachment to be carried on with the governor "presumptively" in his seat at Council. This fiction enabled the patriots to enter upon the House *Journal* that the Chief Justice had been impeached before the governor and Council in spite of the fact that Hutchinson had not set foot inside the Council chamber during the proceedings.[5]

But Adams's efforts to purge the Massachusetts judiciary were rudely cut short by the measures taken by the British government to punish Boston for the Tea Party. By act of Parliament, the port of Boston was so effectively closed to trade that Lord North remarked he had shoved the metropolis back twenty miles from the Bay; and, by subsequent legislation, the administration of justice in the colony was reformed and the elective Council filled with royal appointees. British politicians expected the townspeople to wilt when confronted with these harsh measures, as they had in 1768 when British troops took possession of Boston. But much to the surprise of the Ministry, the citizens showed no sign of weakening. The Port Bill was denounced in the town meeting with "a freedom and energy becoming the orators of ancient Rome"; Sam Adams exclaimed that "for flagrant injustice and barbarity, one might search in vain among the archives of Constantinople to find a match for it"; Thomas Hutchinson was declared responsible for Boston's plight; and Paul Revere was sent galloping off to New York with an appeal for aid to the Sons of Liberty.[6]

[4] *Boston Gazette*, April 11, 1774. Hutchinson, III, 446.
[5] *Ibid.*, III, 447, 449, 453. *The Works of John Adams*, X, 238; II, 328–329.
[6] *The Writings of Samuel Adams*, III, 112, 117. Isaac Q. Leake, *Memoir of the Life and Times of General John Lamb* (1857), 84, 85.

Sam Adams saw in the Boston Port Bill another attempt by the British government to separate the colonies from Massachusetts Bay in order that the "leading colony" might be singled out for punishment. His course was clear: he must convince Americans that if they deserted Massachusetts in this crisis, the colonies would be beaten down singly and British tyranny imposed upon the whole continent. "This Attack, though made immediately upon us," said the Boston committee of correspondence, "is doubtless design'd for every other Colony, who will not surrender their sacred Rights and Liberties into the Hands of an Infamous Ministry. Now therefore is the Time, when *ALL* should be united in opposition to this violation of the Liberties of *ALL*." Sam Adams warned the Philadelphians: "*You* will be called upon to surrender your Rights, if ever they should succeed in their Attempts to suppress the Spirit of Liberty *here*." "It is not the Rights of Boston only, but of ALL AMERICA which are now struck at," declared the Boston Sons of Liberty. "Not the Merchants only but the Farmer, and every order of Men who inhabit this noble Continent." [7]

In the midst of the excitement over the Port Bill, Adams and the Whigs learned that "that damn'd *arch traitor*," Thomas Hutchinson, had been recalled to England. Just before he left Boston, Hutchinson was presented with addresses approving his administration as governor, signed by over one hundred and twenty of the principal merchants, lawyers, magistrates, and Episcopal clergymen of Boston. Sam Adams was dismayed by the number and prominence of Hutchinson's well-wishers, for he feared that if the addresses got abroad, the patriots in the neighboring colonies upon whom Boston depended for support against the British government would be led to believe that the Massachusetts Whig Party was in fact a small blustering faction discountenanced by the substantial citizens of the colony. Therefore, Adams told his friends outside Massachusetts that the greater part of those who signed the addresses

[7] *Committee of Correspondence Papers,* Boston Committee to the Westborough Committee, June 24, 1774; Boston Committee to the Philadelphia, New York, New Jersey, Rhode Island, etc., Committees, May 13, 1774. *The Writings of Samuel Adams,* III, 110. *Boston Evening Post,* May 16, 1774.

to Hutchinson belonged to the lowest class. "I believe," he said, "I could point out half a Score Gentlemen in Town able to purchase the whole of them." The only lawyers who signed, Adams declared, were obscure pettifoggers or young clerks who had recently purchased their books.[8] Yet, in fact, the names of many of the first families of the province appeared in these addresses; and Hutchinson sailed away from Boston on the day the Port Bill went into effect secure in the knowledge that he retained the support of the well-born and conservative. Most of these gentry, however, were exiled during the Revolution, and Hutchinson never returned to America. He did well to give Massachusetts a wide berth, for Sam Adams and John Hancock quickly came into power after the outbreak of war. And Sam Adams lost none of his hatred for Hutchinson: Bernard, he said, he could forgive, but Hutchinson's offenses were too great to be pardoned.[9]

For many years, Sam Adams had made it his policy to provoke the British government to attempt the punishment of the colonies — a step certain to put provincial radicals in power. Hutchinson and Bernard believed Adams baited the Ministry because he wished to see the Massachusetts charter under attack and British "tyranny" weighing heavily upon the colony.[10] Certainly, after the Tea Party, Adams was prepared to "make the best Improvement" of the expected British retaliation. The Boston Port Bill had been no more than received in New England before Adams produced his counterblast: a "Solemn League and Covenant" suspending all commercial intercourse with the "Island of Great Britain" until the privileges of the metropolis had been restored. This plan went beyond previous American nonimportation agreements inasmuch as both the exportation of colonial products to Great Britain and the importation of British commodities to the colonies were prohibited and the common people, rather than the merchants, were entrusted with its enforcement. Adams did not repeat his former mistake of

[8] *Mass. Hist. Soc. Proceedings,* VIII, 328. Hutchinson, III, 459. *The Writings of Samuel Adams,* III, 124–125.

[9] *The Writings of Samuel Adams,* III, 171–172.

[10] Mass. Archives, 27, *Hutchinson Corr.,* III, 40, 609. Hutchinson, III, 439.

putting "gentlemen in trade" in charge: the Solemn League and Covenant provided that the boycott was to be wholly in the hands of those "two venerable orders of Men stiled Mechanicks & husbandmen the Strength of every Community." [11]   He had learned from the ill-fated agreement of 1768–1770 to dread "mercantile Avarice" and to pin his faith to the yeomanry and town laborers whose firm patriotism, it was said, "must finally save this Country." [12]   He believed that after the Solemn League and Covenant had been accepted by these stout Whigs it little mattered whether or not *messieurs les marchands,* will be graciously pleased to come into it," since they could not import when there was no one to buy.

To stir up enthusiasm for another economic war with Great Britain, the Boston patriots declared the Solemn League and Covenant to be the only alternative to "the horrors of slavery, or the carnage and desolation of a civil war."   Although the mother country had shown conclusively in 1770 that it was not to be driven from its ground by the colonies' commercial reprisals, Adams continued to tell the people that they could bring Great Britain to terms merely by "a firm Resolution to insist upon their Rights." [13]   He still said that "degenerate Britons" would give up the struggle when they saw the provinces swarming with "Old Romans" and Puritans who steadfastly refused to touch British merchandise.   Adams attempted to make Americans believe they were so important to the mother country that Great Britain could not punish them without ruining herself.   Once England ceased to draw wealth and power from the colonies, he prophesied her speedy end.   "Britain may fall sooner than she is aware," he said; "while her Colonies who are struggling for Liberty may survive her fate & tell the Story to their Childrens Children." [14]   With over four million pounds of British money tied up in loans to American merchants and planters, colonial patriots felt confident that the

[11] *Committee of Correspondence Papers,* MSS. N. Y. Public Library, "The Solemn League of Covenant."   *The Writings of Samuel Adams,* III, 129.

[12] *Committee of Correspondence Papers,* Boston Committee to New York Committee, June 18, 1774.   Leake, 89.

[13] Mass. Archives, 26, *Hutchinson Corr.,* II, 305.

[14] *The Writings of Samuel Adams,* I, 447.

British government would hesitate long before endangering this investment by interfering in the colonies. Therefore, they regarded British menaces as mere bluff. "The consequences are feared by nobody," said Dr. Thomas Young when the mother country threatened to punish the colonies, because "every old woman" in America knew that Englishmen did not dare to jeopardize their credits and trade. Even such moderates as Thomas Cushing were convinced there was no need to fear coercion: when he was told by Hutchinson that the patriots' activities would bring down quo warranto proceedings against the Massachusetts charter, Cushing answered that "there had been none since the Reigns of the Stuarts and they dare not send one here." [15] As long as it was believed that Great Britain's "future glory" depended upon keeping in the good graces of her American subjects, all signs of yielding by the mother country merely aggravated the controversy with the colonies because Sam Adams had "art enough to improve them to raise the people higher by assuring them that if they will but persevere they may bring the nation to their own terms." [16] Indeed, until the outbreak of war, Sam Adams kept the people firm in the patriot cause by promising them a speedy, peaceful redress of grievances from the "tottering" British government.

From his experience in the last nonimportation agreement, Adams knew that the Solemn League and Covenant would be more warmly received in the country than in the seaport towns where the merchants were reluctant to begin another boycott. His plan, therefore, was to try the temper of New England yeomen before sending the Covenant among the townspeople. Adams and the Boston committee of correspondence worked so stealthily that few townspeople knew what was going on until they were startled to find the covenant sweeping the rural districts. Although it had scarcely been heard of in the metropolis, Adams told the Massachusetts farmers that it had already been adopted by an overwhelming majority of the citizens of

[15] Thomas Young to Hugh Hughes, Aug. 31, 1772, MS. through courtesy of Mr. G. P. Anderson. Mass. Archives, 26, *Hutchinson Corr.*, II, 530.

[16] *Boston Gazette*, Aug. 24, 1772. Mass. Archives, 27, *Hutchinson Corr.*, III, 550.

Boston. This trick worked so well in the country that thousands of yeomen trooped to town to sign the Covenant, swearing they would support the patriotic Bostonians. Nevertheless, many townsmen were outraged to discover they had been hoodwinked by Adams and the committee. Conservative Whigs joined with Tories in wailing that to defend themselves against British tyranny the people had created a far more oppressive tyranny at their very doors. A vigorous effort was made in the Boston town meeting to abolish the committee of correspondence on the ground that it had exceeded its authority by drawing up a nonimportation agreement and foisting it upon the country behind Bostonians' backs. For several hours, Sam Adams and the committee of correspondence were in serious danger of being thrown overboard by the irate citizens. Although the storm was finally weathered, a large number of Bostonians showed themselves heartily in favor of destroying the revolutionary steam roller which now threatened to flatten conservative Whigs and Tories alike.

The chief opposition to the Solemn League and Covenant came from the Boston merchants, who denounced it as a harebrained scheme calculated to ruin New England's trade and enrich other colonies. They protested that the whale and fishing industry, the backbone of New England's commercial prosperity, would be completely destroyed because Adams had neglected to provide for the importation of many articles essential to fishing which the colonies themselves could not supply. They believed that Massachusetts could not survive if cut off from the West Indies as Adams proposed; and they groaned that they would be put out of business because Adams had left nothing to sell. It became a common saying among Boston merchants that Adams and his crew were "determined to bring total destruction upon us" by plunging New England into a quarrel with the mother country before making sure of support from the Southern colonies.[17] But Adams paid little heed to these mutterings from "gentlemen in trade": all shortcomings of the

[17] *Massachusetts Gazette*, June 16, 1774; July 7, 1774. *The Letters and Diary of John Rowe*, edited by Annie Rowe Cunningham (1903), 276. *Mass. Hist. Soc. Proceedings*, VIII, 329. Gordon, I, 378.

Covenant he called mere "Punctilios" and reproached Bostonians for their "utterly unbecoming" behavior in complaining of hardships. "The Virtue of our Ancestors inspires us," he exclaimed, " — they were contented with Clams & Muscles." [18]

In spite of this unpromising reception in Boston, the committee of correspondence accompanied its appeals to the Southern colonies for aid against the Port Bill with copies of the Solemn League and Covenant. But instead of falling in with Sam Adams's plan to extend the boycott over America, most of the colonies gave him a point-blank refusal. The struggle, they declared, was against Great Britain, not against the American merchants, who would certainly be ruined by another nonimportation agreement. Jeremy Belknap in New Hampshire said the Boston committee of correspondence were "acting like persons out of their senses & blindly rushing upon their own Ruin," and he held the Covenant to be as arbitrary "as any Act of the British Parliament which it is intended to oppose." Philadelphia's answer to the Boston committee of correspondence was so cool that there seemed a "stroke of insulting pity in it." All "*moderate prudent* Measures" ought to be employed before resorting to economic war, the Philadelphians said, lest the "many Wise & Good Men in the Mother Country" who supported the colonial cause be alienated and the American Whig Party disunited. The Solemn League and Covenant was forwarded from New York and Philadelphia to Baltimore, Annapolis, Williamsburg, and Charleston, South Carolina, but everywhere it met with the same response: a nonimportation agreement was to be used only after all means of reconciliation had failed. [19]

This overwhelming rejection of the Solemn League and

---

[18] *The Writings of Samuel Adams*, III, 115, 128. *Boston Gazette*, June 27, 1774.

[19] *Mass. Hist. Soc. Proceedings*, Second Series (1886), II, 484–485. Lee, II, 318. *Samuel Adams Papers*, Thomas Mifflin to Sam Adams, May 26, 1774. *Committee of Correspondence Papers*, Philadelphia Committee to Boston Committee, May 21, 1774. Marblehead Committee to Boston Committee, June 18, 1774; Philadelphia Committee to Boston Committee, May 21, 1774. Peter Force, *American Archives*, Fourth Series, I, 303, 304, 323. Drayton, I, 128.

Covenant revealed how greatly Sam Adams had misjudged the strength of his supporters in the Southern and middle colonies. He depended upon "those worthy members of society, the tradesmen . . . under God, to form the revolution of the other ranks of citizens" in New York and Philadelphia.[20] If the merchants attempted to sell American liberty to the British government in exchange for bounties and privileges, Adams believed the mechanics would rise and "forbid the auction." But in 1774, when Sam Adams set on foot the Solemn League, the lower-class town radicals were not yet sufficiently strong to force it upon the more conservative classes. New York was in the throes of a violent struggle for supremacy between the merchants and Sons of Liberty; and, as conservatives or radicals gained the upper hand, the complexion of the city changed with bewildering suddenness from a stronghold of the "champions of liberty" to one of renegade Tories "hugging their chains." Pennsylvania — a province "which has hitherto been distinguished for its moderation" — was under the sway of John Dickinson, who declared, when he learned of Adams's scheme: "Nothing can throw us into a more pernicious confusion but one colony's breaking the line of opposition by advancing too hastily before the rest." [21] Until radicals like Isaac Sears of New York and Charles Thomson, "the Sam Adams of Philadelphia," came into power, Adams's plans of revolutionizing America made slow progress in the Southern and middle colonies.

Rather than adopt the Boston-made Solemn League and Covenant, the New York Whigs proposed that a Continental Congress be held to petition for redress of grievances and to determine by united counsel what steps should be taken against the mother country. Almost all the colonies supported a Congress as against the Solemn League — many because it appeared less dangerous than riding on the tail of Sam Adams's kite.

No American patriot had demanded more vigorously than

[20] Leake, 89.

. [21] Frothingham, 317. Quincy, 118, 148. *Sam Adams Papers*, Isaac Sears and Alexander McDougall to Sam Adams, July 25, 1774. *Documents relative to the Colonial History of New York*, VIII, 433. *Correspondence of Thomas Gage*, edited by C. E. Carter (1931), I, 361.

Sam Adams a Continental Congress to unite colonial opposition to Great Britain. In 1773, for example, he told Hutchinson that only a Congress of representatives from the various provinces could undertake to draw a line between the supreme authority of Parliament and the total independence of the colonies; and it was the fashion among Boston patriots to look forward to "some future Congress as the glorious source of the salvation of America." [22] His writings are filled with exhortations to Americans to unite: "The Colonies are all embark'd in the same bottom," he frequently said. "The Liberties of all are alike invaded by the same haughty Power." [23] Nevertheless, New York's proposal of a Continental Congress in 1774 left him cold. Adams feared that it would be too slow in bringing pressure to bear upon the mother country. "A Congress," he said, "is of absolute Necessity in my Opinion, but from the length of time it will take to bring it to pass, I fear it cannot answer for the present Emergency." [24] Delay, he exclaimed, would be fatal to Boston. And, indeed, the plight of the Puritan metropolis was deplorable: practically all business had ceased; hundreds of workmen had been thrown out of employment; and most of the inhabitants were "render'd wretchedly miserable." Moreover, quick action was necessary because the Tories were raising a storm against the patriots by whispering in the people's ears that it was "our Vile Sons" who were responsible for the town's misfortune.[25]

Sam Adams was well aware that the Tories and lukewarm Whigs expected to wield sufficient power in the Congress to prevent the use of economic weapons against the mother country. This prospect gave rise to many misgivings among the Sons of Liberty; and Sam Adams dreaded nothing more than being thrown in with a large number of "half-way Whigs" who were certain to clamor to go home as soon as they had dispatched a petition to the King and Parliament. Rather than run such risk, Adams wished the Sons of Liberty in each province to take

[22] Wells, II, 82.

[23] *The Writings of Samuel Adams*, II, 25.

[24] *Ibid.*, II, 115, 123–124.

[25] R. Lechemere to Messrs. Lane Son and Fraser, May 30, 1774, MS. Mass. Hist. Soc.

the reins in their own hands and follow Massachusetts into rebellion against the British government. Therefore, the Boston committee of correspondence protested to the New York and Philadelphia committees against summoning a Congress before adopting a nonimportation agreement. The stoppage of British trade to America, said the Boston patriots, would have "a speedy and irresistable operation" upon hardheaded Britons who ignored colonial petitions and remonstrances as long as their pocketbooks were untouched.[26]

But it was soon made clear to Sam Adams that he would be compelled to take his chances with a Continental Congress. The colonies would not touch his Solemn League and Covenant, yet they greeted the proposal of a Continental Congress with enthusiasm. Swallowing his disappointment, Adams quickly set about securing the election of delegates from Massachusetts Bay. After General Gage, the new governor of the colony, adjourned the General Court to Salem, Adams took care that a report reached the governor's ears that the House of Representatives was preparing moderate measures for his approval, while in fact it was taking steps to join the Continental Congress. On June 17, 1774, when all was in readiness, the doors to the representatives' chamber were locked and the key pocketed by Sam Adams. Gage soon learned what was going on in the House and dispatched the secretary to dissolve it. The secretary pounded on the door in vain: no one would admit him and, thanks to Adams's foresight, the key could not be found. The best that could be done was to dissolve the meeting by reading Gage's proclamation outside the door. But the Whigs inside continued their work: the adherence of Massachusetts Bay to the Continental Congress was agreed upon; and the "brace of Adamses" were among those elected to represent the colony at Philadelphia.

At the same time that Sam Adams was learning how greatly he had overrated the radical strength in the Southern provinces he was being made uncomfortably aware that Massachusetts conservatism was still very much alive. In closing the port of

[26] *Committee of Correspondence Papers*, Boston Committee to New York Committee, May 31, 1774.

Boston, the British government left a loophole by which the citizens might escape the full penalty of the law: if the tea destroyed at the Tea Party were paid for, royal clemency would be extended the town. When these terms were known in Boston, Adams remarked that if anyone should pay for the tea it was Thomas Hutchinson and his Tory friends whose obstinacy had made its safe return to England impossible. Nevertheless, a strong sentiment began to develop in Boston in favor of making full amends for the "Narrangansett" braves' work. Benjamin Franklin and John Dickinson of Pennsylvania urged payment, and Thomas Hutchinson made the offer more tempting by promising that if Boston paid the first cost of the tea "every thing else would be made easy." [27] The rapid fall in Boston real estate as a result of the Port Bill increased the clamor from the propertied class that reparation be made to the East India Company. Even the threats of the Sons of Liberty failed to silence the conservatives; and the frightened Whigs were forced to confess that the party in favor of paying for the tea was becoming too formidable for them. [28] A call was sent out to Sam Adams, then in Salem attending the General Court, to come to Boston and crush the Tories. Although Adams was busied in Salem laying plans for the first Continental Congress, he sent down to Boston a batch of propaganda calculated to overset the conservatives. He pointed out that Bostonians would make themselves contemptible in the eyes of their fellow colonists if they faltered after their "late glorious Behaviour" in the Tea Party and that, when the British government saw them in retreat, it would load the colony with taxes until the metropolis had been turned into a "poor fishing village." Massachusetts farmers listened eagerly to Adams because they feared that the tea would be paid for with money collected by means of a province tax — thus compelling yeomen to make good the damage done by the Boston Sons of

[27] *The Works of Benjamin Franklin*, VI, 179. Charles J. Stille, *The Life and Times of John Dickinson* (1891), 109. Peter Force, *American Archives, Fourth Series* (1837), I, 344.

[28] Frothingham, 317. R. Lechemere to Messrs. Lane Son and Fraser, Feb. 14, 1774, MS. Mass. Hist. Soc. *Chalmers Papers*, IV, Extracts of some Letters from New England, Dated in July and Aug. 1774.

Liberty. And at the Boston town meeting, Adams's supporters turned out in such numbers that the "better sort" who
favored reimbursing the East India Company were outvoted
"by a great Majority of the lower Class" which roundly damned
the British government and dared it to do its worst against the
"Antient Capital of North America." [29]

By pushing the colonies toward an open rupture with the
mother country, Adams terrified the conservative Whigs, who
believed with John Dickinson that the cause of liberty should
be left in the hands of lofty-minded patriots strongly averse to
the riots, sedition, and outright rebellion practised by Boston
Sons of Liberty. These cautious "half-way Whigs" were certain that America was not yet a match in war for Great Britain:
a premature struggle with the mother country, they exclaimed,
would prove so disastrous that the colonies would be "kept
down another Age." [30] They declared that there was no need
to hasten a quarrel with Great Britain: Americans had everything
to gain by postponing the day of separation, for within a few
years the colonies would be so powerful that the mother country would be unable to deny their demands. It was believed
that the rapidly increasing population in America would soon
outstrip that of Great Britain and that the balance of empire
would be shifted westward across the Atlantic. Some colonists
confidently looked forward to seeing good King George holding
court and opening Parliament in Philadelphia or New York,
and it is probable that George III would have found those
"polite cities" more suitable than Boston as the seat of his
American empire. Boston, he was informed, was inhabited
by rowdy Congregationalists who could no more bear a gentleman than a bishop and who planted their streets with Liberty
trees and broken glass. Dr. Franklin calculated that Americans doubled their population once every twenty years: therefore they had only to keep quiet for a few years more before
they could make their own terms with King and Parliament. [31]
James Otis believed the time was not far remote when one

[29] *Boston Gazette*, May 16, 1774; Aug. 8, 1774.
[30] *The Writings of Benjamin Franklin*, VI, 273.
[31] *Ibid.*, 3–4.

hundred million people would inhabit the colonies, and Dr. Samuel Johnson lamented that His Majesty's overseas subjects were stiff-necked republicans who multiplied "with the fecundity of their own rattle-snakes." [32] With abundant natural resources and a birth rate that put the mother country to shame, America seemed destined to become "the imperial Mistress of the world" after the fall of the tottering British Empire. This certainty of greatness by easy, natural means convinced many colonists that it was foolhardy to take aggressive action against Great Britain. By waiting a few years, war was certain to break out between England and France and then the colonies could separate themselves from the mother country without a struggle, if they chose. But if there was to be fighting, they urged it be left to their children, who, millions strong, would easily overwhelm the puny armies from the "Island" of Great Britain. [33]

No patriot had firmer faith in the future greatness of America than Sam Adams. As early as 1768 he said that America was a great empire that would soon give laws to England; and his conviction had since deepened that "providence will erect a mighty empire in America" while the "Islanders," having lost their colonies, would be "sunk into obscurity and contempt." [34] But, unlike Benjamin Franklin, Adams did not draw the conclusion from the colonies' high birth rate that the Revolution should be delayed in order to make the parting easier. He believed that the present generation of Sons of Liberty should settle the controversy with the mother country rather than hand it on to their descendants who might be "faint & languid" in the defense of liberty. [35] By waiting quietly, Adams maintained, the British government would be encouraged to load more taxes upon the colonists, who might soon become ac-

---

[32] Otis, *Considerations on Behalf of the Colonists*, 30–31. Johnson, 7.

[33] *Samuel Adams Papers*, Arthur Lee to Sam Adams, Dec. 24, 1772. Lee, 237, 241. *The Works of Benjamin Franklin*, VI, 3–4. *Arthur Lee Papers*, Sparks MSS. Harvard College Library, II, Thomas Cushing to Arthur Lee, Feb. 1775. *Letters of Thomas Cushing, Mass. Hist. Soc. Collections*, Fourth Series, IV, 362, 363, 420.

[34] *Boston Gazette*, Aug. 24, 1772; Nov. 2, 1772.

[35] *The Writings of Samuel Adams*, III, 66.

customed to such tyranny. Americans must challenge every
step made by the British government, he said, and keep colonial rights always in the foreground. The very fact that America was gaining strength was "the strongest reason why we
should be watchful over ourselves, lest for the sake of present
peace, we *indirectly* or *implicitly*, or in any manner of way
inadvertently make the least *appearance* of receding from our
just claim of right." The colonies were already strong enough,
Adams told New Englanders, to resist Great Britain successfully: if Americans formed an independent state, he said, "we
certainly have no Cause to doubt of our Success in maintaining
Liberty." Delay merely lessened the colonies' chances of
victory because the Tories were entrenching themselves behind
an army of officeholders independent of the provincial legislatures. "Every day," Adams exclaimed, "strengthens our oppressors & weakens us." If Sam Adams were to be believed,
the wisest course for Americans was to prime their muskets and
pray that the battle would not be long delayed. "It must come
to a quarrel with Great Britain sooner or later," he said; "and
if so, what can be a better time than the present?" [36]

[36] *Boston Gazette*, Sept. 13, 1773; Oct. 11, 1773. *The Writings of
Samuel Adams*, II, 341. Gordon, I, 335, 336.

XIII

SAM ADAMS AND THE CONTINENTAL CONGRESS

SAM ADAMS was certainly not a dressy man; and it was a problem to his friends — although Sam himself seems to have given it no thought — how he was to make a proper appearance in Philadelphia at the Congress.   Adams had one of the slenderest wardrobes in Boston, yet he was so little troubled by its deficiencies that, had he been left to himself, he probably would have gone to Philadelphia in his everyday clothes.   To prevent this calamity, his friends resolved to send him southward in unwonted style.   One asked Adams to call at a tailor's shop to be "measur'd for a suit of Cloaths and chuse his Cloth"; another inquired politely about the condition of his linen; others questioned him concerning the shortcomings of his breeches and hose.   By this means, Adams was presented with an entire new outfit including: —

> a new whig
> a new Hatt
> six pair of the best silk hose
> six pair of fine thread ditto
> six pair shoes.

After he had been suitably arrayed for Congress, a friend "modestly enquir'd" of Adams "whether his finances want rather low than otherways."   Adams replied that although his pocketbook was empty, he was totally indifferent to money as long as "his *poor* abilities was of any service to the Publick." This answer seemed so worthy of an "Old Roman" that Adams's friend pulled out his purse and urged the patriot to accept a small present of "about 15 or 20 Johannes." [1]

[1] *Mass. Hist. Soc. Proceedings* (1866), VIII, 340.   Wells, II, 208.

Sam Adams and his fellow delegates set off from Boston in what, to Adams at least, was unaccustomed luxury.   They rode in "a coach and four, preceded by two white servants who were mounted and arm'd, with four blacks behind in livery, two on horseback and two footmen." [2]   This resplendent procession cantered by the Boston Common, where five regiments of British regulars lay encamped, and proceeded to Watertown, where they were met by gentlemen on horseback who treated them to "an elegant Entertainment." [3]   Connecticut gave them a rousing reception: in every town, the people rang the bells and set off cannon with such fervor that John Adams said "no Governor of a Province, nor General of any army, was ever treated with so much ceremony and assiduity as we have been throughout the whole colony of Connecticut."   In New York, the Bostonians sat down to the most splendid dinner John Adams had ever seen.   Their hosts were the New York merchants and their meeting place the Exchange Tavern, where Silas Deane, the Connecticut delegate to the Continental Congress, found them late that evening "in the highest possible spirits," having passed the glass so briskly that they raised their good humor "just to that nice point which is above disguise or suspicion." [4]   There was little in New York, besides excellent wine, to raise the spirits of Sam Adams and his friends: there was a strange "delinquency and backwardness" in the city; the Sons of Liberty, led by Isaac Sears, had been decisively defeated by the conservative merchants; and it was doubtful whether the party now in power in New York would support the Continental Congress. [5]   Moreover, Philip Livingston alarmed the Bostonians by accompanying his remarks about "Goths and Vandals" with uneasy glances in their direction, which convinced the Adamses that he believed New Englanders at least as dangerous as British tyranny.   Escaping from these un-

---

[2] *Mass. Hist. Soc. Proceedings,* VIII, 339.

[3] *Boston Gazette,* Aug. 15, 1774.

[4] *The Works of John Adams,* II, 343, 345–353.   *Deane Papers, Collections N. Y. Hist. Soc.* (1887), I, 6.

[5] Josiah Quincy, 118, 173.   *Documents relative to the Colonial History of New York,* VII, 433.   *Deane Papers,* I, 6–7.

friendly surroundings, Sam Adams and his party hurried on to Princeton, where they were dismayed to find that the students sang in chapel as badly as did New York Presbyterians. But John Adams pardoned their discords because they studied hard and were all ardent Sons of Liberty.[6]

The antagonism the Boston delegates encountered in New York from Philip Livingston was merely a foretaste of the hostility and distrust which greeted them at Carpenter's Hall. Many Southern Whigs were not free from the fear that, if British rule were removed, Massachusetts would seize the hegemony of America and send governors to all the other provinces. "Boston aims at nothing less than the sovereignty of the whole continent," cried Southern Tories; and they declared that when King George had been turned out of America, Bostonians would overturn the political and social order and set up "a wild Republic of mad Independents."[7]   To Southern patriots who already felt strong prejudice against New Englanders as "a parcel of Canting, Hypocritical, peculating Knaves" who loathed Episcopalians and all gentlemen regardless of denomination, these apprehensions were not altogether fantastic.[8]   Bostonians had already done much to put Virginians and Carolinians on their guard.   By assuming the leadership of the colonies in their quarrel with the mother country, Boston had aroused the suspicion that it was attempting to dupe the other colonies into fighting its battles against the British government.   Colonists were jealous of the "big and haughty airs" assumed by Massachusetts men and feared there was "too great a nationality among the Bay-men" for the good of America as a whole.[9]   Boston's political principles were too far advanced for most Americans: whereas Sam Adams and his followers had long since denied Parliament all authority over the colonies, the majority of Southern Whigs believed with John Dickinson that Parliament had a superintending power over

[6] *The Works of John Adams*, II, 350, 351, 356.

[7] *Mass. Hist. Soc. Proceedings* (1916), XLIX, 445.   *Jonathan Boucher, Reminiscences of an American Loyalist* (1925), 133.

[8] *Samuel Adams Papers*, William Palfrey to Sam Adams, Oct. 3, 1775.

[9] *The Works of John Adams*, IX, 344.   Gordon, II, 38.

them. Moreover, Sam Adams's doings in Boston led many Americans to conclude that the "Saints" were bent upon total independence of the mother country.

The full weight of this distrust of New Englanders fell upon Sam Adams. He was a poor man; he was more of a democrat than most members of Congress; and he was the embodiment of that New England spirit — or, rather, of "mobbish" Boston's spirit — upon which Southerners looked askance. It was remembered that Sam Adams had attempted in Massachusetts Bay to end the "insolent domination in a few, a very few, opulent monopolizing families" — a purpose that was not likely to endear him to monopolizing South Carolina and Virginia aristocrats.[10] It was supposed of Sam Adams, as of most Bostonians, that he was at heart a levelist who wished to lop off the Whig aristocracy after he had finished with the Tories. He was known in Congress as "the *Greatest Republican* in America" and as "the most extravagant partisan of the democracy"; and, when democratic leanings were coupled with lack of property, as in Adams's case, he loomed in Congress as the potential Wat Tyler of the Revolution against whom Whig gentlemen would do well to be on guard.[11] In the eyes of many of Adams's fellow rebels, it was essential that an American patriot be well stocked with material possessions in order that he might not be tempted to divert the struggle against British tyranny into a war upon American property rights. They believed the purpose of the Revolution was to protect property and that there was no room in the Whig Party for one who did not think the inviolability of all private property — except, of course, that which belonged to Tories — was one of the most sacred rights of nature. Furthermore, Adams was a stiff-backed "Bay-man," so partial to all things which concerned Massachusetts that it was said of him that he wished to see Massachusetts at the head of America, Boston at the head of Massachusetts, and himself dictator of Boston. Not only did

---

[10] *The Works of John Adams,* IX, 388.

[11] *Letters of the Members of the Continental Congress,* edited by E. C. Burnett, V, 400. Marquis de Chastellux, *Travels in North America* (1787), I, 276.

he epitomize the brawling, riotous metropolis of the latter-day New England "Saints," but he was suspected of wishing to "Bostonize" the whole continent and to throw his mobs against the conservative Whigs who stood in the way of his levelism.

Southern gentlemen might well have dismissed most of their fears of Sam Adams as fanciful. In spite of his meagre estate, Sam Adams no more contemplated upsetting property rights than did Virginia planters, and he was far too good a student of John Locke to forget that the chief purpose of government was to protect property. In 1768, Adams had pronounced "Utopian schemes of levelling, and a community of goods" as objectionable as the theory which gave the Crown and Parliament absolute power over the colonists' property. But as a Bostonian and a democrat, conservatives had more reason to dread him. His pride in his home town was so intense that he frequently seemed to regard himself as more of a Bostonian than an American. Adams himself admitted that he "showed a Partiality in nothing so much as in regard to the Citizens of that Place"(Boston), and even his fellow New Englanders complained that he had "too great an Idea of the Virtue of the State of Massachusetts Bay." [12] And, until the Massachusetts Constitutional Convention of 1780, he was an equally staunch democrat. Even his cousin, John Adams, began to have serious doubts about him when Sam championed unilateral legislatures for the new states. One of John Adams's chief grievances against Tom Paine was that *Common Sense* urged the "crude ignorant Notion" of one sovereign assembly ruled by means of appointed executive and judicial committees — a scheme of government which destroyed the sharp divisions between executive, legislative, and judiciary as well as the checks and balances which John Adams believed essential in a sound constitution. His fears for the future of the new nation were visibly increased when he saw this political heresy starting up in Sam Adams, who had so little respect for the British Constitution, as interpreted by Montesquieu, that he

[12] *The Writings of Samuel Adams*, I, 137. *Samuel Adams Papers*, N. Y. Public Library, Benjamin Kent to Sam Adams, Aug. 4, 1776; Sam Adams to ——, March 6, 1781.

was "always inclining to the most democratical forms, and even
to a single sovereign assembly." [13]   Sam Adams had none of
John Adams's fears that the people would abuse their power
by making it a "Cloke for Licentiousness."   But it was not
until after the French Revolution, when Sam became the Jacobin
governor of Massachusetts and John the Federalist President
of the United States, that the "brace of Adamses" split upon
the issue whether "Liberty, Equality, and Fraternity" should
become the political and social creed of the United States.

The New England delegates attempted to disarm the suspicion they encountered in Congress by saying little and keeping out of sight as much as possible.   They were "very modest"
in their conversation and acted with "uncommon prudence and
discretion." [14]   Among their friends, however, the Massachusetts men were less reticent, although even to them they
gave only "hints, which like straws and feathers, tell us from
which point of the Compass the wind comes." [15]   The Adamses
knew that if they showed their true colors in Congress and
openly agitated for complete independence they would produce a panic among timid congressmen who were ready to
stampede the moment they scented New England "republicanism."   Although they denied all desire for independence, their
prudence was wasted upon delegates who believed that a
Bostonian who did not publicly preach sedition was in sheep's
clothing for a sinister purpose.   These delegates were more
surprised than deceived by Sam Adams's studied mildness and
they continued to upbraid him as though he were ranting
political radicalism every day from the floor of Congress.

Nevertheless, Adams had in Congress a few staunch friends
with whom he could speak plainly and prearrange the proceedings of the Continental Congress in the same manner he
had controlled the Boston town meetings.   While the Bos-

[13] *The Works of John Adams*, II, 507–509; III, 17, 18.   *Warren-Adams
Letters, Mass. Hist. Soc. Collections*, LXXII (1917), I, 195, 196.
[14] *Aspinwall Papers, Mass. Hist. Soc. Collections*, Fourth Series (1871),
X, 706.   William B. Reed, *Life and Correspondence of Joseph Reed*, I, 78.
The Examination of Joseph Galloway . . . before the House of Commons
(London, 1779), 3.
[15] *Mass. Hist. Soc. Collections*, Fourth Series, X, 706.

tonians sat silent in their seats in Carpenter's Hall, their Southern supporters proposed the radical steps that had been agreed upon in the caucus and held Congress spellbound with their oratory. Christopher Gadsden of South Carolina declared that Massachusetts could not stand alone against British power and that Congress must act with vigor lest the country be "deluged in blood"; and Richard Henry Lee made the motion for a nonimportation and nonexportation agreement against Great Britain which partly fulfilled the purpose of Sam Adams's ill-fated Solemn League and Covenant.[16]

Christopher Gadsden, in particular, came to the rescue of the New Englanders when they found themselves arraigned in Congress as fire-eating republicans. Gadsden "thank'd God there was such a People in America" as New Englanders who had created "an Asylum that honest Men might resort to in the Time of their last Distress, supposing them driven out of their own States." He advised his countrymen to imitate the New Englanders instead of abusing them. From such "a Systematical Body of Men," Gadsden exclaimed, Americans had nothing to fear. The real danger to the American cause, he declared, came not from New England but from the frontier — the backwoods of Virginia, North and South Carolina, Georgia and Florida, where roamed "a numerous Sett of Banditti of no Property or Principles whatever & ready to be made the tools of power for the sake of plunder whenever they could do it with impunity." Why fear New Englanders, who were men of principle, Gadsden asked, when the frontier swarmed with "Catalines" who were ready to sell themselves to the enemy? Gadsden had no more than resumed his seat when a Pennsylvania delegate sprang up to urge him to include the Pennsylvania frontiersmen in his next denunciation of the enemies of American liberty.[17]

One of Sam Adams's most effective ways of putting his enemies in bad repute throughout New England was, as has been seen, to insinuate they were "papist," or, failing this, that they

[16] *The Works of John Adams*, II, 382 (note), 384.
[17] *Samuel Adams Papers*, Christopher Gadsden to Sam Adams, April 4, 1779.

were members of the Church of England. But Adams saw that this method, although eminently successful in Faneuil Hall, was not suited to Carpenter's Hall, which held a large number of Southern delegates who were Episcopalians. It was clear, moreover, that Bostonians had not raised their reputation in the Southern colonies by using the Church of England as a bugbear. To soothe these outraged religious sensibilities, Thomas Cushing moved in Congress that the meeting be opened with prayers by Dr. Duché, a prominent Church of England clergyman. When Jay of New York and Rutledge of South Carolina opposed Cushing's motion on the ground that the members of Congress were of such divergent religious beliefs they could not worship together, Sam Adams took possession of the floor and roundly declared that "he was no bigot, and could hear a prayer from a gentleman of piety and virtue, who was at the same time a friend to his country." [18] Cushing's motion was carried and the next day Duché appeared before Congress in full canonicals. His prayer was an unparalleled success: "even Quakers shed tears," it was said; one delegate declared it was worth riding a hundred miles to hear; and John Adams believed that not even Dr. Cooper of Boston, the mightiest of the "black regiment," could have interceded with the Lord for Boston's salvation with greater fervor. [19] Although Duché later became a Tory refugee, it seemed in 1774 that Adams had made a "masterly stroke of policy" by bringing him before Congress. For the moment, Southern Episcopalians' distrust of New England Congregationalists subsided. But New Englanders had no need to fear that Sam Adams's rigid orthodoxy was weakening in the lax atmosphere of Philadelphia: he had championed Duché solely because he recognized that "many of our *warmest Friends* are *Members* of the *Church of England*" and suspicious of New Englanders' attitude toward their sect. [20]

Even before the opening of the first Continental Congress,

[18] *The Writings of Samuel Adams*, II, 188. *The Works of John Adams*, II, 368–369 (note).

[19] *The Works of John Adams*, II, 369 (note). *Deane Papers*, I, 20.

[20] *Journals of the Continental Congress* (1904), I, 27 (note). *Boston Gazette*, Sept. 26, 1774.

FANEUIL HALL, BOSTON
"THE CRADLE OF LIBERTY"
(From the Massachusetts Magazine for 1789)

The Old State House, Boston

LOOKING DOWN STATE STREET FROM WASHINGTON STREET

Sam Adams had singled out Joseph Galloway as his most dangerous enemy.   Galloway was speaker of the Pennsylvania Assembly, boss of the Quaker political machine, and the leader of
those "half-way patriots" who Sam Adams feared more than
outright Tories.   When a Congress was first proposed, Galloway gave the Boston committee of correspondence fair warning of his intention to create a "political union" between the
colonies and mother country that would be proof against
colonial demagogues.[21]   He earned the ill-will of the Boston
patriots by pointing out that the changes made by the Crown
in the Massachusetts charter, which Sam Adams was using to
stir up opposition to the mother country, immediately affected
only Massachusetts, Rhode Island, and Connecticut — the
charter colonies where the council was elective; Pennsylvanians,
he said, had no grievances in the abolition of the popularly
elected council because they had recently petitioned for a royal
charter in which the King was given power to appoint the members of the Upper House.[22]   Moreover, Galloway hoped to
avert a nonimportation agreement against Great Britain by inducing Congress to send petitions and commissioners to the
mother country to plead for redress.   He dreaded war between America and Great Britain as the certain ruin of the colonies and he set himself in opposition to "New England demagogues, educated under their democratical charter," because
he believed their policy led inevitably to a disastrous conflict
with the mother country.   Sam Adams he regarded as the most
baleful of the New England "demagogues": the leader of the
irreconcilables, "the great director of their councils, and the
most cautious, artful, and reserved man among them." [23]

Sam Adams had brought to Philadelphia his bag of political
tricks from which he intended to serve Galloway as he had
Bernard and Hutchinson.   From the outset, Galloway found
himself forced to breast a powerful current in Congress: he was
deeply offended when the delegates rejected his offer of the
Pennsylvania State House as a meeting place and chose instead

[21] Force, Fourth Series, I, 486.
[22] Galloway, 21, 22.
[23] *Ibid.* 8, 109. *Journals of the Continental Congress*, I, 47.

Carpenter's Hall, a less suitable building, in order to flatter the Philadelphia mechanics; and his mortification became acute when Charles Thomson, whom Galloway had successfully kept from a seat in Congress, was elected secretary to the Continental Congress.   Despite these disappointments, Galloway presented to Congress on September 28, 1774, his plan for the firm "political union" of America and Great Britain.   This scheme might well have come from the pen of a conservative patriot such as James Otis, for, like Otis, Galloway acknowledged Parliament's sovereignty over the colonies.   At the same time he saw the iniquities of its exercise and the need of colonial representation in Parliament.   He agreed with Sam Adams that it was futile to attempt to settle the dispute by putting the colonies in the position they occupied before 1763: the Empire could not be preserved, he said, by resurrecting the old colonial system. Galloway met the crisis, therefore, with a plan which he believed gave Americans the next best thing to representation in the British Parliament: an American Grand Council in which every province should be represented.   This Council was to be an inferior branch of the British Parliament; and within America it was to exercise many of the rights and privileges enjoyed by the British House of Commons in Great Britain.   But the consent of the British Parliament was essential for the validity of its statutes, and a Resident General, appointed by the King, was to preside over its meetings.

Although Galloway framed his proposal so as to "leave no room for any reasonable objection on the part of the republicans, if they meant to be united to Great Britain on any grounds whatever," neither John nor Sam Adams could swallow the Grand Council and the Resident General, with Galloway's heavy seasoning of Parliamentary sovereignty and royal prerogative.   But, in spite of their opposition, it was decided by the Congress, six colonies to five, to resume debate on Galloway's plan at a later day.   With this understanding, the plan was entered upon the minutes of Congress, and Joseph Galloway began marshaling his forces to drive the republicans out of Congress, federate the colonies, and keep America within the British Empire.

Yet Galloway's plan was never again considered by Congress. Sam Adams so inflamed the Philadelphia mob against the scheme that Galloway feared he would be attacked in the streets; and he became panic-stricken when he discovered a halter in his mail with a warning that unless he made use of it he would be put to death. This threat, Galloway firmly believed, came from the "violent party" in Congress led by Sam Adams.[24] By these means, Galloway was so thoroughly intimidated that he did not dare to reopen the debate. Moreover, while Galloway was attempting to rally the conservative Whigs in Philadelphia to the defense of the Empire, the British government passed the Quebec Act, which, by threatening the colonists with a horde of "Popish slaves" in the North and West, disposed thousands of Americans to follow Sam Adams and his fellow radicals "should it be war itself." Galloway's party was overthrown and his plan, which, had it been adopted, might have made possible the development of the United States within the Empire as a Commonwealth, was erased from the minutes of Congress "so that no vestige of it might appear there."[25]

Before leaving for Philadelphia, Adams had pressed upon his friends in Massachusetts Bay a plan to call a convention in Suffolk County to protest against British military rule and infringements of charter rights. Adams's advice was followed: a meeting was called at Milton to evade the prohibition of town meetings and a set of resolutions known as the Suffolk Resolves were drafted by Joseph Warren and adopted by the delegates. The Resolves were immediately sent with Paul Revere, the Patriot "Express," to the Massachusetts delegates at Philadelphia, who, it was planned, were to secure their adoption by Congress. But it seemed doubtful if the Continental Congress could be persuaded to sanction the boldness of the Suffolk patriots, who declared in their Resolves that no obedience was due the Boston Port Bill, urged the people to prepare for a defensive war against Great Britain, and ordered the committees of

---

[24] *The Examination of Joseph Galloway*, 59.
[25] Reed, I, 78. *Boston Gazette*, Dec. 5, 1774. *Journals of the Continental Congress*, I, 51 (note).

correspondence to summon the citizens to arms when the alarm was sounded in Boston. Joseph Galloway exclaimed that the Suffolk convention had made a "complete declaration of war against Great Britain." [26] Nevertheless, after a hot debate and even hotter caucusing, the Virginia-Massachusetts "phalanx" carried the field and the Suffolk Resolves were formally adopted by the Continental Congress.

The Tories screamed that by upholding the republicans in Suffolk County, Congress "gave such a blast from the trumpet of sedition, as made one half of America shudder." [27] The military preparations made by the New England Whigs were now fully approved by Congress, and they were led to believe they would be supported by all British America if it came to war with the mother country. Congress was pledged to the hilt to aid Massachusetts in a defensive war; and, although the delegates refused to promise aid if the patriots provoked war with the British troops in Boston, it was well understood that if the British sallied out of the metropolis with hostile intent or seized a patriot leader, hostilities would be justified in Americans' eyes. Conservatives were terror-stricken at Congress's promise to support Massachusetts, but the Adamses were in high spirits after the adoption of the Suffolk Resolves: Sam Adams said it was now certain that America would aid Boston "to the utmost" and John Adams declared that the day Congress had voted to accept the Resolves was the happiest day of his life because the colonies had shown they would "support Massachusetts or perish with her." [28] War between the colonies and mother country now hung upon the question of whether the fighting, almost certain to break out in Massachusetts, was defensive; and with a master of propaganda such as Sam Adams at work, Americans were certain to be convinced that New Englanders were fighting a defensive war against British tyranny.

Nevertheless, the nonimportation and nonexportation agree-

[26] *Samuel Adams Papers*, Benjamin Kent to Sam Adams, Aug. 20, 1774. Galloway, 68, 69.

[27] *What think ye of the Congress now?* (1775), 31.

[28] *The Writings of Samuel Adams*, III, 156. *Journals of the Continental Congress*, I, 39 (note). Gordon, I, 392.

ment adopted by the first Continental Congress was not all Sam Adams had hoped for: although some of the spirit of the Solemn League and Covenant was retained, the colonists were permitted to import any amount of goods before November 1, 1774; wines and coffee, though still dutied, might be imported after the agreement went into effect; and each colony was obliged to carry out only such resolutions as had been assented to by its delegates — a concession to local sovereignty that Jefferson believed "totally destroys that union of conduct in the several colonies which was the very purpose of calling a Congress." [29]   But most Americans felt certain that the boycott of Great Britain and the West Indies would speedily bring the mother country to terms: Richard Henry Lee believed that the same ship that carried the news of the proceedings of the Continental Congress to England would return with the Ministry's promise of redress.   Adams did not believe Great Britain would be brought to terms so easily; had the government yielded in 1774, however, he would have been the first to exclaim that the colonies had driven a poor bargain with the mother country. Congress acknowledged Parliament's right to regulate colonial trade and refused to go beyond 1763 in enumerating American grievances.   Therefore Adams believed America's terms for reconciliation with England were far too low: as long as Parliament's sovereignty over the colonies was recognized, he said, there could be no lasting settlement of the quarrel. [30]

Thomas Young promised Sam Adams a pleasant surprise when he returned to Massachusetts Bay.   "You will perceive," wrote Young, "the temper of your countrymen in the condition your every wish, your every sigh, for years past panted to find it.   Thoroughly aroused and unanimously in earnest." [31]   New Englanders were indeed as warlike as an "Old Roman" could wish.   When "that illustrious Warrior and firm Patriot,"

---

[29] *The Works of Thomas Jefferson*, edited by Paul Leicester Ford (1904), II, 93.

[30] *The Works of John Adams*, II, 362–363; IX, 416, 453.   *Journals of the Continental Congress*, I, 68–69.   *Samuel Adams Papers*, Elbridge Gerry to Sam Adams, Oct. 15, 1774.

[31] Dr. Thomas Young to Sam Adams, Sept. 4, 1774, MS. Mass. Hist. Soc.

Israel Putnam, came down to Boston driving a flock of sheep before him for the relief of hungry Bostonians, he was welcomed as a savior; and both Putnam and Charles Lee, the English adventurer who became famous overnight by offering his services in the patriot cause, were "so much carressed" by Bostonians that they had difficulty in getting out of town. Throughout New England, the citizens were drilling as though war would begin within a few weeks; and "Old Louisbourgh soldiers" were laughing at the British fortifications on Boston Neck and swearing they could storm them as easily as a beaver dam. The "popular Fury" had spread from its source in Boston over the whole country: the British troops were no longer opposed by a "Boston rabble" that might quickly be dispersed with a few regiments, but by the "Freeholders and Farmers of the Country." [32]   New Englanders had never before seemed so much like the founding fathers in Sam Adams's eyes: they prayed while they cleaned their muskets, and there seemed little doubt that in a crisis they would "shew themselves to be worthy of such Ancestors." [33]

But what chiefly led Adams to hope that New Englanders' fighting blood was up was their readiness to march to the defense of Boston. While Adams was at Congress a rumor that British soldiers had killed six Americans and that the fleet had opened fire on Boston put thousands of armed New Englanders, New Yorkers, and Pennsylvanians on the highroad to Boston. Since the news reached eastern Massachusetts and Connecticut on a Lord's Day, most of the citizens were in the meetinghouses, but clergy and congregations leaped out of their pulpits and pews, seized their muskets, and set off for Boston "cursing the King and Lord North, general Gage, the bishops and cursed curates, and the church of England." This false alarm, which perhaps was purposely set to "try the temper of the people," gave Massachusetts patriots "the most exalted idea" of the

---

[32] *Samuel Adams Papers, Dr. Thomas Young to Sam Adams*, Aug. 19 and 21, 1774. Frothingham, 357. Josiah Quincy, 175, 181. *The Correspondence of Thomas Gage*, edited by C. E. Carter (1931), I, 367, 371.
[33] *The Writings of Samuel Adams*, III, 163, 171.

willingness of New Englanders to fight for their liberties.[34] Sam Adams was told that if the British had marched out of Boston five miles they would have been cut off to a man; and on his way home from Philadelphia, he passed through districts where the entire able-bodied population had turned out to drive the "bloody-backed rascals" from the metropolis. Even at Philadelphia, it was believed that if the report that the British were cannonading Boston had not been almost immediately contradicted, forty thousand men would have been on the march to Boston. After this display of military ardor it was clear that "if blood be once spilled, we shall be involved in all the horrors of a civil war." [35]

Adams's joy upon finding New England yeomen preparing for war was sobered by the changes that had taken place in Boston while he remained in Philadelphia. "The once happy Boston is now become a den of thieves," wrote Mrs. Adams to her husband, "a Cage of Every unclean Bird — Consignees, Commissioners and tools of every denomination have made this town their ark of safety — they walk upon Change everyday with great insolence." The town that had begun the Revolution was now a Tory stronghold: rather than face mobs of Whig farmers, more dangerous than the Boston mob in its ugliest mood, New England Tories, from "Mandamus" councilors down to the petty squires, took refuge in the metropolis under the guns of royal troops and men-of-war. Although some Whigs left Boston for quieter parts, Mrs. Adams stoutly remained at her house in Purchase Street, where she was joined by her husband after his return from Philadelphia.

The Provincial Congress that had been called in Massachusetts during Adams's absence anxiously awaited his return in the autumn of 1774. Although it claimed no authority, taxes were paid into its treasury and it superseded the royal government of the province. But before the Congress took decisive

[34] *Boston Gazette*, Oct. 24, 1774. *The Correspondence of Thomas Gage*, II, 656. *What think ye of the Congress now?* 27. Frothingham, 356. *The Works of John Adams*, II, 404.

[35] Reed, I, 78.

action, the presence was required of "one who never failed to animate" — Sam Adams.[36] Having sounded public opinion in the middle colonies, Adams was well aware that no aggression could be undertaken against the British troops in Boston. The necessity of respecting the Southerners' prejudice against attacking the redcoats seriously hampered Adams's plans: he was certain early in 1775 that "the publick Liberty must be preserved though at the Expense of many Lives," yet he hesitated to risk losing the support of the Southern colonies by precipitating war.[37] Congress had agreed, however, that if the British marched out of Boston with hostile intent, resistance was justified. Therefore, Sam Adams urged that a New England army be created to lie in wait for the British outside Boston. The proceedings of the Provincial Congress were kept secret, but information leaked through to Gage which convinced him that Adams's plan was to put New Englanders on a war footing, yet at the same time to keep them from "being censured for their rashness by the other Colonies & that made a pretence for deserting them."[38] It was planned to establish a New England military confederation and to put an army of eighteen thousand men in the field, raised by quotas upon the members. Behind this army, New England was to be declared independent of Parliamentary authority and the King recognized as the only bond with the mother country. Many country delegates, however, were unwilling to burden themselves and their constituents with an expensive armament; the Essex members were fearful that the British would retaliate by laying waste the seaports; and it was difficult to convince the majority that there was any immediate necessity for a New England Confederation. Many rural representatives were so frightened by the radicals' war talk that they pleaded illness as an excuse to go home, but Sam Adams administered some strong physic by proposing that as soon as a sick delegate reached his home town he should be compelled to resign his seat in order that a more healthy representa-

---

[36] *Samuel Adams Papers*, John Pitts to Sam Adams, Oct. 16, 1774; Elbridge Gerry to Sam Adams, Oct. 15, 1774.

[37] *The Writings of Samuel Adams*, III, 180, 195.

[38] Allen French, *General Gage's Informers*, 20.

tive might take his place. This immediately put an end to the
epidemic of bowel disorders, agues, and rheums that threatened
to invalid half the Congress, but it did not convince the country patriots that they should raise eighteen thousand men on
the chance that the British would sally out of Boston.[39] Adams,
Warren, and a few other leaders gave Congress the appearance
of "an assembly of Spartans or ancient Romans," but the greater
number of delegates showed the virtues of thrifty, cautious New
Englanders who thought more about the expense of war than
its glory. These men showed "great irresolution" in making
military preparations against the British until they were certain
of support from the other colonies. As a result, the utmost
Adams was able to get from the Provincial Congress was a
promise that if General Gage marched out of Boston with artillery and baggage, the country should be called to arms to oppose the invader "to the last extremity," and that delegates
should be sent from Congress to the New England colonies to
learn their attitude toward the proposed confederation. On
the eve of Lexington and Concord, the Provincial Congress adjourned to await the response of the other New England colonies.
Little had been done to create the army of which Sam Adams
foresaw Massachusetts would soon stand in need.[40]

With Boston full of British troops, trouble was expected at
the annual Massacre Oration in March 1775. Because the
soldiers regarded this commemoration as a deliberate insult, a
large number of officers crowded with the patriots into the Old
South Meetinghouse prepared to "resent any expressions made
use of by the Orator, reflecting on the Military." When Sam
Adams saw the meetinghouse filling up with redcoats he immediately suspected they had come to "beat up a Breeze," but
he took care, as moderator, to treat them civilly and invite them
to take the best seats, in order that they might have no pretext
to start a row. Adams firmly believed that "it is a good Maxim
in Politicks as well as War to put & keep the Enemy in the

---

[39] French, 20, 21, 23, 27. *The Diary of William Pynchon*, edited by
F. E. Oliver (1890), 43 (note). Gordon, I, 416.
[40] French, 18, 21, 24, 27. Josiah Quincy, 177. *The Correspondence of
Thomas Gage*, I, 388.

wrong." To begin the ceremonies, Joseph Warren, the speaker of the day, clad in a "Ciceronian Toga," mounted the black-draped pulpit, attended by "the most violent fellows in town" — the Adamses, Hancock, Church, Cooper, and the Boston selectmen. After taking uneasy note of the large number of officers in the audience, Warren threw himself into a "Demosthenian posture, with a handkerchief in his right hand, and his left in his breeches," and "began and ended without action." [41] Warren was careful not to risk a riot by waving the bloody shirt too brazenly and he particularly avoided mention of the "*bloody* Massacre.*" This restraint saw him safely through his oration: he was "applauded by the mob" and "groaned at by the people of understanding," but when he finally sat down, amidst cheers and hisses, all danger of a free-for-all between soldiers and civilians seemed past. But apparently Sam Adams was disappointed by this tame ending to a promising tussle with the redcoats, for, after Warren had finished, he came forward to propose that "the thanks of the Town should be presented to Doctor Warren for his Elegant and Spirited Oration, and that another Oration should be delivered on the 5th of March next, to commemorate the *Bloody Massacre* of the 5th of March, 1770." Adams's mention of the "bloody Massacre" was the spark that set off the explosive matter within the Old South: officers immediately leaped to their feet and began crying, "O fie, O fie," at the speaker. This created a panic in the galleries, where the Whigs, believing that the soldiers were crying, "Fire, fire," "bounced out of the windows, and swarmed down the gutters like rats, into the street." [42] To add to the confusion, a regiment of British regulars happened to be passing outside at this moment, and when the patriots indoors heard the beating of drums and tramping of feet they assumed they were about to be slaughtered in the meetinghouse. After a large number of Whigs had taken to cover, order was at last restored

---

[41] *Diary of Frederick MacKenzie* (1930), I, 9–10. Frank Moore, *Diary of the Revolution* (1860), I, 35. *The Writings of Samuel Adams*, III, 206.

[42] Moore, I, 35. *Diary of Frederick MacKenzie*, 9, 10.

and the meeting broke up peacefully. Although the patriots had suffered a severe fright, Sam Adams covered their confusion by declaring that the soldiers, not the civilians, had been in danger and that if it had not been for the Whigs' self-control not an officer would have left the meetinghouse alive.[43]

Sam Adams had been frequently warned by his friends that he was in danger of being seized by the British military authorities, clapped in irons, and taken to England to be tried as a rebel. It was said that the British officers who attended Warren's Massacre Oration planned to carry off Adams and other Whig chiefs when the signal — throwing an egg into Warren's face — was given. The patriots believed they had escaped unscathed because the soldier who had been entrusted with the delicate business of throwing the egg slipped and broke it on his way to the meetinghouse. Although Tories jeered that Adams could not bear to look at a hemp rope and blanched at the mention of Tyburn, his friends said he showed *"amazing* fortitude, *noble* resolution, and *undaunted* courage" in his contempt of danger. He voted with other members of the Boston committee of correspondence to "attend the business of the Committee of Correspondence, as usual, unless prevented, by brutal force"; and he continued to remain in Boston after the military occupation, an easy mark for an assassin. General Gage was reluctant to lay hands on the patriot leader because he feared such action would be the signal for hostilities against the King's troops — which, he observed, New Englanders already seemed "very ripe to begin."[44] Nevertheless, as Sam Adams continued to preach rebellion and prepare for war with the mother country, it became clear that he "must be tucked up at all adventures." Most Massachusetts "top Tories" confidently expected to see him safely stowed away in the brig of a royal man-of-war before Congress met. But when the British government dispatched orders to Gage to take up the leading Massachusetts Whigs, Adams knew of them before Gage; and he

[43] *The Writings of Samuel Adams*, III, 206. *Mass. Hist. Soc. Proceedings*, VIII, 340. *Committee of Correspondence Papers*, July 5, 1774.
[44] *The Correspondence of Thomas Gage*, I, 376.

was in hiding at Lexington with John Hancock when the British general began the hunt.[45]

Because fighting usually broke out between New Englanders and British troops when Sam Adams was in the vicinity, it has been suggested that he may have had a hand in the fighting at Lexington and Concord. Parker and his men ignored the protection of forest and walls and took an open position along the Lexington road on April 18, 1775, as though inviting fire from the British; therefore it is said that Parker was acting under orders from Sam Adams, who was lodging near by with John Hancock at Parson Clark's.[46] It had already been agreed in the Continental Congress that if the British troops marched into the country, the people ought to be called to arms; and although it is certain that Adams was eager to see bloodshed hasten the separation of mother country and colonies, there is nothing to show that he was responsible for the military movements made by the embattled farmers at Lexington or Concord. Nevertheless, he was overjoyed when he heard the rattle of musketry on Lexington Common. "Oh," he exclaimed to Hancock, "what a glorious morning is this!"[47]

If Adams had by any chance planned to make patriot martyrs at Lexington, he did not intend to be one himself. He and Hancock slipped out of Massachusetts during the fighting around Boston and headed southward in Hancock's phaeton for Philadelphia. Since British and Americans had begun the "cutting of throats," it was now Adams's purpose to persuade Congress to adopt the New England army besieging the British troops in Boston and to involve the other colonies in the war against the mother country.

Until Sam Adams reached middle age, he was a very inexpert rider — as John Adams said, Sam "never would be persuaded to mount a Horse." This lack of equestrian skill greatly disturbed John Adams, who firmly believed horsemanship essential

[45] *The Works of John Adams*, IX, 345. *Mass. Hist. Soc. Collections* (1858), IV, Fourth Series, 371–372.
[46] Harold Murdock, *Historic Doubts on the Battle of Lexington*, *Mass. Hist. Soc. Proceedings*, XLIX (1916), 374.
[47] Gordon, I, 479.

"to the Character of a Statesman."   He determined, therefore, to make an effort while on the road to Philadelphia in 1775 to get Sam Adams on a horse and thereby complete his education in statesmanship before he reached Congress.   After much coaxing, Sam was induced to mount one of John's horses, — "a very genteel and easy little Creature," — and John taught him to mount and dismount without the aid of the two servants he usually required.   During the first few days of travel, Sam Adams suffered from the soreness inevitable to an inexperienced rider, but his cousin induced him to keep on, and to buy some linen cloth which their landlady made into "a Pair of Drawers" which eased the friction and "entirely healed the little Breach which had been begun."   Before the travelers had been many days on the road, their servants who rode behind in the carriage were commenting on Sam's superiority as a rider over John Adams; and when they reached Philadelphia, John had the mortification of hearing it said that Sam rode 50 per cent better than he.[48]   After this auspicious beginning, Sam Adams rode frequently, to the great benefit of his health.   And later in the war, when Congress was forced to flee from Philadelphia to escape capture by the British army, the full significance of John Adams's connection of horsemanship and statesmanship no doubt struck Sam Adams.   For certainly the ability to make a quick getaway on horseback was indispensable to American statesmen of the revolutionary period.

Although Sam and John Adams wished ardently in 1775 to see a New Englander in command of the troops about Boston, the prospect of a Northern army under a New England general brought visions to many Southerners of "Goths and Vandals" who, after finishing with the British, would turn upon their fellow colonists and make themselves the rulers of America. The prejudice against a New England general was, however, so strong in Congress that John Adams quickly saw it was useless to put forward even as redoubtable a warrior as "that Thunderbolt of War, the intrepid Putnam."[49]   Meanwhile, the situation in Massachusetts was daily growing more acute:

[48] *Warren-Adams Letters*, I, 110–111.
[49] *Samuel Adams Papers*, Benjamin Church to Sam Adams, Aug. 2, 1775.

appeals poured in to Congress to take over the besieging troops
and the Adamses were threatened with a serious loss of prestige
if they failed to spur Congress to action. Sam Adams was ir-
resolute and hampered by his reluctance to see any but a New
Englander in command; when John Adams urged the necessity
of action to Sam, he received no more helpful reply than, "What
shall we do?" [50] By his own account, John Adams alone had a
plan with which to meet the emergency. The only member
of Congress who attended the meetings in military uniform was
George Washington, a delegate from Virginia. Although his
military qualifications were not impressive, he caught the eye
of John Adams, who was in search of a general acceptable to
the Southern congressmen and yet capable of taking command
of the New England army and driving the British out of Boston. John Adams believed that in George Washington he had
found his man; and, during a walk with Sam Adams in the State
House yard, he suggested Washington as commander in chief.
Sam Adams "seemed to think very seriously of it, but said
nothing." [51]

Sam's lack of enthusiasm for George Washington is easily
explained. Washington was not that "Cromwell" Adams and
other Boston Sons of Liberty had vainly sought in 1768 when
British troops were sent to keep order in the metropolis. His
military record was not such as to convince Sam Adams that he
was the long-awaited deliverer of America from British tyranny;
and his political opinions — always an important item in Adams's
judgment of military men — were decidedly not Bostonian.
Washington still thought in terms of reconciliation and redress
of grievances rather than of independence and war with the
mother country, and it was well known that he would oppose
the politicians in Congress who favored complete separation
from the mother country. Nevertheless, the necessity of persuading Congress to take the New England army under its wing
forced the Adamses to act contrary to their convictions. On
June 15, when Thomas Johnson formally nominated Washington as general, John and Sam Adams supported the motion,

[50] *The Works of John Adams*, II, 416.
[51] *Ibid.*, II, 416, 417.

and, after a few days of brisk caucusing, the army was adopted by Congress and put under Washington's command.[52]

The most deeply offended of the amateur generals who hoped to lead the American army was John Hancock, now, by grace of the Adamses, president of the Continental Congress. Hancock nursed a deep ambition for martial glory and thought himself a serious contender for the command of the Continental army, although his best claim to the post was that he knew how to put the governor's cadets through their manœuvres on the Boston Common and that he looked uncommonly well in gold braid. Yet, if the commander in chief were to be appointed on the strength of his services and sacrifices in the patriot cause, Hancock stood far above Washington and every other military man on the continent. With few prominent candidates in the field, Hancock considered his chances excellent, and when John Adams rose to speak in favor of Washington as commander in chief, he felt certain that Adams's long preamble was leading up to his own appointment. He sat in the president's chair listening with obvious pleasure until Adams came to the point where he suggested Washington as the best man to command the American army. Since Adams stood on the floor facing Hancock, he was able to observe the sudden change of expression that passed over Hancock's face: "mortification and resentment" flared in his eyes and revealed how deeply his vanity had been hurt.[53] When Sam Adams rose to second Washington's name, Hancock's wounded feelings received another stab. From that day, Hancock no longer even pretended friendship for the Adamses; and, as will be seen, he was not reconciled with Sam Adams until the rise of the Federalist Party in New England.

Sam Adams was not troubled because Hancock sulked when he was not allowed to play at being a general, but he was deeply alarmed to find him deserting the New Englanders and picking his friends from the aristocratic Southern and New York Whigs whom Adams distrusted as possible Tories. To repay Adams for his slight, Hancock favored all the enemies

[52] Gordon, II, 38.
[53] *The Works of John Adams*, II, 416, 417.

of the Massachusetts delegates in Congress: he courted Dickinson, Duane, and other leaders of the "cold party" and threw his influence against Adams and Richard Henry Lee.[54] The estrangement between Hancock and Adams was made complete when the president of Congress fell a victim to "the glare of Southern manners and the parade of courtly living" and surrounded himself with all the "outlandish state and pageantry of an Oriental Prince." [55] Hancock had always been known as a man of fashion, but even his closest friends were taken aback by the finery in which he now burst forth. Because he had not been appointed general of the Continental army, Hancock determined to make his office of president of Congress do double duty in reflecting splendor upon its occupant. "King Hancock," as he was called, always appeared in public in an "elegant chariot" attended by four servants dressed in livery mounted on richly caparisoned horses and escorted by fifty horsemen with drawn sabres, half of whom rode before and half behind his carriage.[56] This unrepublican ostentation outraged the Whigs: Sam Adams spoke in private of Hancock "with great asperity" and deplored his delight in seeing "the honest Country Folks gapeing & staring at a Troop of Light Horse" and himself furiously tearing along the road. Hancock and his entourage became the dread of tavern keepers for leagues around Philadelphia: when John Adams traveled through the country he found innkeepers everywhere complaining that they had been cheated out of their money by Hancock's cavalry, who usually pranced off on their chargers in company with the president of Congress without paying their bills. The Adamses were at a loss to explain how a New Englander could turn out so badly and they began to fear that Massachusetts had done itself a serious injury by giving "Such *Samples* of her Sons to the World." [57]

Hancock further scandalized the Adamses and made them wish heartily he was not a New Englander by continuing to

[54] *Massachusetts Gazette*, Jan. 11, 1776.

[55] Gordon, III, 20. Wells, II, 385. Lorenzo Sears, *John Hancock, The Picturesque Patriot* (1912), 226.

[56] *Ibid.*, 223.

[57] *The Works of John Adams*, III, 35, 441. *Warren-Adams Letters*, I, 157.

occupy the chair of president of Congress long after he was bound by good manners to surrender it. He had been appointed to the presidency when Peyton Randolph, the first president, was called away to Virginia, it being understood that Hancock was to hold office only during Randolph's absence. Hancock had other plans, however, and when Randolph returned to Philadelphia the president of Congress made no move to step down. Although Randolph died shortly after resuming his place in Congress, the Adamses continued to demand that Hancock resign in order that a new election might be held. Sam and John Adams proceeded from hints to forthright denunciations of Hancock's conduct, but he paid no attention and remained in office until he grew weary of it. Only when, in 1777, it appeared to Hancock that he could better himself by going to Massachusetts, where a state government was being formed, did he determine to resign as president of Congress. Sam Adams was delighted to see him go, but he groaned throughout Hancock's farewell speech because the president took leave of Congress "with almost as much Formality as if he was on his dying Bed." [58] To show Hancock how little they thought of his work as president, Sam Adams and the other Massachusetts delegates voted not to thank him for his services on the ground that it was improper for Congress to thank a man for discharging the duties of office. But in spite of all that Adams could do, Hancock set out for Massachusetts with Congress's thanks in his pocket.

Sam Adams's habit of believing that conservative Whigs who opposed independence were enemies to America and in the pay of the British government brought the Massachusetts delegation into hot water during the second Continental Congress. Adams had been warned by his English correspondents to be on his guard against British spies and traitors in Congress who were selling the patriots' secrets to the Ministry. It could not be denied that there was a dangerous leak in Congress by which the British government learned of its proceedings; and Adams therefore immediately put certain delegates under suspicion. Among them were Philip Livingston, who was described as a "Sort of

[58] *The Writings of Samuel Adams*, IV, 178.

political Hermaphrodite," half Whig and half Tory, and his colleague, John Jay.[59] Jay, in particular, was suspect by Adams because Arthur Lee declared he was betraying the Whigs; and Adams always gave full credence to Lee's reports. Moreover, Jay had aroused Adams's distrust by advocating a conservative policy in Congress. Adams therefore leaped to the conclusion that Jay was a traitor and began to voice his suspicions to other members of Congress. But in fact Jay was guilty of nothing worse than attempting to keep the door open for the reconciliation of mother country and colonies. Instead of raising a storm in Congress against Jay, Adams succeeded only in strengthening the ill will with which the conservative majority regarded him and his fellow New Englanders.

Sam Adams had done much to turn a large part of Congress against the Massachusetts delegates, but John Adams fairly outdid his cousin in making enemies. In a letter to his wife which was intercepted by the British and made public, John Adams called John Dickinson, the leader of the conservative majority in Congress, a "piddling genius." Thus, the "brace of Adamses" succeeded in bringing down wrath from every quarter upon the delegates from the Bay Colony. No Massachusetts man sat upon important committees in Congress during 1775; and Sam Adams, in particular, was excluded from all except a few subordinate ones.[60] Sam, indeed, seems to have borne the brunt of both his and John Adams's mistakes. Jay apologized to John Adams for keeping him off the secret committees of correspondence and commerce and offered him an important place in Congress if he would drop Sam Adams and Richard Henry Lee. Although John Adams declined to purchase political advancement by giving up his friends, he and Jay were on good terms. No doubt Jay, an aristocrat to the core, wondered why John Adams nailed his colors to the mast and insisted on sinking with such a plebeian as Sam. For several months, the latter was almost an outcast in Congress. Even

---

[59] *Samuel Adams Papers,* "The Intelligencer" (Hugh Hughes) to Sam Adams and John Adams, Oct. 17, 1775; Stephen Sayre to Sam Adams, April 4, 1775; William Lee to Sam Adams, April 6 and 10, 1775. *The Works of John Adams,* III, 5.

[60] *Journals of the Continental Congress,* II, 53, 64, 67, 80, 102, 208.

his friendship with Richard Henry Lee made him enemies because Lee had antagonized many powerful Virginia aristocrats by exposing their pilfering of the colony's treasury.[61]

John Adams was a much abler statesman than Sam Adams, but he little understood how a propagandist like his cousin gradually brought public opinion to favor complete separation from the mother country. Had John Adams possessed some of Sam's skill in influencing the public mind he would have been a more effective force in American history, but too often he acted upon the principle, "public opinion be damned." In the Continental Congress of 1775, John Adams displayed all of the unfortunate bluntness and impatience with slow-moving majorities that marked his later public career. John Dickinson and the conservative majority in Congress refused to be pushed deeper into opposition to Great Britain until another petition had been sent the King humbly praying for redress of grievances. Although the radical minority believed that Americans ought not to waste time on George III that could be spent in priming muskets and gathering ammunition, it remained silent in the face of the overwhelming majority that favored petitioning. John Adams, however, was no respecter of majorities and he was never silenced by hostile public opinion. He called the petition a "measure of imbecility" and declared he dreaded further negotiations with the mother country "like Death." [62] His speeches in Congress against petitioning convinced the moderates that New Englanders were so eager for independence that they would not even give good King George an opportunity to restore peace to his dominions. Rather than be forced into war by Northern republicans, Dickinson urged that New England be allowed to go its own way while Pennsylvania and the loyal Southern colonies made terms with the mother country. One day, when Dickinson caught John Adams outside Carpenter's Hall, he exclaimed: "What is the reason, Mr. Adams, that you New Englandmen oppose our measures of reconciliation? . . . Look ye! If you don't concur with us in our pacific system, I and a number of us will break off from you in New England,

and we will carry on the opposition by ourselves in our own way." [63] This "rude lecture" made it clear to John Adams that he must reconcile himself to the petition to the King or see American unity end in "Discord and a total Disunion." [64]

Sam Adams liked petitioning as little as did John, but he recognized that opposition was futile and even dangerous. He believed that the hope nursed by Dickinson and his party that the mother country would adopt a lenient policy toward the colonies was "the Rock which endangers the Shipwreck of America," because it caused a "total Stagnation of the Power of Resentment, the utter Loss of every manly Sentiment of Liberty and Virtue." [65] Among his friends, Sam Adams spoke enthusiastically of the approach of one of "the grandest Revolutions the World has ever yet seen," but he did not join John Adams in publicly attacking John Dickinson's plan of reconciliation. He saw that the petition must be agreed to before Pennsylvania would be ready to join the colonies in declaring independence. It was apparent that as long as hope remained of a change in British policy, the middle colonies would not unite with New England and Virginia in separating from the mother country. However unpalatable petitioning might be to New Englanders who hungered for immediate independence, it was necessary to convince conservatives that King George and Parliament would not have a last-minute change of heart. Moreover, Adams was too well informed on English politics to doubt that Dickinson's petition would go the way of all of Congress's petitions and remonstrances: into the Ministry's wastebasket.

The event proved the wisdom of Sam Adams's policy of waiting "till the Fruit is ripe before we gather it." [66] John Dickinson made the second petition to the King one of the masterpieces of revolutionary rhetoric; and, by avoiding all subjects that had irritated the King and Ministry in the first petition, gave George III an excellent opportunity to show his good intentions toward his American subjects. Nevertheless, Dickinson's peti-

[63] *The Works of John Adams*, II, 410.
[64] *Warren-Adams Letters*, I, 75.
[65] *Ibid.*, I, 280.
[66] *Ibid.*, I, 171. *Letters of Members of the Continental Congress*, I, 284.

tion fared no better than the truculent remonstrances written by Sam Adams in the Massachusetts General Court. Even after this rebuff, Pennsylvania was lukewarm toward the Revolution, but had New Englanders not agreed to the second petition to the King, the middle colonies might have been openly hostile and conservatives everywhere in the colonies would have been given a strong argument against independence.

Congress's delay in declaring American independence caused Sam Adams acute discomfort. He believed that when the British compelled the colonists to take up arms in self-defense at Lexington, America became independent of Great Britain; in fact all that was now required was formal recognition of the separation. Nevertheless, the Whig majority in Congress seemed so unwilling to face this reality that Adams believed the moderates would carry on the struggle against the mother country for a century before they would be able to make up their minds to declare independence and make war in earnest. "Every Day's Delay," he exclaimed, "trys my Patience." His friends in Massachusetts told him that the people were becoming suspicious of Congress: they anxiously asked each other, wrote Joseph Hawley, "what is our Congress about, they are *dozing* or amusing themselves." The postponement of independence, Hawley said, was making Tories saucy and Whigs disheartened, and he pictured to Adams "a Great Mobb" of New Englanders storming Philadelphia, dispersing Congress, and setting up a military dictatorship.[67] From England, Sam Adams received equally alarming news: the only alternative offered Americans was to declare themselves independent or become "Slaves to Scotchmen." Nevertheless, Adams saw he must work cautiously in persuading the timid members of Congress to take the plunge, and he made it his business to "remove old prejudices, to instruct the unenlightened, convince the doubting and fortify the timid." Rather than press the "halfway patriots" too hard, Adams preferred to wait until the efforts of the British government to suppress the rebellion by

[67] *Warren-Adams Letters*, I, 224, 225. *The Writings of Samuel Adams*, III, 276. *Samuel Adams Papers*, N. Y. Public Library, Joseph Hawley to Sam Adams, Feb. 5, 1776.

force had convinced them of the hopelessness of reconciliation. "We cannot make Events," Adams told his friends. "Our Business is wisely to improve them." [68]

But when a committee was appointed by Congress in 1775 to explain to the people that Congress had no intention of declaring independence, Sam Adams was so alarmed that he began to threaten openly a New England Confederation, independent of both Great Britain and the American colonies. The break-up of the American union was no empty menace hung over the heads of congressmen by Sam Adams to frighten them into separation from the mother country: thousands of New Englanders shared Adams's conviction that even alone they were a match for the British. As John Adams said, when New England exerted its full strength it would be found to be that of "a full grown Man, no Infant." [69]

Fortunately for the unity of the American Republic, the obstacles to independence melted away soon after Sam Adams began to threaten a New England Confederacy. Thomas Cushing, who opposed independence, lost his place in Congress to Elbridge Gerry, one of Sam Adams's followers. Henceforth, the Massachusetts delegation ceased to be hampered by internal conflicts: Gerry and the "brace of Adamses" formed a majority in favor of independence and, as a result, the Massachusetts vote was cast for an immediate declaration. [70] Washington was converted to independence; John Adams, — "the main pillar in debate," — Richard Henry Lee, Thomas Jefferson, and Patrick Henry advocated it in Congress; and Sam Adams's "intriguing arts" began to bear fruit. By transplanting the caucus from Faneuil Hall to Philadelphia, Adams overthrew the conservatives in Congress just as he had driven the Tories out of the Boston town meeting. The caucus directed every step taken toward independence: although Sam Adams was seldom seen in the centre of the stage, he was constantly at work behind the scenes. It was decided in the caucus what

[68] *Samuel Adams Papers*, William Lee to Sam Adams, Feb. 6, 1776.

[69] *The Writings of Samuel Adams*, III, 259, 260, 284, 304–305. *Letters of Members of the Continental Congress*, I, 438. *Warren-Adams Letters*, I, 175.

[70] *The Works of John Adams*, III, 25. Wells, II, 340.

parts Richard Henry Lee and Patrick Henry — known respectively as the Cicero and the Demosthenes of the century — were to take in the debates. John Adams took little part in the caucus but he frequently acted under its orders: and it is significant that George Wythe and Richard Henry Lee, two of the chief members of the caucus, proposed in March 1776 that Congress declare the King rather than the Ministry or Parliament the "Author of our Miseries." Without the aid of the caucus, independence might have been long delayed by Dickinson and his conservative followers; but with Sam Adams pulling the wires backstage and marshaling the radical forces in Congress, Dickinson was unable to prevent the separation of mother country and colonies.

By the time of the Declaration of Independence, Sam Adams had attained celebrity as the foremost revolutionist in America. "The whole Continent," cried a Tory, "is ensnared by that Machiavel of Chaos," Sam Adams, and he was dreaded by all conservatives as the "would-be Cromwell of America." [71] Josiah Quincy, Junior, who had been sent to England on a secret mission by the Massachusetts Whigs, found that in London Sam Adams was considered "the first politician in the world" and without a peer in the business of "forwarding a Rebellion." Adams was now recognized as the prime mover of the Revolution — the man who, for many years, had worked indefatigably to make America independent of the mother country. Tories sometimes spoke of the Revolution as "Adams's conspiracy"; and Lord North, with the Boston Massacre and Tea Party still fresh in his mind, nicknamed the American patriots "Sam Adams's crew." After Gage's proclamation excluding Adams from the general amnesty was known in the colonies, no patriot could match Sam Adams's fame in British America; as Thomas Jefferson said, Adams was "truly the *Man of the Revolution*" — the greatest figure yet brought forth by the upheaval. Many years before, Adams's friends had begun to call him the "Father of America," and by 1775

[71] British Museum, Additional MSS. 35913 Hardwicke, Lib. Cong. Transcript; —— to Governor Hutchinson, Sept. 14, 1774. *Independency the Object of Congress in America* (London, 1776), 15.

he seemed to have proved beyond doubt his right to the name.[72] "Would you believe it, that this immense continent from New England to Georgia is moved and directed by one man," wrote an English army officer, "a man of ordinary birth and desperate fortune, who by his abilities and talent for factious intrigue, has made himself of some consequence, whose political existence depends upon the continuance of the present dispute, and who must sink into insignificancy and beggary the moment it ceases!" [73]   John Adams owed much of his early reputation to the fact that he was "the creature and kinsman" of Sam Adams. This reflected glory frequently was highly exasperating to John. When he arrived in France in 1778, one of the first questions he was asked was whether he was "the famous Adams" who had been proscribed by General Gage and who had made himself the ruler of Congress.   John protested that he was plain John Adams and not "the famous" Adams, but his audience replied in chorus: *"Oh, non, Monsieur, c'est votre modestie."* [74]   Obviously, the French did not know John Adams.

Yet, within a brief time, Sam Adams fell from his eminence as the chief figure of the American Revolution.   His career in Congress was marred by factiousness, intrigue, and broils; and, unlike Jefferson and John Adams, he failed to reveal traits of statesmanship.   Although Sam Adams was expert in overturning governments, he knew nothing of rebuilding them.   His weaknesses are most apparent in his attempts to control the American army during the war and in the protracted feuds he carried on with his political enemies in Congress.

At the beginning of the war, Sam Adams wished to fight King George with the American militia rather than with an enlisted regular army.   He dreaded an American standing army almost as much as he had a British, for he suspected that American commanders were not free from ambition to establish a military despotism.   Therefore, Adams praised the militia system as a bulwark against militarism, and in 1775 he went so

[72] Josiah Quincy, 218.   Moore, II, 144.   Wells, II, 418 (note), 424. *Samuel Adams Papers*, Christopher Gadsden to Sam Adams, May 23, 1774; Stephen Sayre to Sam Adams, Sept. 13, 1770.

[73] *Letters of Captain W. G. Evelyn,* edited by G. D. Scull (1879), 46.

[74] Moore, II, 144.   *The Works of John Adams,* III, 189.

far as to advise his friends not to entrust the Massachusetts militia to the command of Continental generals. Military power, he said, "has so often proved fatal to the liberties of mankind" that unless Americans made the militia the backbone of resistance to Great Britain they were in danger of losing their liberties to some aspiring general wearing the uniform of the Continental army.[75] But before many battles had been fought, Adams changed his mind about the effectiveness of the militia. Repeated defeat made him the champion of a strong regular army enlisted not for a year but for the duration of the war — an army that would cross state lines without haggling with their commanders and would remain in the field when the crops at home were ready to harvest.[76] Yet while Adams switched his faith from the militia to the regular army, he did not forget the peril of military dictatorship nor did he cease to be haunted with the fear that the American Revolution would have its Cæsar or Cromwell. Although most Americans seemed so unwilling to serve in the regular army that the real danger was not of military dictatorship but of submission to Great Britain for want of a sufficient number of effective troops, Sam Adams tormented himself, Congress, and the military leaders with apprehensions that "the Sins of America may be punished by a standing army." He proposed to avert such disaster by putting the generals securely in leading strings to Congress and making them instruments to execute the commands of the sovereign legislature. He joined in establishing the Board of War by which Congress intended to put itself in control of the Continental army; and he became exceedingly sensitive to slights cast upon the supremacy of Congress in both civil and military affairs. For example, when the King of France and George Washington were given precedence over Congress in the toasts at a public celebration in Boston, Adams said that he and other "old fashion Whiggs" regarded it as a portent of approaching military tyranny.[77] But Congress's control of

[75] *The Writings of Samuel Adams*, III, 230, 247. *Warren-Adams Letters*, I, 198.

[76] *De Chastellux*, I, 275–276. *Samuel Adams Papers*, Sam Adams to Samuel Cooper, April 23, 1777.

[77] *Warren-Adams Letters*, II, 58, 67.

the army soon proved unworkable and Adams was compelled to give Washington practically dictatorial powers — a gift which Adams bestowed with many misgivings for American liberty.

Sam Adams once confessed that he knew nothing of military matters; and many American commanders would have found it easier to fight the British had Adams recognized that his ignorance unfitted him for meddling in the war department. His faculty for supporting mediocre generals was frequently detrimental to the American cause: through his influence, Charles Lee was appointed one of the major generals in command of the Continental army. Had Adams been able to dispel more of the "Dismal Bugbears" which hung thickly about Lee, that singular adventurer would probably have been given even higher rank. Lee had made strong converts in John and Sam Adams, who judged him largely upon the strength of his political opinions and tall stories of his exploits in the British army. Both "Sam and John fought for him . . . through all the Weapons" — with the result that Washington was given a subordinate who considered his abilities far superior to his chief's, and who refused in several emergencies to obey Washington's orders.[78] Nevertheless, Sam Adams continued to pass judgment upon commanders, strategy, and military matters in general as though he had spent a lifetime in the field. Like many amateur generals, he invariably blamed the commanders for reverses and overlooked the real causes of defeat, although many of them lay under his eyes in Congress. In 1778, after a succession of American defeats, he urged that there be a congressional examination of the "idle cowardly or drunken" general officers whom he held responsible. He saw treachery, intoxication, or gross incompetence in every American military setback: when Schuyler and St. Clair were forced to evacuate Ticonderoga, Adams said they were cowards or traitors who had acted upon "the worst of Principles." [79] He lent a willing ear to the defamatory reports which reached Philadelphia of Schuyler's generalship and he was one of the leaders of Gates's

[78] *Warren-Adams Letters*, I, 61, 64, 69–70, 331. *The Writings of Samuel Adams*, III, 387.

[79] *Ibid.*, III, 403, 404, 407.

party in Congress who intrigued for Schuyler's removal while Burgoyne was advancing upon Albany. Adams was told by Elbridge Gerry that Schuyler was the "evil Genius" of the Northern army, who was so heartily hated by the New England troops that unless he was displaced they would retreat to Philadelphia for the winter.[80] After the command of the Northern army had been juggled between Gates and Schuyler until it became a matter of doubt which was in command from one day to another, Gates's partisans in Congress finally triumphed. When Burgoyne surrendered at Saratoga to Gates (largely because of Benedict Arnold's attack), Sam Adams's estimation of his own wisdom in military matters began to soar and he was soon planning to bring down George Washington in the same manner he had worked Schuyler's downfall.

After the siege of Boston, Washington's strategy deeply pained Sam Adams. Adams was eager to give the British "a handsome Drubbing" and he was utterly unable to comprehend any military manœuvres that did not lead to a speedy annihilation of the invaders. He felt it intolerable that "a small Hand full of ragged discontented unpaid Mercenaries" should overrun the Jersies and Rhode Island, "plundering Houses, cruelly beating old Men, ravishing Maids, murdering Captives in cold Blood, and systematically starving Multitudes of Prisoners" while the American army rested on its muskets. Adams believed that it was the duty of the army to fight the British to a finish: in 1777, he considered that Washington could easily have driven the British into the Atlantic and put an end to the war had he made an energetic campaign.[81] As General Mifflin complained, the "Gentry at Philadelphia" who set themselves up for military geniuses loved fighting as long as they could remain in their cozy quarters in Philadelphia; and they longed for a smashing victory, forgetful of the raw, undisciplined troops and meagre stores with which the commanders were expected

[80] *The Writings of Samuel Adams*, III, 388. *Samuel Adams Papers*, Joseph Trumbull to Sam Adams, July 25, 1776; Roger Sherman to Sam Adams, Aug. 25, 1777; Elbridge Gerry to Sam Adams, July 21, 1776.

[81] *Warren-Adams Letters*, I, 278, 293, 331. *Samuel Adams Papers*, Sam Adams to Samuel Cooper, April 23, 1777. *The Writings of Samuel Adams*, III, 374.

to overwhelm the British.[82] The situation appeared in very
different light when viewed from Congress and from the battle-
field; and, because Adams could account for American defeats
only by the shortcomings of the officers, he soon fell out with
Washington. In spite of much prodding from Congress,
Washington refused to hasten the end of the war by risking a
decisive battle. He adopted, instead, the Fabian policy upon
which his military reputation is now based. Sam Adams was
far too impatient for victory, however, to approve such dilatory
methods: Howe, he cried, was no Hannibal and, if Washington
would only stand and fight, the British would be swept out of
America.[83]

After Gates's victory at Saratoga, Adams thought he had at
last found the man to win the war. When he called upon
Washington to give America another Saratoga at Howe's expense, Washington did no more than fight a few battles around
Philadelphia, evacuate the city, and retire to Valley Forge for
the winter. Sam Adams wasted little sympathy on defeated
generals, but Washington lowered himself even further in
Adams's eyes by advocating half pay for officers in the Continental army — a scheme which the Massachusetts delegates
regarded as final proof of Washington's ambition to establish
a military dictatorship by means of a "set of haughty idle im-
perious Scandalizers of industrious Citizens & Farmers."
Adams now considered the removal of Washington and the
elevation of Gates to the supreme command essential to the success of the war. He was already convinced that the only
soldiers in America who could be relied upon to do their duty
in battle were New Englanders. Although Gates had not the
powerful recommendation of New England ancestry, his political opinions were as sound, in Adams's opinion, as though he
had been born and bred in Boston.[84]

Sam Adams always denied that he had attempted to throw

[82] Collections N. Y. Hist. Soc. (1878), 405.
[83] The Writings of Samuel Adams, III, 371, 374. Warren-Adams Letters,
I, 64, 69–70, 331.
[84] Samuel Adams Papers, James Lovell to Sam Adams, Jan. 13, 1777;
Jan. 20, 1778. Gordon, III, 57. The Writings of Samuel Adams, III, 325,
329, 388.

Washington overboard during those stormy days that followed the British occupation of Philadelphia. But every other member of the "Conway Cabal" later disavowed any parts in the conspiracy against Washington as vehemently as did Adams. The only question really in dispute is to what lengths Adams went in active intrigue to displace Washington. Both Congress and the army were divided in the contest between the rival generals for supreme command, with most of the Northern delegates favoring Gates and the Southerners on the side of Washington.[85] An important break in the Southern support of Washington was Richard Henry Lee, the Virginian, who was one of Gates's most active partisans in Congress and who put his head so close to John and Sam Adams's that they appeared "all so many heads under one bonnet." General Thomas Mifflin, James Lovell, and Benjamin Rush were likewise eager to oust Washington. Although it cannot be shown that Gates actively engaged in a plot to make himself commander in chief of the American army, he knew what his friends in Congress were about and kept in close touch with Sam Adams.[86] Adams and Lee welcomed every defeat suffered by Washington and magnified his failures among their partisans in Congress: when news of Brandywine reached Congress, Adams and Lee could scarcely conceal their joy that he had met with such a signal reverse when his fate as commander hung in the balance.[87] But even when undermining an enemy doomed as hopelessly as Washington appeared to be at Valley Forge during the winter of 1777, Sam Adams preserved all his customary caution. Lest Washington unexpectedly recover his prestige, Adams carefully covered up all traces of his work in the Conway Cabal. This prudence displayed by Washington's enemies eventually saved them from full exposure and it is not yet known precisely how they planned to make Gates the chief in command. Undoubtedly, when Gates was put at the head of the Board of War,

[85] *New Materials for the History of the American Revolution*, edited by John Durand (1889), 23, 28, 173. *Samuel Adams Papers*, Samuel Parsons to Sam Adams, July 9, 1778.

[86] *Ibid.*, Horatio Gates to Sam Adams, May 27, 1778. *Dictionary of American Biography*, VII (1931), 184–190, "Horatio Gates."

[87] Edmund Quincy, *Life of Josiah Quincy* (1868), 415.

which had been given powers superior to Washington's, the conspirators believed that Washington's downfall was inevitable. Their next move was to attempt to induce the Massachusetts House of Representatives and the Virginia House of Burgesses to give their delegates in Congress instructions which would either make Washington's resignation mandatory or shame him out of the army. Although the leading members of Congress from Massachusetts and Virginia, Sam Adams and Richard Henry Lee, were important figures in the cabal, even such proficient intriguers failed to dislodge Washington. Both Virginia and Massachusetts refused to take part against Washington, and when Conway visited Congress at Yorktown in June 1778 he wrote disconsolately to Gates that he had been warmly received only by Sam Adams and Lee "and a few others who are attached to you but who cannot oppose the torrent." Washington quickly regained his popularity; the French alliance put a new complexion upon the war; and Gates's bubble was pricked by the British evacuation of Philadelphia and the battle of Monmouth.[88]

Another reason why Sam Adams's popularity steadily dwindled during the Revolution was that he permitted his passion for intrigue, inherited from his early days in Boston, to have full sway in Congress. If there was a plot being carried on in his neighborhood, Sam Adams could not resist the temptation to get into the thick of it; and Congress gave him ample opportunity to exhibit his talents in the cabal. His skill was useful in bringing about Galloway's downfall and the declaration of independence, but unfortunately for his reputation as a statesman he continued to use the same methods of attack against all his numerous enemies in Congress. Although he had earned the ill will of a formidable group of congressmen through his own efforts, his friendship with Richard Henry Lee and Arthur Lee vastly increased the number of his enemies. Arthur Lee, the Virginia Whig whose letters from London had been Adams's main source of information concerning the designs of the British government, was a man with amazing faculty

[88] Gordon, III, 57. *Letters of Members of the Continental Congress* (1926), III, 278 (note). *New Materials, etc.*, 174.

for making enemies. He habitually assumed that other people acted from the worst motives: he had no sooner been made the confidential London correspondent of the congressional secret committee of correspondence than he began to calumniate the men who had appointed him. Through the influence of Sam Adams and Richard Henry Lee, Arthur Lee was made one of Congress's agents in France. In Paris, Lee made enemies by the score, the most important of whom were Luzerne, Franklin, Carmichael, and Silas Deane. Lee particularly distrusted Deane, the agent sent out by Congress to negotiate aid from the French government, and he quickly convinced himself that Deane was attempting to swindle the American government out of many thousand dollars by representing that the supplies furnished secretly by the French government through Beaumarchais's fictitious firm of Roderique, Hortalez & Cie were given with the understanding that they were to be paid for by the United States. To the joy of the parsimonious statesmen at Philadelphia, Arthur Lee declared that there was no necessity for payment, as the French government had intended from the beginning that these supplies should be a free gift to the United States. Both agents appealed to Congress for support with the result that Congress itself was soon divided into Deane and Lee parties. At the head of Arthur Lee's friends, opposing payment, stood Sam Adams and Richard Henry Lee.

All the jealousies and hatreds within Congress burst forth during the Deane-Lee controversy. Indeed, the delegates fell to quarreling with such good will that they expended almost as much time and energy upon Deane and Lee as upon the Articles of Confederation. Sam Adams was in a heaven of plots and counterplots. On the strength of the material sent him by Arthur Lee, Adams procured Deane's recall and John Adams's appointment as agent. But Arthur Lee continued to send alarming news across the Atlantic: corruption was still rampant; the French ministers were playing a double game with the United States; and there was a conspiracy in Congress to keep "all vigilant Patriots" off important committees in order that powerful merchants might monopolize the trade and

richest lands of America.[89] Although Adams and Lee ruled
Congress "as absolutely as the Grand Turk does in his own
Dominions," their support of Arthur Lee cost them heavily.
After years of futile controversy, Arthur Lee was thrown over
by Congress; and the New York party, led by William Livingston, defeated him for the office of minister of foreign affairs.[90]
After six years of service in Congress, Sam Adams could still
boast that he was a poor man. He was, indeed, in his usual
financial difficulties throughout his congressional career: salaries
were so low that John Adams complained the total amount he
had received for four years' labor at Philadelphia was not sufficient to pay a laborer on his farm; and when a story was cir-
culated by the Tories that a certain member of Congress was
"keeping Mrs. ———," the scandal was refuted by pointing out
that a congressman could not support himself, much less a
mistress.[91] With this poor pay went long hours of drudgery
and extended periods of separation from Adams's "beloved
town": Sam was sometimes so busy he had not even time to write
his "Betsy" a love letter; and Elbridge Gerry was so over-
worked that he was said to be almost "past the salutary power
of Vegetables." [92] Nevertheless, there were odd moments in
the hurry and bustle of Philadelphia, York, and Baltimore,
when the busiest congressman found relaxation. Sam Adams
took pleasure in strolling with John Adams in the State House
yard; talking politics with other delegates over pipes and tea;
eating a Saturday night's dinner with his landlady, Mrs. Yard;
"smoaking a pipe in the political club at the Indian Queen";
holding a tête-à-tête at George Wythe's lodgings opposite
Israel's Garden; and "rambling towards Kensington" with a
few boon companions.[93] When the Marquis de Chastellux
called upon Sam Adams he was shocked to find that redoubtable

[89] *Samuel Adams Papers*, Richard Henry Lee to Sam Adams, Nov. 23,
1777. *Deane Papers*, III, 277; IV, 447.
[90] *The Writings of Samuel Adams*, IV, 113, 127.
[91] *The Works of John Adams*, 111, 89. James T. Austin, *The Life of
Elbridge Gerry* (1828), I, 332.
[92] *The Writings of Samuel Adams*, IV, 238. *Samuel Adams Papers*,
James Lovell to Sam Adams, Jan. 13, 1777.
[93] *Ibid.*, George Wythe to Sam Adams, Aug. 1, 1778.

Puritan *tête-à-tête* with a young girl of fifteen who was preparing his tea, but the Marquis dismissed all thought of scandal when he remembered that Adams was nearly sixty. Having thus acquitted Adams of any moral lapse, de Chastellux entered into a lively discussion with his host of the causes of the American Revolution, until they were interrupted by "a glass of Madeira, a dish of tea, and an old American General." [94]

Although Sam Adams shared comfortable quarters with John Adams in Philadelphia and found the atmosphere of intrigue in Congress to his taste, he liked neither the city nor its inhabitants. The true religion of Quakers, he said, was making money and sleeping in a whole skin. Even the "Mud & Mire" of Yorktown and the "infernal sink" of Baltimore, where even John Hancock, the president of Congress, had difficulty in living "tolerably decent," did not make Adams love Philadelphia the more. [95] He was incurably homesick for Boston; and, as most of his friends dropped out of Congress, he, too, found the only cure for his loneliness was long vacations in Boston with his Betsy. Moreover, he was disturbed by his failure to "Bostonize" Philadelphia by proscribing balls, theatres, and other entertainments frowned upon in the Puritan metropolis. Adams believed that congressmen should set an example for the people by praying often, watching their morals, and staying away from dances and horse races. During the early meetings of Congress, the New England delegates secured the passage of a law forbidding members of Congress to take part in public entertainments. Southern gentlemen who had diverted themselves at balls in Williamsburg and Charleston found this restraint irksome; and it was soon observed that the congressmen were seldom at their prayers but frequently at balls where they appeared in open violation of the law. To the mortification of the "rigid Republicans," many Northerners began to show they had been softened by daily contact with "Southern sensuousness." Sam Adams's puritanism had not been sweetened by

[94] De Chastellux, I, 267–276.
[95] *Warren-Adams Letters*, I, 280. *Letters to Robert Morris, Collections N. Y. Hist. Soc.* (1878), 410, 413. *Samuel Adams Papers*, James Lovell to Sam Adams, April 23, 1778.

Southern influences, however, and he demanded that further steps be taken to keep congressmen and army officers away from dances, theatres, and horse races. Congress agreed, but the day on which this legislation went into effect, the Whig citizens of Philadelphia and officers of the Continental army attended the theatre as usual; and on the next day, the ball given by the Governor of Pennsylvania was crowded. The contemptuous treatment accorded its moral code aroused Congress to such a pitch that it was ordered that every officer present at such revels should be cashiered.[96]   But Sam Adams's efforts to stamp out sin in Philadelphia were rudely cut short by news that the Devil was making long strides in Boston itself.

[96] *The Writings of Samuel Adams*, III, 414–416. *New Materials, etc.*, 166–167.

XIV

SAM ADAMS AND THE NEW REPUBLIC

AFTER the outbreak of war between the mother country and colonies, Massachusetts failed lamentably to take the lead in framing a new state constitution. The Bay State was almost the last of the states to adopt a settled form of government, although its need had been urgent since the beginning of the Revolution. The upheaval in Massachusetts completely destroyed the authority of the central government; and the towns became petty sovereignties that clung tenaciously to the powers they had usurped from the old royal government. The towns had already rejected one constitution, in fact, when in 1779 another attempt was made to establish a central government and Sam and John Adams were elected to the Constitutional Convention.

The absence of a central government in Massachusetts was far more disturbing to John than to Sam Adams. The former was greatly alarmed by the "rage for innovation" and levelism which began to spring up in the state during the Revolution.[1] He strove at all times to keep the Revolution in a well-defined, conservative channel and to wage war against English oppression rather than against English principles of government. When the two Adamses were undermining the royal government in Massachusetts, John Adams was careful to blot out in Sam Adams's state papers all reference to the principles of liberty, equality, and fraternity. He believed that the war was being fought to protect property rights and ancient principles of government which must be safeguarded against popular tyranny in America as well as against overseas tyranny. He wished no violent break with the past: the old provincial form of govern-

[1] *The Works of John Adams*, II, 328; IX, 393, 410.

ment with its two legislative branches and separate executive should, he said, be carried over into the state constitution. If Massachusetts followed Pennsylvania's example in establishing a single legislative chamber, John Adams declared he would be grieved "to the very soul" and would never be happy under such a government.[2]

To broaden the franchise would, in John Adams's eyes, be the surest way of undoing the work of the Revolution. Propertyless voters, he exclaimed, would form a "Fountain of Corruption" which, in turn, would destroy the commonwealth. Even slight alterations in the qualifications for voters he regarded as disastrous: if the franchise were tampered with, women would demand the right to vote; boys over twelve years old would insist they be given equal rights with their mothers; and "every man without a farthing" would clamor for the suffrage. To prevent this train of evils, Adams urged that the property qualifications for voting under the royal government be preserved in the new state constitution.[3]

Although Sam Adams did not share his cousin's fears of giving the vote to the mass of the people, he had no deep conviction in its favor. There was little crusading fire in Sam Adams to enfranchise the unprivileged, and he certainly did not believe it was a purpose of the Revolution. He never made suffrage extension a part of his revolutionary propaganda in Massachusetts; he was no democrat in the Jacksonian sense because, although he wished to put power in the people's hands, he was willing to accept the "people" as they existed in 1776. The important business, in his mind, was to make certain that the people doled out power cautiously to those they had appointed to govern. He feared tyranny in rulers far more than the discontent of the unenfranchised masses. But, unlike John Adams, he had little love for the old charter form of government under which such "oligarchs" as Thomas Hutchinson had prospered. Rather than revert to that system, he wished to create a single-chamber legislature in Massachusetts on the

[2] *The Works of John Adams*, IX, 430.
[3] *Ibid.*, IX, 378.

Pennsylvania model which would execute its laws by appointed committees.[4]

At the Massachusetts Convention which met in Boston during the winter of 1779–1780, James Bowdoin and the "brace of Adamses" were appointed a subcommittee to draw up a constitution for the approval of the Convention and the Massachusetts towns.   Sam Adams and Bowdoin immediately gave full power to John Adams, who proceeded to write the entire Massachusetts Constitution with the exception of Article III. Several motives may have influenced Sam Adams in thus giving his cousin free rein: he was ill during the greater part of the Convention and his pet scheme of a single-chamber legislature met with little support from the delegates.   Bostonians made it clear that they wished to retain the fundamental principles of the old charter government; and, as he was to do a decade later when Massachusetts ratified the Federal Constitution, Sam Adams swallowed his own opinions, bowed to Boston's will, and abandoned "systems in which he loved to stray, for less sublime, but more practicable projects." [5]   The only part of the Massachusetts Constitution in which Sam Adams had a hand and which can be said to represent his true convictions was Article III, dealing with religion.   Because of his fame as a staunch churchman, Adams was placed at the head of the committee appointed to draw up the revolutionary religious settlement.   His work in Article III reveals how little he believed the Revolution had ushered in a period of religious liberalism. Even in the conservative Massachusetts Constitution of 1780, Article III stands out as notably reactionary: indeed, it makes the old provincial religious system seem lenient by comparison. Under the royal charter, Baptist, Quakers, and members of the Church of England were granted exemption under certain conditions from paying taxes for the maintenance of the Congregational Church.   In Article III, Sam Adams provided that the members of these sects were to pay taxes to their own pastors — with the result that unbelievers, non-churchgoers, and minorities too small to maintain a minister were compelled to

---

[4] *The Works of John Adams*, III, 18; IX, 618.
[5] De Chastellux, I, 275.   *The Works of John Adams*, III, 18.

pay directly to the support of the Congregational Church. Moreover, Article III obliged every new sect that appeared in Massachusetts after 1780 to wage a costly legal battle to win recognition as a religious body.   In spite of the opposition raised against Sam Adams's work in many quarters, — four hundred and twenty Boston voters protested against Article III and clamored for a more liberal religious system, — it became a part of the Massachusetts Constitution and endured until 1833.[6]

What Sam Adams did for vested religion in the Massachusetts Constitution, John Adams did for secular interests.   He provided that the requirements for voting for governor, senator, or representatives should be 50 per cent higher than under the charter.   Although the House of Representatives was supposed to represent the persons of the Massachusetts voters, the ballot was confined to a propertied electorate.   Men "who will pay less regard to the Rights of Property because they have nothing to lose" were excluded from the franchise.   Certainly, the Massachusetts Constitution of 1780 did not establish the democracy which in 1776 the people were said "almost universally & most ardently [to] desire & are now aiming at." [7] Joseph Hawley, the Northampton patriot, declined his seat in the Massachusetts Council in 1780 because of his dissatisfaction with the civil and religious provisions of the Constitution.   The old revolutionary watchword of no taxation without representation was thrown in the patriots' faces by soldiers who had fought in the Revolution believing they were struggling for their own liberty.[8]   But Sam Adams was not among these dissenting voices: once the Massachusetts Constitution had been adopted by the majority, he became one of its staunchest champions.   He regarded it as a final settlement of the Revolution; and he told the Marquis de Chastellux that the Constitution of 1780 had been established in "the most legitimate manner of which there

[6] S. E. Morison, *The Struggle over the Adoption of the Constitution of Massachusetts, Mass. Hist. Soc. Proceedings*, L (1917), 371, 379.

[7] *Sam Adams Papers*, N. Y. Public Library, Benjamin Kent to Samuel Adams, May 24, 1776.

[8] *Hancock Papers*, MSS. Mass. Hist. Soc., Samuel Talbot and Lemuel Gray to his Excellency John Hancock, Esq., Nov. 16, 1780.

is any example since the days of Lycurgus." [9] He acclaimed it as "truly *Republic*"; praised mixed government on the British model; defended property qualifications for voting; and pleaded the necessity of a governor and council "to check the human Passions, and controul them from rushing into exorbitances." [10] It is apparent that, with the adoption of the Massachusetts Constitution, Sam Adams ceased, for the time being, to be a revolutionist.

After Thomas Hutchinson and the Tories had been driven into exile, Sam Adams hoped for great things from New England. The chief obstacle to the return of Puritanism, he believed, was the old aristocracy which, by setting the people an example of high living and loose morals, had attempted to destroy their "Sense of true Religion & Virtue, in hopes thereby the more easily to carry their Point of enslaving them." As one of the first fruits of the Revolution, Adams anticipated the resurrection of "that Sobriety of Manners, that Temperance, Frugality, Fortitude and other manly Virtues which were once the Glory and Strength of my much lov'd native Town." After such "vermin" as the Commissioners of the Customs and British army officers, whose balls and feasts had shocked Boston Whigs for a decade, had been driven out of town for the last time, Adams believed that he might look forward to "the ancient purity of principles and manners" again flourishing in the Puritan metropolis. Instead of dressing in the height of London fashion as Bostonians had done during Hutchinson's régime, Adams hoped to see British "frippery" banished from the commonwealth and "that Simplicity which is the Ornament and Strength of a free Republick" among all classes. [11] In Sam Adams's eyes, the American Revolution was to do far more than establish an independent state: it was to purify society, revolutionize manners and morals, and pave the way for another Puritan Age. Its most important consequences were to be felt in Boston, where another "Christian Sparta" would rise and where "Old Puritans" and "Romans" would restore to the

[9] De Chastellux, I, 271.
[10] *The Writings of Samuel Adams*, IV, 348.
[11] *Ibid.*, III, 231, 286; IV, 68, 251.

metropolis its fame as a refuge for the virtuous. But before this transformation could be wrought, it was necessary that the old pleasure-loving Tory aristocracy be succeeded by an upper class of sober republicans who would guide the people to Virtue.

Much to Adams's dismay, the "Happy Era of Republicanism" was ushered in not by the righteous Whigs who had made and fought the Revolution, but by men who had "Hid in Holes and Corners" during the struggle for liberty.[12]   Profiteers, speculators, and privateers were the material heirs of the Revolution in Massachusetts; the old merchants were driven out of business and their places were taken by new men who amassed fortunes and political power that put the Tories to shame. Certainly, this unforeseen result was due to no laxness on Adams's part in sweeping the country clear of Tories: those who revisited Boston after the war saw scarcely "any other than new faces" and found a change in the upper classes "as remarkable as the Revolution itself."[13]   Few of these "mushroom gentry" who moved into the Tories' abandoned homes, bought up their confiscated estates, and seized their places in society, could claim distinguished birth.   It was a bitter humiliation, exclaimed the Massachusetts republicans, to stand with empty hands on Boston street corners and watch "the Scum of Creation Rideing in State"; "fellows who would have cleaned my shoes five years ago," said James Warren, now rode in chariots while he drudged for "a Morsel of Bread."   In this "world turned topsy turvy," the patriots complained, "one forfeits all title to the respect of a gentleman, unless he is one of the privileged order."   Was this, the old Whigs anxiously asked themselves, to be the end of their labors: were the fruits of the Revolution to be gathered by men who had started up from nowhere and were for all the world like the exiled Tories?   None viewed their rise with greater apprehension than did Sam Adams. "The Seeds of Aristocracy," he said, "began to spring up before the Conclusion of our Struggle for the natural Rights of Man,

<hr />

[12] *Warren-Adams Letters, Mass. Hist. Soc. Collections*, LXXIII (1925), II, 20, 42, 147.
[13] *Mass. Hist. Soc. Proceedings* (1862), V, 245.

Seeds which like a Canker Worm lie at the Root of free Government." [14]   He was horrified to find the Massachusetts upper class imitating the British in "every idle amusement & expensive Foppery" which, Adams firmly believed, was invented by cunning Englishmen to sap American virtue.   Indeed, "British Frippery" was imported into Massachusetts in such large quantities after the Revolution that the General Court felt obliged in 1785 to dam the flood of foreign luxuries "unknown to our ancestors." [15]   It was clear that Adams could expect no aid from the revolutionary aristocracy in purging Massachusetts of "British gew-gaws, etiquette and parade" and restoring Puritanism.   From the standpoint of the puritanical "patriots of '75," there was little to choose between the old Tories and the new Whigs.

Had the banished Tories in "Hell, Hull, and Halifax" known the bitterness of the revolutionary patriots toward the new upper class, they might well have exulted that they had the last laugh on Sam Adams and his "crew."   But Adams had not yet tasted the sourest draught in his brimming cup of disappointments.   John Hancock, it will be remembered, had resigned as President of the Continental Congress to fish in Massachusetts waters.   Although his friends gave out that Hancock returned to Boston because "the Airs of Philadelphia doth not sute him," his real purpose in coming to Massachusetts was to angle for the governorship of the state — a prize which, in 1778, appeared far more desirable than the presidency of the Continental Congress. [16]   While Adams toiled in Congress, Hancock began to turn Massachusetts into an impregnable political stronghold.   To Adams's consternation, he quickly became the most popular man in the state and took Boston by storm: the citizens began to burn incense before a "Guilded puppet," as James Warren now described Hancock.   It was soon clear that Hancock intended to pay Sam Adams back for not having made him commander in chief of the Continental

---

[14] *Samuel Adams Papers*, N. Y. Public Library, Thomas Chase to Sam Adams, Jan. 26, 1781.   *Warren-Adams Letters*, II, 105.   Austin, II, 86.   *The Writings of Samuel Adams*, IV, 325.

[15] *Ibid.*, IV, 315.   *Independent Chronicle*, Nov. 23, 1786.

[16] *Mass. Hist. Soc. Proceedings* (1910), XLIII, 333.

army: all who would not "Bow down and worship a very silly Image," it was said, were marked for ruin; and Sam Adams, in particular, was set apart as a fat offering for the sacrificial altar.[17] As soon as he had consolidated his party in Massachusetts, Hancock began a backfire in Boston against Sam Adams that almost succeeded in driving Adams out of political office. Hancock spread a report that Adams was opposed to long-term enlistments in the army; that he was a factious meddler who distracted Congress by stirring up the Deane-Lee controversy; and that he was a secret enemy of George Washington who had been deeply implicated in the Conway Cabal. In 1778, while Adams was attending Congress in Yorktown, he was informed that he had been "severely reprehended" by the Boston town meeting for taking part in an intrigue against Washington.[18] Adams immediately put his affairs in order and hurried to Boston, much to the relief of the French ministers, who welcomed a vacation from Sam Adams. In Boston, Adams denied that he had plotted to remove Washington and asserted that the gossip on which the town meeting had condemned him was a "pityful Contrivance" of Hancock's to make him unpopular and ruin his political career.[19] The only general he had removed from command, Adams said, was Schuyler — and in New England, where Schuyler was hated, this was regarded as a highly meritorious act. Adams's speedy return to Boston saved his seat in Congress, but it was now apparent that he would be forced to keep a watchful eye on John Hancock, who was clearly determined to take his political scalp.[20]

Instead of making a stiff-backed "Old Puritan" first governor of the state of Massachusetts, the people elected John Hancock, who had no sympathy whatever for Sam Adams's somewhat querulous eagerness to restore the days of Winthrop and Cotton. To Adams's great disgust, Hancock celebrated his inauguration with a round of parties and balls such as had not

---

[17] *Samuel Adams Papers*, N. Y. Public Library, Samuel A. Otis to Sam Adams, Nov. 10, 1780. *Warren-Adams Letters*, II, 14, 87, 147, 150.

[18] *Ibid.*, II, 12.

[19] *The Writings of Samuel Adams*, IV, 140, 246.

[20] *Belknap Papers*, II, *Mass. Hist. Soc. Collections* (1877), Fifth Series, III, 151. Wells, II, 466, 501.

been seen in Boston since the "routs" and "Turtle Feasts" of
the Commissioners of the Customs.   Where Adams looked for
republican austerity he found a lively night life topped with
brilliant "Governor's Balls" which even the "sober Inhabitants"
of Boston attended to pay court to Hancock.   The old Whigs
groaned that "Addresses, Assemblies, Entertainments and Balls
have ushered in the Happy Era of Republicanism" and bitterly
exclaimed that Hancock was surrounding himself with "the
Pomp and retinue of an Eastern Prince."   Hancock's example
spread such a plague of feasts and entertainments over the
metropolis that James Warren said Boston society was "more
suitable to the effeminacy and ridiculous manners of Asiatic
slavery, than to the hardy and sober manners of a New-Eng-
land republic."   Sam Adams exclaimed that Bradford, Wins-
low, and Winthrop would have "revolted at the Idea of opening
Scenes of Dissipation & Folly," but, actually, as Adams soon
learned, Bostonians were little concerned how they might appear
in the eyes of these puritanical worthies.[21]   Adams and his
fellow Whigs scolded and fretted in vain: Massachusetts was
possessed by such "a rage for Ease, Luxurious Living, and Expensive Diversions" that they got only jeers for their pains and
were ridiculed "in polite assemblies as *rigid republicans*, men of
contracted minds, only because they will not conform to gaming,
sabbath breaking, drinking and every other vice practiced by
persons of (What is called) the bon ton."   Boston was no
longer regarded as a stronghold of patriotism: it became instead
so notorious for fashionable reveling that the Whigs lamented
that the love of liberty could be found only "in the sober and
manly retreats of husbandmen and shepherds."[22]

James Warren said his ardor for the Revolution would have
cooled very rapidly in 1776 had he known he was laboring
for John Hancock's glory and the transformation of Boston
into a haven for prodigals and *nouveaux riches* who aped British
manner and fashions.   Boston's shaky puritanism aroused Sam

[21] *Samuel Adams Papers*, J. Scollay to Sam Adams, Jan. 17, 1781.   *Warren-
Adams Letters*, II, 20, 147.   Lee, II, 273.   *The Writings of Samuel Adams*,
IV, 238.
[22] *Boston Gazette*, Oct. 30, 1780; Jan. 24, 1785.   Lee, II, 273.

Adams's deepest anxiety: "I am greatly concerned for my dear native Town," he wrote, "lest after having stood foremost in the Cause of Religion and Liberty she lose her Glory." [23] Each time he set off for Philadelphia to resume his duties in Congress it was with greater uneasiness for Boston's "manly Virtue" which, he feared, was being undermined by a "Torrent of Vice." He longed to remain in Boston and again become the "Gadfly" of the Puritan metropolis, buzzing warnings in the citizens' ears and pricking them along the road to virtue. The people had forgotten him and had given the highest regard to his enemy, but Adams was not yet convinced that the citizens of Boston were past saving and that he was not the man to save them.

In Adams's eyes, it was necessary to take action against Hancock because he felt that the first governor of the state of Massachusetts would have decisive influence in forming the people's manners and morals for at least a generation. If he set the people a bad example, Adams believed the fruits of the Revolution would be sour indeed. From the Greeks and Romans to Bernard and Hutchinson, Adams said, all tyrants attempted to destroy the people's love of liberty with luxury and temptations to high living. He was convinced that Hancock was using the same methods that Hutchinson had unsuccessfully employed before the Revolution; the question was no longer whether Hutchinson would be able to keep the people quiet while he forged "Chains and Shackles" upon them, it was rather whether "the judicious Citizens of Boston be now caught in the Snare, which their artful, insidious Enemies, a few years ago laid for them in vain." "Should Levity & Foppery ever be the ruling Taste of the Great," Adams warned, "the Body of the People would be in Danger of catching the Distemper" and losing their liberties.[24] By bringing to the surface these "mushroom Gentry" who now sat in the seats of the Tories and by making such a bad example as John Hancock governor of the commonwealth, Adams believed the Revolution had

---

[23] *Mass. Hist. Soc. Proceedings*, XLIII, 333.
[24] *Warren-Adams Letters*, I, 376. *The Writings of Samuel Adams*, IV, 229, 238.

made a return to Puritanism even more imperative than in George Whitefield's day.   Hancock's influence must be offset by a revival of puritan morality and the "old patriotick Feelings" that guided the Whigs of the first Continental Congress.[25]

Sam Adams's puritanism soon brought him into conflict with the "Coxcombs and Coquettes" of Boston.[26]   His direst forebodings of the metropolis's sinking virtue seemed fulfilled in 1784 when the establishment of the Sans Souci Club brought the depravity of the younger generation clearly into view. The Sans Souci or "Tea Assembly" was designed to give Boston a night life comparable to that of the "polite" cities of New York and Philadelphia.   Young men of fashion keenly resented that the metropolis of New England still forbade all forms of public entertainment except fortnightly assemblies where dancing was permitted and lectures where the gospel was expounded. In the winter of 1784, Adams was startled to learn that a plan was on foot to begin in Boston a club for dancing and card playing where girls over sixteen would be admitted.   He immediately leaped to the conclusion that Boston was to be given over to Roman orgies, and, although his pen had been idle for several years, this menace to morals again put it in motion.   He attacked the proposed Sans Souci Club in the *Massachusetts Centinel* with a flash of his old fire; and, as usual, he used the occasion to take a back-handed slap at England: "Why," he asked, "do you thus suffer all the intemperances of Great Britain to be fostered in our bosom, in all their vile luxuriance?" [27]   This club, he gloomily prophesied, would work Boston's downfall: after the passion for gaming had seized the people, "every necessary restraint" would be cast aside; parents would set the example for their children by becoming hardened gamblers; and "those glaring spectres luxury, prodigality and profligacy" would rob the metropolis of its little remaining virtue.   He cited Greece and Rome as dreadful examples of how states declined when the citizens lost their habits of frugality.   The Sans Souci, he said, should alarm all the righteous in New England: it was "totally

[25] *The Writings of Samuel Adams*, IV, 251.
[26] *Warren-Adams Letters*, II, 120.
[27] *Massachusetts Centinel*, Jan. 15, 1785.

repugnant to virtue" and foreign to the principles of puritanism
and the Revolution alike.   Rather than permit its existence in
Boston, he urged that the citizens follow New York's example
by forcibly breaking it up with a mob.   "Be not behind your
sister States in extirpating vice," Adams said, "however marked
with the epithet of polite." [28]

Sam Adams apparently believed in fighting the Devil with
the same rough-and-tumble methods that had proved so successful against the British.   Although he did not start a mob
uprising, he made the Sans Souci a storm centre for many
months and a "subject for farces, newspapers, broken heads
and legs."   It is plain that Adams's proneness to view
with alarm greatly exaggerated the evils of the Sans Souci
Club: there was a twenty-five-cent limit on betting and, as one
of its defenders complained, its parties were "decent even to
dullness." [29]   The gilded youth at Cambridge in particular
found Adams's moralizing sour and they rushed into print to
ridicule his fears.   Harrison Gray Otis, the nephew of James
Otis, Adams's old political ally, made the liveliest of these
attacks upon Adams and his school of "rigid Republicans."
He peppered him with such stinging names as "a baleful comet"
and "son of sedition"; and he replied to Adams's use of Greece
and Rome as examples that the "reckless intrigues of disappointed ambition, and the seditious speeches of their popular
leaders, produced more important calamities in those Republics"
than had luxury and Sans Souci clubs.   Adams was accused of
being a bigot, a would-be dictator of morals, and a riot lover
who was up to his old tricks of raising mobs.   But if Otis and
his friends expected their invective to get under Adams's skin,
they were sorely disappointed: he had withstood so much abuse
from New England Crown officers during the revolutionary
period that he was able to disregard the Sans Souci boys and to
turn against them Calvin's words: "I KNOW BY THEIR ROARING
I HAVE HIT THEM RIGHT."   His friends quickly came to his
aid: Dr. Benjamin Waterhouse and Ben Austin, Junior, railed

[28] *Massachusetts Centinel,* Jan. 15 and 22, 1785.
[29] Charles Warren, *Sam Adams and the Sans Souci Club in 1785, Mass.
Hist. Soc. Proceedings,* LX (1929), 318, 344.

against the young upstarts who were "reviling an *old Senator*" and calling him Cato "by way of reproach!" [30]   The quarrel was gradually dragged into politics, where it became one of the issues of the campaign of 1785 when James Bowdoin finally succeeded in bringing about the temporary eclipse of John Hancock.

Although Sam Adams believed the dissolution of the Sans Souci Club saved Boston from the worst vices of declining Rome, he found keeping watch and ward over the morals of the metropolis an increasingly arduous and thankless task.   In spite of his vigilance, he was beginning to fear that "the poison of dissipation has choked even the latent sparks of virtue" and entered into the very marrow of the citizens he hoped to make "Old Puritans." [31]   Boston seemed to be a leaky vessel that kept its Puritan crew scurrying from stem to stern plugging its worn seams.   After the Sans Souci affair, Adams made a desperate but futile effort to keep the theatre out of Boston. In 1792, a company of strolling actors fitted up a stable in Board Alley as a theatre and began performances under the name of "moral lectures."   But Sam Adams was not to be deceived by juggling names: theatrical performances were going on in Board Alley and therefore the Devil was getting a foothold in Boston.   Instead of rallying round their puritanical leaders, however, most Bostonians clamored that the theatre be continued: when Adams and Hancock attempted to jail the actors, the Suffolk Grand Jury refused to indict them.   The republican leaders thereupon arrested an actor under an information *ex officio*; but when this was known in Boston, Hancock's picture was torn down from the stage box of the theatre and trampled underfoot and Adams was hooted down at the town meeting for speaking against what the citizens called their "natural Theatrical rights." [32]   Three quarters of the voters in the metropolis demanded the repeal of the law prohibiting theatres and declared that the issue was between liberty and slavery —

[30] *Sam Adams and the Sans Souci Club*, 325, 329.
[31] *Massachusetts Centinel*, Jan. 15, 1785.
[32] Thomas C. Amory, *Life of James Sullivan* (1859), 271.   *Independent Chronicle*, Dec. 27, 1792.

whether or not a remnant of "Feudal Tyranny and Despotic Enthusiasm" and "an encroachment on the RIGHTS OF MAN" should be tolerated in free America.[33]   To Sam Adams and his followers, on the other hand, the only question at stake was whether or not morals and constitutional laws were to be "trampled upon with impunity by Stage players." [34]   Adams proved himself too strait-laced for many of his warmest admirers: Charles Jarvis quarreled with him; and Elbridge Gerry, who had moved to New York, married a rich wife, and become an ardent theatregoer, expostulated warmly in favor of a theatre in Boston.   Despite Gerry's assertion that the actors scrupulously avoided everything that gave "offense to delicacy," Adams was not won over.[35]   But Sam Adams was fated in his old age to be the champion of lost causes and to go down fighting staunchly against a less rigorous moral code.   In 1793, the Massachusetts General Court repealed the Act of 1750 and thereby legalized theatres in Boston.   Although this act did not receive the governor's signature, the theatregoers had so completely routed the old-guard Puritans that in 1794, while Sam Adams was governor of Massachusetts, the Boston theatre was formally opened.

John Hancock owed his power in Massachusetts not to party machinery, — still in a very rudimentary stage, — but to his personal popularity with the mass of the people.   He capitalized on his early reputation as a patriot and loudly proclaimed himself a champion of popular liberty: "I will not give up the Liberties of the people to the last drop of my blood," he cried.[36]   Hancock had received his political training from Sam Adams and he now showed how well he had learned his lessons: he stole most of Adams's thunder and used all Adams's tricks to keep the people in a ferment for their liberties.   But despite his pose as a friend of freedom and the common man, it was said that he was "an attentive listener to every popular buzz, & whirled about

[33] *Columbian Centinel*, Jan. 30, 1793.

[34] *Independent Chronicle*, Oct. 25, 1792.

[35] S. E. Morison, *Two "Signers" on Salaries and the Stage*, Mass. Hist. Soc. *Proceedings* (1930), LXII, 58, 60.

[36] *Samuel Adams Papers*, N. Y. Public Library, John Hancock to Sam Adams, Aug. 31, 1793.

by every wind of doctrine." [37]   John Adams called Hancock "an empty barrel," but John Quincy Adams saw that he had a "peculiar talent of pleasing the multitude" which made him "King of the Rabble," leader of the "true Republican party," and political boss of Massachusetts.[38] The tendency to look toward the aristocracy for political leadership, inherited from colonial days, was still strong in the state, but there were few men in New England who could claim to be blue-blooded aristocrats after Sam Adams had purged the country of Tories. John Hancock, however, was particularly acceptable to the people of Massachusetts, for not only was he a gentleman born, he was a patriot who talked fully as convincingly as did Sam Adams — the man of the people — of his love for popular liberties.

With Hancock upholding the radical cause in Massachusetts, Sam Adams turned perforce to the conservatives. He was convinced after the adoption of the Massachusetts Constitution in 1780 that the Revolution was at an end and that all men should devote themselves to making wise use of the liberties they had won during the struggle. In 1781, his election as president of the Massachusetts Senate obliged him to turn his back upon his earlier radicalism. The Senate was designed by the Constitution to represent the property in the state and to act as a check upon "the vices and follies" of the House of Representatives, which served the people. Senators were required to have an estate of at least four hundred pounds — which, it was believed, would ensure their whole-hearted defense of property rights against democratic encroachments. Sam Adams fell in so completely with the prevailing spirit in the Senate that he became a stickler for senatorial rights and demanded a rigid formality in intercourse with the Lower House that infuriated the democrats. As president, Adams made the Senate a bulwark against the attempts of the refugees and "old Tories" to return to Massachusetts or repossess their land: when the House of

---

[37] *Samuel Adams Papers*, Samuel A. Otis to Sam Adams, Jan. 4, 1780.
[38] A. E. Morse, *The Federalist Party in Massachusetts to the Year 1800* (1909), 22 (note). *The Writings of John Quincy Adams*, edited by Worthington Chauncey Ford (1913), I, 31.

Representatives passed a bill for admitting loyalists according to the terms of the treaty with Great Britain, the bill was killed in the Senate by Sam Adams and his supporters who were "keen in their resentments and rigid in their notions." [39] Adams admitted that he was in a "Fit of Zeal against the Refugees"; indeed, his resentment was so strong that he used the Massachusetts committees of correspondence, inspection, and safety to keep the people in constant alarm for their liberty and the property they had confiscated from the Tories. John Adams protested against this "silly warfare" against the Tories, but Sam Adams endeared himself to the Massachusetts reactionaries by raising a hue and cry. Conservative leaders now spoke of Sam Adams as "the good, the worthy old patriot Mr. Adams." [40]

Adams's conservatism reflected the changing temper of the people after the close of the Revolution. Revolutionary zeal had slowly cooled in Massachusetts after 1776; and the war lasted so long that by the time the revolutionary settlement was made, conservatives were in complete control. When young John Quincy Adams returned to Massachusetts from Europe, he feared that his continental education had not made him sufficiently republican for the taste of his fellow countrymen, but he found himself the "best republican" at Harvard College and compelled to defend democratic principles against his classmates. [41] Before independence had been won, it was clear that patriotism and love of liberty, which "at first ran through the whole state like wild-fire," had burned themselves out. French officers discovered that Boston Whigs, "like the Carthaginians, know to a penny the value of life and liberty" and had learned to turn patriotism to profit. [42]

As a defender of the established order, Sam Adams was kept

[39] *Journal of the Convention for Framing a Constitution of Government for The State of Massachusetts Bay* (1832), 257. *Report of the American Historical Association* (1896), I, 757. *Massachusetts Centinel*, Nov. 23 and 26, 1785.

[40] *The Writings of Samuel Adams*, IV, 312. *The Works of John Adams*, IX, 548. Wells, III, 181. *Historical Collections of the Essex Institute* (1889), XXV, 18.

[41] *The Writings of John Quincy Adams*, I, 29.

[42] *Boston Gazette*, May 6, 1782. Morse, 15.

almost as busy as when he was undermining royal government in the colonies. Dangers seemed to loom on every side. It was feared by Massachusetts patriots that the Society of the Cincinnati, founded by military officers of the Revolutionary War, was a "political Monster" from which would be hatched a government by kings, lords, and commons; as Sam Adams said, the congresses held by the Cincinnati would take the place of the constitutional assemblies of the states and a hereditary military nobility would establish feudalism and military tyranny. Although Adams himself had created more unconstitutional institutions during the Revolution than any other patriot, he now violently denounced all extra-legal political organizations. In particular, he singled out for attack the County Conventions which were beginning to spring up throughout western Massachusetts in protest against the inequalities and oppression to which the Massachusetts Constitution had given rise. These County Conventions were no more illegal than were the committees of correspondence of 1773, but Adams now regarded with dread all assemblies which brought the constitutional legislature into contempt; men who "under any Pretence or by any Means whatever, would lessen the Weight of Government lawfully exercised," he said, "must be Enemies to our happy Revolution & the Common Liberty." [43]   Both John and Sam Adams raged against these "pestilential county conventions" at which the citizens resolved not to pay taxes, called for the abolition of the Massachusetts Senate, and demanded the revision of the Massachusetts Constitution. Unquestionably, the religious and political settlement made by the "brace of Adamses" in the Constitution of 1780 was "not democratick enough in the opinions of these Geniouses" who summoned the County Conventions in western Massachusetts. [44]

Equally dangerous, in Sam Adams's opinion, with County Conventions and the Society of the Cincinnati was the spirit of

[43] *Samuel Adams Papers*, N. Y. Public Library, Elbridge Gerry to Stephen Higginson, March 4, 1784. *The Writings of Samuel Adams*, IV, 296, 301, 305.

[44] *The Works of John Adams*, IX, 556. *The Writings of Samuel Adams*, IV, 296, 301. *Historical Magazine*, 1869, *Thacher Papers*, 257. *The Diary of William Pynchon*, edited by F. E. Oliver (1890), 239.

levelism.   He certainly did not believe it one of the purposes
of the American Revolution that all classes be placed on an
equal plane: he asked, he said, for no more equality than was
"consistent with the true design of government."   Adams still
clung to the principles he had held before the Revolution.
"I am not of levelling principles," he said, in 1771.   ". . . Subordination is necessary to promote the purposes of government."
Indeed, until he fell under the spell of the spirit of "Liberty,
Equality, and Fraternity" during the French Revolution, he
was so little of an equalitarian that he complained to John
Adams that luxury and easy wealth in post-revolutionary New
England were "confounding every Distinction between the Poor
& the Rich." [45]

In 1785, to the accompaniment of "indecent joy" on one
side of the House of Representatives and "unmanly blubbering"
on the other, John Hancock announced his intention of withdrawing from politics.[46]   Although Hancock pleaded ill-health,
his enemies suspected that he was eager to vacate the governor's
chair before the storm he saw brewing in rural Massachusetts
burst upon him.   In the election which followed, Hancock's
nominee for the governorship was defeated by James Bowdoin,
leader of the conservative party with which Sam Adams was
allied.   Adams heartily rejoiced in Hancock's discomfiture and
the success of the conservatives: "I confess," he said, "it is what
I have long wished for."   With men in office who set the people
an example of patriotism and piety there seemed hope that the
long-delayed Reign of Virtue was at hand.[47]   Adams himself
was appointed to the Council which assisted the governor in his
executive duties.   But Daniel Shays in western Massachusetts gave Adams and Bowdoin far greater problems than the
return of Puritanism to wrestle with.

Like other revolutionists, Sam Adams disapproved of revolutions when they were begun by other people; and in 1785
he shared John Adams's conviction that "it can never be the

[45] *The Writings of Samuel Adams*, II, 152; IV, 315.
[46] *The Life and Correspondence of Rufus King*, edited by C. R. King
(1894–1900), I, 81.
[47] *The Writings of Samuel Adams*, IV, 316.

Duty of one Man to be concerned in more than one Revolution." [48]   When Daniel Shays began to kindle the discontent in rural Massachusetts into open rebellion, Sam Adams denounced the Shaysites just as Luther hurled anathemas against the peasants during the Peasants' Revolt.   He regarded Shays as a rebel who richly deserved the halter, not as a defender of popular rights carrying on the principles of the Revolution. The struggle for liberty was over, Adams exclaimed; no people could be more free than those who lived under a constitution they themselves had established; and if the citizens of western Massachusetts had grievances, they should express them at the elections.   There was no justification of forcible resistance to law in a government where voting was free: whatever the provocation, citizens must remember that "republics could only exist by a due submission to the laws." [49]   Had Thomas Hutchinson heard Sam Adams inveighing against the Shaysites in 1786 he would scarcely have believed that it was the one-time incendiary of the colonies speaking.   But there was good reason why Sam Adams was to be found in the conservative camp in 1786.   Shays's Rebellion grew out of the unrest and privation in western Massachusetts and assumed the character of a movement of country against town: one of the insurgents' demands, in fact, was that the capital be moved from Boston.   Sam Adams was a staunch townsman who so little understood rural economic problems that, while western Massachusetts was drifting toward rebellion, he was far more concerned with immorality in his beloved Boston than with the economic breakdown in the country.   When the artisans and small tradesmen of the metropolis were quiet, Adams was apt to think all was well in the commonwealth; when the country people rose in revolt he was utterly unable to understand their grievance.

Sam Adams became one of the strongest advocates of the "passionate measures" taken by the government against the insurgents.   As president of the Senate, he pushed through a

[48] *Warren-Adams Letters*, II, 189.
[49] Wells, III, 235.   *The Writings of Samuel Adams*, IV, 373.   *The Works of John Adams*, IX, 551.

bill suspending the writ of habeas corpus during the crisis; he served on the committee which urged Governor Bowdoin to take energetic action against the Shaysites; and he attempted to rouse Lieutenant Governor Cushing — called the "Old Lady" because of his timidity — to show the Shaysites cold steel. He hounded the insurgents so relentlessly and pleaded so strongly that blood be shed in western Massachusetts that his enemies later said he had shown himself "fitter for a Venetian Doge than for the second Magistrate in a free republick." After the rebels had been dispersed, Adams called for the leaders' blood: in monarchies, he exclaimed, treason and rebellion might be pardoned, but no mercy could be shown in a popular government — "the man who dares to rebel against the laws of a republic ought to suffer death." [50] By pardoning the insurgent chiefs, Governor Hancock revealed himself a more astute politician and a more humane man than Sam Adams.

Shays's Rebellion added strength to the demand for a revision of the Articles of Confederation. There were usually portentous clouds on Sam Adams's horizon and in the proposal for a closer federation of the states he believed he beheld the certain approach of a tempest. He had sat on the committee in the Continental Congress that drew up the Articles of Confederation; and the experiences of the "critical decade" had not convinced him that they must be essentially changed. In 1785, he warned that a revision would endanger the hard-won liberties of the Revolution through the "Artifices of a few designing Men & a general Inattention of the many." But, because he longed to retaliate against Great Britain for placing restrictions upon American trade and refusing to carry out the provisions of the peace of 1783, Adams proposed giving Congress a "properly guarded" control of trade. Adams made clear, however, that revision ought to go no further. Outside the lack of power in the central government to control trade, he found the Articles of Confederation very much to his taste: under them, the states were sovereigns which gave the federal government sufficient authority to maintain their "mutual Safety and

Happiness . . . and *no more*." As he said to John Adams, only "petit politicians" could wish to decrease the powers of the states and make the Congress at Philadelphia an overweening sovereign.[51] Sam Adams believed that the British Empire had been disrupted because King George and Parliament were bent upon "governing too much"; and he was resolved to prevent the national government of the United States from falling into the same error. The best government, he said, played the least part in men's daily affairs; and, after the Revolution, his mind was never free from the dread of seeing a tyrant at Philadelphia who would rule America as George III and Parliament had ruled from Westminster. His negative political theory of natural rights caused him to fear every increase in the central government's power; like Richard Henry Lee, Adams believed that "the first maxim of a man who loved liberty should be, never to grant to Rulers an atom of power that is not most clearly and indispensably necessary for the safety and well being of Society."[52] Since his Harvard College days, Adams had been firmly attached to Locke's theory of the supremacy of the legislature; no principle of government was more fundamental to him than that "in a constituted commonwealth . . . there can be but one supreme power, which is the legislative, to which all the rest are and must be subordinate." For every ounce of authority the people, represented in the legislature, doled out to the executive, they should keep a pound of checks and balances. Instead of strengthening the executive as the Federalists proposed, Adams wished to keep it weak and to preserve the fences he had erected during the Revolution "to protect & cover the rights of Mankind" against the menace of a strong central government.[53] To Adams, as to the most of the older revolutionary patriots, a "strong government" meant only one thing — tyranny.

With the menace of Federalism looming on the horizon,

---

[51] *The Writings of Samuel Adams*, IV, 322–327, 329. *Samuel Adams Papers*, N. Y. Public Library, Sam Adams to Elbridge Gerry, Sept. 19, 1785.
[52] *Samuel Adams Papers*, Richard Henry Lee to Sam Adams, March 14, 1785.
[53] *Mass. Hist. Soc. Proceedings*, L, 383. *The Writings of Samuel Adams*, IV, 322–327.

Sam Adams saw that republicans could not yet rest from their revolutionary labors. Although he had paid no heed when the Shaysites cried that liberty was in danger, he regarded the proposed Federal Constitution as an alarm bell to the "patriots of '75." He never ceased to doubt that the United States was too vast in extent and too divided by local differences to form a successful national government. Under the Articles of Confederation, the separation of the states in education, manners, and religion was clearly recognized. But if an attempt were made to override American localism, Adams believed the result would be "Mistrust, Disaffection to Government and frequent Insurrections, which will require standing Armies to suppress them," [54] if not wars between the different sections. Seventy years later, the Civil War was to bear out Adams's prophecy.

Adams's fears were strengthened by the outcry raised against the proposed Constitution by some of his oldest friends. Richard Henry Lee led the opposition in the Constitutional Convention, and Elbridge Gerry, one of the Massachusetts delegates, refused to sign the Convention's report. Gerry sounded the alarm in Massachusetts by writing Sam Adams that the Constitution gave inadequate protection to popular liberty. Having thus put Massachusetts republicans on guard, Gerry returned to the state and began to damn the Constitution by exclaiming to the citizens: "Beware! beware! — you are forging chains for yourselves and children — your liberties are at stake." [55]

Nevertheless, Sam Adams made no effort to denounce the Federal Constitution openly. As he later explained in the Massachusetts ratifying convention, he withheld judgment until he had carefully weighed its advantages and shortcomings; and, above all, he wished to take soundings in Boston to determine the townspeople's attitude. His observations convinced him that there was a serious backsliding from the "principles of '75" in the metropolis. As James Madison said, the seaboard was everywhere in favor of the Constitution; the chief demand for a strong central government came from the merchants and

---

[54] *The Writings of Samuel Adams*, IV, 324–325, 332.
[55] *Massachusetts Centinel*, Nov. 17, 1787.

traders who suffered from British commercial restrictions.[56]
The Boston mechanics and artisans were such strong Federalists
they could not be frightened by warnings that the metropolis
would lose its trade with Philadelphia if the Articles of Confederation were tampered with.   Far from sharing Sam Adams's
misgivings toward the Constitution, Bostonians were "in raptures
with it as it is, but would have liked it still better had it been
higher-toned." [57]   Boston's eagerness to ratify the Constitution had been foreseen by the Federalist leaders, who relied
upon the metropolis to turn the scales against rural opposition.
Resistance to the adoption of the Constitution in Massachusetts
came principally from the country districts where it was believed to be the work of rich men who hoped to create two social
orders, "one comprehending the opulent and great, the other
the poor and illiterate."   It was the "black cloud" rolling down
from the western counties that aroused Federalist apprehensions:
the seaboard would unquestionably vote for ratification, but
would it be able to overcome back-country anti-Federalism? [58]

Boston's enthusiasm for the Constitution caused Adams to
hold his fire against it.   His silence kept the Federalists in
great uneasiness, expecting every moment he would launch a
bitter attack upon the Constitution and start an anti-Federalist
backfire in the metropolis itself.   They anxiously scanned the
newspapers for signs of that pen "dipped in venom" with which
Adams upset so many of his enemies' best-laid schemes.   Although they believed Adams to be "Helvidius Priscus," the
author of a virulent arraignment of the Constitution, the writer
was in fact James Warren.[59]   Sam Adams gave the Federalists
no definite proof of his anti-Federalism until after his election
to the Massachusetts Convention.   At a banquet given the
Boston delegates it was found that all favored its adoption except Adams, who was "open & decided" against it, arguing that
"such a Govt. could not pervade the United States — that in-

[56] *The Writings of James Madison*, edited by Gaillard Hunt (1901), V,
8.   *The Life and Correspondence of Rufus King*, I, 69.

[57] Morse, 45.   *Mass. Hist. Soc. Proceedings*, LXIV, 149.

[58] *The Life and Correspondence of Rufus King*, I, 263, 266, 317.

[59] *Mass. Hist. Soc. Proceedings*, LXIV, 155.

ternal taxes ought not to be given to the Union — that the representation was inadequate," and that a large number of amendments must be made before liberty was properly safeguarded.[60] This was no more than the Federalists had expected. Sam Adams had at last come into the open and revealed himself an enemy to the Constitution; and it could no longer be doubted that he must be prevented from putting himself at the head of the anti-Federalist forces in the Massachusetts Convention.

Although Adams was old and retained little of his former political influence, the Federalists recognized that his sturdy republicanism was a difficult hurdle in the way of Massachusetts' ratification of the Constitution. They still entertained a healthy respect for Sam Adams — an attitude that might well be taken by aristocrats toward a revolutionist who had already overthrown one aristocracy. The Federalist bugbear was the same as the Tories': to be "entrapped by the craft of A[dams]." [61] But the Federalists soon showed themselves quite as crafty as Adams had been in his best days. Because it was clear that Adams's support of the Constitution could not be won by argument, the Federalists determined to convert him by other means. Adams's habit of making the wishes of Boston mechanics his guide in public conduct was well known to the Federalists. Unlike the Tories, the Federalists carefully cultivated the friendship of Boston mechanics and artisans, and by the time of the Massachusetts Convention they had a strong following among Adams's constituents. It only remained, therefore, to bring the men Adams looked upon as his political oracles to declare themselves in favor of the Constitution. Clark, Rhodes, and Freeman, three of the most powerful politicians in the North End, who had kept the district loyal to Sam Adams for many years, promised the Federalist leaders that they could call "the most numerous caucus ever held in Boston" to rebuke Adams for his anti-Federalist outburst at the delegates' banquet. Early in January 1788, the mechanics assembled at the Green Dragon Tavern and voted unanimously in favor of ratifying the Constitution. Resolutions drafted by Paul Revere and

---

[60] *The Life and Correspondence of Rufus King,* I, 311.
[61] *Ibid.,* I, 267.

Benjamin Russell were adopted by the mechanics, who declared their "warmest wish and prayer" was that the Constitution be ratified by Massachusetts. Sam Adams was given unmistakably to understand that if he opposed its adoption he would "act contrary to the best interest, the strongest feelings, and warmest wishes of the tradesmen of the town of Boston." [62] Adams was so stunned to find such heresy starting up among his followers that, upon learning what had been done at the Green Dragon, he is said to have exclaimed: "Well, if they must have it, they must have it." The story is doubtless false because Adams soon showed that even Boston mechanics could not immediately overcome his reluctance to part with the Articles of Confederation. Nevertheless, Adams's hands were henceforth tied by Federalist strategy and he was unable to play the part of an anti-Federalist leader in the Massachusetts Convention. [63]

The Green Dragon vote fairly muzzled Sam Adams, but the Federalists were well aware that he was at heart no friend to the Constitution. Moreover, there were signs that Adams might turn against his constituents and rally the anti-Federalists about him. Early in the Convention, he became an "Arch Devil" in the Federalists' eyes by moving that Elbridge Gerry, the Massachusetts delegate to the Constitutional Convention that had been held in New York, should be admitted to the Massachusetts Convention to give his reasons for opposing the Constitution. Sam Adams's proposal was carried and Gerry was brought in, much to the joy of the anti-Federalists. But the result was bitterly disappointing to Adams and his friends: Gerry was quickly silenced by the Federalists and forced to sit "biting the head of his cane" until he finally "left the Convention in dudgeon." [64] Adams's second fling at the Federalists was equally unsuccessful. When he interrupted young Fisher Ames to ask why biennial elections should be preferred over

[62] *Historical Collections of the Essex Institute* (1899), XXXV, 89. *Massachusetts Centinel,* Jan. 9, 1788.

[63] *Historical Magazine,* 1869, *Thacher Papers,* 263.

[64] *Historical Collections of the Essex Institute,* XXXV, 92, 93. *Belknap Papers,* II, *Mass. Hist. Soc. Collections,* Fifth Series (1877), III, 7. *Correspondence of the Revolution, edited by Jared Sparks,* IV, 204.

annual elections, Ames answered with a speech of such cogency and force that Adams dropped the matter as though he had touched a red-hot iron and meekly remarked that "he only made the inquiry for information, and that he had heard sufficient to satisfy himself of its propriety." The haste with which Adams backed away from an encounter with Ames disconcerted the anti-Federalists, who had hoped to hear him attack the Constitution. The Federalists, on the other hand, were exultant and they dated the turn of the tide in the Convention in their favor from the day Adams was worsted by young Ames. "This was the first dawn of the Triumph of Reason in the Convention," they exclaimed.[65]

Although John Hancock had been elected president, he had not yet made his appearance in the Convention. Swathed in bandages and keeping to his sickroom as tenaciously as Lord Chatham, Hancock refused to take his seat until he was sure which party in the Convention would triumph. It was well known that as soon as Hancock was satisfied from which direction the wind was blowing his health would show immediate improvement and he would be on hand to lead the winning party to victory; but while the "balance of power was each day vibrating, as the mercury in a thermometer," Hancock's ailments kept him bedridden in Beacon Street.[66] There was nothing more fatal, in Hancock's eyes, than not to be on the winning side; and had the Constitution been ratified or rejected without his aid he would have been a sick man indeed. If he can be said to have had any convictions, they were anti-Federalist. As the governor of one of the strongest states in the Union, Hancock was reluctant to help create an office of greater dignity and power than his own. Nevertheless, he was haunted by the fear that the Constitution might be carried in spite of him and that the rising Federalist tide would overwhelm him, as it threatened to overwhelm all other enemies of the Constitution. He was well pleased with the present order, but he had no in-

---

[65] *Massachusetts Centinel*, Jan. 19, 1788; Dec. 31, 1788.

[66] *Historical Magazine* (1869), *Thacher Papers*, 266. *Historical Collections of the Essex Institute*, 87. Theophilus Parsons, *Memoir of Theophilus Parsons* (1859), 78.

tention of lashing himself to the Articles of Confederation and sinking with them should the Federalists' broadside strike home.

Shrewdly gauging Hancock's weakness, the Federalist caucus leaders hit upon a plan to draw him out of his sickroom and bring him into the Convention an avowed Federalist. Hancock was willing to listen to offers and he soon learned that the anti-Federalists had little to give in comparison with the tempting fruit the Federalists dangled before him. In exchange for urging the ratification of the Constitution, the Federalists promised Hancock their support for the presidency of the United States in case Virginia failed to ratify the Constitution. At the same time, they convinced him that Virginia would not ratify — thereby eliminating George Washington as a rival for the President's chair. Hancock had no aversion to a strong central government provided he could be at its head and therefore he eagerly swallowed the Federalist bait.[67]

While the Federalist chiefs were making certain of Hancock's aid they were tampering with Sam Adams's devotion to the Articles of Confederation. Most of the work was done behind the locked doors of the caucus, where Federalists worked "as hard as in the Convention" and with far more important results. In this secret meeting, Adams made his terms with the Federalists. Unlike Hancock, he could not be tempted with political office, but the Federalists were well stocked with bait to land even the stoutest anti-Federalist in their basket. Adams was promised that amendments would be added to the Constitution to protect the liberty of states and individuals under a centralized government. The Green Dragon vote had sown the first seed of doubt in Adams's mind that perhaps he had misjudged the Constitution; and the arguments of the Federalists began to convince him that even "old fashioned Whigs" could swallow it if it were heavily seasoned with amendments. It was agreed that the amendments drawn up by the Federalist caucus should be introduced into the Convention by Hancock as a "conciliatory proposition" to unite both parties in favor of ratification, and that Sam Adams should second Hancock's pro-

---

[67] *The Life and Correspondence of Rufus King,* I, 319, 344. Parsons, 78. *Historical Collections of the Essex Institute,* XXV, 94.

posal.[68]   The delegates outside the caucus were kept in the dark as to the way Sam Adams would vote, but it was known to the Federalist chiefs that his opposition had been removed ten days before he openly spoke for ratification in the Convention.   As had been expected, Hancock's health quickly improved after he had made his bargain with the Federalists and he was able to take his seat as president of the Convention.   With Adams and Hancock securely pocketed, the exultant Federalists believed nothing more stood in the way of ratification.

The failure of the two leading revolutionary Whigs in Massachusetts to come to the aid of the anti-Federalists worked the downfall of the enemies of the Constitution.   Although the anti-Federalists were in a majority when the Convention opened, they were unwieldy, poorly led, and unequipped with the "whips" and caucuses possessed by the Federalists.   The anti-Federalist leaders, Widgery and Bishop, were uneducated back-country politicians who repeatedly allowed themselves to be outgeneraled by the Federalist minority.   It was one of the anti-Federalists' chief grievances that all the professional and educated men in the Convention were in favor of the Constitution, leaving them only a handful of orators who, it was said, were "very clamorous, petulant, tedious, and provoking." There were so many Shaysites among them that Federalist newspapers traced their genealogy from *"bankrupt tories* in '74 — *fiery whigs* in '75 — *disappointed jockies* in '83 — *insurgents* in '86 and *antifederalists* in '88." [69]   Unquestionably, most of the talent was on the side of Federalism; and the anti-Federalists sorely needed a strategist such as Sam Adams to counterwork the oratory of Judge Dana, who "thunders like Demosthenes," and the skill of the Federalist caucus.   But Adams made no effort to take command; and, as the Convention drew to a close, the anti-Federalists were panic-stricken to see their strength melting away.   "The more the Constitution is canvassed," wrote a Federalist, "the brighter it shines." And, after Hancock made his "conciliatory proposition," seconded by Sam Adams, the anti-Federalists were so weakened

---

[68] *Belknap Papers,* II, *Mass. Hist. Soc. Collections,* Fifth Series, III, 15.
[69] *Massachusetts Centinel,* April 30, 1788.

by desertions that the Federalists began to believe themselves in a majority for the first time since the opening of the Convention.[70]

The Federalists flattered themselves they had taken Sam Adams securely in tow, but on the last day of the Convention he revealed how little to his taste was sailing in the wake of the Federalist man-of-war. Just when the Constitution seemed about to be ratified, Adams "almost overset the apple-cart" by unexpectedly introducing a set of new amendments to the Constitution in an effort to safeguard liberty further against the central government.[71] Both parties in the Convention were alarmed by Adams's motion; and a murmur ran through the anti-Federalist ranks that "such a man as Mr. A[dams] would not have guarded against these evils, if he had not seen a foundation for them in the Constitution." Indeed, he threw the meeting into such consternation that the Constitution's fate was in doubt for some hours. Finally, after it had become apparent that his amendments would create another protracted struggle between the weary delegates, Adams withdrew his motion. The damage was not repaired so easily, however, because some of the anti-Federalists revived the motion and Adams was compelled to vote against his own measure. Although it was ultimately defeated, it cost the Constitution precious votes and almost wiped away the small Federalist majority of seventeen that made possible the ratification of the Constitution. It was suspected by some that Adams introduced those last-minute amendments in order to keep Hancock from stealing the whole show "with *his* amendments and to increase his *own* popularity, as Hancock had his, by the midwifeing the other amendments into the world." [72] More probably, Adams acted from a sincere fear that individual liberty was not yet sufficiently protected from encroachments by the Federal government. The Federalists had silenced him for the greater part of the Convention,

[70] *Belknap Papers*, III, *Mass. Hist. Soc. Collections*, Fifth Series, III, 5, 17. *Historical Collections of the Essex Institute*, XXXV, 94.

[71] *Belknap Papers*, II, *Mass. Hist. Soc. Collections*, Fifth Series, III, 17. *Debates and Proceedings in the Mass. Convention*, 266.

[72] *Belknap Papers*, II, *Mass. Hist. Soc. Collections*, Fifth Series, III, 17. *Massachusetts Centinel*, Dec. 17, 1788.

but they had not succeeded in quieting his fears that the Constitution would undo the work of the Revolution by creating a despotism in Philadelphia. In Adams's justification, his friends later pointed out that most of the amendments he proposed in the Massachusetts Convention — particularly, the prohibition of standing armies, the guarantee of liberty of the press, the power of the people to petition Congress for redress of grievances, and the inviolability of "persons, papers, or possessions" against unreasonable searches and seizures — were later incorporated in the Constitution of the United States.[73]

In spite of Adams's filibustering, the Convention ratified the Constitution "to the great Joy of all Boston." The Federalists had transformed the citadel of Whig republicanism into a "federal metropolis" in which Sam Adams found few familiar landmarks. Boston mechanics who had been the staunchest friends of Sam Adams and the Revolution now paraded the streets in celebration of the Federalist victory, cheering the delegates who had voted for the Constitution and burning a longboat, called the "Old Constitution," on the Common.[74]

Sam Adams had gained no new laurels in the Massachusetts Constitutional Convention. Federalists scented treachery in his "insidious motion" for further amendments and believed his real intention had been to overturn the whole Constitution; and the anti-Federalists reproached him for precipitately withdrawing his amendments under the enemy's fire.[75] It was clear that Adams's reputation acquired in the American Revolution was wearing thin. He seemed completely out of touch with the new order that was being created in America; he could expect no honors under a centralized government; and even in his native state his influence had almost completely vanished. The new generation was as indifferent to most of the "heroes of '75" as it was to the old Whig principles and prejudices. The French traveler, La Rochefoucauld, found that the citizens of Boston retained little of the hatred toward Great Britain for

[73] *Independent Chronicle*, Aug. 6, 1789.
[74] *Historical Magazine* (1869), *Thacher Papers*, 270. *Massachusetts Centinel*, Dec. 17, 1788. *Independent Chronicle*, Feb. 14, 1788.
[75] *Belknap Papers*, II, Mass. Hist. Soc. Collections, Fifth Series, III, 17, 18. *The Writings of Laco* (1789), 49. *Massachusetts Centinel*, Dec. 17, 1788.

which they had been famous during the Revolution.[76]   Sam
Adams, it was plain, would receive no high political reward by
resting upon his fame as "the Man of the Revolution."

Misfortune had done much to show Sam Adams the futility
of further opposing John Hancock, the political "boss" of Massachusetts.   Adams had learned from his disappointments of
the past ten years that Hancock had power to make or unmake
any politician in the state and that, as long as he remained at
odds with Hancock, the highest offices would be barred against
him.   Moreover, in spite of the amendments, Adams regarded
the Constitution as a menace to popular liberty and he believed
that the republicans of the revolutionary period were now called
upon to make peace among themselves in order to combat centralized government and the new "Tory" aristocracy.   Hancock, as well, was eager for a reconciliation.   When Hancock
saw his chances for the presidency of the United States go glim-
mering with Virginia's ratification of the Constitution, he
abruptly broke off relations with the Federalists and, much to
the amazement of all parties, he and Adams went off arm in
arm on a new honeymoon, with Adams enthusiastically singing
the praises of a man whom for the past fourteen years he had
denounced as a wastrel and compared with Thomas Hutchinson.   Just as in 1772, when Adams and Hancock interrupted
their quarrel to make common front against the Tories, so in
1788 they erased old scores to make war against the Federalists.
But despite their parade of friendship, it was understood that
Sam Adams, the one-time leader of the patriot party, was now
merely a lieutenant in Hancock's party: "John is the first of the
tribe, and Samuel is second," it was said.[77]

Unfortunately, Sam Adams's humiliation in the Massachusetts Constitutional Convention at the hands of Fisher Ames
did not teach him that young Ames — soon to be known as the
"Colossus of Monocrats" — was a very dangerous political
opponent.   In 1788, Adams entered the race for the Federal
Congress from the Suffolk district, with Fisher Ames, the Fed-

---

[76] Duc de la Rochefoucauld Liancourt, *Travels through the United States
of North America*, I, 403, 404.

[77] *Independent Chronicle*, March 27, 1788.

eralist candidate, as his adversary. Ames was of the class of 1774, Harvard College, and his revolutionary service consisted in having once turned out with militia. It seemed incredible that such a stripling could defeat the veteran Sam Adams; and, indeed, the Federalists apologized to each other for having picked a novice to oppose him. Hopefully they pointed out that Ames was as old as Sam Adams when he first entered public life and that the Federalist candidate was older than Pitt when he became Prime Minister of Great Britain. But it was agreed that Ames's chances of winning the election were slight.

The principal issue between Ames and Adams was the necessity of further amending the Constitution. Now an avowed anti-Federalist, Adams ran as a "violent stickler for amendments," while Ames belabored the "disappointed jockies" who, having failed to prevent the adoption of the Constitution, would cripple it with amendments.[78] Although it had been a matter of doubt where Sam Adams stood while the Constitution was being debated in the Massachusetts Convention, there was no question of his position now: there were far too few checks and balances and safeguards to popular liberty in the Constitution, he exclaimed, to dispel his fears of despotism.[79] Adams now anxiously sniffed the breeze that blew from Philadelphia for whiffs of tyranny; and he was as determined in 1788 as in 1775 to resist the centralization of American government.

Fisher Ames and his friends pictured Adams as an enemy of the Constitution who wished to enter Congress in order to wreck the newly established Federal government. They urged the Boston mechanics whose support had been vital to Massachusetts' ratification of the Constitution to elect to Congress a "*firm decided* FEDERALIST" who would defend the Constitution against the States' rights republicans.[80] Federalist propaganda put Adams in the light of a destroyer of the Constitution and Ames as its savior — to the great perplexity of the voters of

[78] *Massachusetts Centinel*, April 30, 1788; Sept. 27, 1788; Dec. 17 and 31, 1788.

[79] *The Writings of Samuel Adams*, IV, 337.

[80] *Massachusetts Centinel*, Sept. 27, 1788; Dec. 13 and 17, 1788. Austin, II, 96.

the Suffolk District, who were torn between their loyalty to the Constitution and their respect for Sam Adams. But their desire to see a strong central government in the United States ultimately prevailed and Ames was elected by a large majority. Even Boston turned against Sam Adams and gave Ames 445 votes to Adams's 439. It was an impressive victory for the Federalists; but Adams might well have comforted himself with the reflection that he would have found, as did Elbridge Gerry, that Congress was a very unhappy place for a republican of the vintage of '75.

Fisher Ames's victory was the result of the growing conviction among a large body of Massachusetts voters that Sam Adams's ideas were more suited to solving the problems of 1775 than those of 1788. He seemed to belong to a past generation. "The spirit of '75 was a glorious spirit for *that period*," it was said, "but do its principles apply at the present day?" As the Federalists pointed out, the question was no longer "Shall we be free" but "How shall we use our freedom?" — and to this last question Sam Adams could give no answer.[81] Since the Revolution, Massachusetts had become a great commercial state that demanded from its representatives in Congress wide knowledge of commerce and finance rather than obsolete Whiggish hatred of Great Britain. It was well known that Sam Adams had little interest in trade and that he was openly hostile to commerce with Great Britain. He unhesitatingly confessed his ignorance of commercial matters: "I get out of my Line when I touch upon Commerce," he once wrote; "it is a Subject I never understood." [82] This shortcoming might have been overlooked in 1775, but it was a serious handicap to a Massachusetts politician in 1788. Federalists saw Adams's vulnerability and heckled him ceaselessly with questions concerning his fitness to lead "this Commercial Commonwealth": "What," they asked, "are his acquirements upon the great subject of Finance; has he ever attended to System of Revenue; what are his ideas of trade and Commerce; are they matter of great importance in *his* estimation?" Sam Adams certainly did not seem to be

[81] *Massachusetts Centinel*, May 10, 1788.
[82] *The Writings of Samuel Adams*, III, 353.

the man upon whom Massachusetts businessmen should rely
to foster commerce and dispel the danger of *"Insurgents, Mobs,
Antifederalists, Paper Money,* or *Tender Laws."* [83]

Adams's greatest political weakness, however, was his unpopularity in rural Massachusetts. In the congressional elections of 1788, for example, he received only eighty-two votes
outside of Boston. Just as he had been looked upon with suspicion by many members of the continental Congress as representing too exclusively the interests of Massachusetts, so he was
distrusted by New England countryfolk as being too much of a
Bostonian. Like the Tories before them, the Federalists attempted to destroy Boston's influence in the country and to
keep the farmers "out of the power of the tempters in the seaports, and their mobs." Their policy was to create "an enlightened Yeomanry" that would stand firm against "all the
seditious, and desperate" Boston demagogues.[84] But, unlike
the Tories, they were not satisfied with merely winning the support of New England yeomen: by making allies of the "steady
going Mechanics" of the metropolis they cut the ground from
beneath Sam Adams's feet. Whereas the Tories had regarded
the artisan class of the metropolis as "the rabble" and "the
scum" and ignored their political importance, the Federalists
courted and flattered them as ardently as did Sam Adams. As
a consequence, Boston radicals found themselves opposed with
their own weapons: Federalists called town meetings, held
caucuses of mechanics and shopkeepers, and dispensed liberal
quantities of rum and flip among the electorate.[85] But it was
not until French Jacobinism had begun to infect Americans that
the true value of this missionary work among Boston mechanics
was clearly seen.

The Federalists were so successful in weaning Bostonians

[83] *Massachusetts Centinel,* Dec. 13 and 17, 1788.
[84] *The Works of Fisher Ames,* edited by Seth Ames (1859), I, 182.
Pickering Papers, MSS. Mass. Hist. Soc., XX, T. Williams to Timothy
Pickering, July 17, 1795, 21. *The Works of Alexander Hamilton,* edited by
J. S. Hamilton (1851), V, 571.
[85] *The Correspondence of Rufus King,* I, 361. *Federal Orrery,* April 6,
1795. *The Works of Fisher Ames,* I, 146. *The Works of Alexander
Hamilton,* 571.

away from Sam Adams and arousing hostility in the country districts against him that even John Hancock, the most powerful man in the state, had difficulty in putting his new ally into high office. Adams was defeated in 1788 when he ran for the lieutenant governorship; and it required all the strength the Hancockians could muster in 1789 to hoist Adams beside Hancock in the second highest office in the state.

In his political campaigns after the adoption of the Federal Constitution, Sam Adams was put forward as the "old tried republican" who would "preserve the republick of Massachusetts from being swallowed up in a merciless Aristocracy." He was declared to be the enemy of the "British Faction" in Massachusetts, "the black band of Tories," "British Agents," refugees seeking to recover their estates, and "the filchering gang of speculators" who robbed the people through the Bank of the United States.[86] Before elections the old hatred of Great Britain was turned into votes for Sam Adams by a prearranged British scare; King George's agents were said to be swarming in the state; Tories were plotting to regain their property and political influence; and republicans exclaimed that the British were beginning "to show their teeth" again because Americans had forgotten the men and principles of 1775. Readers of Massachusetts anti-Federalist newspapers might well believe that British redcoats would soon be camping on the Boston Common unless Sam Adams were given an overwhelming vote to prove to King George that New Englanders were still true to their "first love." Adams was not merely a bulwark against the British peril: he was, as well, a staunch opponent of encroachments from the national government and a guardian angel of local liberties. His favorite toast was, "The States united and the States separate"; and, the Federalists complained, he thundered against "every thing that is federal and rational."[87]

Had Sam Adams died before the adoption of the Federal Constitution and the outbreak of the French Revolution created new party struggles in the United States, he would have ended

---

[86] *Herald of Freedom and the Federal Adviser*, April 3, 1789. *Massachusetts Centinel*, March 14, 1789. *Independent Chronicle*, Jan. 15, 1795.
[87] Wells, III, 273. *Salem Gazette*, March 25, 1794.

his days in the conservatism that frequently comes upon revolutionists in their old age. Like John Wilkes, Adams might
have exclaimed that he was an "exhausted volcano" and settled
down to the dreary business of repressing radicalism in the
younger generation. Fortunately, the menace of a centralized
government and a Federalist oligarchy, together with the spread
of the spirit of "Liberty, Equality, and Fraternity" to the
United States, saved Adams from decaying in the conservative
backwaters into which he had fallen and plunged him again into
the centre of those revolutionary eddies which were his true
element.

Sam Adams's faith in the common people remained unshaken,
despite their preference for Hancock and high living. For
many years, John Adams had felt doubtful of the success of
the republican experiment, but Sam Adams was firmly convinced
that democracy would flourish as long as education was extended
to the masses. Sam Adams had much of the zeal for popular
education that his Puritan ancestors had carried to New England. The way to perpetuate republican government, he said,
was to take the children young, clap them into a grammar school
run on sound New England lines, and instill Whig principles
into them until they emerged upright citizens who loathed British luxuries and monarchy alike. As long as these "nurseries of
Virtue" kept turning out young Whigs, there was no danger
of dictatorship or monarchy in America because the people
would be wise enough to elect only the best men to office.[88]
Sam Adams's faith in the common man was fully as strong as
Jefferson's, but there was this significant difference between
these two staunch republicans: whereas Jefferson put his trust
in the American farmer, Sam Adams's common man was a
townsman and usually a Bostonian. Far from being a Jeffer-
sonian democrat in the usual sense of the word, Sam Adams
represented that unruly town democracy which Jefferson later
took into the Republican Party with deep misgivings.

Adams's belief in the wisdom of the common people and devotion to a democratic form of government brought him again

[88] *The Writings of Samuel Adams*, III, 231; IV, 124, 125, 347. *Warren-
Adams Letters*, I, 171, 172, 197.

into the thick of the struggle when, in 1793, the French Revolution began to awaken a revolutionary spirit in the United States and divide the American people into Jacobins and anti-Jacobins. From the beginning, Adams believed the French Revolution to be "a war of Kings and Nobles against the equal Rights of Men," and he was eager to spring to the defense of popular liberty in the United States, jeopardized, as he supposed, by the Federal Constitution and the new aristocracy. "From my Youth," Adams said, "my mind has been strongly impressed with the Love of Mankind; and tho' I am old, the lamp still burns." [89]   Unlike his cousin, John Adams distrusted the French Revolution as early as 1790, when most Americans were strongly Francophile, because he suspected that the French people, like too many Americans, panted "for equality of persons and property." [90]   John Adams, it was clear, would have no sympathy with Sam Adams's efforts to preserve American liberty by making French Jacobinism a rallying cry.

The Federalists' opposition to the spread of French revolutionary principles in the United States sounded an alarm among the old guard of American patriots. The battles of the Revolution must be fought again, they cried, and the Tories once more struck down. "I am alarmed," wrote Hancock to Adams in 1793. ". . . It is time to step forth & oppose the torrent of opinions & pursuits that are attempting to establish a system foreign to your ideas & mine." Adams had lost none of his eagerness to do battle with Tories and he answered that Hancock's call to arms had "cheer'd the Spirit and caus'd the blood to thrill thro' the Veins of an Old Man." [91]   The Whigs forgot their internal quarrels and once more formed themselves into that "phalanx" that had struck terror among the Tories during the Revolution. As Elbridge Gerry said, Hancock, with all his faults, was still a Whig and sorely needed the help of his old comrades against the Federalist aristocracy. [92]

[89] *The Writings of Samuel Adams*, IV, 358. *Samuel Adams Papers*, N. Y. Public Library, Samuel Adams to Pierre Auguste Adet, July 28, 1795.

[90] *The Works of John Adams*, IX, 563, 564.

[91] *Samuel Adams Papers*, N. Y. Hist. Soc., John Hancock to Sam Adams, Aug. 31, 1793; Sam Adams to John Hancock, Sept. 3, 1793.

[92] Austin, II, 86.

After John Hancock's death in 1793, Sam Adams was given an opportunity to become one of the chief apostles of Jacobinism in the United States. He inherited the leadership of the Hancockian party that had controlled Massachusetts politics for over a decade, and, as Hancock's heir, seemed likely to dominate the political scene for the remainder of his life. But to the Federalists it was intolerable that Massachusetts, a strong Federalist state, should elect a "doting antifederalist" to the governorship. They hoped to break up Hancock's party after Adams had taken command and they made a vigorous effort to tumble this "scapegoat of seventy-five" out of the governor's chair in the elections of 1794.[93] But Adams kept the loyalty of Hancock's former followers by lauding the deceased governor in public and praising his "virtuous and patriotic example."[94] With the Hancockians' support, Adams surprised the Federalists by soundly beating their candidate for governor in 1794, but the best John Quincy Adams could say of Adams was that he "may do less harm than some others, but he will certainly never do any good." Conservatives seldom expected good from Sam Adams; and when "all the wise, and good, and the rich," as Fisher Ames characterized the Federalist Party, saw Adams seated firmly in the governor's chair, they threw up their hands in dismay and declared that all was lost.[95] Sam Adams, it was said, was looking forward to a second revolution in the United States — this time with French Jacobinism as his creed and the Federalist aristocracy as his victims.

During Shays's Rebellion, Sam Adams had inveighed against all unconstitutional institutions as vigorously as the Tories had once denounced his committees of correspondence. But the necessity of crushing Federalism in Massachusetts led Adams to alter sharply his attitude toward unconstitutional organizations and he enthusiastically gave his blessing to the Constitutional Clubs — the "self-created Societies" that were designed to keep alive the principles of the American Revolution and, the Federalists suspected, to keep the United States abreast of

[93] *The Writings of John Quincy Adams*, I, 185.
[94] *The Writings of Samuel Adams*, IV, 354.
[95] *The Writings of John Quincy Adams*, I, 183. Charles Warren, *Jacobin and Junto*, 50.

France in the march toward "Liberty, Equality, and Fraternity." [96] These Jacobin Clubs with their corresponding committees and secret caucuses — where radicals were as busy as "Old Nick and his imps" — bore strong resemblance to the machinery which Sam Adams had created during the American Revolution. Like the earlier committees of correspondence they were the terror of the "Tories": Fisher Ames exclaimed they were "born in sin, the impure offspring of Genêt," and some apprehensive Federalists, who fancied they already saw the shadow of the guillotine on Boston Common, were unable to pass a lamppost without casting an uneasy glance in its direction. French tricolor cockades and liberty caps began to give Boston an uncomfortably Parisian atmosphere: "loud and saucy" Jacobins paraded through the streets and were heard to "yelp & howl and Trumpet sedition at every corner." [97] Boston Federalists found to their dismay that they were unable to hoot down the republicans when they broke into the chorus of *"Ça Ira"* in Boston taverns and theatres. But even more alarming than these portents of the Boston Jacobins' eagerness to see the metropolis play the part of an American Paris in the second American Revolution was the spectacle of the governor of Massachusetts, arm in arm with Jacobins and Frenchmen, surrounded by "Sattelites of Anarchy" and proclaiming the doctrine "Liberty, Equality, and Fraternity" from the governor's chair.

Indeed, Governor Adams seemed to be as enthusiastic a Jacobin as ever came out of "Equality Alley." Whenever his failing health permitted, "Citizen" Adams was the guest of honor at the "Civic Feasts" where Boston democrats celebrated French military victories and indulged themselves in such disquieting sport as slaughtering an ox, labeled "Aristocracy," as a "PEACE OFFERING TO LIBERTY AND EQUALITY." Federalists vainly protested against Governor Adams lending the sanction of his person to meetings which, they declared, consisted only of gallows birds and a few "hungry immigrants, happy to pick

[96] *Independent Chronicle*, Dec. 9, 1793.
[97] *The Works of Fisher Ames*, I, 148. *Columbian Centinel*, Aug. 7, 1793; Nov. 1, 1794; Dec. 20, 1794. Parsons (Appendix), 472. Warren, 57. *Massachusetts Mercury*, Nov. 29, 1793. *Independent Chronicle*, April 25, 1793.

up a dinner." These gatherings, it was said, were properly
called tricolor festivals because the company was composed of
whites, mulattoes, and negroes.[98]   But Adams continued to attend these Jacobin frolics regardless of the scandalized Federalists: at the great Civic Feast held in Boston in January 1793,
with Faneuil Hall decorated with French flags and mottoes of
"Liberty, Equality, and Fraternity," Citizen Adams sat beside
the French consul and led the toasts of France.   He was present at the feast held in celebration of the abolition of monarchy;
and when news arrived of a great French victory, Adams ordered
that a collation be served in the Senate chamber and a military
corps parade through the streets.   Adams took such prominent
part in these democratic revels and connected himself so closely
with the Jacobin Club that Federalists exclaimed he acted more
like a French agent than the governor of the commonwealth
of Massachusetts.   But Adams's popularity with Jacobins
throughout the United States was so great that he ran Governor
Clinton a close race for highest honors.   The French ministers
now found him greatly changed from the days of the Continental Congress when he had been a thorn in the side of every
French emissary.   They were charmed by Adams's speeches
to the Massachusetts General Court, "every sentence, every
word" of which, they said, breathed "the purest republicanism"
and proved the governor a "friend of liberty and France."
Particularly exhilarating to the French ministers and perturbing
to the Federalists was Adams's address to the Massachusetts
legislature delivered in 1794, in which the governor pointed
out that liberty and equality were essential parts of the "political
creed of the United States" and that the American and French
Constitutions were based upon the same principles.   Truly, said
the Federalists, Sam Adams had become a Frenchman.[99]

[98] Warren, 57. *The Works of Fisher Ames*, I, 146. *Salem Gazette,*
March 29, 1796. *Massachusetts Mercury*, Sept. 22, 1795. *Massachusetts
Centinel,* Jan. 17, 1794.
[99] Warren, 47. *The Correspondence of Rufus King*, I, 545. *Massachu-
setts Mercury*, Sept. 22, 1795. *Independent Chronicle*, April 2, 1795. *Salem
Gazette*, March 25, 1795. *Samuel Adams Papers*, N. Y. Public Library,
Antoine Charbonnet Duplaine to Governor Samuel Adams, April 10, 1794.
Report of the American Historical Association (1903), II, 893.

Sam Adams further outraged the Federalist aristocracy by surrounding himself with the boon companions of his revolutionary days and with Jacobins from the Boston Constitutional Society. After his election as governor, Adams's best friends continued to be Thomas Hewes, a constable; William Cooper, — "an old Baboon," — the former town clerk; Ben Austin, Junior, — "lank HONESTUS, with his lanthorn jaws," — and "birds of such sort, which," said the Federalists, "would disgrace the kitchen of any other Chief Magistrate." [100] Governor Adams was decidedly not a prize for fashionable hostesses and he was left as much alone by Boston society while he was governor as when he was plain Sam Adams, the South End rebel. The Adamses entertained little and continued to live in an ugly old-fashioned frame house off Winter Street which showed traces of once having had a coat of yellow paint. Sam still dressed in the style that had been popular before the war: his old-fashioned tie wig, cocked hat, buckled shoes, knee breeches, and red cloak were reminiscent of the last generation when Whigs had railed against finery in dress as unrepublican. With characteristic simplicity, Adams would have walked on foot when carrying out his official duties as governor had not his friends presented him with a horse and carriage. He was no longer a poor man, however, because his son's pension and his own lucky investments in Jamaica real estate had dispelled the poverty which pinched him throughout his earlier life. But lifelong habits of frugality were not easily broken and Adams showed how highly he prized his reputation for poverty by indignantly denying the Federalists' insinuations that he had become well-to-do.

That Governor Adams was an arrant Jacobin and no friend of orderly government, few Federalists could doubt after the rough treatment Jay's treaty received in Boston. The Boston mob, strongly anti-British in feeling, greeted the treaty with the cry that Jay had sold them to the British, and vented their anger by burning the treaty and effigies of Jay in the streets. Federalists saw the futility of appealing to Governor Adams to

---

[100] *Massachusetts Mercury*, Feb. 16, 1796; Warren, 62. Dr. John S. J. Gardiner, *Remarks on the Jacobiniad* (Boston, 1795), 15.

prevent indignities to Jay and the United States Senate, which, by ratifying the treaty, incurred the wrath of the Jacobins. "This weak old man," remarked a conservative, "is one of the loudest brawlers against the treaty, and the boldest in proposing schemes of opposition to the federal government."[101] Yet when the Boston mob got out of control and began to attack the houses of prominent aristocrats, it seemed possible that even Governor Adams might be persuaded to take action against his headstrong friends who were carrying matters further than most radicals approved. A body of frightened citizens rushed to Adams with news that the mob was loose in the metropolis and urged him to stop the riot. Governor Adams, however, seemed to relish a return to the days when the Sons of Liberty had fallen upon the Tories and he refused to act against the mob: "It was only Boys water melon frolicks," he told the townspeople. But Mrs. Adams, with a keener eye for the dangers of inaction, is said to have warned her husband that "it was time to look about, for the thing became serious and alarming." [102] When it was known that the governor had refused to restore order in Boston, the mob rioted for six nights, terrorizing Federalists and thoroughly intimidating the government. When the attorney general and sheriff attempted to disperse the mob by reading the Riot Act, they were "hustled" out of the way; and the rioters in Liberty Square made bloodcurdling threats to tear out and roast the hearts of any who tried to infringe their natural right to riot.[103] That the mob was finally driven off the streets was no fault of Governor Adams: it was only after the Boston citizens had organized themselves against the rioters that the town was quieted. The governor would have done well had he taken his wife's advice, for he did his reputation no good by openly countenancing disorder. Federalists immediately raised the cry that Adams was using the mob to satisfy his rancor against the Federal government and its supporters; and henceforth Adams's party was called the "Water Mellon Boys" and Adams himself was known as "our mob-loving Governor."

[101] *The Life and Correspondence of Rufus King*, II, 31.
[102] *Massachusetts Mercury*, Feb. 16, 1796.
[103] *Federal Orrery*, Sept. 28, 1795. Amory, 301.

But it was clear that Adams's influence was being gradually destroyed by the rising Federalist tide. The Federalists had long looked forward to making Massachusetts completely Federal: and with the rallying cry of "not a single Jacobin in the Senate," they purged the Upper House of all Adams's supporters in 1795, including the arch-Jacobin, "Honestus" Austin.[104] With the passing of the parent Constitutional Club at Philadelphia, the other clubs declined — with the result that in 1796 Austin lost political control of Boston and the Federalist nominees for the Boston seat defeated the Republicans. In spite of Adams's efforts to induce the Massachusetts General Court to adopt the Virginia Resolves, they were overwhelmingly defeated by the conservative majority. His assertion that Jay's treaty was "pregnant with evil" because it gave Great Britain an opportunity to carry out its plans to dominate the United States was greeted "with almost universal disgust" in the legislature, and the governor was rebuked by the representatives for interfering in the business of the Federal government.[105] Adams's Jacobinism cost him the support of the New England clergy, — that "black regiment" of revolutionary days, — who fulminated against the infidelity and license of the French Revolution as energetically as they had preached rebellion during the American Revolution. "Shall our Sons become the disciples of Voltaire and the dragons of Marat," exclaimed the Reverend Timothy Dwight; "or our daughters the concubines of the Illuminati?" And New England congregations answered with a hearty "Nay!" Moreover, Adams was greatly embarrassed by the publication of a letter he had written Citizen Genêt. Although Washington had already demanded Genêt's recall, Adams assured him that his conduct as Minister Plenipotentiary would "greatly tend to promote the common cause of Liberty, and the Rights of Man" — an indiscretion that had the unfortunate effect of encouraging the French minister to appeal to the people over Washington's head.[106] New England Fed-

---

[104] *Federal Orrery*, April 6, 1795. *The Correspondence of Rufus King*, I, 511; II, 55.

[105] Morse, 158. *The Writings of Samuel Adams*, IV, 391.

[106] Morse, 171. *Columbia Centinel*, April 3, 1794. *Report of the American Historical Association*, II (1903), 277.

eralists were not slow to take advantage of Adams's mistakes
and discredit the Republican Party in New England.   It was
made abundantly clear to Adams that Federalist domination of
Massachusetts was inevitable.   The "great Incendiary of the
province" who had brought about the downfall of so many
royal governors of Massachusetts Bay was well aware that he
could not long remain the anti-Federalist governor of the
strongest Federalist state in the Union.

Before he gave up the struggle against Federalism, Adams
determined to fight one last pitched battle.   In 1796, John
Adams was the Federalist candidate for President of the United
States to succeed George Washington.   In Massachusetts, Sam
Adams ran as a presidential elector opposed to John Adams's
election; and the bitterly fought campaign that followed revealed how completely the "brace of Adamses" had parted
company.   The Republican newspapers warned the people that
John Adams, "the advocate of kingly government, and of a
titled nobility to form an upper house, and to keep down the
'swinish multitude,' would make Senate and President hereditary, and is to be your President unless you turn out THIS DAY
and support the old tried patriot SAMUEL ADAMS, who is the
friend of the people, a republican in principles and manners."
Sam Adams believed John Adams had betrayed the "principles of '75," but the younger Adams was convinced that he
alone had kept them pure and undefiled — Sam Adams, in his
eyes, had cast the doctrines of the American Revolution into the
sewer of French Jacobinism.   "What is the reason," John
Adams asked, "that so many of our 'old standbys' are infected
with Jacobinism?   The principles of this infernal tribe were
surely no part of our ancient political creed."   He declared that
his ideal was the same in 1796 that it had been in 1775: a government "well ordered, mixed, and counterpoised."   Unlike
Sam Adams, John Adams believed that one revolution in a lifetime was enough.[107]

Despite the warm support of all the Jacobins in the Green
Dragon Tavern, Sam Adams was defeated for presidential elec-

---

[107] *Independent Chronicle*, Nov. 7, 1796.   *The Works of John Adams*,
IX, 562, 584.

tor. Indeed, he was given such a drubbing by John Adams's friends that the Republicans roared that the Federalists had packed Boston during the election with "Foreigners and Strangers" who had voted illegally. To Sam Adams, governor of the commonwealth, and to Sam Adams, the Boston rebel, illegal voting appeared in a very different light; and he now complained as bitterly as had Hutchinson of frauds in Boston elections. It made vast difference to Sam Adams whether the unqualified voters who crowded into Faneuil Hall on meeting days were Sons of Liberty or Federalist hirelings. Adams's position was now similar to Hutchinson's during the Revolution; and therefore he became as staunch a defender of purity in elections as any royal governor of Massachusetts Bay.[108]

Adams's failure to carry Boston as an anti-John Adams elector led him to take a step he had contemplated for several years: to retire from the governorship before the Federalists had the satisfaction of turning him out of office. Toward the close of 1796, therefore, Adams announced that he would not be a candidate for governor at the next election; and his retirement marks the virtual end of the early Republican Party in Massachusetts and the complete triumph of Federalism. As Ben Austin bitterly exclaimed in 1797: "Every attempt to restore the liberties of mankind, or to check the progress of arbitrary power is now styled Jacobinism." Massachusetts had fallen into the hands of a Federalist oligarchy; and the new aristocracy so closely resembled the old Tories that John Adams lamented a few years later that the Higginson family had more influence than had Thomas Hutchinson at the height of his career, "and upon the same Principles and by the same means."[109]

Sam Adams lingered on several years after his retirement from the governorship — a broken-down old man who shuffled wearily about his house on Winter Street and lived in the past when he had been the foremost Son of Liberty in New England. His old age was not happy or beautiful: it was John Adams's

---

[108] *Columbian Centinel*, Nov. 2, 1796. *Independent Chronicle*, Nov. 7 and 10, 1796. *The Writings of Samuel Adams*, IV, 400, 401.

[109] Benjamin Austin, Jr., *Constitutional Republicanism* (1797), 52. W. C. Ford, *John Adams, Statesman and Friend*, 96.

prayer that he be spared the fate of Sam Adams, "a grief and distress to his family, a weeping, helpless object of compassion for years." [110]   Palsy, which attacked him early in life, had long since made it impossible for him to write, and he was forced to depend upon his "faithfull friend and amanuensis" John Avery, the one-time secretary of the Boston Sons of Liberty. He lived to see the triumph of Jefferson, which he regarded as a victory for the principles he had maintained throughout his life.   "The Storm is over, and we are in port," he wrote Jefferson when the Republicans came into power.   He still kept faith in the French Revolution and he looked upon the coalition against France as a league of "Tyrant Kings to exterminate those rights and liberties which the Gracious Creator has granted to Man."   He remained a "consistent Republican" to the end; although age and ill-health had made it impossible for him to aid in carrying on the principles of the Revolution, he wrote Jefferson, he could still give his blessing to the defenders of liberty.[111]

In 1803, Sam Adams died.   It was fitting that as his funeral cortege wound through the streets of Boston it passed the spot on which Liberty Tree had stood and Chase and Speakman's distillery, where Sam Adams and the Sons of Liberty had smoked their pipes, drunk flip, and plotted the overthrow of the Tories and the royal government.   He was buried in the Old Granary Burying Ground, near where "old Endicott lies."

Sam Adams was at last among the Puritans.

[110] *The Works of John Adams*, X, 100.
[111] *The Writings of Samuel Adams*, IV, 409–410.

BIBLIOGRAPHY

Since 1936, when *Sam Adams, Pioneer in Propaganda* was published, no full-length biography of Adams has appeared. There is no danger, however, that Adams will become a forgotten man of American history; thanks to the labors of historians and biographers, his stature as a revolutionary leader is rising steadily. Among the books published in the last twenty-three years which attempt to evaluate his contribution to the American Revolution, the following studies merit special mention:

Alden, John Richard. *The American Revolution, 1775–1783*. New York, 1953.

Bowen, Catherine Drinker. *John Adams and the American Revolution*. Boston, 1950.

Brown, Robert E. *Middle Class Democracy in Massachusetts*. Ithaca, New York, 1955.

Chidsey, Donald Barr. *July 4, 1776*. New York, 1958.

Davidson, Philip. *Propaganda and the American Revolution, 1763–1783*. Chapel Hill, 1941.

Douglass, Elisha. *Rebels and Democrats: the Struggle for Equal Political Rights and Majority Rule During the American Revolution*. Chapel Hill, 1955.

Falkner, Leonard. *Forge of Liberty*. New York, 1959.

Gipson, Lawrence H. *The Coming of the Revolution, 1763–1775*. New York, 1954.

Lengyel, Cornel. *Four Days in July*. New York, 1958.

Meigs, Cornelia. *The Violent Men*. New York, 1949.

Morgan, Edmund S., and Helen M. Morgan. *The Stamp Act Crisis: Prologue to Revolution*. Chapel Hill, 1953.

Rossiter, Clinton. *Seedtime of the Republic*. New York, 1953.

Sanford, Allan H. *John Hancock, Patriot in Purple*. New York, 1948.

Taylor, Robert J. *Western Massachusetts in the Revolution*. Providence, 1954.

Tourtellot, Arthur Benton. *William Diamond's Drum*. New York, 1959.

INDEX

Bass, Henry, cousin of Sam Adams, and member of the "Loyall Nine," 53

Bay State, name for Massachusetts, 271

Beacon Hill, Boston, pole placed on, for a rallying device, 154

Beaumarchais, and part played in Revolution by him and his fictitious firm, Roderique, Hortalez & Cie, 351

Belcher, Governor, proclamation against Land Bank, 11–12; jails Land Bank leaders, 14; removed from office, 15; mentioned, 37

Belknap, Jeremy, of New Hampshire, quoted on Boston Committee of Correspondence, 305

Bernard, .Governor Francis, succeeds Thomas Pownall, 28–29; impressions of Massachusetts, 29, 40; disregards threats of Adams and Otis, 35; factions and opposition in Massachusetts, 35, 37; popularity in Massachusetts, 41, 46; and Stamp Act, 56, 73; on reaction in Boston to Virginia Resolves, 57; admits Massachusetts cannot stand more taxes, 57; dismay over October 1765 Assembly meeting, 60; fear of Stamp Act mob, 68, 72; at Castle William, 70, 72; quoted on colonial militia, 71–72; on publication of Massachusetts House of Representative papers, 95; dismisses Whigs from military posts, 105; attitude toward James Otis, 105, 121; attacks Sam Adams in General Court, 107–108; nicknamed "Verres," 108; feels secure again, 112; treatment by Whigs, 122; and circular letter, 130; writes Lord Hillsborough on royal government, 131; belief about Sam Adams, 136, 301; prepares to return to England, 142; tells Councillor, September 3, 1768, of British troops on way to Boston, 147; obeys Lord Hillsborough's instructions, 147; gives

orders for troops from Halifax and Ireland, 154; remarks on Massachusetts Convention, 160–161, 165; quoted on power of Adams and Otis, 170; fears Boston mobs, 171; loses favor in England, 171; as scapegoat, 171; Suffolk Grand Jury indicts for libel, 173; impeachment proceedings dismissed in England, 173; quoted on Adams's *Journal*, 175; alarm over withdrawal of English troops, 177; quoted on New England manufactures, 199; removal from office, 282; made a baronet by George III, 230; attended Church of England, 231; quoted on Boston Whigs, 251

Bernard, Lady, does not go back to England with Governor Bernard, 173

"Black List" of Tories in General Court, 104; published in *Boston Gazette*, 105

"Black regiment," of Congregational ministers, James Otis wins their support, 129; compliments Hutchinson on governorship of Massachusetts, 233

Board of Trade, British, mention of, 15

Boston, and the Great Awakening, 6; politics in, 7–9; aristocrats hated in, 10; gentlemen in, oppose the Land Bank, 13; has wave of materialism, 1748, 18; Sam Adams as clerk in Boston Market, 22; quarrels with Governor Shirley, 25; Hutchinson loses popularity there, 26; praise for Pownall, 28; Bernard's changing estimate of, 29; visitor's estimate of, in 1760, 30–31; merchants desire free trade, 31; James Otis at head of vice-admiralty court, 33; opposes Hutchinson as lieutenant governor, 35; clubs and secret societies in, 37; not enough representatives to House of Representatives, 45; heads Massachusetts revolutionary party, 46; business failures at, in

of become Jacobins or anti-Jacobins during French Revolution, 391; importance of Jacobin principles in, 392

VALLEY FORGE, Washington and army at, winter of 1777, 348
Vice Admiralty Courts, establishment of, 117
Virginia, first colony to deny right of British government to impose internal taxes on colonies, 56; leads in protest against Stamp Act, 61, 131; legislature supports Massachusetts circular letter, 131; Whig prestige lost in, 251; patriots go ahead of Sam Adams on intercolonial correspondence, 270–271; attitude in, on Federal Constitution, 381
Virginia Resolves, adopted in the House of Burgesses, 56; defeated by conservatives in Massachusetts General Court, 397

WAR, FRENCH, lags, 28
War, with French and Indians on New England frontier, 1756–1766, prevents local political growth, 22–23; enthusiasm for, stirred up in Boston, by Sam Adams, 145; rapid growth of feeling in Boston, in 1768, 145; response to Adams's appeal to arms, 155; plans of radicals crippled, 158–159; question of, between Massachusetts and Great Britain, 324
War of 1812, marks the time when New England took its place in the industrial world, 199–200
Ward, Artemas, of Shrewsbury, as delegate to General Court, 46
Warren, James, and description of John Hancock, 361–362; as "Helvidius Priscus," author of virulent attack on Federal Constitution, 377–378
Warren, Dr. Joseph, as political pupil

of Sam Adams, 99; his house used as secret meeting place for town-meeting resolutions, 149; quoted on "mushroom" gentry, 360–361; drafts Suffolk Resolves, 323; on fashionable revelries in Boston, 363–364; as speaker at Massacre Oration, March 5, 1775, 330
Washington, George, estimate of in New England, 334; converted to independence, 342; given precedence in toasts at Boston, 345; suffers from Charles Lee's insubordination, 346; retires to Valley Forge for winter, from Philadelphia, 348; plot for his downfall, 350; as presidential candidate, 381; asks recall of Citizen Genêt, the French minister to the United States, 397
Waterhouse, Dr. Benjamin, comes to aid of his friend, Sam Adams, 366–367
Watertown, Massachusetts, received Boston delegates to First Continental Congress, on their way to Philadelphia, 314
Wealth, increase of in colonies, 30
Wedderburn, Solicitor General, on Sam Adams's twelve-penny book on colonial rights and grievances, 266; on absurdities of rural towns resolves, 270
Welles, Elizabeth, second wife of Sam Adams, 83
West Indies, Spanish and French, and trade with American colonies, 31; British, unable to supply needs of New England distilleries, 43
Whaling industry and fisheries, importance of in America, 304
Whately, Thomas, former Member of Parliament, writes to Hutchinson, 278; Benjamin Franklin sends letters to Massachusetts with instructions as to their use, 279–280; Sam Adams uses them to incense people against Hutchinson, 281–282
Wheelright's Wharf, Molineux's